Myth, Materiality, and Lived Religion

In Merovingian and Viking Scandinavia

*Edited by Klas Wikström af Edholm,
Peter Jackson Rova, Andreas Nordberg,
Olof Sundqvist & Torun Zachrisson*

STOCKHOLM
UNIVERSITY PRESS

Published by
Stockholm University Press
Stockholm University
SE-106 91 Stockholm, Sweden
www.stockholmuniversitypress.se

Supporting Agency (funding): Department of Ethnology, History of Religions
and Gender Studies at Stockholm University

First published 2019
Cover designed by Karl Edqvist, Stockholm University Press

Stockholm Studies in Comparative Religion (Online) ISSN: 2002-4606

ISBN (Paperback): 978-91-7635-099-7
ISBN (PDF): 978-91-7635-096-6
ISBN (EPUB): 978-91-7635-097-3
ISBN (Mobi): 978-91-7635-098-0

DOI: https://doi.org/10.16993/bay

Suggested citation:
Wikström af Edholm, K., Jackson Rova, P., Nordberg, A., Sundqvist, O.
& Zachrisson, T. (eds.) 2019. Myth, Materiality, and Lived Religion: In
Merovingian and Viking Scandinavia. Stockholm: Stockholm University Press.
DOI: https://doi.org/10.16993/bay. License: CC-BY.

To read the free, open access version of this book online,
visit https://doi.org/10.16993/bay or scan this QR code with
your mobile device.

Stockholm Studies in Comparative Religion

Stockholm Studies in Comparative Religion (SSCR) (ISSN 2002-4606) is a peer-reviewed series initiated by Åke Hultkrantz in 1961. While its earlier emphasis lay in ethnographic-comparative approaches to religion, the series now covers a broader spectrum of the history of religions, including the philological study of discrete traditions, large-scale comparisons between different traditions as well as theoretical and methodological concerns in the study of cross-cultural religious categories such as ritual and myth.

SSCR strives to sustain and disseminate high-quality and innovative research in the form of monographs and edited volumes, preferably in English, but in exceptional cases also in the French, German-, and Scandinavian languages.

SSCR was previously included in the series Acta Universitatis Stockholmiensis (ISSN 0562-1070). A full list of publications can be found here: http://www.erg.su.se/publikationer/skriftserier/stockholm-studies-in-comparative-religion-1.38944. Volumes still in stock can be obtained through the editors.

Editorial Board

Titles in the series

36. Jackson, P. (ed.) 2016. *Horizons of Shamanism. A Triangular Approach to the History and Anthropology of Ecstatcic Techniques*. Stockholm: Stockholm University Press. DOI: https://doi.org/10.16993/bag
37. Rydving, H. & Olsson, S. 2016. *Krig och fred i vendel- och vikingatida traditioner*. Stockholm: Stockholm University Press. DOI: https://doi.org/10.16993/bah
38. Christoyannopoulos, A. & Adams M. S. (eds.) 2017. *Essays in Anarchism & Religion: Volume I*. Stockholm: Stockholm University Press. DOI: https://doi.org/10.16993/bak
39. Christoyannopoulos, A. & Adams M. S. (eds.) 2018. *Essays in Anarchism & Religion: Volume II*. Stockholm: Stockholm University Press. DOI: https://doi.org/10.16993/bas
40. Wikström af Edholm, K., Jackson Rova, P., Nordberg, A., Sundqvist, O., & Zachrisson, T. (eds.) 2019. *Myth, Materiality, and lived Religion. In Merovingian and Viking Scandinavia*. Stockholm: Stockholm University Press. DOI: https://doi.org/10.16993/bay

Peer Review Policies

Stockholm University Press ensures that all book publications are peer-reviewed in two stages. Each book proposal submitted to the Press will be sent to a dedicated Editorial Board of experts in the subject area as well as two independent experts. The full manuscript will be peer reviewed by chapter or as a whole by two independent experts.

A full description of Stockholm University Press' peer-review policies can be found on the website: http://www.stockholm universitypress.se/site/peer-review-policies/

Recognition for reviewers

The Editorial Board of Stockholm Studies in Comparative Religion applies single-blind review during proposal and manuscript assessment. We would like to thank all reviewers involved in this process.

Special thanks to the reviewers who have been doing the peer review of the manuscript of this book:

Frands Herschend, Professor at the Department of Archaeology and Ancient History, Uppsala University

Britt-Mari Näsström, Professor emerita, History of Religions, University of Gothenburg

Håkan Rydving, Professor, History of Religions, University of Bergen

Contents

Introduction

Andreas Nordberg, Klas Wikström af Edholm and Olof Sundqvist

"The Old Norse Mythology Conferences", also called "The Aarhus Mythology Conferences", were introduced and held in Aarhus, Denmark, between 2005 and 2008. The original initiative for these conferences was taken by Pernille Hermann and Jens Peter Schjødt. As Pernille mentioned at the 2014 conference in Aarhus, the original concept was that the meetings should have a relatively informal character, and should provide the possibility of presenting new ideas rather than final thoughts. It was not the intention that the papers were to be published afterwards. Over the course of time, however, the conferences have grown in size and have become more formal than their early forerunners. There is no doubt that they have in recent years meant much to interdisciplinary research on Old Norse mythology,* not only in Aarhus, but for all scholars who are dealing with these matters generally.

In 2009 the conference started to circulate between universities. It has since been held in Aberdeen, Reykjavik, Zürich, Bonn, Harvard, and – in 2014 – at Aarhus again. Every year the

---

* By the concept Old Norse mythology, we refer to the mythic traditions transmitted orally and occasionally written down in medieval manuscripts in Old West Nordic, which embraces Old Norwegian, Old Icelandic, Old Faroese etc. In this presentation we use the term Old Norse mythology in a wide sense, and also include mythic traditions, which may have been rendered in Old East Nordic and Old Gutnish. For a discussion on the concept Old Norse religion, see Nordberg 2012:124–130.

How to cite this book chapter:
Nordberg, A., Wikström af Edholm, K. & Sundqvist, O. 2019. Introduction. In: Wikström af Edholm, K., Jackson Rova, P., Nordberg, A., Sundqvist, O. & Zachrisson, T. (eds.) *Myth, Materiality, and Lived Religion: In Merovingian and Viking Scandinavia*. Pp. 1–8. Stockholm: Stockholm University Press. DOI: https://doi.org/10.16993/bay.a. License: CC-BY.

organizers have managed to set up excellent research events, so admittedly it was a great challenge to take responsibility for the programme and activities in Stockholm, in November 2015.

Each of these conferences has been organized with an eye to the local research community and has thus been an integral part of the different research environments. At Stockholm University, the collaboration between scholars in the departments of History of Religions and Archaeology had been ongoing for some years, and we wanted this interdisciplinary milieu to reflect the theme for the Stockholm conference.

Looking back a century or so, the boundaries between comparative religion, archaeology, philology, history and place-name studies were diffuse, and to a certain degree the fields may at the time even be viewed as aspects of a common grand cultural historical discipline. In Scandinavia at least, this began to change in the 1930s. There are several reasons for this, but the most salient one was probably the increasing institutionalization of individual disciplines at the universities, which lead to the emergence of academic territorial claims and institutional boundaries. This, in turn, resulted in specializations of research interests within each discipline. In the late 1930s and 1940s, Carl Wilhelm von Sydow and generations of Swedish folklorists under his influence broke with scholars of comparative religion and disputed the possibility of studying religious history from a folkloristic perspective. In the 1940s and 1950s, Jöran Sahlgren, and some of his disciples, stated that historical place-names could not be used in the study of Old Norse religion. In the 1960s, the emergence of the so-called New Archaeology fashioned some generations of archaeologists, who found the study of religion uninteresting or even archaeologically impossible. As a result, the academic study of Old Norse religion became for a long time almost the same thing as the study of Old Norse mythology, conducted by philologists and historians of religion dealing with Old Norse texts.

This situation lasted well into the late 1980s. In the early 1990s, however, several interdisciplinary seminars and conferences announced the beginning of a new direction in Old Norse scholarship. Again, scholars insisted on the necessity of the study of pre-Christian Scandinavian religion being an interdisciplinary project. As organizers of The Old Norse Mythology Conference of 2015, we can proudly state that many of the scholars who initiated this significant change of direction some 20 to 25 years ago, were present at the meeting in Stockholm.

The Theme of the Stockholm Conference 2015

The theme and title of the Stockholm conference 2015 was *Myth, Materiality, and Lived Religion*. As this title suggests, the conference focused on the material dimension of Norse mythology and the role played by myths in everyday life. More broadly expressed, the theme referred to the social, ritual and material contexts of myths. To some extent this theme was also related to the novel theoretical understanding, often called "the ontological turn", or "the stance to materiality" visible in anthropology and the human sciences more broadly (see e.g. Miller 2005; Henare *et al.* 2007; Meyer *et al.* 2010). This issue has not been fully featured in previous research on Old Norse myths, especially considering the theoretical implications it has had (see, however, for example Hedeager 2011; Sundqvist 2016:26ff.). The discussion concerning materiality (in a more general sense) has, on the other hand, for a long time been crucial for historians of religions and especially archaeologists, and we think it has become relevant for historians of literature and philologists as well. Several questions related to this theme may be posed, for instance: What do myths tell us about the material culture of the periods in which they were narrated? In the mythic traditions we encounter several interesting concepts and descriptions of things which refer to the materiality of religion, such as *hǫrgr*, *hof*, *trémaðr*, and the hapax legomenon *hlautviðr*. People probably encountered such concepts and things in their everyday life, and it is interesting to explore how these could have been perceived. Another relevant question is whether material things and iconographic expressions contribute to our knowledge of Norse mythology, for instance the Gotlandic picture stones, the so called "guldgubbar" (gold foil figures), and the symbol of Þórr's hammer. Another aspect of this theme is the significance of myth in everyday life, i.e. in the "lived religion" (see also below). What role did myths or mythical beings play in connection with, for instance, illnesses and remedies during the Viking Period and the Middle Ages? How did ordinary people experience taking part in a more formal sacrificial feast led by ritual specialists? In addition to this, also more general and classical issues were addressed at the conference, such as the question of whether mythical traditions preserved in medieval texts and other types of sources actually tell us anything about the pre-Christian mythology and religion. "The Old Norse Mythology Conferences" have always adopted such perspectives on myths, and, of course, such contributions are always relevant in this context. The major aim of the Stockholm conference was, however, to contextualize the myths, to go beyond the texts and discuss their historical and material backgrounds as well as their social and ritual settings. As this book shows, the contributors have approached the dimensions of *Myth, Materiality, and Lived Religion* using a variety of methods and from different perspectives. These approaches and perspectives could be summarized in three different themes, which also constitute the basic disposition of the present book: Part I "Myths and Texts", Part II "Myths and Pictures" and Part III "Myths and Lived Religion".

Outline and Themes

During the Stockholm Mythology Conference, the participants took a decision to publish their contributions by rewriting them as articles. Since there were commentators to each presentation, we also decided to publish these contributions. The outline of this book follows the three themes mentioned above.

Ever since the research on Old Norse myths became an important issue for scholars at universities in the early 19th century, the source material has mainly been made up of old texts. This is, of course, natural, since myth in its form is a narrative which is transmitted in verbal accounts and/or texts. The most important sources of the ancient Scandinavian myths in the scholarly undertakings have often been the Old Norse poetry, that is, the Eddic lays and the skaldic poetry. These poetic traditions were written down in medieval Icelandic manuscripts, but some of them may have been composed during the Viking Age. This poetry was thus passed on by oral tradition into later centuries when it was fixed in texts. There are also some prose texts which have played a crucial role in this research on myths, especially Snorri Sturluson's *Edda* (c. 1220) and Saxo Grammaticus' *Historia Danorum* (c. 1200) written in Latin. They were composed during the High Middle Ages and must be regarded as the medieval reception of the old mythic accounts. In addition to the intense discussion of the age and background of these mythic traditions, conducted by Sophus Bugge, Eugen Mogk and others, a number of different themes and questions have been investigated in these materials, for instance, the function and significance of individual gods and goddesses in the myths, the relationship between the different groups of mythical beings and the issue of whether the myths had a relation to specific cultic contexts. This variety of questions and themes is also featured in Part I ("Myths and Texts") in the present anthology. Jens Peter Schjødt, for instance, discusses the origins and development of the god rendered as "Óðinn" in Old Norse prose and poetry, and how the older conceptions of the god Wotan, and through *interpretatio romana* Mercury, may be crucial for our understanding of certain aspects and characteristics of the Old Norse god. Tommy Kuusela draws attention to the question of whether Gullveig in the Eddic poem *Vǫluspá* st. 21 should be identified as a giantess, rather than Freyja or some unspecified female being. Kuusela suggests that she is a giantess and that the war in *Vǫluspá* st. 24 was between the giants and the gods, rather than between Æsir and Vanir, unveiling a deeper structure of conflict and dependence in the relation between the two categories of gods and giants in the Old Norse mythology. Merrill Kaplan, on the other side, investigates some gifts (funerary goods) offered by Brynhildr to the females attending at her death, as mentioned in *Sigurðarkviða in skamma*, and the associations between the colours red and gold in this context.

A myth could also be brought to life by means of a ritual drama, a religious dance, and also via religious art, icons, symbolic signs and other types of illustrations. Thus, myths do not have to be verbalized (cf. Honko 1972). This fact has been noticed in the study of Old Norse myth, especially when investigating the Gotlandic picture stones, images on runic stones, bracteates, gold foil figures, figurines and symbols such as the hammer of Þórr. Most of these materials are contemporary with Late Iron Age society and have as sources a more direct character for the researcher when reconstructing pre-Christian myths. The iconographic manifestations of the myths reflect how people in contemporary society perceived the mythic accounts, divine beings and cosmic world in different contexts. Several contributions to the present book take this approach to the Old Norse myths, and they have been gathered in Part II "Myths and Pictures". Stephen Mitchell, for instance, focuses on the *drakormar* ("dragon serpents") and certain female figures as depicted on the Gotlandic picture stones. He discusses the role they may have played in the lives of the Gotlanders during the Merovingian Period and later. A critical assessment of scholarly interpretations of Ragnarök motífs in Viking Age iconography, both on stones and tapestries, is presented by Anders Hultgård. His answer to the question: "Do we find Ragnarøk motifs in pictures?" is neither a clear "yes" nor a definite "no". Sigmund Oehrl studies the iconography of the Gotlandic picture stones with support from the new RTI-method. For instance, he investigates the motif traditionally called "Gunnar in the snake pit" as represented on the stone from Hunninge in Klinte Parish. From the RTI-picture, Oehrl can conclude that the person in the snake pit is not a man but a woman, which calls for a new interpretation of the image. In her contribution to the present volume, Margrethe Watt focuses on the relationship between the gold foil figures from the Merovingian Period and Old Norse mythology. Rather than entering into a discussion identifying specific gods or mythical scenes on these foils, Watt prefers to look at the general concepts as expressed in the iconographic details, such as the concept of "the warlord", "the king of gods", "the seer" and "the legally binding marriage".

The concept of lived religion has been formulated and developed especially by North American scholars, in an effort to bridge the problematic dichotomy between the categories of official religion and popular religion (see e.g. McGuire 2008). In this regard, the lived religion includes all religious aspects of life. It includes the fundamental, common structures of religion as well as its many individual variations, among common people as well as the specialists of the religious institutions. The lived religion includes formal feastings and institutionalized cult and official rituals, as well as varied religious traditions in everyday life. It comprises the official theology and personal beliefs, as well as the professional mythical epics and popular narratives. In Part III of the present book, "Myths and Lived Religion", some of these kaleidoscopic aspects of the lived religion are explored. The contributions written by Ola Magnell, and Christina Fredengren and Camilla Löfqvist, for instance, highlight how pre-Christian sacrificial feasts are reflected in the archaeological materials. Rudolf Simek discusses religious beliefs and rites in the context of diseases and remedies in medieval Northern Europe, focusing especially on magical charms on amulets, both in the vernacular and Latin. Frederik Wallenstein illuminates some central aspects of the pre-Christian conception of the soul as reflected in *Hávamál* st. 155, while Frog discusses ideas about "embodiment" in Viking Age society. Andreas Nordberg proposes that Old Norse religion was never homogeneous, but rather that people in Viking Age Scandinavia shifted between four overall configurations of the lived religion, linked to four corresponding socio-cultural contexts.

The volume points future research in a direction of considering the long continuation and widespread roots of Old Norse mythology. The results emphasize the fact that we cannot always expect to find a clear-cut divide between pre-Christian and Christian religious motifs and conceptions in the religion during the Viking Age or Early Middle Ages, or between Old Norse religion and the religion of its bordering cultures. The lived religion seems to have been more complex than the sources sometimes appears to indicate. New methods and perspectives in the analysis may prevent the expectations from shaping what we read, or want to read, into the source material. A close reading of the textual sources may also give new insights into possibly underestimated and infrequently represented ideas possibly found in other source materials, such as human grave goods. The aggregation of different source materials shows a discrepancy between the archaeological finds of animal and human remains, and the descriptions of sacrificial traditions in the written sources. The lived reality seems to have been more complex and perhaps less formally structured when it comes to sacrificial gifts and the killing of animals and humans in a ritual manner than the written accounts may tell us. This is inspiring for the future interdisciplinary study of sacrificial traditions and customs, as neither discipline may be given the sole role of interpreting the lived reality. The need for interdisciplinary cooperation is growing with the new finds.

The manuscripts to this book were submitted by the contributors during 2015 and 2016. We apologize for the delay in this publication.

References

Hedeager, Lotte. 2011. *Iron Age Myth and Materiality. An Archaeology of Scandinavia AD 400–1000.* London & New York: Routledge.

Henare, A., M. Holbraad, & S. Wastell. 2007. Introduction. Thinking Through Things. In A. Henare et al. (eds.). *Thinking Through Things. Theorising Artefacts Ethnographically.* London: Routledge, 1–31.

Honko, Lauri. 1972. The Problem of Defining Myth. In H. Biezais (ed). *The Myth of the State.* Scripta Instituti Donneriani Aboensis 6. T. Ahlbäck. Stockholm: Almqvist & Wiksell, 7–19.

McGuire, Meredith B. 2008. *Lived Religion. Faith and Practice in Everyday Life.* Oxford & New York: Oxford University Press.

Meyer, B. *et al.* 2010. The Origin and Mission of Material Religion. *Religion* (40:3), 207–211.

Miller, Daniel. 2005. Materiality. An Introduction. In Daniel Miller (ed.). *Materiality.* London: Durham, 1–50.

Nordberg, Andreas. 2012. Continuity, Change and Regional Variation in Old Norse Religion. In C. Raudvere & J. P. Schjødt (eds.). *More than Mythology. Narratives, Ritual Practices and Regional Distribution in Pre-Christian Scandinavian Religion.* Lund: Nordic Academic Press, 119–151.

Sundqvist, Olof. 2016. *An Arena for Higher Powers. Ceremonial Buildings and Religious Strategies for Rulership in Late Iron Age Scandinavia.* NuS vol. 150. Leiden/Boston: Brill.

PART I:
MYTHS AND TEXTS

Gold is Red: *Sigurðarkviða en skamma* 49–50

The Ohio State University

Brynhildr Buðladóttir knows how to make a grand exit. Having brought about the death of Sigurðr and told her own version of her sad tale, she is bent on self-destruction. In *Sigurðarkviða en skamma*, she stages for herself a final scene in which the gifts of gold she proffers to her maidservants are an invitation to join her on the pyre. But we may have overlooked a further gruesome implication of Brynhildr's words, the specifics of the promised death. The idea hinges on an oft-mentioned detail of the lexicon: in Old Norse, gold is red.

In st. 46, we find Brynhildr distributing her riches (*mǫrc menia /meiðmom deildi;*[1] tree of necklaces (= lady) shared out treasures), which I take to be her executing her own will, a hands-on approach to inheritance. She gazes upon her property, including already sacrificed maidservants. When Brynhildr dons her golden mail-coat in st. 47, she is preparing her own funerary goods. Only once thus attired does she deal herself the mortal sword blow. She still has plenty to say. In st. 49, she invites any who would receive gold from her to come forward. These are her words:

> Nú scolo ganga, þeir er gull vili
> oc minna því at mér þiggia;
> ec gef hverri um hroðit sigli,
> bóc oc blæio, biartar váðir.[2]

How to cite this book chapter:
Kaplan, M. 2019. Gold is Red: *Sigurðarkviða en skamma* 49–50. In: Wikström af Edholm, K., Jackson Rova, P., Nordberg, A., Sundqvist, O. & Zachrisson, T. (eds.) *Myth, Materiality, and Lived Religion: In Merovingian and Viking Scandinavia.* Pp. 11–24. Stockholm: Stockholm University Press. DOI: https://doi.org/10.16993/bay.b. License: CC-BY.

I'll render the lines this way:

> Now should come forward those who would have gold
> And remember that they receive it from me;
> I'll give to every woman an ornamented necklace,
> A figured coverlet and sheet, bright clothes.

The women in the audience know that those gifts would also be their own funerary goods, that Brynhildr is offering a spot on the pyre. There are no takers: they turn her down in st. 50. Brynhildr seems to shrug in st. 51: she doesn't want anyone to die unwillingly (*Vilcat ec mann trauðan / né torbœnan / um óra sọc / aldri týna*), but (st. 52) when they do follow her, she warns them, their bones will burn without any riches at all! (*Þó mun á beinom / brenna yðrom / fœri eyrir, / þá er ér fram komið, / neit Menio góð, / mín at vitia*). The essential action is clear. Less clear is the best translation of *hroðit sigli*, which I treat in detail below. Taken together, reading *hroðit sigli* as "ornamented necklace," as have many before me, and the famous redness of gold, Brynhildr's offer of gold, jewelry, and bright clothing becomes an offer of red rings around the neck and stained cloth, or, more bluntly, slit throats and fabric soaked in gore.

This interpretation relies on a very close association between gold and the color red. Quite a lot of things are red in the Old Norse corpus, but, as it happens, gold is very red indeed. Here I rely on Jackson Crawford's 2014 dissertation *The Historical Development of Basic Color Terms in Old Norse – Icelandic*. Crawford's corpus is extensive though not exhaustive, including the Eddas, the skaldic corpus, the sagas and *þættir* of Icelanders, *Heimskringla*, *Physiologus*, *Elucidarius*, and *Hauksbók*. In this corpus, things red include blood, fire, angry human faces, human hair, horses, oxen, mythological roosters, and internal organs. Red is emblematically the color of blood – the lexicon includes blood-red (*blóðrauðr*), but not horse-red, hair-red, or fire-red – and the most frequent referent of the word *rauðr* is blood or things covered with blood, in fact 33% of all usages. No color term is more consistently associated with a specific referent than *rauðr* with blood. Gold is the second most frequent referent of *rauðr*: 10% of occurrences of *rauðr* refer to gold, and of all color terms and all referents the second-most consistent correlation is of *rauðr* with gold.[3] Put another way, gold is redder than anything save blood itself. The vocabulary of material culture of this stanza is also relevant, and some of the words are difficult or rare. *Sigli* is often translated simply as "jewel," but older lexicographers such as Finnur Jónsson, Hugo Gering, and Sveinbjörn Egilsson understood it as more likely a necklace or neck-ring than anything else. They reasoned in part from the Anglo-Saxon cognate, *sigle*, which is unproblematically a necklace.[4] *Hroðit* is also unique, and scholars have likewise had recourse to Anglo-Saxon, where the cognate past participle *hroden* (from a lost verb **hreóðan*), means ornamented or adorned. (Cleasby and Guðbrandur Vigfússon understood the Anglo-Saxon verb **hreóðan* to have meant 'to paint or stain', an interpretation that fits very nicely with my bloodstained ideas, but for which I do not see supporting evidence.) Cleasby and Guðbrandur Vigfússon read Old Norse *hroðit* as 'gilt'. For *hroðit sigli*, Sveinbjörn Egilsson offered *monile inauratum*, 'gilded necklace,' a reasonable conjecture based on limited evidence. We cannot know exactly what manner of ornamentation the Old Norse word signified – gilding or inlaying or stamping in already precious metal – but whatever its proper sense, it was consonant with the gold (*gull*) promised in the first line of the stanza. "Gilded" captures that idea even if it may miss the precise semantics of *hróðit*.

We already know that, when Brynhildr offers gold, she offers death. But when she offers specifically a *hróðit sigli*, she offers a red ring around the neck, a ring the color of blood, and in that image, it is easy to see a slit throat or a decapitation.

Red Ring Around the Neck

There is precedent for this sort of imagery elsewhere in the literature, in dream, and rather more explicitly.[5] Recall the dismal end of Hákon jarl and Þórmóðr Karkr in *Ólafs saga Tryggvasonar* 49 in *Heimskringla*.[6] Karkr and Hákon are hiding in the famous pigsty; Hákon frets that Karkr will betray him, but Karkr insists on his loyalty. They were born the same night, after all, and their fates are intertwined. Hákon is keeping watch while Karkr sleeps fitfully. Hákon wakes him, and Karkr says he's dreamt of being at Hlaðir, *ok lagði Óláfr Tryggvason gullmen á háls mér* (Olaf Tryggason set a gold necklace around my neck). Hákon interprets the dream immediately: *Þar mun Óláfr láta hring blóðrauðan um háls þér, ef þú finnr hann* (Olaf will put a blood-red ring around your neck there, if you meet him); *Vara þú þik svá* (So watch yourself accordingly). *En af mér muntu gott hljóta, svá sem fyrr hefir verit, ok svík mik eigi* (But from me you will receive only good, as has been the case before, and do not betray me). Gold is red – red as blood – and receiving a blood-red ring about the neck is the opposite of being treated well. Hákon does not completely unpack the *hringr* as being a wound; the text does it for us. Dreams being what they are, and the depiction of slaves in this literature being what it is, Karkr gets spooked and kills Hákon in his sleep. When he brings Hákon's head to Olaf Tryggvason in hope of reward, yes, Olaf has Karkr's own head cut off. End of Chapter 49.

Thus the case for the red ring around the neck. It remains to locate the resultant blood on the named textiles: *bók, blæja*, and *bjartar váðir*. *Bók* is a very uncommon word when it does not mean simply "book." This other *bók* is an embroidered cloth, or so we extrapolate from the verb *gullbóka* in *Guðrúnarkviða ǫnnur* 14, where one woman entertains another by *gullbóc*-ing a textile with southern halls and Danish swans: *hon mér at gamni / gullbócaði / sali suðrœna / oc svani dansca.* The usual translation is "embroidered with gold," by analogy with Anglo-Saxon *gibōkod*, perhaps borrowed from northern German[7] – perhaps in this very context. More relevant than the specific technique is the narrative associations it is likely to have had for the poem's medieval audience. Aside from here in *Sigurðarkviða en skamma*, *bóc* by itself appears only in *Guðrúnarhvǫt* and *Hamðismál*, where it seems to be part of the bedlinen. The two stanzas tell the same moment: Guðrún awakening in her marital bed, her slain husband beside her. The sole narrative function of the *bœcr* is being covered in blood.

bœcr vóro þínar,	*inar bláhvíto*
roðnar í vers dreyra,	*fólgnar í valblóði* (Hhv.)[8]
ofnar vǫlondom,	*fluto í vers dreyra.* (Hm.)[9]

Your blue-white *bœcr* were
(in *Guðrúnarhvǫt*) reddened in a man's gore, drenched in
   slaughter-blood
(in *Hamðismál*) woven by skilled craftsmen, (they) were floating
   in a man's gore.

When Brynhildr offers embroidered coverlets in *Sigurðarkviða
en skamma*, they are not explicitly soaked in blood, but for the
medieval audience of Eddic poetry the very word *bóc* may have
been colored by its role in the scene of Sigurðr's murder, the only
surviving context in which it appears. To a contemporary mind,
bœcr might have been the kind of embroidered coverlets one has
on one's bed if one's bed is soaked in blood. We might compare
English "veranda." The word means "porch," but functionally it
means the kind of porch you have if you live in an antebellum
mansion in the American South.

The much more common word *blæja* is less colorful by comparison. *Blæja,* a cloth covering, sheet or spread, is used of the linen
of the marital bed – in Eddic poetry especially of the extra-marital
bed, as in *Oddrúnargrátr* 6 and 25. The older *Frostaþingslǫg* mentions *blæja* in the context of the blood-stained site of possibly non-
consensual intercourse.[10] In *Grágás, blæja* is a shroud,[11] in *Laxdœla*
55, *blæja* is Guðrún's shawl, on which Helgi Harðbeinsson wipes
the blood of the new-slain Bolli.[12] It would be too much to claim
that *blæja*, like *bóc*, was stereotypically bloody, but it was, at
least, often a cloth for lying down with and not always while still
alive. The use of *blæjur* here suggests the serving women's bodies
stretched out rather than standing attentively.

Váðir are cloths or clothes depending on the register. In prose, *váð*
is the raw material wool cloth measured and traded by the ell or the
mark, except in the compound *hvítaváðir* "baptismal whites." In
poetry, *váðir* is clothing. Here, and only here, are *váðir* bright, *bjartar*.[13] *Bjartr* is an interesting word of itself. Like English "bright," it
tells us nothing about color in the sense of hue. Cloth and wool are
not normally "bright" in Old Norse. Things typically *bjartr* include
weather, fire, light, the countenances of handsome people, and
metals – especially gold, which is bright twice in *Skáldskaparmál*
40.39; 41.8.[14] Fire can be *rauðr* as well as *bjartr*.[15] That gold was

stereotypically bright is reflected in the word *gullbjartr*, attested twice in Eddic verse. Referring to Valhǫll in *Grímnismál* 8.2, it might mean "bright-with-gold" owing to the shields making up the roof; it could mean "bright as gold" as in *Hárbarðsljóð* 30.5, where it refers to a radiant woman. Compared to the rest of the corpus, *bjartr* seems inappropriate to its object, *váðir*, on the level of the materials. Are the *bóc* and *blæja* also *bjartar*? Grammatically, as feminine nouns, they could be. Semantically, the same problem applies. The mismatch sends the reader searching for the nearest material thing that can partake of brightness. The nearest thing, the promised thing, is the gold offered in the first line of the stanza. The juxtaposition of somehow "bright" textiles of no specified color with gold itself invites us to see the clothing as having taken on the color of bright gold, and bright gold is red, like blood. Blood, too, can be bright as in Sighvatr Þórðarson's *Erfidrápa Óláfs helga* st. 8.[16] At this point we can see the gory image float to the surface: slit throats, bright blood flowing down to stain dresses, sheets, and coverlets on and around the bodies of the serving women.

Thus the textual case for this essay's gory interpretation. Archaeology confirms that human sacrifice was sometimes part of burial custom in the Old Norse cultural area in the Viking Age, though the method of execution is not always discernable from the human remains. The body at Gerdrup shows a broken neck; the Stengade sacrifice was decapitated, which would have given him the same red ring Karkr received; the young woman at Ballateare was killed with a sword blow to the back of the head, which just might reflect a botched decapitation.[17] Methods aside, *Sigurðarkviða en skamma* appears to preserve a cultural memory of heathen practice, at least as far as funerary sacrifice goes. We might credit both oral tradition and centuries of grave robbing and less larcenously motivated grave opening[18] with helping keep some knowledge of pre-Christian funerary customs alive. One does not need an archaeology degree to notice a sliced-open cranium or a skull lying far from its ribcage. Here we begin to veer towards speculation, however, and might profitably return to the poem for some final thoughts.

Brynhildr can make a grand exit, taking with her trappings of wealth both animate and inanimate, but if the interpretation presented here is correct, she is less than straightforward about just how bloody she intends that grandeur to be. Therein lies the pleasure of the text at this juncture. Therein too, lies the scholarly anxiety that one has pressed the source material too hard and found meaning that would not have been apparent to the audience of the poem's own days. The intertextual case for that interpretation has been made above. One last intratextural point should be mentioned. Brynhildr's words in st. 49 need some unpacking, but the rhythm of the text suggests that they are meant to be understood. The poem gives us time to do so by building a pause into the action: in stanza 50, everyone falls silent.

> 50   *Þǫgðo allir,*   *hugðo at ráðom,*
>   *oc allir senn*   *annsvor veitto:*
>   *"Œrnar soltnar,*   *munum enn lifa,*
>   *verða salkonor*   *sœmð at vinna."*[19]

>   All were silent,   considered their courses,
>   and all together   gave answer:
>   "Enough have died, we would yet live,
>   Be serving-women in hall, earning honor."

Brynhildr says her bit about gold and bright clothing, but those addressed are silent in response for two whole, tension-building lines. People in Eddic poetry do not fall silent very often. The only other place I can find is in response to Brynhildr saying something confusing. In *Brot af Sigurðarkviðu* 14, Sigurðr has already been killed when Brynhildr wakes before dawn and cries out:

> *Hvetið mic eða letið mic*   – *harmr er unninn* –
> *sorg at segia*   *eða svá láta!*[20]

> Urge me on or hinder me   – the harm is done now –
> to tell my sorrow   or so leave be!

At that, all fell silent:

> *Þǫgðu allir*   *við því orði,*
> *fár kunni þeim*   *flióða látum,*
> *er hon grátandi* *gorðiz at segia,*
> *þat er hlæiandi* *hǫlða beiddi.*[21]

At that, all fell silent.
Few understand the behavior of women,
when, crying, she spoke of the deeds
she had, laughing, ordered men to do.

Silence falls to mark an interpretive crux: how should Brynhildr's words and actions be understood? (Or perhaps that of women in general, as per *Hyndluljóð* 84.) The answer is both ways. Brynhildr wanted Sigurðr dead *and* yet mourns him. Her whole story is about a double bind of conflicting obligations that reflects an internal conflict between love and a need for revenge. The silence in *Sigurðarkviða en skamma* falls at a similar moment, though less obviously so. The sudden silence signals to the audience that we, too, might *huga at ráðum* and consider whether we missed anything in the preceding stanza.

Gold is red, sometimes it is bloody, perhaps especially so in the Burgundian material. After all, the cycle revolves around the hoard that, thanks to Wagner, we think of as the Rhinegold, but that is just where it ends up. It all starts with a killing and the first payment of compensation. Fáfnir's treasure, the Niflung gold, the gold ring that reveals Sigurðr's betrayal of Brynhildr. It is the original blood money. In Snorri's Edda, after Loki kills Ótr, he and his companions owe the family enough red gold to fill his flayed skin and then cover it entirely: *fylla belginn af rauðu gulli ok sva hylia hann allan;*[22] In the prose before *Reginsmál*, the line is *Fylla otrbelginn með gulli oc hylia útan oc með rauðo gulli.* They must literally replace the body of the slain kinsman with gold and then bury the body completely with more gold, effectively making a burial mound. This gold is wergild and grave mound in one. It acquires as guardian Fáfnir, in the shape of a dragon, an animal not infrequently mentioned in realms of the dead like Nástrǫnd. The Burgundian gold circulates from the chthonic and watery Otherworld to a recently vacated skin and a burial mound via a serpent-like monster's hoard to the world of men, where it drags many to their own deaths – and then ultimately back underwater, where it shines like fire. Fire is red, like gold, like blood. In heroic legend and myth, gold may always be an Otherworld material, hailing from and returning to the world of the dead, leaving a crimson trail behind it.

These are larger ideas than the rather small point of interpretation to which this essay is dedicated – perhaps they will resonate with others besides myself. The hope is rather to have convinced the reader that the striking image painted here is not this author's own fantasy, but a real part of the poem as it has come to us, an especially gruesome scene in an already violent cycle of narratives.

Notes

1. All quotations are taken from (Neckel/Kuhn 1983).

2. *Sigurðarkviða en skamma* 46.

3. Crawford 2014:131.

4. Bosworth and Toller 1972.

5. Thanks go to Jonas Wellendorf for reminding me of this episode.

6. Bjarni Aðalbjarnarson 1941:297–298.

7. de Vries 1962:48.

8. *Guðrúnarhvǫt* 4.

9. *Hamðismál* 7.

10. Frostatingsloven IV 39, Keyser & Munch 1846–1849:169–170.

11. Vilhjálmur Finsen 1852 I:238.

12. Einar Ól. Sveinsson 1934:168.

13. *Klæði* can be *bjart* when translating Latin: I find one instance of *klæddr með bjǫrtu klæði* (clad in bright clothing) in A Dictionary of Old Norse Prose, where *bjǫrtu* renders *candente*.

14. Crawford 2014:28–31.

15. Bjarni Aðalbjarnarson 1945:60.

16. Finnur Jónsson 1912, A1:259, B1:240.

17. Christensen 1981; Skaarup 1972; Bersu & Wilson 1966.

18. Jankuhn 1978; Soma 2007.

19. *Sigurðarkviða en skamma* 49.

20. *Brot af Sigurðarkviðu* 14.

21. *Brot af Sigurðarkviðu* 14.

22. Faulkes 1998:45.

References

Primary sources

Den Norsk-Islandske Skjaldedigtning. Finnur Jónsson. 1912. *Den Norsk-Islandske Skjaldedigtning.* København and Kristiania: Gyldendal Nordisk forlag.

Edda. Neckel, Gustav & Kuhn, Hans. (eds.). 1983. *Edda. Die Lieder des Codex Regius nebst verwandten Denkmälern.* 5. verbesserte Auflage. Vol. I. Text. Heidelberg: Carl Winter.

———— Larrington, Carolyne. 2014. *The Poetic Edda.* 2nd ed. Oxford World's Classics. Oxford: Oxford University Press.

Frostathing Law. Larson, Laurence (trans.). 1935. *The Earliest Norwegian Laws, Being the Gulathing Law and the Frostathing Law.* New York: Columbia University Press.

———— Keyser, R. & Munch, P. A. (eds.). 1846–1849. *Norges gamle Love indtil 1387.* Vol. I. Christiania: Chr. Grøndahl, n.d.

Grágás. Vilhjálmur Finsen. 1974. *Grágás. Konungsbók. Islændingernes Lovbog i Fristatens Tid, udgivet efter det Kongelige Bibliotheks Haandskrift og oversat af Vilhjálmur Finsen.* Reprint of 1852 edition. Odense: Odense Universitetsforlag.

Heimskringla. Bjarni Aðalbjarnarson (ed.). 1941. *Heimskringla II.* Íslenzk Fornrit XXVII. Reykjavík: Hið íslenzka Fornritafélag.

———— Bjarni Aðalbjarnarson (ed.). 1945. *Heimskringla III.* Íslenzk Fornrit XXVIII. Reykjavík: Hið íslenzka Fornritafélag.

Laxdæla saga. Einar Ól. Sveinsson. 1934. *Laxdæla saga. Halldórs þættir Snorrasonar, Stúfs þáttr.* Íslenzk Fornrit V. Reykjavík: Hið íslenzka Fornritafélag.

Skáldskaparmál. Faulkes, Anthony. 1998. *Edda. Skáldskaparmál. 1. Introduction, Text, and Notes.* London: Viking Society for Northern Research.

Secondary Literature

A Dictionary of Old Norse Prose. http://onp.ku.dk/english/.

Bersu, Gerhard & Wilson, David. 1966. *Three Viking Graves in the Isle of Man*. London: SMA.

Bosworth, Joseph & T. Northcote Toller. 1972. *An Anglo-Saxon Dictionary, Based on the Manuscript Collections of the Late Joseph Bosworth*. London, New York: Oxford University Press.

Christensen, Tom. 1981. Gerdrup-graven. In *Romu. Årsskrift fra Roskilde Museum* 2, 19–28.

Cleasby, Richard & Guðbrandur Vigfússon. 1957 *An Icelandic-English Dictionary*. 2nd ed. Oxford: Clarendon Press.

Crawford, Jackson. 2014. *The Historical Development of Basic Color Terms in Old Norse–Icelandic*. Ph.D diss. Madison: The University of Wisconsin. Germanic and Slavic Languages and Literatures Faculty Contributions. 1. https://scholar.colorado.edu/gsll_facpapers/1.

Finnur Jónsson. 1931. *Lexicon poeticum antiquæ linguæ septentrionalis: Ordbog over det norsk-islandske skjaldesprog*. 2. udg. ved Finnur Jónsson. København: SLMøllers bogtr.

Gering, Hugo, & Barend Sijmons. 1931. *Kommentar zu den Liedern der Edda*. 2 vols. Halle (Saale): Buchhandlung des Waisenhauses.

Jankuhn, Herbert, et al. 1978. *Zum Grabfrevel in vor- und frühgeschichtlicher Zeit. Untersuchungen zu Grabraub und "Haugbrot" in Mittel- und Nordeuropa*. Göttingen: Vandenhoeck & Ruprecht.

Skaarup, J. 1972. Rejsekammeraten. In *Skalk* 1, 4–9.

Soma, Rune. 2007. *Haugbrott og herskermakt. Om gravrøveri som ritual*. Master of Arts, University of Oslo. https://www.duo.uio.no//handle/10852/26673.

Sveinbjörn Egilsson. 1854. *Lexicon poëticum antiquæ linguæ septentrionalis*. Hafniæ (Copenhagen): Kongelige Nordiske oldskriftselskab.

de Vries, Jan. 1962. *Altnordisches etymologisches Wörterbuch*. Leiden: Brill.

Response

Agneta Ney
Uppsala University

Merrill Kaplan's interpretation of Brynhild's funerary goods in
Sigurðarkviða in skamma is based on a close association between
gold and the colour red, and this in turns means blood and death.
She particularly emphasizes Brynhild's gifts to the maidservants.
The question is what kind of funerary goods she is proffering
them. Gold is only one of the gifts mentioned. However, Kaplan
includes *hroðit sigli*, 'ornamented necklace', to the golden goods.
According to Kaplan, it is "easy to see a slit throat or a decapitation" behind *hroðit sigli*. She supports her interpretation with one
example from another literary genre and another context, but in
which it is told that one man is decapitated by a king.[1] It is not
fully convincing, and furthermore, in an archaeological aspect,
maidservants, as far as I know, were neither decapitated nor had
their throat slit before following their matron to death.

But what of the textile gifts *bók*, *blæja* and *bjártar váðir*? Merrill
Kaplan argues that they also are associated with red, and thus
with blood. That the audience would associate *bók* with something bloody depends, according to Kaplan, on evidence from
two other heroic poems. That the medieval audience had heard
of other poems belonging to the Sigurðr tradition is a reasonable
assumption, but I doubt that the word *bók* in *Sigurðarkviða in
skamma* would conjure the bloody bedlinen from the death of
Sigurðr from other poems. However, a grammar detail may question this interpretation. In the two poems referred to, the plural
form *bœkr* is used and not the singular *bók*.[2]

Blæja means linen sheet and is bright in colour, and cannot
generally be associated with red gold or blood, so what is the
function of linen sheet as funerary goods? In comparison with the
other grave goods, *blæja* can, according to Kaplan, not immediately be associated with red, but via the adjective *bjártr*, it would
still be possible. I would like to point out another possible interpretation: the word *blæja* could also mean grave-clothes, as it is

used in *Guðrúnarkviða I* (stanza 13): *Svípti hún* [Guðrún] *blæju of Sigurði* [...].[3]
Brynhildr also wants to give away *bjártar váðir*. The phrase is similar to *hvítaváðir*, which in previous research has been perceived as white grave-clothes, something that would fit within the context.[4] As the word *bjártr* is not associated with *váðir*, the "reader", according to Kaplan, therefore is looking for something else that can, namely *gull* (gold), and the red gold can "colour" the textiles red or blood-red. Kaplan's interpretation actually leads to the conclusion that all Brynhild's gifts can be associated with blood. This leads Kaplan further to decapitated human sacrifices as part of Nordic burial customs during the Viking Age.

In her concluding arguments, Merrill Kaplan inter alia reflects on whether the source material, after all, might have been pushed too hard and "found meaning that would not have been apparent to the audience of the poem's own days." One difficulty is rather what "the poem's own days" refers to. Is it the contemporary audience or the audience in a more indefinite period of oral tradition?[5] None of Brynhild's women accepts the funerary gifts (stanza 50). This is in my opinion the text's own evidence of a present contemporary ideology that also provides for an alternative interpretation. If both stanzas (49–50) can be said to preserve the cultural memory of a pre-Christian custom, the women would not have rejected the gifts. It would hardly have been a choice in the context. Since this kind of grave ritual was no longer in general use in the Medieval Ages, or was disappearing, the poet can let the women reject the gifts and also argue that too many have already been killed.[6]

Notes

1. *Ólafs saga Tryggvasonar en mesta*. Vol 1:236.

2. *Guðrúnarhvǫt*, in *Eddukvæði* II, *Hetjukvæði*:403, *Hamðismál*, in *Eddukvæði* II:408.

3. *Guðrúnarkviða I*, in *Eddukvæði* II:331.

4. When *hvítaváðir* appears on Swedish runic monuments, on at least seven rune stones in Uppland, it generally refers to men who died in baptismal clothing, for example at U 243 in Vallentuna

Parish:"Holmlaugr ok Holmfríðr latu ræisa stæina æftir Fasta ok
Sigfast, sunu sina. Þæir dou í *hvítavaðum*." Cf. Larsson 2007:255ff.,
285f., 332ff., and her references to other works.

5. Gräslund 2001:9–10, 43ff.; Larsson 2007:249ff.

6. Brynhild's suicide can be a later motif in relation to other heroic
poems belonging to the Sigurðr legend, *Eddukvæði* II:87, cf. Klaus
von See et al. 2009:317 and their references to other works.

References

Primary Sources

Guðrúnarhvǫt. Jónas Kristjánsson & Vésteinn Ólason. 2014.
Eddukvæði II, *Hetjukvæði*. Íslenzk fornrit. Reykjavík: Hið íslenzka Fornritafélag.

Guðrúnarkviða I. Jónas Kristjánsson & Vésteinn Ólason. 2014.
Eddukvæði II, *Hetjukvæði*, Íslenzk fornrit. Reykjavík: Hið íslenzka Fornritafélag.

Hamðismál. Jónas Kristjánsson & Vésteinn Ólason. 2014.
Eddukvæði II, *Hetjukvæði*, Íslenzk fornrit. Reykjavík: Hið íslenzka Fornritafélag.

Ólafs saga Tryggvasonar en mesta. Ólafur Halldórsson. 1958. *Ólafs
saga Tryggvasonar en mesta*. Udgivet af Ólafur Halldórsson. Series
A. Vol. I. København: Editiones Arnamagnæana.

Sigurðarkviða in skamma. Jónas Kristjánsson & Vésteinn Ólason.
2014. *Eddukvæði* II, *Hetjukvæði*, Íslenzk fornrit. Reykjavík: Hið
íslenzka Fornritafélag.

Secondary Literature

Larsson, Annika. 2007. *Klädd krigare. Skifte i skandinaviskt dräkt-
skick kring år 1000*. Opia 39. Uppsala: Uppsala University.

Gräslund, Anne-Sofie. 2001. *Ideologi och mentalitet. Om religionsskiftet i Skandinavien från en arkeologisk horisont*. Opia 29.
Uppsala: Uppsala University.

Klaus von See et al. (ed.). 2009. *Kommentar zu den Liedern der Edda
6. Heldenlieder*. Heidelberg: Winter.

Halls, Gods, and Giants: The Enigma of Gullveig in Óðinn's Hall

Tommy Kuusela
Stockholm University

Introduction

The purpose of this article is to discuss and interpret the enigmatic figure of Gullveig. I will also present a new analysis of the first war in the world according to how it is described in Old Norse mythic traditions, or more specifically, how it is referred to in *Vǫluspá*. This examination fits into the general approach of my doctoral dissertation, where I try to look at interactions between gods and giants from the perspective of a hall environment, with special attention to descriptions in the eddic poems.[1] The first hall encounter, depending on how one looks at the sources, is described as taking place in a primordial instant of sacred time, and occurs in Óðinn's hall, where the gods spears and burns a female figure by the name of Gullveig. She is usually interpreted as Freyja and the act is generally considered to initiate a battle between two groups of gods – the Æsir and the Vanir. I do not agree with this interpretation, and will in the following argue that Gullveig should be understood as a giantess, and that the cruelty inflicted upon her leads to warfare between the gods (an alliance of Æsir and Vanir) and the giants (those who oppose the gods' world order). The source that speaks most clearly about this early cosmic age and provides the best description is *Vǫluspá*, a poem that is generally considered to have been composed around 900–1000 AD.[2]

How to cite this book chapter:
Kuusela, T. 2019. Halls, Gods, and Giants: The Enigma of Gullveig in Óðinn's Hall. In: Wikström af Edholm, K., Jackson Rova, P., Nordberg, A., Sundqvist, O. & Zachrisson, T. (eds.) *Myth, Materiality, and Lived Religion: In Merovingian and Viking Scandinavia.* Pp. 25–57. Stockholm: Stockholm University Press. DOI: https://doi.org/10.16993/bay.c. License: CC-BY.

The Problem of Gullveig in *Vǫluspá*

Gullveig is only mentioned in *Vǫluspá*. The poem narrates how Óðinn seeks out a *vǫlva* who recounts the major events in the Creation, and the eventual destruction, of the world. In the beginning, after the world has been created, the *vǫlva*, who herself might be a giantess,[3] speaks of a "golden age" for the gods, which is broken by the coming of three mighty giantesses. The episode is hard to comprehend, and many commentators seem to identify the three female figures with the Norns (even though they actually appear later, in stanza 20). Nothing more is said of these women. After this, the poem speaks of the creation of dwarves, humans, and how fate is measured by the three Norns. After the fates have been introduced, the poem again returns to the topic of the gods and describes how the *vǫlva* remembers the first war in the world, and how the gods immolated a figure known as Gullveig. As John McKinnell[4] has pointed out, the following two stanzas: "constitute one of the most familiar problems in the study of Eddic poetry".

> 21   *Þat man hon fólcvíg fyrst í heimi,*
> *er Gullveigo geirom studdo*
> *oc í hǫll Hárs hána brendo;*
> *þrysvar brendo, þrysvar borna,*
> *opt, ósialdan, þó hon enn lifir.*[5]

> She remembers the first war in the world,
> when they stuck Gullveig with spears
> and in the High-One's hall they burned her;
> three times they burned her, three times she was reborn,
> over and over, yet she lives still.[6]

> 22   *Heiði hana héto, hvars til húsa kom,*
> *vǫlo velspá, vitti hon ganda;*
> *seið hon, hvars hon kunni, seið hon hug leikinn,*
> *æ var hon angan illrar brúðar.*[7]

> Bright One [Heiðr] they called her, wherever she came to houses,
> the seer with pleasing prophecies, she practised spirit-magic,
> she knew seid, seid she performed as she liked [practised
>   magic in a trance],
> she was always a wicked woman's favourite.[8]

Both stanzas are as fascinating as they are challenging, but it is primarily stanza 21 that is the motivation for this article. In that stanza, the *vǫlva* says that she remembers *fólcvíg fyrst í heimi* and speaks of how "they" (most likely the gods) stabbed a figure called Gullveig with spears and burned her in the High One's hall. Not just on one occasion, but three times – and every time she is reborn. The subsequent stanza speaks of yet another figure, called Heiðr, who practise *seiðr*, and say that she was a wicked woman's favourite.

The name *Gullveig* is mentioned in *Vǫluspá* on one single occasion, in a mythical context that is difficult to interpret. The stanza that mentions her is puzzling and opens up for many interpretations. What is the meaning of this, and who, or what, is this cryptic figure called Gullveig? Why do the gods torture her, and how does this affect them? Was this incident considered significant, and how can it be explained? In the following, I will try to argue that Gullveig can be explained, and that she fits into a pattern of conflict and interaction between gods and giants in Old Norse mythology. Before I present my own point of view, it is necessary to give a brief summary of earlier interpretations.

How Was this Episode Explained in Earlier Studies?

Naturally, there have been many different explanations for the Gullveig episode, from the 1800s until the present day. There is not enough space to mention all of them and I will only refer to those that I believe have been most significant. This will be done chronologically and as briefly as possible, before I present my own reading of the text.

An early – and probably the most influential – analysis of the Gullveig episode was presented by Karl Müllenhof,[9] who believed that Gullveig was a personification of gold. For him, she represented the destructive powers of gold, as well as its seductive and ensnaring influences. He argued that she was the same person as Heiðr and that she could be identified with the *vǫlva* who speaks in the poem.[10] Sophus Bugge, on the other hand, thought that Gullveig was one of the Æsir and that she was killed by the Vanir in Óðinn's Hall. For him, the episode explained how the war broke out. He did not believe that Heiðr was the same being as Gullveig and assumed that she (Heiðr) was a giantess and the narrator in the poem.[11]

Elard Hugo Meyer argued for a Christian context and believed that the influence of Christian literature was evident in Vǫluspá. He compared Gullveig with Ambrose's comment on Eve in Paradise, who was beguiled into sin by the Devil's poisonous arrows. This, in turn, was associated with descriptions in the Bible of the Whore of Babylon, both in the Book of Revelation and in Jeremiah, where she is called the golden goblet (calix aureus) and it is said that she must burn. He also thought that the war in Vǫluspá referred to God's war with the fallen and rebellious angels.[12]

Another line of thought was to try to trace Gullveig back to classical sources. Wolfgang Krause[13] compared Gullveig with Pandora, while H. W. Stubbs[14] tried to find a link between Norse and Greek myths, where Gullveig was seen as a combined version of Eris and Aphrodite. Georges Dumézil presented yet another explanation. He compared the episode with a Roman legend that speaks of how the city of Rome was founded. In the Roman narrative, two different tribes, the Sabines (compared with the Vanir), and another group that follows Romulus (compared with the Æsir) wage war for the region that would later become Rome. The Sabines have almost conquered the city by bribing a woman, Tarpeia, from their opponent's side (with gold or love, according to two different accounts). Dumézil thought that this legend could be used to explain the fact that Gullveig was sent to the Æsir by the Vanir, where she corrupts them with a strong craving for gold, a desire that manifests itself among the Æsir goddesses.[15]

Robert Höckert[16] claimed that the war between the gods was at the heart of Vǫluspá, and that it was its major topic. He believed that the poem described a religious war between two people, an older agriculturally oriented Vanir religion, and a younger war-oriented Æsir religion. In his thesis[17] he argued that Gullveig was identical with Heiðr and the vǫlva who speaks in Vǫluspá, and that they could be interpreted as a personification of the mythical mead as a mythical female being that belonged to the Vanir; as such, she was associated with the mythic mead and its mythical source.[18]

Sigurður Nordal believed that Gullveig was identical with Heiðr and that she was to be identified with one of the Vanir.

Nordal essentially followed Müllenhof (above) when he assumed that she represented the power of gold and its intoxicating and seductive qualities.[19]

Yet another approach was to compare Gullveig's immolation with ritual activity. Anne Holtsmark[20] thought that the torture of Gullveig might have something to do with some kind of "battle magic", where she represented an image of the enemy. Torment of that image meant that the same kind of injury would befall the one the imitation was meant to represent. The purpose was to give the Æsir an advantage in the approaching war with the Vanir. Another theory was proposed by Rudolf W. Fischer.[21] He thought that the spears that strike and pierce (or are used to prop up) Gullveig three times, as well as her burnings, were a reflection of ancient ritual used in the purification of gold. Heino Gehrts[22] also thought that the episode reflected ancient cultic practice; in his view it represented a ritual sacrifice and the battle that follows was consequently identified as a ritual combat. Initiation and warfare were also the perspectives preferred by Andreas Nordberg[23] who argued that the ritual of spearing Gullveig was imitated in the cult and that the cosmological meaning was to spread the desire for gold and consequently to stimulate war in the world.

John McKinnell compared the burning of Gullveig with an episode from *Grímnismál*, where Óðinn is tortured between two fires with the purpose of obtaining knowledge from him. According to McKinnell, the gods try to do the same thing with Gullveig – they want to win gold, or learn how to create it themselves. The madness this results in is that the gods wage war against the Vanir.[24] McKinnell has also suggested that Gullveig might be an idol or a gold foil figure ("guldgubbe") of Freyja, which is attacked by spears and burned: "Just as gold emerges refined from the fire, the cult of the goddess herself lives on; she is re-born, not as Heiðr, but as herself".[25]

Margaret Clunies Ross argued against the idea that Gullveig was an invention by the *Vǫluspá* poet(s), as the figure fits general themes in Old Norse mythology.[26] Gullveig and Freyja are performing the same mythological functions, whether or not they were understood as being one and the same. She argues convincingly that there are some similarities between the arrival of the three giant maidens in stanza 8 and the advent of Gullveig. The reason is that the gods reject the possibility of a marriage alliance with these women and their own group. She explains that it might have been the Vanir who sent her in the hope of getting something in exchange, but that they become outraged when the Æsir attack and try to destroy Gullveig.[27] This falls into her theoretical pattern of negative reciprocity, social relations between the Æsir, the Vanir, and the giants, in Old Norse mythology.[28]

Gullveig could also symbolically represent female powers. Gro Steinsland and Preben Meulengracht Sørensen thought that Gullveig and Heiðr were identical figures. They were not convinced that she should be interpreted only as Freyja. They suggested that she is rather a mythical feminine force that lives on in different forms: as Freyja, as the vǫlva who speaks in Vǫluspá, and as Heiðr. Her killing is seen as a ritual killing.[29] A different interpretation was presented by Else Mundal. In her opinion, a good way to approach Gullveig is to compare her with other mythical females that have been scorched by fire and associate them as personifications of "female chaos". Mundal thinks that Gullveig has been reborn in new shapes and that Angrboða could be one of them. Her argument partly rests on Hyndlulióð 41, in which Loki devours a woman's burnt heart, upon which he becomes pregnant and gives birth to all the troll women (flagð) in the world.[30] Another woman who was scorched by fire is, of course, the giantess Hyrrokkin.

One of the most common identifications of Gullveig is that she is to be understood as a hypostasis of Freyja. This idea is usually traced back to Gabriel Turville-Petre. The theory has been favoured by many scholars.[31] In the words of Turville-Petre:

> Gullveig can hardly be other than Freyja, the Vanadis and foremost of the Vanir [...]. It is not known how Freyja came to Ásgarð[r] or the hall of Óðinn, but if we can identify her with Gullveig, it was because of her that the war of the gods broke out. It could be suggested that Gullveig (Freyja) had been sent to Ásgarð[r] by the Vanir in order to corrupt the Æsir with greed, lust and witchcraft. Attempts by the Æsir to destroy her were vain, and she still lives.[32]

Ursula Dronke[33] links Gullveig to the mysterious Þorgerðr Hǫlgabrúðr, who is also associated with gold. In an earlier article, she identified Gullveig with Freyja and proposed, with an imaginative reconstruction of the earlier stages of the myth, that Gullveig is an idol that is burnt to get back at the Vanir, whose forces were led by Freyja herself.[34]

The last theory to be presented here is not the latest, but has recently been picked up by Katja Schulz,[35] and can, therefore, serve as a good bridge extending from earlier theories to my own. Eugen Mogk[36] proposed that the war described in *Vǫluspá* is a Nordic version of a Gigantomachia, i.e. it concerns a war fought between the gods as a group and the giants. The gods march together against the giants but fare ill and are almost defeated; in the end they must offer Freyja, the sun and the moon to the giants. His idea is repeated by Katja Schulz in her thesis.[37] Both of them consider Gullveig to be a giantess, and not one of the Vanir.[38] This interpretation is worth considering, and I will return to this question below.

Gullveig and Heiðr

Before we turn the spotlight on Gullveig, a few words need to be said about an earlier stanza of the poem that introduces *þriár þursa meyiar*, as I think they are of importance for solving the puzzle and can shed light on the elusive Gullveig-episode.

8   *Teflðo í túni, teitir vóro,*
    var þeim vættergis vant ór gulli,
    unz þriár qvómu, þursa meyiar,
    ámátcar miǫk, ór iǫtunheimom.[39]

   They played chequers in the meadow, they were merry,
   they did not lack for gold at all,
   until three ogre-girls came,
   all-powerful women, out of Giant-land.[40]

Some critics have identified these three giantesses with the fates, but, in my opinion, there is no reason for doing so, as they actually appear in stanza 20. What is clear, however, is that the arrival of the three giant maidens somehow breaks the golden age that the gods up until now have prospered in. The *tafl* "board game" seems to indicate an aristocratic setting, which is confirmed by the abundance of gold, the very symbol of power and wealth. We know, then, that the poet(s) identified these three maidens with deterioration and the end of a peaceful and prosperous age. This narrative ends with the arrival of the giant women and moves on to speak of the creation of dwarves and list dwarf names (stanza 9–16), and then explains how human beings came into being (stanza 17–18), and after that speaks of the appearance of the three fates (stanza 20). Reading this, it seems as if the narrative of the gods and their primordial age of prosperity is somehow broken off. When the narrative returns to the gods, it speaks of the torturing of Gullveig in the High One's Hall and the outbreak of the first war in the world.

Gullveig is, as mentioned previously, found nowhere else. The first element of her name, *Gull-*, is uncomplicated and means "gold", but the second element, *-veig*, is harder to interpret, because it can be associated with many different words and usages. It is usually, after Karl Müllenhof,[41] understood as "intoxication by gold", that is, as an allegorical figure that symbolizes the greed for gold. Lotte Motz[42] interpreted the name as "golden (coloured) drink" and suggested that both Heiðr and Gullveig represented the first brewing of mead. John McKinnell[43] has argued for another meaning, supported by a careful lexicographical study, where the second element should be understood as something that refers to "military power", or simply "woman". When linked to military power, the root is that found in ON *víg* "war" and Gothic *weihan* "to fight".[44] The name is therefore interpreted as "woman made of gold", "gold-adorned woman", or "gold-adorned military power".[45] In other words, McKinnell opens up for the possibility of interpreting her name in ways other than the common reading of its elements as "gold" and "drink".

In stanza 22, just after the immolation of Gullveig, the poem speaks of a female figure called Heiðr, skilled in *seiðr*, who came to houses. Who is she, and why is she specified as the favourite of a wicked woman? The name *Heiðr* can be found in several sagas as the name of a *vǫlva*.[46] The name in the sagas probably goes back to a mythical prototype. According to Jan de Vries, the name is just an epithet for a *vǫlva* in general and not the personal name of a given person. Maybe the *vǫlur* from the sagas have been given their name from a similar oral tradition to the poem? The name Heiðr can also be found in *Hyndlulióð*, stanza 32, listed with Hrossþjófr as children of the giant Hrímnir. It is uncertain whether the poem lists two brothers, or a brother and sister (I prefer the latter reading). Nevertheless, the name is being used in this source as the name of someone who is of giant kin. The same poem, in stanza 33, also says that all *vǫlur* derive from Viðólfr; a name that can be interpreted as "forest wolf" and therefore links the figure with uncultivated land and wilderness. The connection is interesting compared to the troll woman, probably a giantess, in *Vǫluspá* 39, who sit in Iron-wood (*Iárnviði*) and give birth to Fenrir's offspring (all the wolves in the world). Therefore, there might be some basis for considering Heiðr in *Vǫluspá* as a giantess who knew how to practice *seiðr*. Giants skilled in sorcery are a common motif in the Old Norse sources, especially in myths about Óðinn. In the poem, Heiðr is said to be a wicked woman's favourite.

Who is this wicked woman? There are a couple of female giants that are said to be wicked; one can be found in *Hyndlulióð* 41 and is the one from whom Loki eats a burned heart and becomes pregnant: "Lopt was impregnated by the wicked woman (*af kono illri*), from whom every ogress on earth is descended". The other giantess who is said to be wicked and mother of benign giants, is the *vǫlva*/speaker of *Baldrs draumar*. In stanza 13, Óðinn says, in a heated exchange of words, that she is not a seeress (*vǫlva*), nor a wise woman (*vís kona*), but a mother of three giant women (*þriggia þursa móðir*). Some of the giantesses that Þórr encounters on his journeys can also be considered wicked, for example the daughters of Geirrǫðr (in *Þórsdrápa* and in Snorri's *Skáldskaparmál* 18) or the giantesses he brags that he has killed in *Hárbarðslióð* (stanzas 23, 37–39).

The wicked woman who does harm to the gods, referred to in *Vǫluspá*, is probably a giantess; it might even be a reference to the *vǫlva* herself or to Gullveig (or both). Else Mundal thinks that Heiðr is the joy of Gullveig, because she promotes disorder by way of her witchcraft and that they are both dangerous to the gods' world order.[47] I think this is a reasonable explanation. Clunies Ross noted that in the whole of the Old Norse mythological corpus, Gullveig is the only non-giant female being who is killed by a male or by a group of males.[48] The most common way to kill a sorcerer or witch was execution by destroying the individual by fire, something that is supported by continental Germanic and Scandinavian legal codes, as well as in the penal codes of the majority of the Indo-European peoples.[49] Gullveig/Heiðr can be related to the three mighty giantesses mentioned earlier, that somehow managed to ruin the gods' prosperous age. If we consider that Gullveig/Heiðr is sent by the giants to the gods, and that she is a great practitioner of sorcery who wreaks havoc among the gods with her magic, and that the gods respond by trying to destroy her in flames, then the anomaly that Clunies Ross noted would simply disappear; she is indeed a female giant that a group of male gods try to kill. It would also be a reasonable cause for starting a war with the giant race.

When considering what we can glean of the principal elements of the mythical narrative about Gullveig so far, we can identify the following: the first war in the world was caused in some way by the actions of unnamed beings ("they stuck Gullveig with spears") in spearing and then burning her in the High One's (likely Óðinn's) Hall; they burned her three times, but she was reborn three times and she still lives. No information is given in stanza 21 as to who "they" were and who Gullveig was, but I think we can reasonably assume that "they" in this case were the gods (who are the inhabitants of Óðinn's Hall). The next stanza (22) then mentions that "they" called her Heiðr, wherever she came to houses. Who "they" are is not specified, but I will, following Clunies Ross, interpret them as "humans".[50] Following the discussion above, this seems to indicate that Gullveig has transformed herself into a vǫlva who practises seiðr. Consequently, this episode can be interpreted as a narrative that takes us from the mythic to the mundane. This contrastive sphere of activity, from a divine hall to a house, suggests that Gullveig/Heiðr has been translated from the divine to the human world.[51] This might also explain why the name is used for vǫlur in the sagas; it might even suggest that it was meant to point to hostile elements known from mythological traditions, where it is used as a name for a perilous giantess, skilled in sorcery.

A Proto-typical War Fought Between Gods and Giants

Immediately after the immolation of Gullveig and the appearance of Heiðr, the gods have a meeting and deliberate whether they ought to pay a tribute or share sacrificial feasts. Who they should pay tribute to is not mentioned, nor who should share the sacrificial feasts with them. It seems as if the gods decide not to pay tribute or share their feasts. Instead, it seems as if Óðinn's answer to this crisis is a declaration of war. In the next verse (stanza 24), Óðinn hurls his spear at (or over, as a sign of symbolic supremacy) the host of his enemies.[52] But the war goes badly and the gods see their battlements broken down by their enemies. In this context, the Vanir and their proficiency with magic are mentioned. It does not say who they aim their spells at, but I think that they are marching out from the stronghold, entering the battlefield, wielding war-spells (*vígspá*). Their magic skills and the element of surprise are just what the gods need to turn the tide and strike back at their overwhelming enemies.

> 23 *Þá gengo regin ǫll á rǫcstóla,*
> *ginnheilog goð, oc um þat gættuz,*
> *hvárt scyldo æsir afráð gialda*
> *eða scyldo goðin ǫll gildi eiga.*[53]
>
> Then all the Powers went to the thrones of fate,
> the sacrosanct gods, and considered this:
> whether the Æsir should yield the tribute
> or whether all the gods should share sacrificial feasts.[54]

> 24 *Fleygði Óðinn oc í fólc um scaut,*
> *þat var enn fólcvíg fyrst í heimi;*
> *brotinn var borðveggr borgar ása,*
> *knátto vanir vígspá vǫllo sporna.*[55]
>
> Odin hurled a spear, sped it into the host;
> that was war still, the first in the world;
> the wooden rampart of the Æsir's stronghold was wrecked;
> the Vanir, with war-spell, kept on trampling the plain.[56]

Most commentators have interpreted the first war in the world as a war between the Æsir and the Vanir.[57] This interpretation is dependent on Snorri Sturluson's narratives (*Ynglinga saga* 4 and *Skáldskaparmál* G. 57), where he makes it clear that the two tribes of gods fought. But his accounts do not resemble the one found in the poem. Snorri places it as a part of the creation of the mead of poetry; he never mentions Gullveig or Heiðr. It might be, as Clunies Ross[58] has pointed out, that Snorri, for some reason, might have chosen to omit the passage of Gullveig, from his narrative as he also did with the sacrifice of Óðinn.[59]

If we look closer at stanza 24, it could as easily mean that the giants had broken down the god's defences. The Vanir mentioned in the next line, *knátto vanir vígspá vǫllo sporna*, could be interpreted as a synonym for "gods", or simply indicate that the Vanir attacked the giants with their magic. Therefore, the poet(s) might have understood the two separate groups of gods as fighting a battle, not among themselves, but as allies against a common foe – the giants. The poet(s) use different synonyms for "gods" in the poem, and this instance is probably no exception.[60]

Lately, there has even been a discussion concerning the existence of the Vanir as a group. The idea was put forward by Rudolf Simek,[61] who used philological arguments against the existence of the Vanir as a distinct group of gods. This heated debate is not really of interest here, although I would like to propose that there is nothing in the poem itself that supports a battle between Æsir and Vanir.[62] Besides, if we turn to Snorri and his narrative of the Master Builder tale (*Gylfaginning* 42), it is quite clear that the giant who is the master builder is supposed to build a fortress that can protect the gods, not against the Vanir, but against the threat of giants:

> *Þat var snimma í ǫndverða bygð goðanna, þá er goðin hǫfðu sett Miðgarð ok gert Valhǫll, þá kom þar smiðr nokkvorr ok bauð at gera þeim borg á þrim misserum svá góða at trú ok ørugg væri fyrir bergrisum ok hrímþursum þótt þeir komi inn um Miðgarð.*[63]

> It was right at the beginning of the gods' settlement, when the gods had established Midgard and built Val-hall, there came there a certain builder and offered to build them a fortification in three seasons so good that it would be reliable and secure against mountain-giants and frost-giants even though they should come in over Midgard.[64]

Another reason for considering the war as a war fought between gods and giants is that the following two stanzas (25–26) make it obvious that the giants are involved in a conflict with the gods.[65] They have somehow stolen a goddess, and Þórr, the biggest enemy of the giants, becomes furious and seemingly breaks all kinds of oaths and sacred vows, presumably to get her back.

25   *Þá gengo regin ǫll á rǫcstóla,*
     ginnheilog goð, oc um þat gættuz,
     hverir hefði lopt alt lævi blandit
     eða ætt iǫtuns Óðs mey gefna.[66]

Then all the Powers went to the thrones of fate,
the sacrosanct gods, and considered this:
which people had troubled the air with treachery,
or given Od's girl to the giant race.[67]

26   *Þórr einn þar vá, þrunginn móði,*
     hann sialdan sitr, er hann slíct um fregn;
     á genguz eiðar, orð oc sœri,
     mál ǫll meginlig, er á meðal fóro.[68]

Thor alone struck a blow there, swollen with rage,
he seldom sits still when he hears such a thing;
the oaths broke apart, words and promises,
all the solemn pledges which had passed between them.[69]

Þórr is inflamed by rage: all pledges, oaths and promises are broken apart (stanza 26). The reason is that Óðr's maid (*Óðs mey*) has been given to the giant race (stanza 25). This female figure can likely be understood as Freyja, who deceitfully has been given to the giants, something that must have resulted in a crisis for the gods (as a group). The person responsible for this trickery could very well be Loki; indeed, it would fit his trickster character and unreliable nature as we know him from the sources.[70] It is up to Þórr to get her back, probably by the use of force and violence. This follows a mythological pattern where the giants try to steal the goddesses that we can easily recognize from other sources.[71]

There are, I believe, reasons for considering the primeval battle between gods and giants as an old mythic motif. A primordial war between gods and another race of beings is not unique for Old Norse mythology. It might be fruitful to consider comparative material from other mythological traditions, both Indo-European as well as other traditions. There are some parallels in oriental mythology, particularly among different succession myths and the conception of ancient gods vanquished to the underworld, for example in Greek, Hittite, Phoenician, and Babylonian mythology.[72] The Babylonian god Marduk won his sovereignty by overthrowing Kingu, Tiamat, and their armies; while the Vedic god Indra won his by overcoming Vritra and Vritra's hosts.[73] If we turn to Greek mythological traditions, there are descriptions of two great wars that the gods fought, first against the Titans and later against the Gigantes. As Walter Burkert says, "Power is latent violence which must have been manifested at least in some mythical once-upon-a-time. Superiority is guaranteed only be defeated inferiors".[74]

The giants (known as Titans and Gigantes) in Greek mythology are famous for waging wars against the Olympian gods – the Titanomachy and the Gigantomachy. There are various descriptions of these wars; the most detailed is the one between the gods and the Titans as an older generation and rival group for supremacy. The most comprehensive account is given in Hesiod's *Theogony* (e.g. line 617–735), a poem that is usually dated to the decades before or after 700 BC. A similar, but by no means identical, narrative can be found in Apollodorus' *The Library*.[75] A brief account of the main events can be summarized as follows: just as Kronos overthrew his father Ouranos, Kronos in turn is overthrown by his own son Zeus. It is this battle that is called the Titanomachy, where Zeus alongside his supporters and his brothers and sisters fought from Mount Olympos, while Kronos and many of the Titans fought from Mount Othrys. The war shook the universe to its foundations and the tumult is described as immense. It was as if heaven and earth collided. In the end, Zeus summoned the Cyclopes and the Hundred-handed. With their help they managed to overcome Kronos and his Titans. The Hundred-handed were set as prison guards over the Titans in the depth of Tartarus. The mother of the Titans, Gaia, became furious and urged her other children, the Gigantes, to go to war against the gods. Their overwhelming attack on Olympos could only be defeated with the help of a mortal, Herakles. After the Gigantes were beaten, another fearsome monstrous being called Typhon attacked the gods and challenged Zeus, who in the end managed to defeat the monster with his thunderbolts.[76]

The beings who challenge the gods' position as supreme, be it giants or something else, did not only represent primeval disorder, but all the terrible and frightening forces that still remain in the world and that could periodically threaten the order that the gods had secured by force: hurricane, flood, fire, volcanic eruption, earthquake, eclipse, disease, famine, war, crime, darkness, death, freezing cold, and so on.[77] After the gods have fought with the giants in Vǫluspá, the world will slowly degenerate and ultimately be destroyed in a final battle. Most of the catastrophic and traumatic events listed above influence this period of disaster, among the gods as well as on earth. It will increasingly do so before the gods and the giants fight one last time and the earth is scorched by fire and sinks into the depths of the sea. Disastrous events of this kind are indeed described in Vǫluspá, especially from stanza 39 to 56.

Many of the suggested comparative sources can be used to argue that it might as well fit a war between two different tribes of gods, i.e. the Æsir and the Vanir, but most of the material found in comparative mythology seems to concern a generational schism between an older and a younger group of gods. There is nothing in the sources to suggest that the Æsir and the Vanir were related. But the giants on the other hand are, however, clearly described as an older generation of beings that are indeed related by blood to the Æsir (at least on their mother's side).[78] Therefore, it is much more fruitful to associate the comparative mythological traditions with the gods and the giants, not between two separate groups of gods (albeit the giants in Old Norse religion were not considered to be an older generation of gods). In the mythological traditions, the primeval giants served as an explanation for how the world came into being and are regarded as mythological beings (without any cult).

The main point of these mythological traditions is to explain how the gods, with their use of force and cunning, defeated the giants. It also gives a reason for how they continue to fight and compete with them for power over the cosmos. This cosmological conflict and tension is a part of life for the sacred and the profane. In the end, this fight for dominance will end with Ragnarøk, a final powerful confrontation between the gods and the giants, which will affect all living things, and be the end of the world as we know it.

Breaking the Sacred Rules of the Hall

My arguments relating to the account given in *Vǫluspá* are linked to my general theory of interactions between gods and giants from the perspective of a hall. What really intrigues me is that the scene presented in the poem actually takes place in Óðinn's Hall, and that it is the gods who first resorts to violence, not the giants. From my point of view, sacrilegious acts in a hall and the breaking of the truce therein, might explain why the downfall of the gods starts with this episode and eventually leads to warfare and the breaking of words, promises, solemn pledges, and oaths.

When the gods try to shed blood and kill Gullveig, they break the *grið* "truce, pardon, peace"[79] of the hall, and this very act has severe consequences. The account of this violence in Óðinn's Hall seems to be important, even though it is hard to fully comprehend. I think that when the gods resort to violence against her, they also break the truce and sanctity of the hall (*grið*). The result might be that a new figure, by the name of Heiðr, appears. She might be Gullveig reborn, or another figure that represents wicked witchcraft. The episode is a part of the first war in the world. It was by pre-Christian moral standards considered shameful for men to injure women; physical aggression aimed at a woman was disgraceful. It was, furthermore, particularly insulting for the woman's male relatives. Therefore, it could be used as a weapon or strategy for serious defamation that demanded blood vengeance from the women's male relatives. The mythical episode mirrors a state of war. In this world, an extreme and hostile situation (war, violent conflicts, feuds, raids etc.) meant that women were killed or led away as slaves: rough treatment and assault against women, even rape, was not uncommon in this context.[80] The *vǫlva* who speaks in the poem is perhaps trying to insult Óðinn with this information; something that must have been truly shameful, as he actually *failed* to kill Gullveig.

Even though it is nowhere stated that the Æsir are Gullveig's aggressors, the mere fact that she is speared in Óðinn's Hall, is, I believe, strong indications that Óðinn is thought to be responsible for her immolation. Breaking the sacred rules of the hall leads to the downfall of the gods. In many myths, the hall serves as the centre for interaction between giants and gods. Like halls in this world, the mythic halls seem to be protected by the same sets of rules and prohibitions. When the gods are torturing and trying to kill a guest in their hall, the very rules that the gods are meant to uphold and care for are torn apart. Gullveig is not exactly described as a guest, but if we give it some thought, then the gods can be interpreted as representing hosts that act in a way that in every way is considered dishonourable. This kind of behaviour is, as is made clear in *Hávamál*, something that a host should avoid at all costs. The episode might also be an example of how *grið* became institutionalised. As Jarich G. Oosten reminds us of myths: "Many myths explain how the world arouse out of chaos, order out of disorder, and culture out of nature. This is often expressed in a paradoxical way in the structure of the myth itself: a cultural rule or norm is instituted because of the very act it prohibits".[81] This ill treatment of the unexpected guest can perhaps also, in the chronological order of the poem, be seen as progressing Ragnarøk. This is even more emphasized when Þórr breaks oaths, words, promises, and all the solemn pledges (stanza 25, after the first war). Again, it is the giants who are the enemy, and the battle that is fought in *Vǫluspá* is between gods and giants.

I believe that it is possible to assume that gold plays a major part in this episode and that it is also a major reason for the war. But it is hard to say whether the Gullveig-episode is the reason for the war or a result of it. I believe that Gullveig and Heiðr (even if we consider them as two different characters or one and the same) can be traced back to the advent of the giant maidens and the ending of a "golden age". The gods violate the rules of hospitality when they torment and try to kill her in their hall. This was not a minor offence, but a major breach of hospitality, that would lead to a war with the giants.

Gullveig could symbolize a greed for gold, and gold had a major symbolic and powerful value and impact in Old Norse society, not least among chieftains and warriors. Power and wealth went hand in hand and are accompanied by war. We can perhaps understand Gullveig's role as someone who was sent by the giants to spread discord and desire among the gods – principles that could easily be understood by the audience of the poem. A crazed desire and craving for gold. It seems that it is the gods who are acting wrongly when they attack Gullveig in their hall, not the giants. This started the first great struggle for dominion in the world, not between different gods, but a war of gods against giants that will be continued until the breaking of the world.

In his study of *Vǫluspá*, Finnur Jónsson supports Müllenhof's notion that Gullveig's name has something to do with the powerful desire of gold and argues: "Det lå nu meget nær at antage at, at det var jætterne, der havde sendt Guldvég afsted; men det forholder sig dog ikke så."[82] I disagree; the giants have probably, in my opinion, sent Gullveig to the gods, an action that makes the gods break sacred bonds in their hall, and leads to an ongoing conflict and fight for domination and power between gods and giants that characterizes Old Norse mythology as a whole.[83]

Conclusion

When I first wrote about Gullveig for my thesis, I was not aware that Mogk, Mundal and Schulz had already preceded me in thinking that she was a giantess, nor that Mogk and Schulz also thought that the war that followed was fought between gods and giants. I do, however, believe that this theory merits more attention. My main conclusion, as well as my own contribution to the study of Gullveig, is that the brutal treatment of her is a direct violation of *grið*; it is an act that breaks the sanctity and the truce that is supposed to be sustained in a hall. This, in turn, leads to a war with the giants. I believe that this is the first war in the world; therefore, I believe it was proto-typical. A war that is fought between gods and giants can also be found in Greek and Roman mythology and fits with a mythological pattern found in other mythological traditions.

How does this reflect on a hall culture? The mythical tradition of a war between gods and giants in a primordial time can be seen as prototypical for warriors, warlords and chieftains. War and violence were glorified and praised, at least within a warrior ideology. Gullveig is a guest in Óðinn's Hall, and as such she is treated in violation of the rules and norms for a host-guest-relationship that the hall is supposed to secure and maintain. The gods violate *grið* and show how a cultural rule or norm is instituted because of the very act it prohibits. In a hall, rules and norms exist to maintain a status quo between a guest and a host. When someone, as a guest, entered and crossed the threshold of a hall, a suspense and uneasiness, both for the host and for the guest, manifested in the hall. The norm guaranteed safety and security within the hall building.

The narrative of Gullveig takes us from the divine to the human world, something we can gather from the description when, after she is immolated, it can be argued that Gullveig (a threat to the gods in the divine hall) is transformed and returns as Heiðr (a threat to humans in this world). The figure of Gullveig is, as we have seen, usually interpreted as Freyja. The torturing of her has consequently been seen as one of the crucial factors that lead to a warfare between two tribes of gods, the Æsir and the Vanir. I do not agree with this conclusion and have tried to consider another approach. In my opinion, Gullveig does not represent Freyja, nor anyone sent from the Vanir, and the war is not fought between two different tribes of gods. Instead, I believe this to be a version of the first clash between the gods and the giants as two conflicting groups, and I consider Gullveig to be a giantess, sent out by the giants to spread discord among the gods and make them break sacred vows. In the narrative, in the chronological order of events as presented in *Vǫluspá*, this is one of many factors that eventually lead to *Ragnarøk*.

Notes

1. See Kuusela 2017. In this text I will use the term gods as a word that signifies divinities of both sexes (both gods and goddesses).

2. Only two different versions of *Vǫluspá* have survived, in the manuscripts *Codex Regius* and *Hauksbók*. Parts of the poem are quoted in Snorri Sturluson's *The Prose Edda*, but he does not mention Gullveig.

The audience of the poem, however, ought to have known who she was, or at least have been able to figure it out without much effort. Gullveig is probably one of these figures that we only know of from one source, but who might have been well-known in oral tradition. Old Norse oral tradition must have been diverse, with numerous versions of myths and motifs than we no longer know of. In the following, the text quoted from *The Poetic Edda* is taken from the edition of Neckel and Kuhn (1962) and all of the translations are quoted from Carolyne Larrington (2014).

3. I base this statement on the fact that she refers to herself as being nurtured by giants, and that her first memory is of giants (stanza 2).

4. McKinnell 2014 (2001):34.

5. Neckel/Kuhn 1962.

6. Larrington 2014.

7. Neckel/Kuhn 1962.

8. Larrington 2014.

9. Müllenhof 1883.

10. This had actually been suggested earlier by Jacob Grimm (1876–1877:334).

11. Bugge 1867:38–39.

12. Meyer 1889:92–114.

13. Krause 1959.

14. Krause 1959.

15. Dumézil 1973:24.

16. Höckert 1916.

17. Höckert 1926.

18. E.g. Höckert 1926:51–52, 85. I will not repeat many of his, in my opinion, far-reaching ideas that echo Viktor Rydberg's (1886–1889) excessive attempts to bring together a diverse assembly of different female mythical beings from Germanic and Indian mythological traditions. Höckert repeated many of his ideas in 1930, after severe

criticism in a review of his thesis by Elias Wessén (1926) – a defence that was more extensive than his original thesis!

19. Nordal 1927:52–53.

20. Holtsmark 1950.

21. Fischer 1963.

22. Gehrts 1969.

23. Nordberg 2003:94–99.

24. McKinnell 1994:118.

25. McKinnell 2014 (2001):53.

26. The idea that Gullveig was a figment of a composer's imagination was proposed by Sigurður Nordal (1927:61) and was later repeated by Jan de Vries (1962:194).

27. Clunies Ross 1994:198–211.

28. Clunies Ross 1994:103–143.

29. Steinsland & Meulengracht Sørensen 1999:51–53.

30. Mundal 2002:191–193. Even though the stanza does not actually say that the heart belongs to Angrboða.

31. In the influential article on Gullveig in *Reallexikon der Germanischen Altertumskunde* Heinrich Beck (1999:190) trace the theory of Gullveig-Freyja back to Turville-Petre. Edgar C. Polomé (1995:585) mentions, in his article on Freyja, that she is identical to Gullveig and cause for the war between Vanir and Æsir. Cf. Näsström 1995:63; Simek 2006:160.

32. Turville-Petre 1964:159.

33. Dronke 1997.

34. Dronke 1988:229.

35. Schulz 2004.

36. Mogk 1925.

37. Schulz 2001:108–109.

38. As far as I know, Katja Schulz is the first person, since Eugen Mogk, to classify Gullveig as a giantess. The same identification was also proposed by Else Mundal (2002), but she does not make a reference to neither Schulz nor Mogk.

39. Neckel/Kuhn 1962.

40. Larrington 2014.

41. Müllenhof 1883.

42. Motz 1993.

43. McKinnell 2014 (2001).

44. Hugo Gering & B. Sijmons (1927:27) also adds the Latin *vīc-i* to this group and argues for a connection with conquest and battle.

45. McKinnell 2014 (2001):48.

46. The parallel between the names Gullveig and Heiðr is usually considered to be semantic; as ON *heiðr* 'fame', adj. 'shining' is in agreement with Gullveig, *if* the name is understood as "gold intoxication". The name *Heiðr*, however, can also be derived from the feminine noun *heiðr*, meaning "heath"; probably semantically related to the adj. *heiðinn* "heathen" (McKinnell 2014 (2001):35).

47. Mundal 2002:193.

48. Clunies Ross 1994:208 n. 16.

49. Ström 1942:189–198.

50. Clunies Ross 1994:204.

51. I am indebted to Margaret Clunies Ross for proposing this interpretation (private correspondence).

52. Cf. Nordberg 2003:107–112.

53. Neckel/Kuhn 1962.

54. Larrington 2014.

55. Neckel/Kuhn 1962.

56. Larrington 2014.

57. Cf. Weinhold 1890; Eckhardt 1940; Dronke 1988; Nordberg 2003:107–120.

58. Clunies Ross 1994:200.

59. The same could be said of the framework of *Vǫluspá* where Óðinn gains cosmological insights from the *vǫlva* or in *Vafþrúðnismál* where he gets it from Vafþrúðnir in the giant's hall.

60. Cf. stanza 4: *Burs synir*; stanza 6, 9, 23, 25: *regin ǫll, ginnheilǫg goð*; stanza 23: *goðin ǫll*.

61. Simek 2010.

62. Cf. Simek 2010; Frog & Roper 2011; Tolley 2011; Schjødt 2014.

63. Snorri Sturluson 2005:34.

64. Transl. Anthony Faulkes 2005:35.

65. In the *Hauksbók*-manuscript, this episode (21–22) occurs earlier and is placed before the war (26); it is followed by a reference to Heimdallr's hearing (23), and then the giantess in the Iron-Wood giving birth to Fenrir's offspring that is said to threaten mankind and acts as a harbinger of *Ragnarøk* (24–25). Cf. Quinn 1990.

66. Neckel/Kuhn 1962.

67. Larrington 2014.

68. Neckel/Kuhn 1962.

69. Larrington 2014.

70. Cf. de Vries 1933:253–254.

71. Cf. Clunies Ross 1994:107–127.

72. Burkert 2004:32–33.

73. Fontenrose 1980:239.

74. Burkert 1985:128.

75. Apollodorus 1997:27–28, 34–35.

76. Cf. Nilsson 1941:480–486, Dowden 2006:35–39.

77. Fontenrose 1980:219.

78. Óðinn and his brothers descended from Burr on their father's side, the son of the primordial ancestor Búri, and the giantess Bestla on their mother's side, who is the daughter of the giant Bǫlþorn

(*Hávamál* 140). Þórr is the son of Óðinn (in some sources) and a giantess (called Jǫrð, Hlóðyn or Fjǫrgyn). Heimdallr is descended from nine giant women (*Hyndluljóð* 35–37). Týr is described as the son of a giant woman (*Hymiskviða* 11).

79. Fritzner 1954:642–644.

80. Cf. Holtsmark 1964, Jochens 1991, Brink 2012:85–91, Charpentier Ljungqvist 2015.

81. Oosten 1985:6.

82. Finnur Jónsson 1911:23.

83. See Kuusela 2017 for more examples and arguments for the strained relationship between the gods and the giants and how they interact, many times with the aim of humiliating each other, especially in the context of a hall culture.

References

Primary sources

Apollodorus. Hard, Robin. 1997. *The Library of Greek Mythology*. Transl. Robin Hard. Oxford, New York: Oxford University Press.

Edda. Neckel, Gustav & Hans Kuhn. 1962. *Die Lieder des Codex Regius nebst verwandten Denkmälern. I. Text*. 3rd Edition. Heidelberg: Carl Winter.

———— Larrington, Carolyne. 2014. *The Poetic Edda*. Transl. by Carolyne Larrington. 2nd Edition. Oxford: Oxford University Press.

Snorri Sturluson, *Edda*. Faulkes, Anthony. 2005. *Edda. Prologue and Gylfaginning*. Edited by Anthony Faulkes. 2nd Edition. London: Viking Society for Northern Research.

Secondary literature

Beck, Heinrich. 1999. Gullveig. In H. Beck et al. (eds.). *Reallexikon der Germanischen Altertumskunde*, 13. 2nd Edition. Berlin & New York: Walter de Gruyter, 190–191.

Bugge, Sophus. 1867. *Norrœn fornkvæði: islandsk samling af folkelige oldtidsdigte om Nordens guder og heroer: almindelig kaldet Sæmundar Edda hins fróða.* Christiania: P. T. Mallings forlagsboghandel.

Brink, Stefan. 2012. *Vikingarnas slavar. Den nordiska träldomen under yngre järnålder och äldsta medeltid.* Stockholm: Atlantis.

Burkert, Walter. 1985 (1977). *Greek Religion.* Transl. John Raffan. Cambridge: Harvard University Press.

Burkert, Walter. 2004. *Babylon, Memphis, Persepolis. Eastern Contexts of Greek Culture.* Cambridge, London: Harvard University Press.

Charpentier Ljungqvist, Fredrik. 2015. Rape in the Icelandic Sagas. An Insight in the Perceptions about Sexual Assaults on Women in the Old Norse World. In *Journal of Family History* 40:4, 431–447.

Clunies Ross, Margaret. 1994. *Prolonged Echoes. Old Norse Myths in Northern Society. Vol. 1: The Myths.* (Viking Collection, 7). Odense: Odense University Press.

Dowden, Ken. 2006. *Zeus.* (Gods and Heroes of the Ancient World) London and New York: Routledge.

Dronke, Ursula. 1988. The War of the Æsir and the Vanir in Vǫluspá. In G. W. Weber (Ed.). *Idee-Gestalt-Geschichte. Festschrift Klaus von See.* Odense; Odense University Press, 223–238.

Dronke, Ursula. 1997. *The Poetic Edda. Vol. 2: Mythological Poems.* Oxford: Clarendon.

Dumézil, Georges. 1973 (1959). *Gods of the Ancient Northmen.* 2nd Edition. Publications of the UCLA Center for the Study of Comparative Folklore and Mythology, 3. Berkeley & Los Angeles: University of California Press.

Eckhardt. Karl A. 1940. *Der Wanenkrieg.* Germanenstudien, 3. Bonn: Schriften des Deutschrechlichen Instituts.

Fischer, R. W. 1963. Gullveig Wandlung: Versuch einer läutender Deutung des Kultes in Hars Halle. In *Antaios* 4, 581–596.

Fontenrose, Joseph. 1980 (1959). *Python. A Study of Delphic Myth and Its Origins.* Berkeley: University of California Press.

Fritzner, Johan. 1954 (1886). *Ordbog over det gamle norske sprog*, I–III. Oslo: Møller.

Frog & Jonathan Roper. 2011. Verses versus the 'Vanir': Response to Simek's 'Vanir Obituary'. In *Retrospective Methods Network Newsletter* 2, 29–37.

Gehrts, Heino. 1969. Die Gullveig-Mythe der Vǫluspá. In *Zeitschrift für deutsche Philologie* 88, 312–378.

Gering, Hugo & Sijmons, B. 1927. *Die Lieder der Edda. Kommentar zu dem Lieder der Edda*. Germanistische Handbibliotek. Halle: Buchhandlung der Waisenhauses.

Grimm, Jacob. 1876–1877 (1835). *Deutsche Mythologie*, I–III. 4th Edition. Gütersloh: Bertelsmann.

Holtsmark, Anne. 1950. *Forelesninger over Vǫluspá, hösten 1949* (Universities studentkontor). Oslo: Skrivmaskinstua.

Holtsmark, Anne. 1964. Kvinnerov. In *Kulturhistoriskt lexikon för nordisk medeltid* IX. Malmö: Allhems förlag, 574–576.

Höckert, Robert. 1916. Vǫluspá och vanakriget. In *Festskrift tillägnad Vitalis Norström på 60-årsdagen den 29 januari 1916*. Göteborg: Wettergren & Kerber, 293–309.

Höckert, Robert. 1926. *Vǫluspá och vanakulten*. Uppsala: Almqvist & Wiksell.

Höckert, Robert. 1930. *Vǫluspá och vanakulten*, II. Uppsala: Almqvist & Wiksell.

Jochens, Jenny. 1991. The Illicit Love Visit. An Archaeology of Old Norse Sexuality. In *Journal of the History of Sexuality* 1:3, 357–392.

Jónsson, Finnur. 1911. *Völu-spá. Völvens spådom*. Studier fra sprog- og oldtidsforskning. Det philologisk-historiske samfund, 84. København: Tillge's boghandel.

Jónsson, Finnur. 1932. *De gamle Eddadigte*. København: Gads Forlag.

Krause, Wolfgang. 1959. Gullveig und Pandora. In *Skandinavistik* 5, 1–6.

Kuusela, Tommy. 2017. *"Hallen var lyst i helig frid": Interaktion mellan gudar och jättar, belyst från perspektivet av en fornnordisk hallmiljö*. Stockholm: Stockholms universitet.

McKinnell, John. 1994. *Both One and Many. Essays on Change and Variety in Late Norse Heathenism*. Philologia: saggi, ricerche, edizioni, 1. Roma: Il Calamo.

McKinnell, John. 2014 (2001). On Heiðr and Gullveig. In D. Kick & J. D. Shafer (eds.). *Essays on Eddic Poetry*. Toronto Old Norse and Icelandic Series, 7. Toronto: University of Toronto Press, 34–58.

Meyer, Elard H. 1889. *Völuspa. Eine Untersuchung*. Berlin: Mayer & Müller.

Mogk, Eugen. 1925. Zur Gigantomachie der Vǫluspá. In *Folklore Fellowship Communications* 58, Helsinki: Suomalainen tiedeakatemia, 1–10.

Motz, Lotte. 1993. Gullveig's Ordeal. A new interpretation. In *Arkiv för nordisk filologi* 108, 80–92.

Müllenhoff, Karl. 1883. Ueber die Völuspá. In *Deutsche Altertumskunde* 5:1. Berlin: Weidmann, 1–157.

Mundal, Else. 2002. Austr sat in aldna ... Giantesses and Female Powers in Vǫluspá. In R. Simek & W. Heizman (eds.). *Mythological Women. Studies in Memory of Lotte Motz (1922–1997)*. Studia Medievalia Septentrionalia, 7. Wien: Fassbaender, 185–195.

Nilsson, Martin P. 1941. *Geschichte der Griechischen Religion*, 1. München: C. H. Beck.

Nordberg, Andreas. 2003. *Krigarna i Odins sal: dödsföreställningar och krigarkult i fornnordisk religion*. Stockholm: Stockholms universitet.

Nässtrom, Britt-Mari. 1995. *Freyja. The Great Goddess of the North*. Lund Studies in History of Religions, 5. Lund: University of Lund.

Oosten, Jaarich G. 1985. *The War of the Gods. The Social Code in Indo-European Mythology*. London: Routledge.

Polomé, Edgar, C. 1995. Freyja. In *Reallexikon der germanische Altertumskunde*. 2nd Edition. Band 9. Berlin, New York: de Gruyter, 584–587.

Quinn, Judith. 1990. Vǫluspá and the Composition of Eddic Verse. In T. Pàroli (ed.). *Poetry in the Scandinavian Middle Ages. Proceedings of the Seventh International Saga Conference.* Spotelo: Presso la Sede del Centro Studi, 303–320.

Rydberg, Viktor. 1886–1889. *Undersökningar i germanisk mythologi,* I–II. Stockholm: Albert Bonnier.

Schjødt, Jens-Peter. 2014. New Perspectives on the Vanir Gods in Pre-Christian Scandinavian Mythology and Religion. In T. R. Tangherlini (ed.). *Nordic Mythologies. Interpretations, Intersections and Institutions.* Berkley, Los Angeles: North Pinehurst Press, 19–34.

Schulz, Katja. 2004. *Riesen. Von Wissenshütern und Wildnisbewohnern in Edda und Saga.* Skandinavistische Arbeiten, 20. Heidelberg: Winter.

Simek, Rudolf. [1984] 2006. *Lexikon der germanischen Mythologie.* 3rd revised edition. Stuttgart: Alfred Kröner.

Simek, Rudolf. 2010. The Vanir. An Obituary. In *Retrospective Methods Network Newsletter* 1, 10–19.

Steinsland, Gro & Preben Meulengracht Sørensen. 1999. *Voluspå.* Oslo: Pax forlag.

Stubbs, H. W. 1959. Troy, Asgard, and Armageddon. In *Folklore* 70, 440–459.

Schjødt, Jens Peter. 2014. New Perspectives on the Vanir Gods in pre-Christian Scandinavia Mythology and Religion. In T. R. Tangherlini (ed.). *Nordic Mythologies. Interpretations, Intersections, and Institutions.* Berkeley & Los Angeles: North Pinehurst Press, 19–34.

Sigurður Nordal. 1927 (1923). *Völuspá. Vølens spådom.* Transl. Hans Albrectsen. København: Aschehoug, dansk forlag.

Ström, Folke. 1942. *On the Sacral Origins of the Germanic Death Penalties.* Lund: Håkan Ohlssons boktryckeri.

Tolley, Clive. 2011. In Defence of the Vanir. In *The Retrospective Network Newsletter* 2, 20–28.

Turville-Petre, Gabriel. 1964. *Myth and Religion of the North. The Religion of Ancient Scandinavia*. New York: Holt, Rinehart and Winston.

de Vries, Jan. 1933. *The Problem of Loki*. Folklore Fellowship Communications, 110. Helsinki: Suomalainen Tiedeakatemia.

de Vries, Jan. 1962. *Altnordisches etymologisches Wörterbuch*. 2nd Edition. Leiden: Brill.

Weinhold, Karl. 1890. Über den Mythus vom Wanenkrieg. In *Sitzungsberichte der Könglich Preußischen Akademie der Wissenschaft zu Berlin* 1890, II, 611–625.

Wessén, Elias. 1926. Anmälan. Vǫluspá och vanakulten, I. Akad. Afhandl. af Robert Höckert. In *Arkiv för nordisk filologi* 43, 72–87.

Response

Eldar Heide
University of Bergen

Kuusela draws attention to quite a number of points in the sources which fit best with understanding Gullveig in *Vǫluspá* 21 as a giantess, rather than Freyja or some unspecified female being, and the war in *Vǫluspá* 24 as a war between the giants and the gods, rather than between the two groups of gods. It is a good point that stanza 25 refers to a conflict involving the giants, and that Snorri, too, says that the wall around *Ásgarðr*, which is generally understood as being identical with the *borðveggr ása* in *Vǫluspá* 24, is supposed to protect the gods from the giants. I agree that the mention of the Vanir and their war magic in stanza 24 does not require that the Vanir are the Æsir's opponents in the battle; the idea may well be that war magic is the Vanir's responsibility in their alliance with the Æsir. It also seems very significant that the Æsir's killing of Gullveig would be an anomaly if she were not a giantess, because the Æsir sometimes kill giantesses but not other female beings. In addition, it fits well with this understanding that *Heiðr* is the name of a giantess in several sources, because most scholars believe that Heiðr in stanza 21 and Gullveig in stanza 22 are one and the same. Finally, it makes sense to see the cruelty inflicted upon Gullveig in Óðinn's Hall in relation to the hostility between the gods and giants that accelerates through the mythological history and ends with victory for the giants in the apocalyptic *Ragnarøk* battle. It is not correct, however, that "the downfall of the gods starts with this episode". As Kuusela himself notes earlier in the article, the downfall of the gods in *Vǫluspá* starts with the arrival of the enigmatic giantesses in stanza 8.

As Kuusela points out, it is a problem in the interpretation of Mogk, Schulz, Mundal and himself that Snorri presents the war in question as one between Æsir and Vanir.[1] Rejecting Snorri's version is not in itself too problematic, if there are strong reasons for doing so, because there are several cases (when we know Snorri's sources) where his presentation is disputed by today's scholars (e.g.

the idea that the Norse gods live in heaven[2]). It is hard, though, to see a plausible reason why Snorri would, in a myth about a war between gods and giants, replace the giants with the Vanir. (In the case of the gods living in heaven, Christian influence is an obvious explanation.) After all, the antagonism between gods and giants is essential to his presentation of Old Norse mythology, so we should expect that a primordial war between these two groups would suit him well. Also, Snorri's version to some degree is supported by other Eddic poems. According to *Vafþrúðnismál* 38–39 and *Lokasenna* 34–35, Njǫrðr was sent from the Vanir to the Æsir as a hostage. This would normally imply a settlement of a conflict between Vanir and Æsir,[3] and it happened, apparently, at a very early point in mythological history. The Vanir's magic in the world's first war in *Vǫluspá* 24 fits well into this. For this reason, I find it problematic to reject Snorri's account.

Kuusela says that interpreting Gullveig in *Vǫluspá* 21 as a giantess implies "a new analysis of the first war in the world according to how it is described in Old Norse mythic traditions". We might, however, have to distinguish between the first war in the world and the information about it found in *Vǫluspá* 21–26. If we look at *Vǫluspá* in isolation, the more plausible interpretation may be that the first war was one between the gods and the giants. But, there is evidence of such a war between the Vanir and the Æsir, too. This could mean that there were two myths about this, or two versions of it, similar to how there were two myths of how the world was created (raised from the sea, in *Vǫluspá* 4, or made from the giant Ýmir's body, in *Vafþrúðnismál* 20–21). It is also conceivable that the Vanir and the giants were allies in the same war against the Æsir. Perhaps this could shed light on the enigmatic link between the hostage exchange of Njǫrðr and his humiliation by the giant Hymir's maidens in *Lokasenna* 34 – because, in retrospect, such an alliance would probably be seen as deeply humiliating. This would also be a good reason for Snorri not to mention the alliance. Could it also make sense of *Hymiskviða*'s information that Týr was the son of Hymir? We have no information about how Týr came to the gods, but could he, too, have come there as a hostage? He functions as a hostage guaranteeing a deal with one of the powers of chaos in the only preserved myth about him, the one about the binding of the Fenrir wolf.[4] And in this myth, the gods break their own promises, similar to how they act in Kuusela's interpretation of *Vǫluspá* 21 and in *Vǫluspá* 26. About these questions, we can only speculate.

This is an interesting and well-argued article about an essential, but, alas, probably unsolvable, question in Old Norse mythology. It is no accident that around 10 previous interpretations of the *Vǫluspá* stanzas in question are mentioned in Kuusela's research overview.

Notes

1. *Ynglinga saga* 1941 ch. 4:12–13; *Skáldskaparmál* 4, *Edda Snorra Sturlusonar* 1931:82

2. *Edda Snorra Sturlusonar* 1931:25, 19–20, 22, 25, 29–31, 33 (*Gylfaginning* 9, 6, 8, 9, 10, 11, 13, 18). Cf. Schjødt 1990:40ff., Heide 2014, especially p. 110.

3. Olsson 2016.

4. *Gylfaginning* 21, *Edda Snorra Sturlusonar* 1931:37.

References

Primary Sources

Snorri Sturluson, *Edda*. Finnur Jónsson. 1931. *Edda Snorra Sturlusonar*. Ed. Finnur Jónsson. København: Gyldendal.

Ynglinga saga. Bjarni Aðalbjarnarson. 1941. *Heimskringla I*. Ed. Bjarni Aðalbjarnarson. Íslenzk fornrit XXVI. Reykjavík: Hið íslenzka fornritafélag, 1–83.

Secondary Literature

Heide, Eldar. 2014. Contradictory Cosmology in Old Norse Myth and Religion – But Still a System?. In *Maal og Minne*, 102–43.

Olsson, Stefan. 2016. *Gísl. Givande och tagande av gisslan som rituell handling i fredsprocesser under vikingatid och tidig medeltid*. Ph.D. thesis. Bergen: University of Bergen.

Schjødt, Jens Peter. 1990. Horizontale und vertikale Achsen in der vorchristlichen skandinavischen Kosmologie. In T. Ahlbäck (ed.). *Old Norse and Finnish Religions and Cultic Place-Names. Based on Papers Read at the Symposium on Encounters between Religions in Old Nordic Times and on Cultic Place-Names Held at Åbo, Finland, on the 19th–21st of August 1987.* Scripta instituti Donneriani Aboensis 13. Åbo: Instituti Donneriani Aboensis, 35–57.

Mercury – Wotan – Óðinn: One or Many?[1]

Jens Peter Schjødt
Aarhus University

The aim of this paper is to discuss some aspects of the problem that we face when we are dealing with the Old Norse god Óðinn from the point of view of the History of Religions. The Óðinn figure, as we meet him in the medieval sources, mainly from Iceland, is surely a multi-facetted god and a very complex figure. Therefore, most scholars have been of the opinion that the medieval reception of Óðinn, whom we meet in the extant sources, should be viewed as the "end result", so to speak, of a development from a much simpler state. And there is certainly no doubt that some development has taken place, since no religious or cultural phenomena (or anything else for that matter) remain the same over longer periods. Change is common for all cultural forms. The problem when we attempt to reconstruct the "history" of Óðinn is that we know, as just stated, mainly the "end result", whereas his earlier stages are very little known to us today, mainly because of the source situation. As is well known by all scholars dealing with Old Norse religion or mythology, there has been a major dispute about the historical development of Óðinn: Is he a latecomer (perhaps no earlier than the beginning of the Germanic Iron Age) in Scandinavia or has he been there since the Indo-European migrants arrived (probably towards the beginning of the Bronze Age) – or something in between. What was his original function, and how can we imagine the process that leads to the complex picture which we get from the medieval Icelandic sources? It is not possible in a short article to address all the problems involved in any exhaustive way, so what we shall deal with here will be

How to cite this book chapter:
Schjødt, J. P. 2019. Mercury – Wotan – Óðinn: One or Many?. In: Wikström af Edholm, K., Jackson Rova, P., Nordberg, A., Sundqvist, O. & Zachrisson, T. (eds.) *Myth, Materiality, and Lived Religion: In Merovingian and Viking Scandinavia*. Pp. 59–86. Stockholm: Stockholm University Press. DOI: https://doi.org/10.16993/bay.d. License: CC-BY.

primarily discussing the relation between Óðinn and some earlier divine figures who have been seen to be cognates among other Germanic cultures, and even earlier; this will also include some of the methodological problems involved in such an enterprise. Since the problematic is of a comparative kind, i.e. comparing Óðinn with gods such as Wotan and Mercury we will be dealing to some extent with some problems involved in comparisons, such as the notions of "sameness" and "difference".[2]

A Brief Outline of Contemporary Research in Connection with Óðinn

It seems as if for most scholars during the 20th century the most-often posed questions were concerned with the origin and historical development of the god, and closely tied to this issue, the question of Óðinn's "original" function: was he originally a death god, a wind god, a warrior god, a god of fate or something else.[3] The reason for this kind of question was, especially in the early part of the century, a kind of vulgar cultural evolutionism, maintaining that a phenomenon which is complex must by necessity have been much simpler in earlier stages, and therefore what we see in the medieval sources from Scandinavia as many functions must have been a single one earlier on.[4] It is obvious that the many, sometimes apparently almost contradictory functions that we have for Óðinn, as for instance those related in the *Ynglinga saga* chapters 6 and 7, call for some kind of explanation,[5] whether historical or structural. And until the 1950s or perhaps even the 1960s the explanatory model for most scholars was historical, sometimes supplied with structural arguments. This is the case, then, with the two most prominent names in the discussion about Óðinn during the mid-20th century, Karl Helm and Georges Dumézil, proposing respectively a late arrival to the North (early 6th century AD)[6] and a very early one, namely with the immigration of the Indo-Europeans, i.e. sometime before 2000 BC.

In more recent times, these questions have continued to dominate the debate about Óðinn: on the one hand, there have been attempts to trace the historical roots of this god, and, on the other hand, attempts have been made to establish what his "original" function was, before medieval Christians composed the sources which we now use for our reconstructions. It seems as if most scholars accept without further ado that the Óðinn of these sources must have originated or at least been strongly influenced from somewhere south of Scandinavia – an important view point which I will discuss later. Thus, an East Germanic origin or strong inspiration has been argued by many scholars.[7] In recent years, however, the favourite theory has been that we should turn to the Rhine area as the place to look for most of the characteristic elements in the Óðinn figure. Two of the most interesting theories have been proposed, on the one hand, by Anders Kaliff and Olof Sundqvist who argue for a strong influence from the cult of Mithras, and, on the other hand, by Michael Enright, arguing that Óðinn (Wotan, Wodan etc.), seen as warlord, simply originated as a Germanic god along the southern part of the *limes* in the centuries around the beginning of our common era.[8] Both Kaliff and Sundqvist and Enright maintain, and no doubt rightly so, that this area was a melting pot for cultural influences among Germani, Celts, and Romans (and individuals from many other cultures). Enright focuses on the Celtic Mercury as the primary source for Óðinn with a strong connection to warrior bands as well as kings and chieftains. Kaliff and Sundqvist, as just mentioned, on the other hand, favour a strong impact from the cult of Mithras which played a huge role among the Roman troops along the *limes*, and they argue, not least on the basis of iconographic material, that it is from this god that we should look for the warrior aspects of Óðinn. So, Enright[9] as well as Kaliff and Sundqvist are open to the possibility that a god of the Óðinn type existed long before any connections with the Romans and Celts, or with the cult of Mithras, but that his role as a war god and ancestor of royal kin was due to such cultural influences. I partly agree with that, since it seems likely that in the Rhine area, just as in the eastern Mediterranean, around the same time (in the so-called Hellenistic Culture), there was an extremely high degree of syncretistic tendencies, so that gods that centuries earlier had been quite different, became identified; perhaps not by everybody, but by some.

Óðinn and his Historical Roots

It is common knowledge that the name of Óðinn is known from several Germanic languages. Thus, among the Anglo-Saxons he was called *Woden*, by the Longobards' *Wotan*, in Old Frankish *Wodan*, and in Old High German *Wuotan*,[10] a clear indication that he was venerated among many Germanic tribes from the early Middle Ages, and probably, as we shall argue below, from at least the beginning of the common era. The proto-Germanic name would thus have been *$Wōðanaz$.[11] It seems as if he is most often translated into the Roman god Mercury in the *interpretatio romana* by the authors of Antiquity and the Middle Ages, to which we shall return. An early Germanic piece of evidence is the so called Nordendorf fibula, found near Augsburg in Bavaria, containing the name Wodan (together with two other gods), and probably to be dated to the 6th century.[12] The root *óð- and thus the noun *óðr* (proto-Germanic *$wōþa$-), means 'excitement' or 'poetry',[13] and as adjective 'furious'. Thus, the meaning of the name Óðinn is most likely 'ecstasy'[14] which is also how it was understood by Adam of Bremen in the 11th century (4, 26), as he says "Wodan that is frenzy", and it seems to fit well with the characterization of the Scandinavian Óðinn, although etymology is not always as important as has often been believed. We also have to acknowledge that Óðinn in particular was a god who had a lot of names, all of them contributing in some way to characterize him, and all with their own etymology.

But we shall begin even further back, namely among the proto-Indo-Europeans. Georges Dumézil saw a tripartite functional structure in the various Indo-European pantheons, and Óðinn was seen here a representative of the magical aspect of the first function, Týr being a representative of the "juridical" aspect, having to do with law.[15] Since these functional gods can be found all over the Indo-European area, it implies that it should be possible to find what we may term "a god of the Óðinn type" in all these pantheons. This notion "a god of the Óðinn type" is certainly rather vague, but, and this is something I shall return to, the vagueness is important in these matters because strong "either/or" solutions seldom fit the historical reality.

Dumézil often used the pre-Vedic Indian situation as a point of reference for his comparisons, and these two aspects of the first function, magic and law, are thus frequently called "the Varunic" and "the Mitraic" aspects. We shall not deal with Týr here, where we shall concentrate on Óðinn, but it is important to note that Mitra and Varuna are in many ways seen as opposites to each other: whereas Mitra is connected to light and the day, Varuna is connected to darkness and the night. Mitra is of this world, Varuna of the other; milk belongs to Mitra, soma to Varuna; Mitra is reliable, Varuna terrifying. Varuna, like many Vedic and pre-Vedic gods, is multifaceted, and has clear connections to natural phenomena, such as the moon and water; he is the protector of the world order and punishes those who do not contribute to this order (among others those who break their oaths). These are elements that we do not recognize in Óðinn, but on the other hand there certainly are such parallel elements, as, for instance, the relation to kingship, horses, and to medicine.[16] Thus, if Varuna, who is also a god of magic, is of the same "type" as Óðinn, it follows logically that at least part of the Óðinn figure will have roots back in Indo-European times,[17] just as is the case with the gods of the three functions, wherever they are found within the Indo-European space. The prerequisite for this, however, is that Dumézil's Indo-European theory is at least partly right, which I think is the case.

Nevertheless, as we saw above, the idea of an Indo-European Óðinn could immediately seem to be in opposition to what many scholars dealing with the pre-Christian religion believe concerning Óðinn's advent to the North. However, this problem is of a rather theoretical kind and has to be solved theoretically – and certainly not empirically: What part of Óðinn do we focus upon, when we talk about continuity and discontinuity from Indo-European times – or Germanic, for that matter. Influences of various kinds from other religions will always have an impact on the way religions and cultures develop; some gods may disappear, and their functions will be shared among the other gods; some gods of neighbouring cultures will be part of one's own pantheon and be transformed in a way that makes it extremely difficult to distinguish such foreign gods from local ones, etc. For example, it seems very likely, as was proposed by Michael Enright,[18] that the particular ties between Óðinn and the war bands were heavily inspired by what went on among the Germani in the Rhine area during the two centuries around the beginning of our era. Nevertheless, there is a strong case that war bands or at least troops of warriors were connected to some god right back from Indo-European times, as suggested by Kris Kershaw.[19] We thus know that the father of the warrior troops (the Maruts in mythological terms) in India is Rudra,[20] whereas they are usually led by Indra[21] – but apparently not Varuna.[22] Rudra, however, shows many similarities to Óðinn,[23] and particularly his engagement in war and fighting and his affiliation with illness and healing reminds us strongly of Óðinn as we shall see in a moment. So, the idea that a god with some ecstatic abilities was connected to bands of young warriors seems clearly to go back to Indo-European times. This could indicate that, in spite of the partial transformation that took place in Óðinn during the Early Roman Iron Age, he was already associated with the war bands in the pantheon of the Indo-Europeans. But it also shows that, even if there are clear similarities between Óðinn and Varuna, functions being performed by other gods have also been applied to Óðinn.[24] This makes it extremely complicated to decide whether Óðinn is "the same" as Varuna. In a certain sense we can, for obvious reasons, say "no". There are huge differences between the two gods, which was also acknowledged by Dumézil, but at the same time there are also many similarities, not least in their structural positions, their "dark" roles in various myths etc. In other words, it does not really make sense to pose the question at all, if we do not qualify it. And as we shall see, this problematic is also to be seen when we ask whether the Nordic Óðinn was the same as Mercury, as Anglo-Saxon Woden, or even if Wodan by Adam of Bremen was the same as Óðinn by Snorri. In all cases we can give the answer "yes and no" – there are similarities as well as differences. I shall return to this important problematic towards the end of the paper.

But, to conclude on Óðinn's Indo-European background, we can state that, at least at a structural level, it makes sense to accept that "a god (or maybe more appropriate 'gods') of the Óðinn type" existed more or less continuously from Indo-European times down to the Viking Age in Scandinavia.[25]

Moving forward into the Roman era we have almost no Germanic names for any of the gods, although the weekday names which probably found their way into the Germanic area during the 3rd century AD indicate that, at that time at least, equivalents to Týr, Óðinn, Þórr and Frigg were major gods in a pan-Germanic pantheon. According to most of the authors of that period the Germanic peoples venerated Mercury, Mars, Hercules, Venus, and others with Roman names. Most scholars agree that Mercury, of whom Tacitus says (*Germania* Ch. 9): "of the gods they venerate Mercury most, and they see it as a sacred obligation to sacrifice human victims for him at certain days", "is" Óðinn, although it has been rejected by some.[26] The acceptance of this identification, which probably owes much to the Celtic Mercurius is based primarily on three arguments: 1) he is the most venerated (at least among the nobility), and he is receiving human victims,[27] exactly like Óðinn in the medieval sources; 2) In the Germanic weekday names *Mercurii dies* is translated into Wednesday, the day of Woden, with cognates to be found in other Germanic languages, and particular in the Scandinavian languages, too;[28] and 3) among later authors, writing in Latin, there is a clear tendency to identify Mercury with Óðinn, although at times he is also identified with other gods such as Mars,[29] to which we shall return in a moment. The identification between the two gods can, as we have just argued, never be a one-to-one relationship: Wodan was not the same as Mercury, but from a Roman perspective, and probably also from that of the Germani acquainted with Roman and Celtic culture, this identification would in most cases be the most sensible way of translating – not the name – but the semantics of Wodan/Óðinn. Thus we meet the identification again by Paulus Diaconus in his history of the Longobards (*Historia Longobardum* 1.9) and in other sources in Latin, such as the *Vita Columbani* I. 27 from the 7th century.[30]

We cannot be certain what the exact reason was for the identification, but it is remarkable that these writers chose to identify the allegedly most powerful god of the Germani (and also the Celts) with a relatively minor god among the Romans. This indicates that it was not just a routine, which could have been the case if they had chosen to identify with Jupiter – our mightiest god is the same as their mightiest god. There must have been some special reason. We may notice that there is a partial similarity between the attributes of the two gods: they both carry a staff and wear a large hat, and they are both "wanderers" moving from place to place. The identification, however, was probably based on much more than these minor parallels. Both Óðinn and Mercury had knowledge of things that were unknown to ordinary people, both were connected to eloquence, and both were connected to the dead: Mercury as a psychopompos and Óðinn as the lord of the dead in *Valhǫll*. And there are further similarities.[31] All in all it seems quite understandable that, if the Germanic peoples in antiquity had a god, who corresponded more or less to the Óðinn of the North, then Mercury would be the natural choice among the Roman gods to identify with. This is not to say, however, that the statement by Tacitus and the identification in general cannot be seen as partly due to influences from the Celts, as has been proposed by both Enright,[32] as we saw, and also Rübekeil[33] and Timpe[34] and many others. There is no doubt that the Celtic Mercurius was not exactly the same as the Roman god due to a process which would be parallel to that of the "Germanic Mercurius" in his relation to both Roman and Celtic versions: the development would involve a complex relation between differences and similarities; therefore, we can state that the mutual identification of gods of the different cultures in the Rhine area around the birth of Christ cannot be reduced to the simple question of whether Mercury "was" Óðinn.[35]

Turning for a moment away from the *interpretatio romana*, it can be mentioned that in the 6th century Jordanes write in his *Getica* (14, 79) that the ancestor of the Amali of the Ostrogoths was *Gapt*, probably to be identified with *Gautr*, a byname for Óðinn, mentioned among other places in *Grímnismál* 54, and thus a further indication of a cult of Óðinn among the southern Germanic peoples. This idea that Óðinn was the progenitor of royal houses or whole tribes is also known from Anglo-Saxon genealogies.[36] Wodan (*Uuodan*) is also mentioned in the second Merseburg charm as a sort of healer of a horse. We know this charm from a 10th century manuscript, but it is likely to be much older. In this connection we should also mention the English *Nine*

Herbs Charm, recorded in the same century, mentioning Woden, as a healer of snake poisoning and the so called Ribe skull fragment,[37] where he is mentioned in connection with some kind of pain. Another noteworthy characteristic is that we are told by, for instance, Jordanes (*Getica* 5, 41) about the Goths and Procopius (*De bello Gothico* 6. 15) about the people in Thule, both writing in the 6th Century, that these peoples sacrificed war prisoners to the war god. In this case, however the war gods are called respectively Mars and Ares, which indicate that the identifications were far from static, but it is hard to think of any Germanic god, apart from Óðinn or "a god of the Óðinn type", to be venerated with human sacrifices in connection with war,[38] so once again we probably see that the *interpretatio romana* was in no way consequent: the associations of the antique and medieval writers were more likely connected to functions and characteristics than to names of the various Germanic gods.[39] And, as stated already by Tacitus and later authors, Mercury was in particular the recipient of human sacrifices, strongly reminicent of myths and rituals connected to the Scandinavian Óðinn.[40] The picture we get from these sources is thus a god who is connected to human sacrifices, who has a clear relation to royalty (and thus may be seen as a kind of "main god"), and to war and who has some magical abilities.

Even if many scholars have cast doubt on most of these individual sources, taken together, they strongly indicate that Óðinn, although not exactly the same as the god that we know from the Nordic sources, has roots reaching far back in time, probably as early as the Indo-European era (at least 3000 BC). During this long period various kinds of major and minor changes inevitably must have taken place due to changing circumstances of all kinds. And particularly during the first half of the first millennium AD, huge changes took place among the Germanic peoples, first in the Rhine area, but soon also in other Germanic areas. The Rhine area was a melting pot with Roman soldiers from various parts of the empire taking part in various cults,[41] as well as Celts and Germani from various parts of their respective homelands being part of the Roman army. Thus, many possible direct and indirect influences were at stake, with strong variations from place to place, from one social stratum to another and from one individual to another according to the relation with different groups of Romans and Celts, soldiers and priests, magistrates and chieftains, etc. that this individual would have. When this is acknowledged, it hardly seems to be worth the effort to attempt to trace the historical development of the semantics of a certain god from the very heterogeneous source material. In my opinion it is in any case doomed to fail, since most of the scholars who have discussed whether Wodan existed among the south Germanic peoples in the guise of Mercury, or if Óðinn existed in the North before a certain time have not even made the effort to define which Óðinn they are talking about. The Germanic gods (not only Óðinn) as well as the gods of other peoples from the Roman Iron Age, we can be pretty sure were all influenced to some degree by ideas about other gods. And some of these ideas would eventually reach Scandinavia; in the case of Óðinn, it was probably among warriors and in the higher social strata, whereas nothing suggests that he was ever a god of importance for the daily life of common people.

This is perhaps also reflected in the place-name material. There are rather few of these connected to Óðinn, either in Scandinavia or among the other Germanic peoples in comparison to some of the other gods. This has been taken to indicate that the cult of Wotan-Óðinn was not very widespread, and has even been used as an argument against the identification of Mercurius-Óðinn. However, we have to take into consideration the character of the place-name material. Although it is far from certain how various places got their names, it is probable that most names were not given by kings and chieftains, but by the people living in the area. The complexity concerning name giving, nevertheless, is overwhelming,[42] and the argument should not be stretched too far. But if Óðinn, as suggested, was not a god of the common people, then we should expect his appearance in place-names to be quite modest.

Conclusion

My main point here has been that, when we compare various gods in order to decide whether they are "the same" or not, it is important that we are explicit about what we are comparing. As mentioned earlier, it is obvious that Óðinn is not the same as Varuna in the sense that everything we know about Óðinn from all the available sources could also be found in Varuna, or vice versa. Now, one way to explain these differences could be, at least theoretically, that once, back in Indo-European times, there was a conception about such a god; and during the following millennia different branches of Indo-Europeans developed different variations, no doubt often influenced by encounters with other cultures. The last part of this is clearly true, but the idea that an original "Varuna-type" ever existed is probably not true, since the natural question then would be: was this god not influenced by any other gods? And, from a logical point of view we have to admit that he must have been so. And furthermore, is it likely that, even back in the pre-migration time of the Indo-Europeans, all held the same conception about a certain god? Again, the answer must be a definite "no". We know from all historical religions that religious notions differed, even within rather small areas; and even from one individual to another there would be minor differences in their religious outlook, and especially so when we speak about religions with no theological élite, telling people how this or that figure should be viewed. This means that there was never one single mythological figure like a proto-Varuna or a proto-Óðinn who were seen in exactly the same way by all individuals. Religious conceptions, like everything else, change all the time, sometimes rapidly and sometimes slowly, but they do change. And the same line of reasoning can be attributed to Mercury, whether we talk about the Roman god or the Celtic one, and to the Germanic *Wōðanaz: None of them would be exact equivalents to the Scandinavian Óðinn. But as noted above, the same problem applies, let us say, to the Óðinn of Snorri and the Wotan of Adam, and perhaps even, for instance, to the Óðinn of *Hárbarðslióð* and the Óðinn of *Hávamál*. The god(s) in these sources were different in regard to some characteristics, but similar when it comes to others, of course dependent of distances in time and space. Therefore, let us repeat, it is as correct to say that Óðinn and Mercury were different gods as it is to say that they were one god. The discussion among some scholars of an older generation, therefore, seems to me to be based on false prerequisites, as if it could be determined as an either-or. So, when we discuss whether Mercury "was" Óðinn, it is necessary to be clear about what we are actually talking about: is it the whole spectrum of attributes and mythic roles that we mean, for if so the answer is "no", but to take this view point to its extreme, we can hardly speak about the "same" god, in the world view of even two individuals. And that, of course, would hardly make any sense; so less will have to do. We could, for instance, focus on etymology: is it the same name we meet; or we can focus on the attributes: one-eyedness, a spear, a certain dress, or so on. From my point of view it would, however, make much more sense to focus on what I have earlier called "the semantic centre" of the god in question.[43] This notion, I suggest, we may use to describe those ideas about a certain god which could be expressed in the discourse about this god, and not least those ideas that cannot be attributed to this figure.[44] From that perspective, because we do not have many pre-medieval sources, so we cannot be certain – it may very well make sense to speak about a semantic centre with considerable similarity, concerning Mercury, Wotan, and Óðinn.

So, to summarize my view of the historical roots of Óðinn, I find it very plausible that part of the semantics that we find surrounding the god, as described in the medieval sources of the North, can be traced back to an Indo-European god of the Varuna type, especially when it comes to the "dark" aspects. I also find it probable that at the same time there existed one or several gods who were connected to bands of young warriors and who were somewhat connected to royalty and leadership. Around the beginning of our era along the *limes*, not least due to strong Roman and Celtic influences (but not only so) and foreign gods such as Mithras and various versions of Mercury, a god, much closer to "the Óðinn type" took shape who eventually also transformed the Wodan of the North from a god of magic and war and connected to death, and to the chieftains into Óðinn who kept many of these characteristics and added others. Are these gods identical, then? *No*; are they historically related? *Yes*. So, the answer to the question asked in the title of this article: "one or many?" must be "both one and many".[45]

Óðinn or Wotan is thus not a latecomer, either in the southern Germanic area, or in the North, but he, like all other gods, was certainly part of a permanent transformation process.

Notes

1. Parts of this paper in a slightly revised version will be part of an extensive chapter on Óðinn in the work *Pre-Christian Religions of the North: Histories and Structures*, edited by Anders Andrén, John Lindow, and Jens Peter Schjødt, planned to be published in 2018.

2. I have been dealing with comparison in a number of articles, i.e. Schjødt 2012; 2013; and 2017a and 2017b. Here I have argued that comparisons of various kinds are necessary in order to make sense of the Pre-Christian religion of the North.

3. A good survey of the scholarship concerning Óðinn up till the beginning of the 20th century can be found in Lassen 2011; and for more recent research in Dillmann 1979. The question of "original" function will only be briefly touched upon in this paper.

4. The idea that "many" earlier on was "one" (functions or gods) can be seen by many researchers during the 20th century, perhaps most clearly by the Swedish historian of religion Folke Ström, who, among other ideas, suggested that Óðinn and Loki were originally one single figure (Ström 1956). It is quite possible that such developments may have taken place, just as it is possible that the opposite, i.e. that several gods have turned into one, can be imagined. A functional area of one god may have been distributed among several gods earlier on. Such processes are definitely not impossible, but they are very difficult to trace, and it is very hard to decide where to stop. For instance: if Óðinn and Loki were "originally" (when?) one and the same, what went on before, then? Could it be that even more "originally" they were two or even more? We do not know, and it is hard to imagine that we ever will.

5. A possibility is that Óðinn in *Ynglinga saga* is actually modelled on some contemporary "shaman" or sorcerer, as has been suggested by John Lindow (2003). This is certainly not unlikely, but it could well be argued that even so, it is not a coincidence that all these attributes

are connected to Óðinn, and not to any other god, and thus that this "sorcery" aspect was already at hand in the conception of the pagan Óðinn.

6. Helm 1946:71.

7. See, for instance, references by Hultgård 2007:776; and Kaliff & Sundqvist 2004:14–16. Lotte Hedeager (2011) argues that, although Óðinn is seen as a pan-Germanic god, the Huns and their famous king, Attila, played a decisive role in the formation of the late pagan Óðinn, enumerating many common traits between the king and the god (2011:221–222). Therefore, her theory can be seen as a variant of the "eastern" hypothesis.

8. Enright, however, seems to accept some "proto-type" for Wodan, as he writes (1996:218): "Dumézilians …….. routinely associated this wisdom/warfare complex with the first function of sovereignty, just as they associate Celtic Lug and Germanic Wodan with Indic Varuna. In a certain ultimate senses, they may be correct".

9. Although Enright has made a very good case for "the warlord" Wodan, originating at that time, it seems as if he is basing much too much of this argument on *argumenta ex silentio*. For instance, even if there is no positive evidence that the Cimbri worshipped Wodan before they left their Scandinavian homeland (1996:238), as was proposed by Jan de Vries (1956–57, II:30), we have to ask the simple question: what evidence could we in any possible way hope for? Such arguments are simply of no value in this case, and the question whether or not Wodan, as a god connected to war, existed before the Roman and Celtic influences were at stake, must therefore be based on another line of reasoning.

10. de Vries 1962:416.

11. For various forms of the name, such as *Godan* in *Origo gentis Longobardorum* and Paul the Deacons *Historia Longobardorum*, see Hultgård 2007:759–760.

12. Discussion of the inscription can be seen in McKinnell & Simek 2004:48–49.

13. de Vries 1962:416.

14. Cf. The runic inscription from the so called Gårdlösa fibula from the pre-Viking Age, according to Krause (1966:35–36) as early as around 200 AD, saying *ek unwod* ....., probably meaning 'I the not frantic....' (Moltke 1976:99–100).

15. Dumézil 1973:26–48.

16. Gonda 1960:73–82.

17. For interesting ideas about both etymology and function of these gods, we can also refer to Jackson 2012:57–59.

18. Enright 1996:218–240.

19. Kershaw 2000:211–221.

20. Gonda 1960:87.

21. In some texts (e.g. *Rigveda* 2.33), however, Rudra apparently takes over many characteristics that we usually see in Indra. The whole distribution of functions among the gods in India is in general rather unsystematic, and there is a great deal of overlap in the functional areas of the various gods.

22. It is not possible to trace the development of the retinue, or the *comitatus* in any detail back from the Indo-European times, but there is no doubt, however, that it must have changed substantially from the times when a chieftain would have had a small band of men, perhaps twelve as could be indicated in some of the Icelandic fornaldar sagas, to a large number of warriors, surrounding the kings in later times because of completely different social situations.

23. Cf. Samson 2011:186–187; Gonda 1960:89.

24. Turville-Petre (1964:41) is no doubt right when he writes that: "Perhaps we should rather doubt the stability of the tripartite system", although it seems to be an understatement of the actual situation. Rather we should say, that, even if, at a rather abstract structural level, as Dumézil has shown in numerous publications, there are clear parallels among the various Indo-European traditions, there is at the same time also room for tremendous variations and transformations.

25. It could be relevant here to ask whether Óðinn can be traced in the Rock carvings of the Scandinavian Bronze Age. But as is often

the case the answer is almost impossible to give. We do have carvings depicting a figure with a spear, which is one of the main attributes of Óðinn. On the other hand, a spear was probably a rather common weapon in the Bronze Age, so that the motif could be either a great warrior, or perhaps a god. But a god of the Óðinn type? It seems as if more attributes would be needed, if such an interpretation is not to be seen as completely arbitrary. For a discussion of that sort of problems we can refer to Schjødt 1986.

26. E.g. Helm 1946:8. Helm argues that this sentence by Tacitus is a convention that can be seen from Herodotus to Caesar, and that it is pure form, whereas it has no real content. Helm certainly has shown that it is *possible* that the sentence by Tacitus is not reliable. On the other hand, however, it is a question of whether his proposition is the most likely one. What if a god of "the Óðinn type" was at stake among the Indo-European peoples that Herodotus as well as Caesar wrote about? What if the Hermes of Herodotus (V, 7) who was venerated by the kings of the Thrachians (as Óðinn was venerated by the kings of Scandinavia) actually was a god of the Óðinn type, and if Cesar's Celtic Mercurius was a god resembling Lug? Then they were both similar to Óðinn and therefore reminded the respective authors of Hermes/Mercury? (for a critical evaluation of the equation between Lug and Mercury, see Maier 1996, and Egeler (2013) casts doubt on the parallels between Lug and Óðinn). How would these authors of antiquity be able to convince the source critics of our time that this was actually the case? They would probably not stand a chance.

27. Maier 1994:231.

28. For the question of the week day names we can refer to Strutynski 1975; and for a critical evaluation of the traditional dating of the acceptance of the theophoric week among the Germanic peoples, Shaw 2007, who proposes a much later dating, namely in the 7th and 8th centuries (Shaw 2007:387).

29. Lassen 2011:90; cf. Ármann Jakobsson 2009.

30. For many other instances of texts mentioning Mercury and various cognates of Wodan from the southern part of the Germanic area, we can refer to de Vries 1956–1957, II:27–42.

31. See for instance Kaliff & Sundqvist 2004:62–63 and Liberman 2016:33–35.

32. Enright 1996:217–218.

33. Rübekeil 2002.

34. Timpe 1992:456–457.

35. Bernhard Maier is no doubt right when he argues that, when it comes to *interpretatio romana* in general, the particular reason for the various identifications would have been similarity in certain aspects which are not necessarily transparent (Maier 1994:180).

36. Cf. North 1997:111–131.

37. Cf. McKinnell & Simek 2004:180.

38. From the week day names it is indicated that Týr is equivalent to Mars, but we do not know which aspects of Mars is in focus here. There is nothing to suggest (except from *Snorra Edda*) that Týr was seen as mainly a war god. It is not possible to deal with this highly interesting problematic in any detail here.

39. A great example of this lack of consequences in the identification, although within the Celtic realm, is the so-called Berner Scholia where almost any Roman god can be identified with almost any Celtic god.

40. Cf. *Orkneyinga saga* Ch. 8, see also below.

41. Therefore, it is also a priori likely that Óðinn of the Viking Age was to some extent influenced by the cult of Mithras – and influences the other way round are just as likely – as has been convincingly proposed by Kaliff and Sundqvist (2004), taking both textual, iconographic, and archaeological material into consideration.

42. Cf. Vikstrand 2001:45–54.

43. I have dealt with this notion particularly in Schjødt 2013.

44. Schjødt 2013.

45. The answer proposed here thus has clear references to the brilliant 1994 book by John McKinnell, *Both One and Many*, which, however, does not have Óðinn as a primary focus.

References

Primary sources

Adam of Bremen. Bernhard Schmeidler (ed.). 1917. *Adam of Bremen, Hamburgische Kirchengeschichte*. Scriptores Rerum Germanicarum in usum scholarum ex Monumentis Germaniae Historicis Separatim Editi. Magistri Adam Bremensis Gesta Hammaburgensis Ecclesiae Pontificum. Hannover, Leipzig: Hahnsche Buchhandlung.

Edda. Gustav Neckel & Hans Kuhn. 1962. *Edda. Die Lieder des Codex regius nebst verwandten Denkmälern*. Germanische Bibliothek, 4ᵗʰ ed. Heidelberg: C. Winter.

Herodotus. T. E. Page & A. D. Godly (eds. and trans.). 1922. *Herodotus. Books 5–7*. The Loeb Classical Library. London: William Heinemann Ltd, Cambridge: Harvard University Press.

Jordanes. Theodorus Mommsen. 1882. *Iordanis. Romana et Getica*. Monumenta Germanie Historica. Inde ab anno Christi Quingentesimo usque ad annum Millesimum et Quingentesimum. Edidit. Societas Aperiendis Fontibus rerum Germanicarum Medii Aevi. Auctorum Antiquissimorum Tomi 5 pars Prior. Iordanis Romana et Getica. Berlin: Weidmannsche Buchhandlung.

Nine Herbs Charm. Elliott van Kirk Dobbie. 1942. *The Anglo-Saxon Minor Poems*. The Anglo-Saxon Poetic Record, 6. London: George Routledge & sons, New York: Columbia University Press, 119–21.

Orkneyinga saga. Finnbogi Guðmundsson (ed.). 1965. *Orkneyinga saga*. Íslenzk Fornrit XXXIV. Reykjavík: Hið Íslenzka Fornritafélag.

Origo gentis Langobardorum. Georg Waitz (ed.). 1878. In G. Waitz (ed.). *Scriptores rerum Langobardicorum et Itaæicarum saec. Monumenta Germaniae historica*. Hannover: Impensis Bibliopolii Hahniani, 1–6.

Paul the Deacon. L. Bethmann & Georg Waitz (eds.). 1878. *Pauli Historia Langobardorum*. Scriptores Rerum Germanicarum. Monumentis Germaniae Historicis Recusi. Hannover: Impensis Bibliopolii Hahniani.

Procopius. E. H. Warmington & H. B. Dewing (ed. and trans.). 1919. *Procopius. History of the wars. Books 5 and 6*. The Loeb

Classical Library. Procopius, 3. London: William Heinemann Ltd, Cambridge: Harvard University Press.

Snorri Sturluson, *Edda*. Faulkes, Anthony (ed.). 2005. *Edda. Prologue and Gylfaginning*. 2nd edition. London: Viking Society for Northern Research.

——— Faulkes, Anthony (ed.). 1998. *Edda. Skáldskaparmál 1. Introduction, Text and Notes*. London: Viking Society for Northern Research.

Snorri Sturluson, *Heimskringla*. Bjarni Aðalbjarnarson (ed.). 1979. *Heimskringla I–III*. Íslenzk Fornrit vols. XXVI–XXVIII. Reykjavík: Hið Íslenzka Fornritafélag.

Tacitus, *Agricola, Germania, Dialogus*. E. H. Warmington & M. Hutton (ed. and trans.). 1970. *Tacitus. Agricola, Germania, Dialogus*. The Loeb Classical Library. London: William Heinemann Ltd, Cambridge: Harvard University Press.

Vita Columbani. Krusch, Bruno. 1905. *Vita Columbani. Ionae Vitae Sanctorum. Columbani, Vedastis, Iohannis*. Scriptores Rerum Germanicarum. Monumentis Germaniae Historicis Separatim Editi. Hannover, Leipzig: Impensis Bibliopolii Hahniani.

Secondary literature

Ármann Jakobsson. 2009. 'Er Saturnús er kallaðr en vér köllum Frey'. The Roman Spring of the Old Norse Gods. In L. Slupecki & J. Morawiec (eds.). *Between Paganism and Christianity in the North*. Rzeszow: Wydawnictwo Uniwersytetu Rzeszowskiego, 158–164.

Dillmann, François-Xavier. 1979. Georges Dumézil et la religion Germanique. L'interprétation du dieu Odhinn. In J.-C. Rivière (ed.), *Georges Dumézil. à la découverte des Indo-Européens*, Paris: Copernic, 157–186.

Dumézil, Georges. 1973. *Gods of the Ancient Northmen*, ed. and trans. Einar Haugen *et al*. Publications of the UCLA Center for the Study of Comparative Folklore and Mythology, 3. Berkeley, Los Angeles, London: University of California Press.

Egeler, Matthias. 2013. *Celtic Influences in Germanic Religion. A Survey*. Müncher nordische Studien, 15. Munich: Herbert Utz Verlag.

Enright, Michael. 1996. *Lady with a Mead Cup. Ritual, Prophecy and Lordship in the European Warband from La Tène to the Viking Age*. Dublin: Four Courts Press.

Gonda, Jan. 1960. *Die Religionen Indiens. I Veda und älterer Hinduismus*. Die Religionen der Menschheit, Band 11. Stuttgart: W. Kohlhammer Verlag.

Hedeager, Lotte. 2011. *Iron Age Myth and Materiality. An Archaeology of Scandinavia AD 400–1000*. London, New York: Routledge.

Helm, Karl. 1946. *Wodan. Ausbreitung und Wanderung seines Kultes*. Giessener Beiträge zur deutschen Philologie, 85. Giessen: Wilhelm Schmitz Verlag.

Hultgård, Anders. 2007. Wotan-Odin. In H. Beck et al. (eds.). *Reallexikon der germanischen Altertumskunde*, 35, 2nd ed. Berlin, New York: Walter de Gruyter, 759–785.

Jackson, Peter. 2012. The Merits and Limits of Comparative Philology. Old Norse Religious Vocabulary in a Long-Term Perspective. In C. Raudvere & J. P. Schjød (eds.). *More than Mythology. Narratives, Ritual Practices and Regional Distribution in Pre-Christian Scandinavian Religions*. Lund: Nordic Academic Press.

Kaliff, Anders & Sundqvist, Olof. 2004. *Oden och Mithraskulten. Religiös ackulturation under romersk järnålder och folkvandringstid*. Occational papers in archaeology, 35. Uppsala: Department of Archaeology and Ancient History, Uppsala University.

Kershaw, Kris. 2000. *The One-eyed God. Odin and the (Indo-)Germanic Männerbünde*. Journal of Indo-European Studies, Monograph, 36. Washington DC: Institute for the Study of Man.

Krause, Wolfgang. 1966. *Die Runeninschriften im älteren Futhark, I, Text*. Abhandlungen der Akademie der Wissenschaften in Göttingen. Philologisch-Historische Klasse, dritte Folge, 65. Göttingen: Vandenhoeck & Ruprecht.

Lassen, Annette. 2011. *Odin på kristent pergament. En teksthistorisk studie*. Copenhagen: Museum Tusculanums Forlag.

Liberman, Anatoly. 2016. *In Prayer and Laughter. Essays on Medieval Scandinavian and Germanic Mythology, Literature, and Culture.* Moscow: Paleograph Press.

Lindow, John. 2003. Cultures in Contact. In M. Clunies Ross (ed.). *Old Norse Myths, Literature and Society.* The Viking Collection, 14. Odense: University Press of Southern Denmark, 89–109.

Maier, Bernhard. 1994. *Lexikon der keltischen Religion und Kultur.* Stuttgart: Alfred Kröner Verlag.

Maier, Bernhard. 1996. Is Lug to be Identified with Mercury (*Bell. Gall.* VI 17.1)? New Suggestions on an Old Problem. In *Ériu* vol. 47, 127–35.

McKinnell, John & Rudolf Simek, with Klaus Düwel. 2004. *Runes, Magic and Religion. A Sourcebook.* Studia Medievalia Septentrionalia, 10. Vienna: Fassbaender.

Moltke, Erik. 1976. *Runerne i Danmark og deres oprindelse.* Copenhagen: Forum.

North, Richard. 1997. *Heathen Gods in Old English Literature.* Cambridge Studies in Anglo-Saxon England, 22. Cambridge: Cambridge University Press.

Rübekeil, Ludwig. 2002. *Diachrone Studien zur Kontaktzone zwischen Kelten und Germanen.* Österreichische Akademie der Wissenschafte, Sitzungsberichte der Philosophisch-Historische Klasse, 699. Vienna: Verlag der Österreichische Akademie der Wissenschaften.

Samson, Vincent. 2011. *Les* Berserkir. *Les guerriers-fauves dans la Scandinavie ancienne de l'âge de Vendel aux Vikings (VI'e – XI'e siècle).* Villeneuve d'Ascq: Presses Universitaires du Septentrion.

Schjødt, Jens Peter, 1986. The 'Meaning' of the Rock Carvings and the Scope for Religio-Historical Interpretation. Some Thoughts on the Limits of the Phenomenology of Religion. In G. Steinsland (ed.). *Words and Objects. Towards a Dialogue between Archaeology and History of Religion.* Oslo: Norwegian University Press, 180–196.

Schjødt, Jens Peter. 2012. Reflections on Aims and Methods in the Study of Old Norse Religion. In C. Raudvere & J. P. Schjødt (eds.),

More than Mythology. Narratives, Ritual Practices and Regional Distribution in Pre-Christian Scandinavian Religions. Lund: Nordic Academic Press, 263–287.

Schjødt, Jens Peter. 2013. The Notions of Model, Discourse and Semantic Centre as Tools for the (Re)Construction of Old Norse Religion. In *The Retrospective Methods Network Newsletter* vol. 6, 6–15.

Schjødt, Jens Peter. 2017a. The Reintroduction of Comparative Studies as a Tool for Reconstructing Old Norse Religion. In S. Brink & L. Collinson (ed.). *Theorizing Old Norse Myth.* Turnhout: Brepols.

Schjødt, Jens Peter. 2017b. Pre-Christian Religions of the North and the Need for Comparativism. Reflections on Why, How, and With What we can Compare. In P. Hermann et al. (eds.). *Old Norse Mythology in Comparative Perspective.* Cambridge: Harvard University Press.

Shaw, Philip. 2007. The Origins of the Theophoric Week in the Germanic Languages. In *Early Medieval Europe,* vol 15, 386–401.

Strutynski, Udo. 1975. Germanic Divinities in Weekday Names. In *Journal of Indo-European Studies* vol. 3, 363–384.

Ström, Folke. 1956. *Loki. Ein mythologisches Problem.* Göteborg Universitets årsskrift, 62.8. Göteborg: Elander.

Timpe, Dieter. 1992. Tacitus' Germania als religionsgeschichtliche Quelle. In H. Beck et al. (eds.). *Germanische Religionsgeschichte. Quellen und Quellenprobleme.* Berlin, New York: Walter de Gruyter, 434–485.

Turville-Petre, E. O. Gabriel. 1964. *Myth and Religion of the North. The Religion of Ancient Scandinavia.* London: Weidenfeld & Nicolson.

Vikstrand, Per. 2001. *Gudarnas platser. Förkristna sakrala ortnamn i Mälarlandskapen.* Acta academiae regiae Gustavi Adolphi, 77. Studier till en svensk ortnamnsatlas. Uppsala: Kungliga Gustav Adolfs Akademien för svensk folkkultur.

de Vries, Jan. 1956–1957. *Altgermanische Religionsgeschichte*, 2 vols, 2nd ed. Grundriss der Germanischen Philologie, 12. Berlin: Walter de Gruyter & Co.

de Vries, Jan. 1962. *Altnordisches etymologisches Wörterbuch*, 2nd ed. Leiden: E. J. Brill.

Response

Peter Jackson Rova
Stockholm University

The old and much-debated problem tackled in Jens Peter Schjødt's paper concerns the origins and development of the god rendered as *Óðinn* by the writers and poets of Medieval and Viking Age Scandinavia. Covering a near half millennium stretching from the earliest recorded Skaldic poetry to Snorri Sturluson's mythographic adaptation of the Old Norse poetic heritage by the first half of the 13th century, the Scandinavian evidence gives a comparatively rich testimony to what most scholars regard as, in Schjødt's own wording, as the "end result" of a god whose functions and features must have gone through significant changes, through time as well as space, from the Roman Iron Age onwards. While there is little doubt that this god – whether Proto-Germanic (PGmc) **Wōðanaz*, **Wōðinaz* or **Wōðunaz* (the form taken by Stefan Schaffner to reflect the most archaic stage) – was being worshiped by most Germanic tribes during the Migration Period, opinions diverge as to the deeper past of the cult. Did it spread late from a more restricted geographical area to the rest of the Germanic speaking world under the influence of Gallo-Roman cults, or was the god rather an original member of the Germanic pantheon with ties back to the Indo-European migrations of the Bronze Age? The answer provided by Schjødt in the concluding sentence of the paper seems altogether satisfying to me, namely that "Óðinn or Wotan is thus not a latecomer, neither in the southern Germanic area, nor in the North, but he, like all other gods, was certainly part of a permanent transformation process."

Since the ancient sources remain far too meagre to allow us to reconstruct the no doubt complex processes through which the gods of the Celts and Germani merged and changed shape as a result of Roman influences, we should avoid the *argumenum e silentio* that a god, whose perfectly transparent name is well-attested in the ancient dialects (excluding only Gothic), was *not* indigenous to all of the Germanic tribes before their first encounters with the Roman-Hellenistic world. The unwillingness to accept the god's early provenance lies in the failure to appreciate the "permanent transformation process" that all cultural artefacts are expected to undergo in a changing socio-economic environment, and especially so with regard to religion in the absence of canon and scripture. Whether gods are to be considered new or old also depends on how we chose to distinguish innovation from tradition: is the latter always endemic to the former, or should the "new" only be treated as such in the absence of a pre-existing model – the introduction, for instance, of an entirely new cult, like emperor Elagabalus' installation of the Syrian god Ilāh hag-Gabal as the new chief deity of the Roman pantheon?

Even when one turns to the much richer documentation of the cult of Mercurius, with whom Wotan/Woden was frequently identified by Roman writers and the colonists of Roman Gaul and Germania from the first century AD onwards, uncertainty still prevails as to whether this god was a direct borrowing from Greek religion (Hermes) – because he is said to have been worshiped "according to Greek rites" (*Graeco ritu*) – or, at least, a comparatively late member of the Roman pantheon without a common Italic origin (BNP, s.v. *Mercurius*). This is just to exemplify how tricky it is to disentangle such matters, even where processes of cultic migration and innovation can be reconstructed in greater detail.

Schjødt makes a moderately positive assessment of George Dumézil's treatment of Óðinn as a manifestation of the dark, magico-religious so-called "Varuṇic" aspect of the first function (as opposed to the light, judicial so-called "Mithraic" aspect). A comparison between Óðinn and Varuṇa in the style of Dumézil implies a systematic treatment of functional (or semantic) correlations, whereas the linguistic dimension is typically disregarded. Suggestive as such an approach may be, a linguistic touch to the operation would in fact – at least in this particular case – substantiate the comparison. I can think of at least three such instances:

1. If Óðinn is the *áss* (Proto-Germanic **ansuz*) par excellence – the chief of the *æsir* as it were –, Varuṇa is the chief representative of the group of divinities referred to as Asuras (or

Ādityas [i.e. descendants of the goddess Aditi]) in the Vedic hymns. He is frequently referred to as *ásura-* 'lord'. The same title (possibly reflecting a Proto-Indo-European [PIE] noun *h_2ṇsu[ro]-*) is also seen in the name of Zarathustra's god of preference, Ahura Mazda ('the Wise Lord').[1]

2. Óðinn and Varuṇa are both conveyers of poetic skills linked to the etymologically compatible nouns *bragr* ('poetic craft' [*Digtekunst* in Fritzner's terms]) and *bráhman* ('sacred utterance' or [in Monier-Williams terms] 'pious outpouring of the heart') (from a PIE noun *$b^hreĝ^h$-*). If the two gods really did develop from a common source, this figure would have been especially linked to the area of poetry and ritual professionalism – a circumstance still reflected in the cases of Varuṇa and Ahura Mazda.

3. A pre-Proto-Germanic realization of the PGmc name *Wōðunaz* would (before the Germanic sound shifts) have sounded something like *Wātunos* (or perhaps *Wātūnos*, with a long *ū* reflecting the so-called *Hoffmannsches Possessivsuffix* [typically expressing lordly qualities, the 'lord of x' {as in Portūnus, the 'lord of the *portus*'}], from an earlier PIE form *Wātuh₃nos). Somewhere and sometime during the long period of gradually dissolving Indo-European tribal networks,[2] perhaps even after the development of Proto-Indo-Iranian, a god worshipped by some groups as *Waruṇa and as *Wātunos by others, could very well have developed out of some common source, in which case one or other would have acquired a consonant epithet replacing an earlier one, perhaps as the result of taboo deformation.[3] A comparable case is seen in the likewise non-etymological consonance between the reconstructed name of the North-West Indo-European god *Perkʷuh₃nos (e.g. Old Norse *Fjǫrgýnn* and Lithuanian *Perkúnas*) ['lord of the oak']) and the reconstructed name of his eastern cousin *Pergenịo (as seen in the name of the Vedic storm-god Parjanya) (possibly from an extension of the root *per* 'to strike'). The latter was a god who, just like Old Norse *Þórr* (a close associate of the relatively bleak divine pair

Fjǫrgyn and Fjǫrgynn) and Perkúnas, 'thundered' (PIE *(s)tenh₂-]), confronted a serpentine monster and wielded a thunderbolt.[4] While the reconstructed epithets are merely vaguely consonant, the divinities so labelled apparently had other attributes in common, some of which can also be grasped linguistically. Divine names are not typical items of everyday communication, but may also be expected to reflect the embellishments of poetic creativity and ritual artifice.

Notes

1. If the initial element *A(n)su-* (PGmc. **ansuz* ['god']) in the Ancient Scandinavian (Runic) name *Asugasdiz* (= *A[n]sugastiz*) is cognate with Old Avestan (OAv.) *ahura-*/Vedic (Ved.) *ásura-* (< PIE **h₂ŋsu[ro]-*) (cf. Hittite *hassu-* ['king']), as hesitatingly acknowledged by Manfred Mayrhofer ("nicht primär auszuschließen") in his *Etymologisches Wörterbuch des Altindoarischen* (EWAia), the second element (*-gastiz* [PIE < **gʰosti-* {'guest, stranger'}]) would be functionally compatible with Proto-Indo-Iranian (PII) **átHti-* (> OAv. *asti-*/Ved. *átithi-*). This means that the recurrent Mitanni-Aryan onomastic element *-atti*, if it really does reflect **átHti-* (> OAv. *asti-*) in the name *Ašuratti*, could belong to the same onomastic tradition (cf. Pinault 1998:454 [with reference to a series of studies on the topic by Mayrhofer {e.g. Mayrhofer 1960:137 ff.}]). The name would thus reflect either a late Proto-Indo-European proper noun **H₂ŋsu(ro)gʰosti* realized as Proto-Indo-Iranaian **AsurātHti*, or a pre-Proto-Germanic calque of the Proto-Indo-Iranian name.

2. An intermediary (Meso-Indo-European) period of relative comprehensibility between different Indo-European branches (or dialect clusters) – including those of Italo-Celtic, pre-Proto-Germanic, Balto-Slavic, Indo-Iranian, Proto-Greek and Proto-Tocharian – may have reached well into the 2nd millennium BC. Compare, for example, the 1) initial members of the Eburonic royal name Catuvolcus with the Ancient Scandinavian (Runic) name Haþuwulfz (500–700 AD), and 2) that of the Greek name Kle(w)óxenos with Ancient Scandinavian Hlewagastiz. Both would have been virtually transparent to speakers

of Celtic, Greek and pre-Proto-Germanic in the early 1st millennium BC: *Katu-* and *Klewo-* respectively.

3. Interaction between speakers of pre-Proto-Germanic and speakers of Iranian dialects, somewhere in the Pontic-Caspian region, must still have taken place during the 1st millennium BC, as attested by the word *hemp* (PGmc *hanapa-* > *kánnabis*), a borrowing from some Iranian dialect (possibly Scythian [cf. Herodotus 4.74]) clearly pre-dating the so-called First Germanic Sound Shift (or Grimm's Law).

4. A historical example of the same basic tendency would be that of Italian *Madonna* replacing the proper noun *Maria* (Ma-CVC-a/ Ma-CV-a) in vernacular piety.

References

Etymologisches Wörterbuch des Altindoarischen. Heidelberg: Carl Winter Universitätsverlag. 1992.

Brill's New Pauly: Encyclopaedia of the Ancient World. Eds. Huber Cancik, Helmuth Schneider and Manfred Landsfester. English translation edited by Christine F. Salazar and Francis G. Gentry. Leiden/Boston: Brill. 2006–2011.

Pinault, Georges. 1998. "Le nome indo-iranien de l'hôte." in *Sprache und Kultur der Indogermanen*. Ed. Wolfgang Meid. Innsbruck: Innsbrucker Beiträge zu Sprachwissenschaft, 451–477.

Mayrhofer, Manfred. 1960. "Indo-Iranisches Sprachgut aus Alalaḫ." *Indo-Iranian Journal* 4, 136–149.

PART II:
MYTHS AND PICTURES

Myth on Stone and Tapestry: Ragnarøk in Pictures?

Anders Hultgård
Uppsala University

Despite its character of being a well-known and still used concept in Scandinavian cultures, the idea of Ragnarøk is based on a limited body of texts preserved on Iceland. No wonder, then, that iconographical evidence has been sought, in order to supplement the meagre textual sources. To take a few examples. In a recent book on Anglo-Saxon stone sculpture, the author, having mentioned the Gosforth Cross, states that "Sculptural evidence from the Isle of Man provides further proof that the events of Ragnarøk were known in the British Isles".[1] The presence of Ragnarøk motifs on Danish and Swedish rune stones suggested by runologists such as Erik Moltke and Sven B.F. Jansson serves to show that the Ragnarøk myth was told all over Scandinavia. The degree of certainty with which scholars present their interpretations varies on a scale from plain statement of facts to a cautious "perhaps". Often one gets the impression that scholars cannot resist the temptation of proposing a Ragnarøk interpretation, but that the insertion of a simple question mark saves them from reproaches for being too speculative. In addition, we may point to the circumstance that interpretations of pictorial scenes tend to be repeated by others without independent reflection.

The purpose of my contribution is to make a critical assessment of the interpretations that suggest Ragnarøk motifs in Viking age iconography. Space does not allow me to review all the material at our disposal. Instead, I will pick out some of the more important monuments and objects that have been associated with the

How to cite this book chapter:
Hultgård, A. 2019. Myth on Stone and Tapestry: Ragnarøk in Pictures?. In: Wikström af Edholm, K., Jackson Rova, P., Nordberg, A., Sundqvist, O. & Zachrisson, T. (eds.) *Myth, Materiality, and Lived Religion: In Merovingian and Viking Scandinavia*. Pp. 89–113. Stockholm: Stockholm University Press. DOI: https://doi.org/10.16993/bay.e. License: CC-BY.

Ragnarøk.[2] For a fuller review of such iconographic material, I refer to my book on the Ragnarøk myth.[3]

The Gosforth Cross

Let us begin with the Gosforth Cross. It has been dated to the first half of the 10th century and is still standing on its original place in St Mary's churchyard at Gosforth in northern England. The four and a half metre-high stone pillar has figurative motifs on all four sides, but the decorative aspect dominates: long bands of elements, interlaced or linked together, that end up in yawning animal heads (Fig. 1). The figurative scenes are generally considered to be a mixture of Christian and pagan elements. The first person

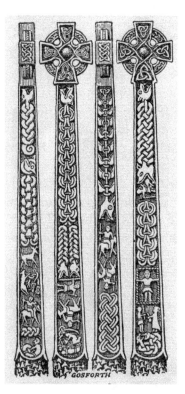

Figure 1. The Gosforth Cross; from Collingwood 1927:156. License: CC-BY-NC-ND.

to interpret the carvings with reference to Old Norse mythology seems to have been the Dane George Stephens at the beginning of the 1880s.[4] He was soon followed by the English antiquarian Charles Arundel Parker in his book on the Gosforth Crosses.[5] Subsequently, a number of scholars have followed this line of interpretation, among them Axel Olrik,[6] Knut Berg;[7] Richard Bailey;[8] Sigmund Oehrl[9] and Lilla Kopár.[10]

I will briefly summarize how the picture scenes of the cross are usually explained. Starting at the bottom of the east face, we are undoubtedly confronted with a crucifixion scene (Fig. 2). Longinus, the Roman soldier, piercing the side of Jesus with his lance; the blood pouring forth; the woman may represent Mary, mother of Jesus, Mary of Magdala, or *Ecclesia*, the Church personified, who

Figure 2. The Gosforth Cross, east side. Crucifixion scene; from Stephens 1884. License: CC-BY-NC-ND.

approaches with her bottle-like bowl to receive Christ's blood. Another interpretation suggests that the woman has been substituted for Stephaton, the sponge-bearer in the Christian standard scenes of crucifixion.[11] She offers a mead cup or a drinking horn to Jesus as a symbol of death. This would suggest an influence of Germanic myth. The crucifixion scene together with the monument's shape and original location makes it clear that the frame of interpretation must be Christian. However, the rest of the figurative scenes seem to be more difficult to place in that context. At this point, Old Norse mythology intervenes and rescues scholars from their bewildering situation. Farther up, on the east face, a man is seen leaning on a staff (less probably a spear; Fig 3); his left arm is raised upwards and his hand touches the upper jaw of the beast. The man's one leg appears as if trapped in the tongue of the beast which is cleft in the way typical of serpents; the foot is hidden behind the inferior jaw. The male figure is generally interpreted in accordance with the description of the *Prose Edda* as being the god Víðarr who is tearing the jaws of Fenrir to avenge his father's death.[12]

At first glance, the interpretation seems convincing, but in my view it is not. The details of the picture do not tally with the

Figure 3. The Gosforth Cross, east side. Man confronting a beast; from Stephens 1884. License: CC-BY-NC-ND.

descriptions of the Poetic Edda which are roughly contemporane-
ous with the date of the Gosforth Cross. According to the *Vǫluspá*,
Víðarr thrusts his sword into the heart of the monster and in the
version of the *Vafþrúðnismál* he splits the jaws of Fenrir (with his
sword). The German philologist Richard Reitzenstein suggested
instead that the male figure represents Christ who is opening the
jaws of Satan or Death in order to liberate the souls of the just
from their captivity in hell. The myth of Christ's *descensus ad
inferos* was well known in Christian antiquity, and its popularity
increased considerably in the Middle Ages which is shown by the
many versions in the vernacular. Reitzenstein's interpretation is not
without problems either, however. The way in which Christ con-
fronts the Devil, as described in the main textual sources, does not
quite agree with the pictorial representation of the Gosforth Cross.
According to the *Gospel of Bartholomew*, Jesus seized Beliar (=
the Devil), flogged him and bound him in fetters that could not be
broken. The *Gospel of Nicodemus*, states that Christ, the King of
Glory, trod Death beneath his feet, seized Satan and delivered him
into the power of Hades. The Old Norse version from the twelfth
century, the *Niðrstigningar saga*, may be closer to the imagery
of the Gosforth Cross in telling that Satan transformed himself
into an enormous serpent or dragon. Having learnt that Jesus was
dying on the cross (*var þá í andláti*), he went to Jerusalem in order
to capture the soul of Jesus. But Jesus had prepared a trap with a
hook hidden in the bait. When Satan attempted to devour Jesus,
he became stuck on the divine hook and the cross fell on him from
above: *þá beit ǫngullinn guðomsins hann ok krossmarkit fell á
hann ofan*. Then Jesus approached, bound the Devil and ordered
his angels to guard him (*varðveita hann*).[13]

The west face shows a similar figure to the one on the east face
(Fig. 4). A man is standing in front of two gaping beasts. Unlike
the animal head of the east side, these are depicted with teeth
similar to those of a wolf. The man holds a staff in one hand and
in the other an object that looks like a drinking horn. The motif
is considered to represent the god Heimdall at the moment when
he is to give a great blast on the Gjallarhorn to warn the gods of
their approaching enemies; he tries to keep them away with his
"spear".[14] However, the figure may as well depict Christ, although

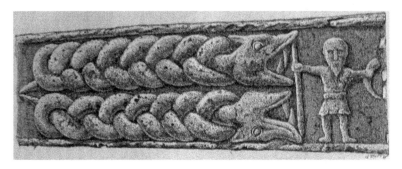

Figure 4. The Gosforth Cross, west side. Man and two gaping animal beasts; from Stephens 1884. License: CC-BY-NC-ND.

the horn appears to be somewhat odd in the context. Below, we see a rider set upside-down holding a spear (note the pointed form of the end unlike the staff). At the bottom, there is a scene showing a male figure with bound hands and feet; something like a snare is hanging around the neck (Fig. 5). The man seems to have his hair arranged in a long braid; in front of him is another figure, also with a braid, usually interpreted as a woman, in a kneeling position and holding a sickle-shaped object. The head of a snake can be distinguished above the figure to the left. A band with a knot seems to protrude from the band along the edges; the two figures are, as it were, encircled. Almost all commentators agree on the interpretation that the motif represents the punishment of Loki bound in the cave and also showing his wife Sigyn with her bowl. Even Reitzenstein had to admit the Scandinavian origin of the scene, but emphasized that it is only a symbol or *typos* for the Devil being fettered in the body of Hades. However, uncertainty about the Loki-Sigyn interpretation was expressed by Jan de Vries,[15] and I am not quite convinced that the scene is inspired by Norse mythology.

The figurative motifs of the north and south faces are more difficult to interpret in a clear-cut manner (see Fig 1). Some scholars find Christian symbolism,[16] others suggest figures such as Týr, the dog Garm, the stag Eikþyrnir and the Fenris Wolf.[17]

To conclude, doubt can be raised regarding the iconographical interpretations relying on Scandinavian mythology, but explaining convincingly all the pictures in the context of Christian ideas

Figure 5. The Gosforth Cross, west side. Bound man, snake and woman. License: CC-BY-NC-ND.

is not without its problems either. The only scene that presents an undisputed picture is the crucifixion scene on the east face. The proponents of the "Scandinavian mythology" interpretation explain the presence of the Ragnarøk motifs by the fact that they serve as symbols to communicate important Christian teachings. But if so, why were they not pictured so as to better fit in with what is told in Old Norse mythology, and the question still remains – how could the viewers know that the figurative scenes should be interpreted symbolically?

The Tullstorp Stone

Several pictures on rune stones have been considered to allude to the Ragnarøk drama. Among them is this large beast of the Tullstorp Stone (DR 271; Fig. 6), usually interpreted as the wolf Fenrir running to attack the gods.[18] The shape of this four-legged animal shows it to be part of a particular type of animal representation known from many other stones and objects, in the first place the Jelling Stone. Examples from Sweden are the Stora Ek Stone (Vg 4) and the Norra Åsarp Stone (Vg 181) both in the province of Västergötland. I call this type of animal the "the big, gaping beast" and have described its characteristics elsewhere.[19] The iconography of this animal type has also been studied by Sigmund Oehrl[20] who terms it "das grosse Tier". As to the image on the Tullstorp Stone, there are two points to be made. First it

Figure 6. The Tullstorp Stone. Photographer: Skånska Akademien (skanskaakademien.se/index.php/publikationer.html) Copyright: Skånska Akademien, License: CC-BY-NC-ND.

should not be interpreted in isolation from other representations of "the big, gaping beast" and secondly, I find it rather improbable that the patron or the artist of the monument had intended to depict the wolf Fenrir. This does not exclude the possibility that onlookers of the eleventh century were able to discover an allusion to this Ragnarøk monster animal.

The Ledberg Stone

The stones belonging to the Tullstorp group show only animal representations. Other stones that have been associated with Ragnarøk motifs display both animal and human figures. The most well-known example is the Ledberg Stone (Ög 181) which has images engraved on three sides. The front side (A) shows two warriors with round shields (Fig. 7). The warrior above holds an axe in one hand and in the other an object that looks like a sword. The body position of the warrior below is different; his right arm is pointing downwards and he holds something that could be a spear. Between the two warriors an animal, dog or wolf, is seen running. Close to the warrior below the contours of a second animal can be distinguished in a position as if attempting a leap. The lowest part shows a ship with mast and shields.

The back (B) presents another scene (Fig. 8) Again we meet two warriors dressed in the same way as those on the front but lacking weapons. The position of their bodies seems to indicate defeat and death. An animal, dog or wolf, is seen biting the foot of the warrior above, whereas the warrior below stretches his arms forward; his legs are missing. One of the edge sides (C) shows a cross, drawn like a tree with its roots (Fig. 9).The inscription says that a man, Bisi, and a woman, Gunna, had the stone set up in memory of his (or their) father Thorgaut, and the text ends with the formula *þistill/mistill/kistill* which probably was intended to protect the monument or perhaps serve as a sort of password formula for the dead person on their way to the other world. The formula most probably had a ritual background and might have been used in private or public worship.

The iconography of the stone, in particular side B, has been linked to the Ragnarøk myth by several commentators, who see

Figure 7. The Ledberg Stone, front (A). Photographer: Ulla-Maj Hultgård. Copyright: Ulla-Maj Hultgård, License: CC-BY-NC-ND.

Figure 8. The Ledberg Stone, back (B). Photographer: Ulla-Maj Hultgård. Copyright: Ulla-Maj Hultgård, License: CC-BY-NC-ND.

Figure 9. The Ledberg Stone, edge (C). Photographer: Ulla-Maj Hultgård. Copyright: Ulla-Maj Hultgård, License: CC-BY-NC-ND.

in it Óðinn's confrontation with the wolf Fenrir.[21] Reference is thereby made to a similar pictorial scene on the Thorvald Cross from Kirk Andreas on the Isle of Man.

In my view, we should keep the two sides (A and B) together when seeking to understand the iconography of the stone. One interpretation could be that the four warrior figures represent one and the same person shown at different moments of a struggle against one and the same animal. Above, on the front (A) we see the warrior at full strength with battle-axe and shield. The wolf is moving around him. In the next scene, the beast prepares to attack and the warrior now appears less forceful and even indecisive. On the back (B) the wolf has seized the foot of the warrior who seeks to escape, having lost his weapons. The final scene (below, side B) shows the defeated warrior sinking to the ground. But who is the warrior and who the wolf?

Erik Brate, the editor of *Östergötlands runinskrifter*, suggested that the four warrior figures depicted Thorgaut himself at different moments of the combat alluded to in the final part of the inscription, which Brate read as "he fell among the men of Tröndelag". But this reading is now abandoned for the formula *þistill, mistill, kistill*. The animals, Brate thought, only had an ornamental purpose. A more likely view is that the figurative scenes are inspired by mythic tradition or some heroic legend. If one prefers the former alternative, all four warrior pictures would then show Óðinn fighting the wolf Fenrir. However, in this case the iconography is not in accordance with the statement in all the textual sources that the wolf will swallow (*gleypir*) the god entirely. Perhaps there is an allusion to some heroic tradition, like the allusion in one of the stanzas of the *Qrvar Odds saga*. Here a seeress predicts that a serpent shall bite the foot of the hero: *naðr mun þik hǫggva neðan á fóti*. On the Ledberg Stone we find a wolf instead, but otherwise the parallel is striking. The pictorial configuration of a wolf or serpent biting a man's foot could also be another way of stating a warrior's death in combat.[22]

The family that had the Ledberg Stone erected lived at a period of religious change when Christianity had penetrated into southern Sweden. The cross on the edge (C; Fig. 9) is evidence, but the inherited faith was still alive and could inspire the choice of pictorial elements and formulae, as well as the adoption of pagan ideas that in their basic sense did not oppose Christian teachings. Such an idea was the final battle at Ragnarøk, the confrontation of Good and Evil. The iconography of the Ledberg Stone could in fact have to do with that myth. After his death, Thorgaut might have hoped to join the host of the *einherjar* and to fight against the powers of evil when the time came.

The Wall-hangings of Överhogdal

The wall-hangings of Överhogdal consist of five pieces or weaves that were later sewn together to form a cover (Fig. 10, 11 and 12). The radio carbon dating (900–1100) brings us back to the late Viking period which sets the frame of interpretation. The textiles have in all probability a local origin somewhere in the region from Tröndelag in the west over Jämtland to Hälsingland in the east. Some of them (**Ia, Ib** and **III**) would have decorated the walls of a chieftain's hall or a wealthy farmer's house; for weave **II** which

Figure 10. The Överhogdal Wall-hangings. Weave II. Photographer: Jämtlands museum. Copyright: Jamtli/Jamtli fotosamlingar, License: CC-BY-NC-ND.

Figure 11. The Överhogdal Wall-hangings. Weave Ia. Photographer: Jämtlands museum. Copyright: Jamtli/Jamtli fotosamlingar, License: CC-BY-NC-ND.

Figure 12. The Överhogdal Wall-hangings. Weave Ib. Photographer: Jämtlands museum. Copyright: Jamtli/Jamtli fotosamlingar, License: CC-BY-NC-ND.

has the most explicit Christian elements its original place in an early stave church seems likely. Weave **Ia** contains a runic inscription that should be read upside down. It was interpreted as *guðbȳ* by Jöran Sahlgren.[23]

Here is not the place to make a detailed description of the wall-hangings and I pass directly to the discussion of their interpretation. Two studies have to be commented upon in the first place, one by Ruth Horneij[24] and the other by Sture Wikman.[25] Taking weave **II** (Fig. 10) as a point of departure, Horneij explains the pictorial contents as being derived from medieval illuminated manuscripts of the biblical *Book of Revelation*. For instance, the tree in the middle and the small animal below could represent the Tree of life and the Lamb, i.e. Christ (*Rev.* 22,1–2); the pictures of this motif in the Trier Apocalypse and on the so-called "Marcus Throne" in Venice in fact provide good parallels. The building to the far left is tentatively explained by Horneij as God's temple in heaven; in the chancel we see Christ holding two book scrolls and the figures in the nave represent the seven apocalyptic angels, following *Revelation* Chapters 8 to 10.

Coming to pieces **Ia** and **Ib** (Fig. 11 and 12), Horneij has to have recourse to Old Norse mythology for her interpretation, although she thinks the overall message is still Christian. The tree with a bird on the top and another bird at the base depicts Yggdrasill at the beginning of Ragnarøk, the birds also alluding to the crowing cocks of the *Vǫluspá*. Some of the animal figures could, according to Horneij, be interpreted as animals taking part in the last battle at Ragnarøk. The beast with a wide-open mouth above the tree is the wolf Fenrir and the ship would then be Naglfar.

The eight-legged animal also appearing twice would be Óðinn's horse Sleipnir which is taking part in the last battle together with the horse of St. Michael shown to the left. The blue animal below the runes would be the dog Garm and the large red animal looking backwards is probably meant to represent a reptile and could thus picture the Midgard serpent. For the figure inside the hexagonal construction, Horneij proposes three different interpretations 1) the bound Loki (but without Sigyn), 2) Gunnar in the snake pit and 3) the fettered Devil.

The building above the runes is explained as the New Jerusalem coming down from heaven and the figures inside would then represent redeemed souls. To support her interpretation, Horneij refers to the runes read as *guðbȳ* which would mean 'God's abode'. Further figurative elements of piece **Ia** could also be seen in a Christian eschatological context and Horneij concludes that weave **Ia** is an early Christian apocalyptic wall-hanging in part inspired by the Ragnarøk myth.

The animal with big hooves or paws could be another representation of the wolf Fenrir and the small human figure on the back who appears to stick something into the mouth of the beast would represent the god Víðarr fighting Fenrir. In my opinion, it is highly improbable that Víðarr performing the most heroic act of Ragnarøk should have been represented by such a tiny figure whose weapon cannot clearly be distinguished. Moreover, we cannot be sure of the narrative connection between the beast and the human figure. In addition, an unprejudiced interpretation could see the ears where Horneij sees the mouth.

Although having a less varied pictorial content, Horneij finds it easier to establish the Christian character of piece **Ib**. She points especially to the rider figures that she believes represent Christ. To the right, he raises his hands triumphantly after having defeated the dragon. The second picture in the middle shows Christ mounted on an ass rather than on a horse, thus recalling the prophecy of *Zechariah* Chapter 9. And the third rider picture would represent Christ when he returns as the Messiah.

The scene in the middle below shows a man with an axe riding up a triangular construction upon which a small human figure is seen sitting or lying on a throne or a bed. The motif which is unique has given rise to rather imaginative explanations: a missionary riding up to the top of a hill to smash an enthroned pagan idol,[26] or Sigurðr Fáfnisbani riding up the mountainside to waken the sleeping valkyrie Sigrdrifa.[27] Piece **III** should be explained, according to Horneij, by Christian legend about the virgin Mary and the infancy history of Jesus.

The study of Horneij merits recognition because she tries to interpret wall-hangings **II, Ia** and **Ib** as a whole from the viewpoint of Christian eschatology. The interpretation is beset with some difficulties, as she herself admits. The problem, as I see it, is to explain convincingly the mixture of Scandinavian and Christian myth on wall-hanging **Ia** in particular. Horneij thinks the missionaries could have included some pagan ideas in order to better illustrate the Christian doctrine about the end of the world. The animals inspired by Norse mythology are there in their function of representing the pagan world and the evil powers that will perish in the Ragnarøk. Thus, even Óðinn's horse Sleipnir seems to belong with the monster animals, as Horneij points out.

The study by Wikman, presents a more consistent Ragnarøk interpretation. He agrees with the identifications of Old Norse motifs proposed by Horneij on piece **Ia**, but adds further elements. The eight-legged horse is of course Sleipnir, here bringing Óðinn to take counsel from Mímir's head, which may be pictured by the object down to the right. In addition to the beast with gaping jaws (Fig. 12), Wikman identifies three further representations of the wolf Fenrir, depicting him in different situations. First, when he is fettered and Týr puts his hand into the mouth of the wolf. Second, the larger animal with its head bent downwards and lines on its body would represent Fenrir tearing dead bodies, an allusion to the *Vǫluspá* st. 50: "the Grey one tears the corpses", *slítr nái niðfǫlr*. The third one shows the wolf at the moment when he has come loose from his chain that can still be seen hanging from his neck. To me, it seems rather unlikely that Fenrir should have been depicted four times on the same piece of tapestry in such varying shapes.

The statement that Surt throws fire upon the earth is, according to Wikman, illustrated by the "combs" of fire depicted above Loki and elsewhere on this textile. However, the most significant details that show the overall theme to be that of Ragnarøk are the three large rider figures with uplifted hands on wall-hangings **Ia** and **Ib**. They represent the three main gods at the moment when they perish in the final battle. To the far left of piece **Ia** we see how Óðinn is being caught up by the wolf Fenrir, and on piece **Ib** the Midgard Serpent turns his head toward the god Þórr to release its venom. The motif in the middle of the same wall-hanging depicts Surt riding up the bridge of Bifrost towards the guardian of the gods, Heimdall. Above, we find the third main god, Freyr, waiting to confront Surt beside the bursting sky.

The interpretation of wall-hangings **Ia** and **Ib** by Wikman is open to several critical remarks. It is not at all apparent that the three large figures should depict gods. We may equally well assume that they represent mounted worshippers or heroes. According to the Prose Edda, only Óðinn rides on a horse to the battlefield at Ragnarøk. The *Vǫluspá* uses the word *ferr* approximately "advances" followed by *vega* "fight" to describe the confrontations of Óðinn and Freyr with their respective opponents, whereas

Þórr is said to walk, *gengr*, when he meets the Midgard Serpent; after the combat he takes, *gengr* (SnE: *stígr*), nine steps before falling down dead (Vsp 56; SnE 51). The figure riding up the "bridge" (or the "hill") having an axe on its shoulder is less likely to represent Surt, since the textual tradition pays much attention to the fact that Surt has a sword. Furthermore, it seems that the artist of the wall-hangings did not have in mind any hostile relationship between the three rider figures and the animals with which they are associated; still less is it possible to distinguish fighting scenes between them.

Wall-hanging II displays, according to Wikman, another aspect of the Ragnarøk myth, namely the new world to come after the destruction. The two figures on the eight-legged horse are considered to show Víðarr and Vali reappearing in the new world on the back of their father's horse, whereas the sons of Þórr, Móði and Magni, arrive riding in a chariot which here looks like a sleigh. One of them is holding Mjǫllnir in his hand. For his Ragnarøk interpretation, Wikman attaches particular importance to the rectangular object with squares that can be seen above the horse and the chariot/sleigh. It represents one of the golden game bricks that the gods will find in the grass on the earth having arisen once again out of the sea (Vsp 59). Wikman cannot deny the fact that wall-hanging II shows obvious Christian elements, and he explains their presence by assuming the wish of the artist to relate pagan views of the world's restoration with the Christian idea of Paradise.

To sum up, looking at the figurative scenes of the Överhogdal Tapestry without any preconceived notions about what should be there, one is far from convinced of their association with the Ragnarøk myth. If the wall-hangings had been designed to reproduce motifs from that myth, one would have expected a more unequivocal Ragnarøk iconography. The pictorial elements are never precise enough to exclude other interpretations.

Conclusions

Interpreting Viking age iconography is an intricate matter. The pictorial details are seldom so apparent as to remove every doubt about what they represent. The image of Christ on the Jelling

Stone and the visit of the Magi on the Dynna Stone in Norway are two notable exceptions, however. With respect to the social and historical context, we have to recognize different actors who are involved in shaping the meaning of the iconography. There is first the person or persons who wished to set up a monument, to make a tapestry or some other object and paid for them, second, the artist who designed and produced them, and third, the viewers who may have associated the pictures with quite different things than those the patron and the artist had in mind. In that respect, the pictures are multivalent and some people looking at them might have found motifs from the Ragnarøk myth where the representation of other ideas was originally intended. The answer to the question first raised: "Do we find Ragnarøk motifs in pictures?" has to be neither a clear "yes" nor a definite "no". It seems more complicated than that, as I have attempted to show.

Notes

1. Kopár 2012.

2. The rendering in English of Old Norse mythic names follows Larrington 2014.

3. Hultgård 2017.

4. Stephens 1884.

5. Parker 1896.

6. Olrik 1902.

7. Berg 1958.

8. Bailey 2003.

9. Oehrl 2011:135–140.

10. Kopár 2012:75–77, 90–94.

11. For this interpretation and a summary of the previous discussion of the Gosforth Cross's crucifixion scene, see Kopár 2012:94–101.

12. For example Olrik 1902:163; Berg 1957–1958:212; de Vries 1956–1957:§514; Oehrl 2011:163, 171; Kopár 2012:77, 91–92.

13. *Soga om nedstinginga i dødsriket* 4.

14. So Berg 1957–1958; McKinnell 2001; Bailey 2000; Oehrl 2011:169; Kopár 2012:92.

15. de Vries 1956–1957:§558.

16. Stephens 1884 and Reitzenstein 1924.

17. Berg 1957–1958; Bailey 2003.

18. E.g. Moltke 1985; Ellmers 1995.

19. Hultgård 2017.

20. Oehrl 2007; 2011.

21. Jansson 1987:152; Moltke 1985:246–248; Gschwantler 1990:521; Düwel 2001:139; McKinnell 2007; Oehrl 2011:229; Kopár 2012:71, 78, 125.

22. Oehrl (2011:229–230) indicates a similar interpretation line.

23. Sahlgren 1924.

24. Horneij 1991.

25. Wikman 1996.

26. Karlin 1920.

27. Branting & Lindblom 1928.

References

Bailey, Richard N. 2000. Scandinavian Myth on Viking-Period Stone Scultpure in England. In G. Barnes & M. Clunies Ross (eds.). *Old Norse Myths, Literature and Society. Proceedings of the 11th International Saga Conference 2–7 July 2000, University of Sydney.* Sydney: University of Sydney, 15–23.

Berg, Knut. 1957–58. Gosforth-korset. En Ragnaroksfremstilling i kristen symbolikk. In *Viking* (English version in *The Journal of the Warburg and Courtauld Institutes* 1958:21), 203–228.

Branting, Agnes & Lindblom, Andreas. 1928. *Medeltida vävnader och broderier i Sverige 1.* Uppsala.

Collingwood, W. G. 1927. *Northumbrian Crosses of the Pre-Norman Age*. London: Faber & Gwyer.

Düwel, Klaus. 2001. *Runenkunde*. 3. Aufl. Stuttgart: Metzler.

Ellmers, Detlev. 1995. Valhalla and the Gotland Stones. In O. Crumlin-Pedersen & B. Munch Thye (eds.). *The Ship as Symbol in Prehistoric and Medieval Scandinavia*. Copenhagen: Copenhagen National Museum, 165–171.

Gschwantler, Otto. 1990. Die Überwindung des Fenriswolfs und ihr christliches Gegenstück bei Frau Ava. In T. Pároli (red.). *Poetry in the Scandinavian Middle Ages. The Seventh International Saga Conference*. Spoleto: Centro Italiano di Studi Sull' Alto Medioevo, 509–534.

Heizmann, Wilhelm & Axboe, Morten (Hrsg.). 2011. *Die Goldbrakteaten der Völkerwanderungszeit. Auswertung und Neufunde*. Berlin, New York: W. de Gruyter.

Horneij, Ruth. 1991. *Bonaderna från Överhogdal*. Östersund: Jämtlands läns museum.

Hultgård, Anders. 2017. *Midgård brinner. Ragnarök i religionshistorisk belysning*. Uppsala: Kungl. Gustav Adolfs Akademien.

Jacobsen, Lis et al. (eds.). 1942. *Danmarks runeindskrifter*. Ved Lis Jacobsen og Erik Moltke under medvirken af Anders Bæksted og Karl Martin Nielsen. København.

Jansson, Sven B. F. 1987. *Runes in Sweden*. Stockholm: Gidlund.

Karlin, Georg J:son. 1920. *Över-Hogdals tapeten. En undersökning*. Östersund: Jämtslöjds förlag.

Kopár, Lilla. 2012. *Gods and Settlers. The Iconography of Norse Mythology in Anglo-Scandinavian Sculpture*. Turnhout: Brepols.

Larrington, Carolyne. 2014. *The Poetic Edda. Translated with an Introduction and Notes*. Oxford: Oxford University Press.

McKinnell, John. 2001. Eddic Poetry in Anglo-Scandinavian Northern England. In J. Graham-Campbell et al. (eds.). *Vikings and the Danelaw*. Oxford: Oxbow, 327–344.

Moltke, Erik. 1985. *Runes and their Origin. Denmark and Elsewhere.* Copenhagen: National Museum of Denmark.

Oehrl, Sigmund. 2007. Das Große Tier. Zur Deutung eines spätwikingerzeitlichen Bildmotivs. In A. Heitmann et al. (eds.). *Tiere in skandinavischer Literatur und Kulturgeschichte.* Freiburg: Rombach, 41–71.

Oehrl, Sigmund. 2011. *Vierbeinerdarstellungen auf schwedischen Runensteinen. Studien zur nordgermanischen Tier- und Fesselungsikonografie.* Berlin, New York: W. de Gruyter.

Olrik, Axel. 1902. Om Ragnarok. In *Årbøger for nordisk oldkyndighed og historie,* 157–291.

Parker, Charles Arundel. 1896. *The Ancient Crosses at Gosforth, Cumberland.* London: E. Stock

Reitzenstein, R. 1924. *Weltuntergangsvorstellungen. Eine Studie zur vergleichenden Religionsgeschichte.* Särtryck ur Kyrkohistorisk årsskrift 1924. Uppsala: A.-B. Lundequistska Bokhandeln.

Sahlgren, Jöran. 1924. Runskriften på Överhogdalsbonaden. In *Festskrift tillägnad Hugo Pipping.* Helsingfors: Mercator, 462–464.

Soga om nedstiginga i dødsriket (*Niðrstigningar saga*), tekst og omsetjing ved Odd Einar Haugen. Bergen 1985: Nordisk Institutt.

Stephens, George. 1884. Prof. S. Bugge's studier over nordisk mythologi. Supplement. In *Aarbøger for nordisk Oldkyndighed* 1884, 1–47.

de Vries, Jan. 1956–57. *Altgermanische Religionsgeschichte, I–II.* Berlin: W. de Gruyter.

Wikman, Sture. 1996. *Fenrisulven ränner.* Östersund: Jamtli.

Response

John Lindow

University of California, Berkeley

The textual tradition tells us that there indeed were images of the mythology in pre-Christian times. From ample internal evidence – the apparent beginning and the *stef* – we know that Bragi Boddason's *Ragnarsdrápa*, which is one of the very earliest skaldic monuments, describes the scenes on a shield, almost certainly from somewhere in Norway in the early ninth century. The same is true of Þjóðólfr's *Haustlǫng*, and, although *Ragnarsdrápa* mixed heroic and mythological material – which should hardly surprise us – what remains of *Haustlǫng* is exclusively mythological. If Eilífr Goðrúnarson's *Þórsdrápa* is based on a shield, we find evidence for mythological images in 10th-century Norway. And we definitely have such evidence from late 10th-century Iceland, in the form of Úlfr Uggason's *Húsdrápa*. It is, of course, true that none of the ekphrases that have survived contain descriptions of Ragnarøk. Myths of Þórr seem to have been the most popular with the skalds, and indeed no one doubts that we have images of Þórr's fishing expedition on stones in Cumbria, Denmark, and Sweden. However, the textual evidence shows us that Ragnarøk was on people's minds toward the end of the Viking Age. I refer here to Óðinn gathering warriors for the last battle in *Eiríksmál,* and the trope that often ends panegyrics, to the effect that the world will be destroyed before another such excellent ruler appears.

Given this background, it is not at all unlikely that images of Ragnarøk may have existed in the Viking Age North. The question raised in the insightful analysis by Anders Hultgård is the degree of certainty regarding the identification of Ragnarøk in the materials he discusses, when it can be shown that details of image and text diverge.

This question raises a fundamental theoretical issue, namely the difference between a canonical and an oral religion. Because Old Norse religion did not have canonical texts, and because there must, therefore, have been extensive variation in time and space, it is possible that a motif in an image, even if it is not found in one of the texts that have survived, may reflect a lost variant. Of course, we cannot be certain, but I think that we can responsibly discuss the implications of such variants within a given myth complex.

A word now on our extant texts. It is a curious fact that we know Ragnarøk largely from Eddic poetry. While it is true that skalds borrowed the trope of the natural phenomena attending the end of the world – mountains falling into the sea, and the like – they did not describe what would happen when the Æsir and Jǫtnar met in battle, or the aftermath. On the other hand, Eddic poets found these to be very fruitful topics. Both versions of *Vǫluspá* can, to some degree, be regarded as more about eschatology than cosmogony, and certainly they are about very little else. The wisdom lore in which Óðinn traffics in *Vafþrúðnismál* and *Grímnismál* also focuses on Ragnarøk and the end.

One consequence of the Eddic focus of the textual material probably complements what I have just said about oral religions. Given the metrical differences, and especially the constraint that skaldic meters would place on textual variation, it is surely likely that Eddic texts changed more in transmission than did skaldic texts – or to put it another way, there was more textual variation in Eddic performance than there was in skaldic performance. This makes it more likely that motifs seen in images may have been paralleled in variants of Eddic poems that were not recorded.

Eddic poetry also gave us the name we use for the mythical phenomenon under discussion here. *Ragna røk* and *tíva røk*, both expressions limited to Eddic poems, are ultimately perhaps the rebirth,[1] more conventionally the 'fate' or 'judgment', of the powers or gods, that is, of a group. This textual focus on a group rather than an individual could well suggest that, of all myths, this is one that might inspire an artist or one who commissioned an artist to think of not just one but a number of images, portraying more than one of the individuals who are involved. The Gosforth Cross and Överhogdal Tapestry meet this criterion, while most of the runestones do not. And if, as Finnur Jónsson suggested,[2] the second component rightly means something like 'elements that make up a whole', 'course of events', or 'development' (an

attractive suggestion when it comes to thinking about the inevita-
bility of Ragnarøk in the mythic system), we might also perhaps
expect artists to depict more than one scene.

It is striking that some possible images of Ragnarøk, especially
those discussed by Hultgård, are found in a demonstrably Christian
context. A program that wished to deny this fact would need to be
able to prove conclusively that *all* the images in an iconographic
suite – not just most – containing possible Ragnarøk motifs or
others from Norse mythology, would have to be unambiguously
interpretable from the perspective of Christian iconography. As
Hultgård's analysis shows, that is simply not possible. We must,
therefore, accept that conceptions of Ragnarøk were part of the
Christianization process. That should surprise no one, although
again, as Hultgård shows, the issue is very complex. Personally, I
find attractive some of the hypotheses put forward in G. Ronald
Murphy's 2013 book *Tree of Salvation. Yggdrasill and the Cross
in the North*, namely that certain symbolic matrices of pre-
Christian religion, far from being shunned or condemned by the
new Church, were particularly adapted to its use. Among them, he
argues, is the tree, which blended with the cross and came to stand
for redemption after death – that is, for salvation. Murphy sees
repackaging of symbolic space around Yggdrasill in the architecture of stave churches and Bornholm's round churches, and of the
tree and its message in the Middleton Crosses in Yorkshire, in the
Old English *Dream of the Rood*, in the structure of the older rune
row, and in folklore. Some of this puts a big burden on a slender
body of evidence, but it is worth paying attention to a challenge of
some traditional Christian interpretations of images on precisely
the grounds that Hultgård brings forth for the potential images of
Ragnarøk: lack of cohesion with textural details. This argument is
particularly cogent when one is dealing with a canonical religion
such as Christianity.

Hultgård's most important point is that those who commissioned images, those who executed them, and especially those
who viewed them, may well have had differing understandings of
what the images portrayed. This point is particularly important
in light of the fact that those who might have seen Ragnarøk in
the images discussed – as well, of course, in others – might have

known variant versions of the myth, including some no longer known to us. Indeed, one could imagine a precursor of this discussion, a thousand or so years ago, in which persons in front of an image tried to determine whether or not it portrayed Ragnarøk. A wise man like Anders Hultgård might then have said: We can reach neither a clear "yes" nor a definite "no".

Notes

1. Haraldur Bernharðsson 2007.

2. Finnur Jónsson 1931:475–476 s.v. *rǫk*.

References

Finnur Jónsson. 1931. *Lexicon Poeticum Antiquæ Linguæ Septentrionalis. Ordbog over det norsk-islandske skjaldesprog.* København: S.L. Møller.

Haraldur Bernharðsson. 2007. Old Icelandic Ragnarök and Ragnarökkr. In: Alan J. Nussbaum (ed.). *Verba Docenti. Studies in Historical and Indo-European Linguistics Presented to Jay H. Jasanoff by Students, Friends, and Colleagues.* Ann Arbor/New York: Beech Stave Press, 25–38.

Murphy, G. Ronald. 2013. *Tree of Salvation. Yggdrasill and the Cross in the North.* Oxford: Oxford University Press.

Ormhäxan, Dragons, Partuition and Tradition

Stephen Mitchell
Harvard University

Medieval Nordic vernaculars routinely use the terms *dreki* (pl. *drekar*), 'dragon', and *ormr* (pl. *ormar*), both 'serpent' and 'dragon', in often overlapping ways, although clearly *dreki*, a word of foreign origin (< Latin *draco*, from Greek *drakōn*) has the more restricted range, never referring to snakes as such, but always, and only, to the kind of serpentine beasts known from myth and legend.[1] By contrast, *ormr*, cognate with Old English *wyrm* 'snake,' 'dragon' and so on, is employed to mean both the actual reptiles of the suborder Ophidia and cryptozoological monsters. So intertwined are the two in medieval texts and in artistic representations that one scholar has suggested the Swedish neologism *drakorm* (pl. *drakormar*) as a means of referring to the two as a group.[2]

In surviving texts concerned with Old Norse mythological and legendary traditions, modern readers encounter three especially well-known dragons: Níðhǫggr, the Miðgarðsormr, and Fáfnir. There are other named dragons and other terms, of course, as Snorri remarks in his *Skáldskaparmál*:

> *Þessi eru orma heiti: dreki, Fáfnir, Jǫrmungandr, naðr, Níðhǫggr, linnr, naðra, Góinn, Móinn, Grafvitnir, Grábákr, Ófnir, Sváfnir, grímr.*[3]

These are the names for serpents: dragon, Fafnir, Iormungand, adder [*naðr*], Nidhogg, viper [*naðra*],[4] Goin, Moin, Grafvitnir, Grabak, Ofnir, Svafnir, masked one.[5]

How to cite this book chapter:
Mitchell, S. 2019. *Ormhäxan*, Dragons, Partuition and Tradition. In: Wikström af Edholm, K., Jackson Rova, P., Nordberg, A., Sundqvist, O. & Zachrisson, T. (eds.) *Myth, Materiality, and Lived Religion: In Merovingian and Viking Scandinavia.* Pp. 115–139. Stockholm: Stockholm University Press. DOI: https://doi.org/10.16993/bay.f. License: CC-BY.

What these legendary *drakormar* of Norse tradition have in common with the well-known dragons of Christian tradition, such as
those that do combat with Christian heroes such as Saint George,
is that they are typically seen to have negative associations, that is,
generally negative and adversarial relations with human society:
according to *Vǫluspá* in GKS 2365 4to, Níðhǫggr, for example, *inn
dimmi / dreki fljúgandi* ('the dark dragon flying') bears corpses *í
fjǫðrom* (lit., in [his] feathers'; *Vǫluspá* (K) st. 63 cf. *Vǫluspá* (H)
st. 58) and is said in *Grímnismál* (st. 35) and *Gylfaginning* to
gnaw (*skerðir*) at the roots of the World Tree.

This adversarial "man versus monster" scenario, the central
image of the various story lines gathered as motifs A876, A1082.3
and so on in *The Motif-Index of Folk-Literature*,[6] is one that has
ancient roots: not only the North Germanic peoples but also many
other Indo-European cultures – i.e., Italic, Indo-Iranian, Celtic,
Greek, Anatolian and other historically- and linguistically-related
traditions – were, according to Calvert Watkins' *How to Kill a
Dragon: Aspects of Indo-European Poetics*,[7] inheritors of a mil-
lennia-old formula of the following sort:

(HERO) SLAY (*g^uhen-) SERPENT (WITH WEAPON; alt., WITH
COMPANION)

It is, of course, a tale that recurs in the myths and legends of many
Indo-European cultures, for example, in the storied confrontations between Zeus and Typhon, Herakles and the Hydra, Perseus
and the Gorgon, Indra and Vṛtra, and, in the Nordic case, Þórr
and the Miðgarðsormr.

Given this well-documented archaic story pattern and such
popular Christian presentations of dragons in the Nordic Middle
Ages as the legend of Saint George, it seems that the principal
way these beasts ought to be understood is within an adversarial
context; however, several scholars have been at pains to argue for
a different perspective on pre-Christian perceptions, and uses, of
dragons. Basing his interpretation on close examination of Bronze
Age rock art and images on bronze objects, Flemming Kaul has
proposed an integrated understanding of what he has termed the
religion of "the solar age" (*solalderen*).[8] According to Kaul's analysis, this is a belief system connected to a social elite exercising

control of, and trade in, bronze.[9] In it, the *drakorm* provides assistance to the sun in its daily movement by leading it below the horizon for its nocturnal aqueous passage.[10]

On the significance of such an understanding of Bronze Age religion in the North for the Germanic Iron Age many centuries later, Kaul thinks such continuity unlikely, mainly due to what he understands to be two periods of disruption: one c. 500 BC with a change in ritual patterns, and another, c. 500 AD, with the establishment of a religion centered on the Æsir. But, even if he thinks the possibility slight of there being any meaningful comprehensive connections between the Bronze Age materials and, for example, later written sources, Kaul concedes that some of the earlier motifs, including the snake motif, may have been transformed in ways that allowed them to survive into the Iron Age.[11]

Birgitta Johansen, also an archaeologist, concludes as well that there may have been generally positive relationships of *drakormar* to human society. Treating the Roman Iron Age up through the Middle Ages (200 CE –1400 CE), Johansen examines the evolution of social and mental constructs, especially as these are to be inferred from the natural and built landscapes (e.g. hill forts, stone walls), and their interrelationships. Johansen's interpretation relies heavily on what she sees as the contrasting views of pagan vs Christian Scandinavia, especially as these perspectives are employed in dragon imagery on rune stones.[12] Johansen argues that the previously positive connection between *drakormar* and women turns negative under Christianity's influence:

> My conclusion is that women are the users of the dragon (even explicitly against men) and that the dragon protects women. The dragon fights with men and it kills men. These roles eventually changed, the dragon increasingly becoming a threat to men and something men could control only by killing. In addition it became, during the Middle Ages and under Christian influence, a deadly threat to women too.[13]

Thus, against the view that human relations to *drakormar* were necessarily negative, as in so many Indo-European sources and such Old Norse narratives as those about Þórr and the Miðgarðsormr, an alternative, positive interpretation also emerges for the pre-Christian era. Recognizing the possibility then that there may have existed two distinctly different interpretations of *drakormar* in the Iron Age, how might our understanding of the *drakorm* figure as seen in Gotland be re-interpreted?

Drakorm elements figure strongly in the island's art tradition, and a number of Gotlandic picture stones provide important clues about the *drakorm*'s status. Frequently, these images come from the earliest era of the Gotlandic picture stones,[14] a turning point in the history of religious and cultural life in northern Europe.

From the earliest periods, Lindqvist's group Aa, now understood to include the 2nd through the 6th centuries,[15] such *drakorm* images as Martebo Church (G 264) (Fig. 1) and Hangvars Austers I, for example, testify to the popularity of the dragon-snake motif within the island's art traditions. For the most part, these depictions appear to fall well within the adversarial dragon tradition.[16] A related, but much more complex and divergent, use of *drakormar* is also one of the best-known Gotlandic picture stones to the world at large, namely, the remarkable monument from Smiss in När Parish, discovered in 1955, sometimes called the "snake witch stone" (Swedish *ormhäxan,* alt., *ormtjuserskan*).[17] När Smiss III (Fig. 2) is usually dated to the 6th to 7th centuries (although some have suggested that it might be from as early as the 5th century).[18] In it, rather than the dominating central whirling solar figures on Martebo Church (G 264) and Hangvars Austers I, När Smiss III

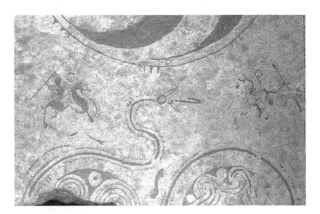

Figure 1. Martebo Church (G 264). Photographer: Stephen Mitchell. Copyright: Stephen Mitchell, License: CC-BY-NC-ND.

Figure 2. När Smiss III. Photographer: Stephen Mitchell. Copyright: Stephen Mitchell, License: CC-BY-NC-ND.

has instead a large triskele of three animals, often interpreted as a boar, a raptor, and a *drakorm*. Beneath this group is the figure of a human, generally, although not always, believed to be a woman, legs outstretched, holding two differing *drakormar*, one in either hand.

Interpretations of this stone's origins, history and meaning have been much discussed, although little agreed on – already its discoverer, Sune Lindqvist, brought not only Norse but also Celtic and Minoan traditions into the debate and these possibilities have tended to dominate discussion ever since. The stone has, for example, been understood to be a product of Celtic artisanship representing Daniel in the lion's den;[19] others have also promoted possible Celtic connections, especially to the degree to which the image has been likened to the god, Cernunnos, as presented on the Gundestrup Cauldron.[20] Karl Hauk sees in the figure a shape-shifted Óðinn in the form of a *Seelenführer*.[21] And comparisons with the famous Minoan snake goddess figurines from the "houses of the double-axe" in Knossos and other Cretan towns are highly suggestive but of uncertain value given our current state of knowledge. The very uniqueness of this stone among Gotlandic picture stones makes the object difficult to assess, although one need not be quite so pessimistic as the Harrisons, who include the stone in their *101 föremål ur Sveriges historia* noting simply that "we haven't a clue about what the stone says".[22]

By contrast, local historians and other enthusiasts have been neither silent nor uncertain about this remarkable stone, and we may, in fact, be able to provide a context which at the very least situates När Smiss III within an empirically-based matrix, such that it no longer seems so utterly *sui generis*. Of particular interest, despite being half a millennium later than När Smiss III, has been a 12th-century stone relief at Väte Church, Gotland:

It has sometimes been suggested that such scenes are legacies of a pre-Christian belief in *Terra mater*, the earthmother, nursing beasts, including serpents. Another, and in my opinion likelier,

Figure 3. Väte Church, Gotland. Photographer: Bengt A. Lundberg. Copyright: Riksantikvarieämbetet, License: CC-BY-NC-ND.[23]

interpretation is that it reflects an interest in such vision literature as e.g. the 4th-century *Vision of Saint Paul*, the 5th-century
Apocalypse of Elijah, or the (contemporary) 12th-century *Vision of
Alberic*, all of which present women condemned to nurse serpents
in Purgatory/Hell, because they have refused to care for orphans,
or, in other instances, their own children. And in Continental
church art, these unusual scenes of multi-specied nursing are
understood to be a punishment for lust and debauchery, an idea
occasionally applied to Väte as well;[24] moreover, similar scenes
are also found in medieval homiletic literature, which again point
to envy and lust as the causes of this unusual suckling.[25] Recent
arguments have pushed back against this ecclesiastical interpretation and contended anew that it is, in fact, *Terra mater* and
not *Luxuria* that is being presented here and elsewhere in Nordic
contexts.[26]

Importantly, one of the other sites comes from the church at
Linde on Gotland, part of a baptismal font described as showing "a standing woman with a 'snake' [*orm*] at one breast".[27]
Naturally, the origin of the medieval *drakorm*-nursing images at
Väte and Linde are most easily explained by these ecclesiastical
references – yet whatever the Church's specifically theological
rationale, nothing about this scene dictates that islanders who
knew of a traditional association of women and *drakormar* could
not interpret it in ways that were convivial to local beliefs and customs, an association that could, in fact, have played a role in the
Church's selection of this theme. The two images at Väte and Linde
are hardly a large dataset and one might reasonably conclude that
these unusual human-*drakormar* interactions are merely examples of the so-called "infinite monkey theorem". Yet, as already
strongly hinted at in Peel's edition and translation of medieval
Gotlandic law and legend,[28] there are, in fact, several other significant indications of a local tradition involving *drakormar*.

Although the human figure on the lower portion of Där
Smiss III is unique on Gotland, the triskele design on the upper
portion is not. In fact, in reviewing the archaeological record from
the period 550–750 CE,[29] it is clear that designs similar to the Där
Smiss III triskele are a common feature of Gotlandic iconography
throughout these pre-Viking periods, as in the following examples
of perforated discs:[30]

The design of these artifacts, of which there are a great many from Gotland, strongly resembles the triskele on När Smiss III (although it shows three different animals), especially when it is presented in a similar style (Fig. 5):

One particularly interesting item in this inventory (item c in Fig. 4), as noted already in Peel,[31] comes from an early 9th-century Gotlandic grave for a woman at Ihre in Hellvi Parish in northeastern Gotland. Although the grave itself dates to the 9th century,[32] it has been argued that the object may date to the period 650–700 CE.[33] One possible interpretation of this chronology would be that the disc, as a noted archaeologist suggests "might have been an antique when it was buried and this raises the possibility of such decorative discs having been heirlooms passed from mother to daughter".[34]

The continuity of these ornamental discs, their style, and their concern with *drakormar* brings to mind, as is occasionally mentioned on online sites about Gotland, that also concerned with women and serpents is an important episode in the so-called *Legendary History of Gotland* from the 13th century:

> Þissi Þieluar hafþi ann sun, sum hit Hafþi. En Hafþa kuna hit Huitastierna. Þaun tu bygþu fyrsti a Gutlandi. Fyrstu nat, sum þaun saman suafu, þa droymdi henni draumbr, so sum þrir ormar varin slungnir saman i barmi hennar, ok þytti henni sum þair skriþin yr barmi hennar. Þinna draum segþi han firir *Hafþa, bonda sinum. Hann *reþ draum þinna so:
> 'Alt ir baugum bundit.
> Boland al þitta varþa,
> ok faum þria syni aiga.'[35]

This same Þieluar had a son named Hafþi, and Hafþi's wife was called Huitastierna. These two were the first to settle in Gotland. The first night that they slept together, she dreamed a dream. It was just as if three snakes were coiled together within her womb, and it seemed to her as though they crawled out of her [womb][36]. She related this dream to Hafþi, her husband, and he interpreted it as follows:

> 'Everything in rings is bound.
> Inhabited this land shall be;
> we shall beget sons three.'

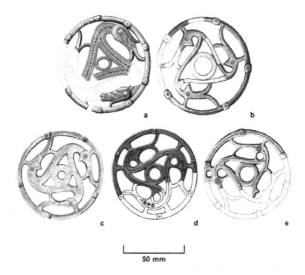

Figure 4. Perforated disks. From Pearl 2014, original drawing from Nerman et al. 1969-1975. Copyright: Pearl, Frederic; The Swedish Archaeological Society; Kungl. Vitterhets Historie och Antikvitets Akademien. License: CC-BY-NC-ND.

Figure 5. När Smiss III triskele presented in the style of an ornamental disc. Copyright: Stephen Mitchell, License: CC-BY-NC-ND.

This legendary text as a whole has been the subject of much discussion over the decades,[37] and although its immediate context – the Laws of Gotland – suggests that it largely functioned as a framing device for these important documents, few doubt that much of the material in the history offers us insights into the early history and traditions of the island.[38] The opening settlement or foundation legend, for example, has numerous parallels, including the three brothers, but virtually without parallel is the notion of Huitastierna dreaming of having three snakes coiled in her womb who are subsequently born and who, as humans, settle the island.

A somewhat similar tale is the dream reported about Clytemnestra in the second of Aeschylus' *Oresteia* trilogy, *Choephoroi* (*The Libation Bearers*), according to which Clytemnestra has given birth to a monstrous and vengeful snake. But even if the basic idea – an elite woman giving birth to one or more snakes – is the same, it is in one instance meant to be a real snake and in the other a dream to be interpreted, like the cows and corn that Jacob reveals to pharaoh (*Genesis* 40–41); moreover, the consequences of the dreams are quite different.[39] On the other hand, the association of snakes with birthing can boast many parallels: the resemblance of entwined snakes to the umbilical cord, a perception that leads to the connection, and perhaps even metonymy, of this funiculus and snakes, is a phenomenon well-documented in a variety of ancient and modern cultures.[40] Moreover, the skin-shedding or sloughing (*edysis*) of snakes has led to the association of these animals with concepts of re-birth in e.g. ancient Egyptian and Mesoamerican cultures.

The occasional attempts to link this episode of the *Legendary History* to När Smiss III might easily be dismissed as an exuberant exercise in local pride, yet viewed in the context of the decorative disc from Ihre and the other Gotlandic *drakorm* triskeles that suggest a long-standing preoccupation with these motifs, it is worth noting that that keen native observer of Gotlandic history and culture, Hans Nielsön Strelow (1580s–1656), makes much of the continued popular importance in his day of Huitastierna and her role in creating the identity of the island, concluding by saying that "The Gotlanders ascribe much to her" (*Hende tilskrifuer Guthilenderne megit*).[41]

Two further data points can be added to this puzzle, one from the Danish "solar age", the other broadly contemporary with the Iron Age materials from Gotland. The Bronze Age votive offering from Fårdal in Jutland – the most impressive of several Bronze Age scenes Kaul sees as representing humans, snakes and

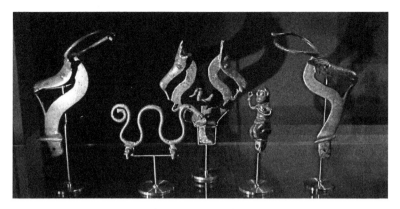

Figure 6. Bronze Age votive figures from Fårdal, Denmark. Photographer: Stephen Mitchell. Copyright: Stephen Mitchell, License: CC-BY-NC-ND.

drinking/suckling – consists of some five bronze pieces (Fig. 6), among them, a kneeling woman and a serpentine beast:

In his interpretation, Kaul argues that the woman is turning toward the snake, "and with her hand she is holding her breast, presenting her breast to the snake, as if inviting it to drink";[42] moreover, he suggests that the hole made by the woman's closed hand and the hole in the head of the serpent indicate that the two had been connected with a line.

Furthermore, recent research by Sigmund Oehrl on Gotlandic picture stones using RTI technology, and presented at the 2015 Stockholm Mythology Conference, considerably strengthens the possible correctness of the argument here. The advanced techniques offered by RTI have led Oerhl to an entirely different understanding of the depiction usually described as being of Gunnar in the snake pit on the Klinte Hunninge I picture stone (*NB:* see Figures 13–15 in his essay in this volume). This monument was assigned by Lindqvist to the 8th century; current research places its group to the late 8th to 10th centuries.[43] The newly revealed tableau, especially in light of the current discussion, looks like nothing quite so much as a birthing scene – a recumbent woman,[44] assisted by one, perhaps two, midwives, and accompanied by *drakormar*. To this, one might add Kaul's understanding that snakes in his reconstructed Bronze Age religion assisted the sun's transition between worlds – perhaps this function has translated over time into *drakormar* helping the child's transition into the world during childbirth.

Is it possible then that we see in these Iron Age materials the echoes of a tradition with deep roots involving women, *drakormar*, and parturition, a tradition which, at least by the time of our medieval text, has become the "myth" of Huitastierna's vision of *ormar* and the origin of the island's population – and also a tradition the Church appropriated to its own ends at Väte and Linde, returning closely, visually at least, to Kaul's lactating Fårdal figurine? That is a long leap, I realize, and, if anything, we should view such a scheme with healthy skepticism, but such an evolution would both explain our data and conform to them. Certainly, I do not insist on such an interpretation, yet I hope by focusing on the Gotlandic materials we now have a better purchase on how *drakormar* may have played a role in the lived lives of Gotlanders in the Merovingian Period and later.

Notes

1. The subject of medieval Nordic dragons has attracted considerable attention in recent years (e.g., Johansen 1997; Lionarons 1998; Evans 2005; Ármann Jakobsson 2010; Cutrer 2012; Acker 2013; and Mitchell *forthcoming*).

2. Johansen 1997. In sympathetic appreciation of the conundrum addressed by this term, I adopt its use here.

3. *Skáldskaparmál*, Faulkes 1998:90.

4. The terms translated as 'adder' and 'viper' – *nadr* and *nadra* – would seem to be most simply understood as the gendered male and female counterparts of the same animal, as both Cleasby-Vigfusson 1982 and Zoëga 1975 treat the terms, yet as an indication of the complexity associated with this category of beast, although Fritzner 1973 accepts *nadra* as a poisonous snake (*vipera*), he suggests that *nadr* might indicate some sort of lizard-like creature (*firben, øgle*). *Ordbog over det norrøne prosasprog* notes some 18 instances of *nadra* but for *nadr*, only the current citation in *Snorra edda* and as

a sword name in *Egils saga Skalla-Grímssonar.* On *drakorm* names and swords, cf. *Skáldskaparmál*, Faulkes 1998, st. 451, 459.

5. *Skáldskaparmál*, Faulkes 1998:137.

6. Thompson 1966.

7. Watkins 1995.

8. Kaul 2004a:408–409. Cp. Nordberg 2013:232, "Kauls solara tolkningar har fått stort genomslag i de senaste decenniernas arkeologiska forskning om bronsålderns religion. Idéhistoriskt sett utgör hans studier en av de senaste länkarna i den solmytologiska skola som har sitt egentliga ursprung i romantikens idévärld, 1800-talets *theologia naturalis,* den evolutionistiska religionsforskningen och Max Müllers komparativa mytologi."

9. See Kaul 2004a:369–406.

10. Cp. Kaul's observation (1998:263), "On the other hand, the possibility cannot be excluded that the snake can have played a role in the morning." I note too that Kaul typically uses the term "snake" (*slange*) in his writings.

11. Kaul 1998:11–16, 221–41.

12. Johansen 1997:63–107.

13. Johansen 1997:253–54.

14. Cf. Karnell 2012:10–21.

15. Cf. Karnell 2012:14–15.

16. Cf. e.g. Andrén 2014:136–38 *et passim.*

17. Regarding this stone, see the detailed information in *Guta saga,* Peel 2015:283–284.

18. Recently, Pearl (2014:137) concludes that it belongs to "an artistic tradition that should be dated conservatively from the beginning of the 5th century AD to the middle of the 7th century AD."

19. Arrhenius & Holmquist 1960.

20. See Hermodsson 2000.

21. Hauk 1983:556.

22. "Vår något nedslående slutsats blir alltså att vi inte har en aning om vad bildstenen berättar" (Harrison Lindberg & Harrison 2013:64).

23. http://www.europeana.eu/portal/record/91622/raa_kmb_16001000 197924.html. Accessed 9 January 2016. Accessed 9 January 2016.

24. On the motif of the *femme-aux-serpents*, especially in medieval church art, see Luyster 2001. I take this opportunity to thank Sara Burdorff for pointing this important connection out to me.

25. From Tubach 1969: #4281 An empress, envious of another who has greater prestige than she, makes her put two snakes at her breasts. #4888 A woman bears two sons in adultery; her first son, a hermit, has a vision of his mother in which she has two toads at her breasts and a snake about her head.

26. Ohlson 1995, who provides a survey of parallels from, e.g. three Scanian baptismal fonts (63–64). Cf. Herjulfsdotter & Andersson 2012, who suggest additional sites, as well Mackeprang (1941:10 *et passim*) on the remarkable baptismal font from Vester Egede, Denmark.

27. Ohlson 1995:63, "en stående kvinna med en orm vid ena bröstet." Cp. Lagerlöf 1981:81, and, especially, the image and detailed description in Stenstöm 1975:109–10.

28. *Guta saga*, Peel 1999:19–20; *Guta saga*, Peel 2015:283–84.

29. As reported in e.g. Nerman 1917–1924 and Nerman et al. 1969–1975.

30. Cf. Nerman et al. 1969–1975, II, Table 174, Nr. 1451 and III:31, "St. u. Lilla Ihre, Ksp. Hellvi. St. 20550: Grab 159."

31. *Guta saga*, Peel 1999:19–20.

32. Nerman 1969–1975.

33. "A small disc with a pierced decoration, about two and a half inches in diameter, was found in a woman's grave at Ihre in Hellvi parish, northeastern Gotland, and seems to depict three intertwined serpents. The grave is dated, on the basis of other finds within it, to the beginning of the ninth century" (*Guta saga*, Peel 2015:283).

34. Quoted in *Guta saga*, Peel 2015:283–284.

35. Peel 1999:2–3.

36. 'Womb' (in square brackets) modifies Peel's translation slightly in order to indicate that Old Gutnish *barmbr* (dative *barmi*) is used in both instances in the original as the site within which the "snakes" apparently gestate and out of which they 'crawl' (*skriþa*).

37. Cf. Mitchell 1984; *Guta saga*, Peel 1999; 2015; and Pearl 2015.

38. Cf. Mitchell 2014; *Guta saga,* Peel 2015.

39. There are, of course, other tales involving kindred beasts, such as the *Tóruigheacht Dhiarmada agus Ghráinne* 'Pursuit of Diarmaid and Gráinne' of the Irish Fenian cycle. On it, Persian and Nordic parallels, see Nagy 2017.

40. E.g. Herskovits & Herskovits 1938 II:248.

41. Strelow 1633:16.

42. Kaul 2004b:36; cf. 2004a:328–330.

43. Karnell 2012:14–15.

44. The character of birthing in the Germanic Iron Age is unknown: images from the Classical world often show the parturient seated, but some authorities (e.g. Soranus, *Gynecology*) also mention lying down. Likewise, in the Eddic poem *Oddrúnargrátr*, several positions are noted, with the maid saying initially (st. 4), *Hér liggr Borgný, of borin verkiom* ("Here lies Borgny, overcome with labour pains"). For other Old Norse examples, see Gotfredsen 1982.

References

Primary Sources

Edda. Jónas Kristjánsson and Vésteinn Ólason (eds.). 2014. *Eddukvæði I–II*. Íslenzk fornrit. Reykjavík: Hið íslenzka fornrítafélag.

———— Larrington, Carolyne. 2014. *The Poetic Edda*. Transl. Carolyne Larrington. Second rev. ed. Oxford: Oxford University Press.

Grímnismál, see *Edda*. Eddukvæði I: 367–79.

Guta saga. Peel, Christine. 2015. *Guta Lag and Guta Saga. The Law and History of the Gotlanders.* Medieval Nordic Laws. Ed. and transl. Christine Peel. New York: Routledge. (Guta Saga originally published as Guta saga. The History of the Gotlanders. Ed. and tr. Christine Peel. 1999. Viking Society for Northern Research. Text Series, 12. London: Viking Society for Northern Research).

———— Strelow, Hans Nielsen. 1633. *Cronica Guthilandorum.* Copenhagen: Prentet aff M. Martzan.

Gylfaginning. Faulkes, Anthony. 2005. *Snorri Sturluson. Edda. Prologue and Gylfaginning.* Ed. Anthony Faulkes. Second ed. London: Viking Society for Northern Research. University College London, 2005.

———— Faulkes, Anthony. 1995. *Snorri Sturluson. Edda.* Transl. Anthony Faulkes. London: J.M. Dent.

Oddrúnargrátr, see *Edda.* Eddukvæði II: 365–71.

Skáldskaparmál. Faulkes, Anthony. 1998. *Snorri Sturluson. Edda. Skáldskaparmál. I. Introduction, Text and Notes.* Ed. Anthony Faulkes. London: Viking Society for Northern Research. University College London.

———— Faulkes, Anthony. 1995. *Snorri Sturluson. Edda.* Transl. Anthony Faulkes. London: J.M. Dent.

Vǫluspá, see *Edda.* Eddukvæði I: 292–391.

Secondary Literature

Acker, Paul. 2013. Dragons in the *Eddas* and in Early Nordic Art. In P. Acker & C. Larrington (eds.). *Revisiting the Poetic Edda. Essays on Old Norse Heroic Legend.* New York: Routledge, 53–75.

Andrén, Anders. 2014. *Tracing Old Norse Cosmology. The World Tree, Middle Earth, and the Sun from Archaeological Perspectives.* Vägar till Midgård, 16. Lund: Nordic Academic Press.

Ármann Jakobsson. 2010. Enter the Dragon. Legendary Saga Courage and the Birth of the Hero. In M. Arnold & A. Finlay (eds.). *Making History. Essays in Fornaldarsögur.* London: Viking Society for Northern Research, 33–52.

Cleasby, Richard and Gudbrand Vigfusson (eds.). 1982 (1957). *An Icelandic-English Dictionary.* Second rev. ed. by William Craigie. Oxford: The Clarendon Press.

Cutrer, Robert. 2012. *The Wilderness of Dragons. The Reception of Dragons in Thirteenth century Iceland.* M.A. thesis, Háskóli Íslands.

Evans, Jonathan. 2005. 'As Rare as They are Dire'. Old Norse Dragons, *Beowulf*, and the *Deutsche Mythologie.* In T. A. Shippey (ed.). *The Shadow-Walkers. Jacob Grimm's Mythology of the Monstrous.* Arizona Studies in the Middle Ages and the Renaissance, 14. Tempe, Arizona: Arizona CMRS (with Brepols), 207–269.

Fritzner, Johan (ed.). 1973 (1886). *Ordbok over Det gamle norske Sprog.* 4th rev. ed. Oslo, etc.: Universitetsforlaget.

Gotfredsen, Edvard. 1982 (1956–1978). Barsel. In J. Brøndsted et al. (eds.). *Kulturhistorisk leksikon for nordisk middelalder.* Copenhagen: Rosenkilde og Bagger: I, cols. 354–365.

Gräslund, Anne-Sofie. 2006. Wolves, Serpents and Birds. Their Symbolic Meaning in Old Norse Belief. In A. Andrén et al. (eds.). *Old Norse Religion in Long-Term Perspective. Origins, Changes, and Interactions.* Vägar till Midgård. Lund: Nordic Academic Press, 124–129.

Harrison Lindbergh, Katarina, & Harrison, Dick. 2013. *101 föremål ur Sveriges historia.* Stockholm: Norstedts.

Hauk, Karl. 1983. Text und Bild in einer oralen Kultur. Antworten auf die zeugniskritische Frage nach der Erreichbarkeit mündlicher Überlieferung im frühen Mittelalter. Zur Ikonologie der Goldbrakteaten XXV. In *Frühmittelalterliche Studien* 17, 510–599.

Herjulfsdotter, Ritwa, & Andersson, Tommy. 2012. Luxuria eller Terra på relieferna i Siene och Strö? In *Skara stiftshistoriska sällskap. Medlemsblad* 20:1, 8–10.

Hermodsson, Lars. 2000. En invandrad gud? Kring en märklig gotländsk bildsten. In *Fornvännen 95*, 109–118.

Herskovits, Melville J. & Herskovits, Frances S. 1938. *Dahomey. An Ancient West African Kingdom.* New York: J.J. Augustin.

Johansen, Birgitta. 1997. *Ormalur. Aspekter av tillvaro och landskap.* Stockholm Studies in Archeology, 14. Stockholm: Arkeologiska institutionen. Stockholms universitet.

Karnell, Maria Herlin (ed.). 2012. *Gotlands bildstenar. järnålderns gåtfulla budbärare.* Gotländskt arkiv, 84. Visby: Fornsalens Förlag.

Kaul, Flemming. 1998. *Ships on Bronzes. A Study in Bronze Age Religion and Iconography.* Studies in Archaeology & History, 3. Copenhagen: National Museum of Denmark.

Kaul, Flemming. 2004a. *Bronzealderens religion. Studier af den nordiske bronzealders ikonografi.* Copenhagen: Det Kongelige Nordiske Oldskriftselskab.

Kaul, Flemming. 2004b. *Bronzealderens religion. Studier af den nordiske bronzealders ikonografi. Dansk resumé. English Summary.* Copenhagen: Det Kongelige Nordiske Oldskriftselskab.

Lagerlöf, Erland. 1981. *Linde kyrka (Fardhems ting, Gotland, VII:2).* Sveriges kyrkor, konsthistoriskt inventarium, 186. Stockholm: Almqvist & Wiksell.

Lionarons, Joyce Tally. 1998. *The Medieval Dragon. The Nature of the Beast in Germanic Literature.* Enfield Lock, Middlesex: Hisarlik Press.

Luyster, Amanda. 2001. The *Femme-aux-serpents* at Moissac. *Luxuria* (lust) or a Bad Mother? In S.R. Asirvatham et al. (eds.). *Between Magic and Religion. Interdisciplinary Studies in Ancient Mediterranean Religion and Society.* Lanham: Rowman & Littlefield, 165–191.

Mackeprang, Mouritz. 1941. *Danmarks middelalderlige Døbefonte.* Copenhagen: Selskabet til Udgivelse af Skrifter om Danske Mindesmærker.

Mitchell, Stephen A. 1984. On the Composition and Function of *Gutasaga.* In *Arkiv för nordisk filologi* 99, 151–174.

Mitchell, Stephen. 2014. The Mythologized Past. Memory and Politics in Medieval Gotland. In P. Hermann et al. (eds.). *Minni and Muninn. Memory in Medieval Nordic Culture.* Acta Scandinavica, 4. Turnhout: Brepols, 155–174.

Mitchell, Stephen. *forthcoming*. Dragons, a Cryptozoological Journey into the Nordic Otherworld. In J.F. Nagy (ed.). *Comparing Dragons. Ancient, Medieval, and Modern*. UCLA CMRS. Mundi. Turnhout: Brepols.

Nagy, Joseph Falaky. 2017. Vermin Gone Bad in Medieval Scandinavian, Persian, and Irish Traditions. In P. Hermann et al. (eds.). *Old Norse Mythology in Comparative Perspectives*. Cambridge: Harvard University Press.

Nerman, Birger. 1917–1924. Gravfynden på Gotland under tiden 550–800 e. K. In *Antikvarisk Tidskrift för Sverige* 22:4, 1–102, I–XXX.

Nerman, Birger et al. 1969–1975. *Die Vendelzeit Gotlands*. Monographien hg. von der Kungl. Vitterhets, historie och antikvitets akademien, 48, 55. Stockholm: Almqvist & Wiksell.

Nordberg, Andreas. 2013. *Fornnordisk religionsforskning mellan teori och empiri. Kulten av anfäder, solen och vegetationsandar i idehistorisk belysning*. Acta Academiae Regiae Gustavi Adolphi, 126. Uppsala: Kungl. Gustav Adolfs Akademien för svensk folkkultur.

Oehrl, Sigmund. 2012. Ikonografiska tolkningar av gotländska bildstenar baserade på nya analyser av ytorna. In M. H. Karnell (ed.). *Gotlands bildstenar. Järnålderns gåtfulla budbärare*. Gotländskt arkiv, 84. Visby: Fornsalens Förlag, 91–106.

Oehrl, Sigmund. 2017. Re-Interpretations of Gotlandic Picture Stones Based on the Reflectance Transformation Imaging Method (RTI). Some Examples. In K. af Edholm et al. (eds.). *Myth, Materiality, and Lived Religion in Merovingian and Viking Scandinavia*. Stockholm: Stockholm University Press.

Ohlson, Elisabeth. 1995. Själajakt och fruktbarhetssymbolik. Romanska reliefer på de gotiska kyrkorna i Grötlingbo och Väte. In *Gotländskt arkiv* 66, 49–66.

Pearl, Frederic B. 2014. The Water Dragon and the Snake Witch. Two Vendel Period Picture Stones from Gotland, Sweden. In *Current Swedish Archaeology* 22, 137–156.

Peel, Christine. 1999. *Guta saga. The History of the Gotlanders*. Ed. and transl. Christine Peel. Viking Society for Northern Research. Text Series, 12. London: Viking Society for Northern Research.

Peel, Christine. 2015. *Guta Lag and Guta Saga. The Law and History of the Gotlanders.* Ed. and transl. Christine Peel. Medieval Nordic Laws. New York: Routledge.

Stenstöm, Tore. 1975. *Problem rörande Gotlands medeltida dopfuntar.* PhD Diss. Umeå: Umeå Universitet.

Thompson, Stith (ed.). 1966. *Motif-Index of Folk-Literature.* Second rev. ed. Bloomington: Indiana University Press.

Tubach, Frederic C. 1969. *Index Exemplorum. A Handbook of Medieval Religious Tales.* Folklore Fellows Communications, 204. Helsinki: Akademia Scientiarum Fennica.

Watkins, Calvert. 1995. *How to Kill a Dragon. Aspects of Indo-European Poetics.* New York: Oxford University Press.

Response

Judy Quinn
University of Cambridge

Of Snakes and Women – The Interpretation of the Early Stone Carvings of Gotland

In their illustrated survey of Romanesque sexual carvings, Weir and Jarman[1] document an extraordinary array of what they term "images of lust", which are linked to detailed maps of church locations across western Europe (should the reader be curious enough to wish to visit the carvings *in situ*). The carvings, designed to serve as admonishment against the sin of fornication, focus on the organs of lust belonging to both male and female bodies. While one carving shows a figure whose testicles are being bitten by a snake,[2] the majority of the depictions are of female bodies, in keeping with Christian theology's fixation on the female body as a locus of sin. To highlight the afflictions that the damned might expect, other animals including toads, fish and unicorns are shown gnawing sensitive bodily areas. Those that target a woman's breasts often present a particularly disconcerting picture, the attachment of mouth to breast closely resembling the maternal suckling of infants. It is possible that viewers of the medieval iconography may have been influenced to some extent in their interpretation of the image by the antique iconography of the so-called earthmother (Terra), who was depicted suckling animals as well as children. A favourite motif among Romanesque carvers, a snake biting a woman on her breast (dubbed *la femme aux serpents*), is attested across a wide geographical area, from northern Spain to Italy, to Britain and Ireland in the west and Germany and Scandinavia in the north. Emile Mâle charted the migration of the iconography across Europe, identifying what he thought were probably its earliest forms in the Languedoc region.[3] Three examples from Denmark (Bråby, Gosmer and Vester Egede) are listed by Weir and Jarman,[4] who also note that the example from Väte Church in Gotland closely resembles a carving from

Saint-Jouin-de-Marnes in northern France.[5] *La femme aux serpents* also shares some characteristics with another well-attested figure from the same period, the *sheela-na-gig*, or 'female exhibitionist', depicted with legs akimbo and often flanked by beasts.[6] Such a posture and composition is, however, also attested in much earlier cultures, including in Etruscan artefacts.

The symbolism of the snake is as complex as its attestation is widespread across world cultures, the reptile sometimes playing a beneficent role in relation to human society, sometimes representing a threat and sometimes twisting and turning between the two. That the island of Gotland preserves some striking carvings that depict a female figure with a snake is intriguing, as Stephen Mitchell has shown in his paper, even if the relationship between the traditions behind them may not go far beyond geographical proximity. The carving on Väte Church, with its clear connection to the Romanesque tradition of *la femme aux serpents*, dates from the twelfth century. The carving on the När Smiss III stone, a stylised depiction of a figure with an ornate headdress or hairstyle, holding a stylised reptile in each hand, facing forward and with widely splayed legs, is dated to at least five centuries earlier (and possibly as many as seven centuries earlier). The implied relationship of woman to reptile is markedly different in each image: in the earlier carving, the sexualised figure is assertive and in command of the reptiles; in the later one, she appears to tug the bodies of the reptiles away from her breasts unsuccessfully with her outwardly-bowed arms. As Mitchell notes, the theological motivation of the carver of the Väte image may have included reference to a punishment specifically designed for negligent mothers, who were condemned to breastfeed inappropriate species.[7]

In situating his interpretation of the När Smiss III and Väte carvings within the "adversarial 'man versus monster' scenario" of Indo-European tradition, and using as his point of reference the popular Christian presentation of dragons in the Nordic Middle Ages to argue that the "principal way these beasts ought to be understood is within an adversarial context", Mitchell downplays the gender specificity of the Gotlandic works. As he notes, another trajectory is taken by scholars such as Flemming Kaul and Birgitta Johansen, whose interpretations accommodate a productive symbiosis in the relationship between humans and snakes in the pre-Christian era, particularly with regard to women. Textual evidence also supports the notion that a snake was a positive symbol in the context of Gotlandic traditions, with an episode in the so called *Legendary History of Gotland* presenting coiled snakelings within a woman's body as a figuration of dynastic prosperity: the snakes emerge as three sons, playing an entirely positive role in a foundation legend for the island.[8] There is considerable evidence, therefore, that, in the semantics of early Gotlandic culture, a woman in the company of snakes was without any negative connotation unless – or possibly until – the image is fully saturated by Christian demonization of the reptile (and to some extent, of women).

In plotting "data points" to facilitate the interpretation of images, some caution needs to be exercised in deducing features that can be considered analogous. The doubt cast by Sigmund Oehrl in his essay in this volume on the standard interpretation of one of the tableaux on the Klinte Hunninge I picture stone and his postulation of other possible scenarios it might reference is a case in point. By fading out Sune Lindqvist's enhancement of the carving, Oehrl has shown that the tableau is unlikely to represent Gunnarr in the snake-pit (the recumbent figure appears to be female) and tentatively proposes two alternative interpretations: a representation of 'the Christian idea of a post-mortem place of punishment', or a depiction of the myth of Loki's punishment, with Skaði affixing a snake above (a feminised) Loki while Sigyn returns to the enclosure with the emptied venom-catching bowl. Citing Oehrl's work as 'strengthen[ing] considerably the possible correctness of the argument here', Mitchell speculates that the scene may represent something else entirely: "a birthing scene – a recumbent woman, assisted by one, perhaps two midwives, and accompanied by *drakormar*". In the interpretation of Gotlandic tradition, a female figure in the company of snakes can certainly fire the imagination!

While it is fair to consider the images on När Smiss II, Klinte Hunninge I and on Väte Church within a matrix – they are all carved on stone and located in Gotland, and they depict female figures and snakes – their cultural semantics seem to me so dissimilar that it is hard to construe one through the other, especially an earlier image through a later one. That is not to say that later medieval parishioners' interpretation of När Smiss III might not have been coloured by the Väte image. A reading of När Smiss III through the data points of Mitchell's matrix, however, does not seem to me to get us any closer to the lived religion or thought-world of pre-Christian Gotland. The Harrisons' conclusion regarding När Smith II that Mitchell quotes is not so much "pessimistic" as an acknowledgement of the wonderful otherness of the past, where images of snakes, and indeed women, may have encoded meanings that centuries of Christian-inflected pondering have not yielded up.

Notes

1. Weir & Jarman 1999.

2. Weir & Jarman 1999:75, Fig. 27a.

3. Mâle 1978:375ff.

4. Weir & Jarman 1999:68–69, Fig. 22.

5. Weir & Jarman 1999:62, Plate 28; 68.

6. Weir & Jarman 1999:11–20; 70ff.

7. This interpretation is based on Luyster 2001.

8. Peel 1999:2–3.

References

Peel, Christine, ed. and transl. 1999. *Guta saga. The History of the Gotlanders*. Viking Society for Northern Research. Text Series, 12. London: Viking Society for Northern Research.

Harrison Lindbergh, Katarina & Harrison, Dick. 2013. *101 föremål ur Sveriges historia*. Stockholm: Norstedts, 61–64.

Johansen, Birgitta. 1997. *Ormalur. Aspekter av tillvaro och landskap*. Stockholm Studies in Archeology, 14. Stockholm: Arkeologiska institutionen, Stockholms universitet.

Kaul, Flemming. 2004. *Bronzealderens religion. Studier af den nordiske bronzealders ikonografi*. København: Det Kongelige Nordiske Oldskriftselskab.

Lindqvist, Sune. 1941–1942. *Gotlands Bildsteine I–II*. Stockholm: Wahlström & Widstrand.

Luyster, Amanda. 2001. "The Femme-aux-serpents at Moissac: Luxuria (lust) or a Bad Mother?" In: S.R. Asirvatham, C.O. Pache and J. Watrous (eds.), *Between Magic and Religion: Interdisciplinary Studies in Ancient Mediterranean Religion and Society*. Lanham: Rowman & Littlefield, 165–191.

Mâle, Emile. 1978. *Religious Art in France, the Twelfth Century. A Study of the Origins of Medieval Iconography*. Princeton: Princeton University Press.

Weir, Anthony & Jerman, James. 1999 (1986). *Images of Lust. Sexual Carvings on Medieval Churches*. First published by Batsford 1986. London: Routledge.

Re-Interpretations of Gotlandic Picture Stones Based on the Reflectance Transformation Imaging Method (RTI): Some Examples

Sigmund Oehrl
Munich/Stockholm University

The picture stones[1] from the Isle of Gotland in the Baltic Sea are a unique source for the study of Germanic history of religion. These stone slabs, which have been inspired by late antique sepulchral monuments and iconography,[2] were raised from the Migration Period until the end of the Viking Age. Even when most of the figures on the Gotland picture stones are still enigmatic, it is clearly proved that their iconography includes mythological and heroic motifs which in certain cases can reliably be interpreted against the background of Old Norse literature. The later picture stones, which offer an abundance of figurative depictions and narrative scenes, were dated by Sune Lindqvist, in his most relevant book *Gotlands Bildsteine*, published in 1941–1942, to the 8th century (type C/D according to Lindqvist's classification).[3] Recent research, however, has attested that monuments of that type were still being erected in the 9th and 10th centuries,[4] the period of the earliest known scaldic and Eddic poetry. Thus, there is a chronological overlap of both sources, the written sources from Iceland and the iconographic sources from the Baltic isle of Gotland. As a result, it can, in favourable cases, be reasonable to connect these disparate traditions in order to interpret the carved pictures.

How to cite this book chapter:
Oehrl, S. 2019. Re-Interpretations of Gotlandic Picture Stones Based on the Reflectance Transformation Imaging Method (RTI): Some Examples. In: Wikström af Edholm, K., Jackson Rova, P., Nordberg, A., Sundqvist, O. & Zachrisson, T. (eds.) *Myth, Materiality, and Lived Religion: In Merovingian and Viking Scandinavia.* Pp. 141–189. Stockholm: Stockholm University Press. DOI: https://doi.org/10.16993/bay.g. License: CC-BY.

Figure 1. Ardre Church VIII (SHM). Photographer: Bengt A. Lundberg (SHM)

The two prominent Viking picture stones (type D) Alskog Tjängvide I[5] and Ardre Church VIII[6] (Fig. 1, on the top of the stone), for instance, bear the depiction of a horseman riding an eight-legged horse. Written sources from Iceland dating to the 13th century talk about Óðinn's miraculous horse Sleipnir that was born with eight legs.[7] Sleipnir is described as the best and the fastest of all horses. Its most special feature seems to be its ability to cross the border between the world of the living and the world of the dead. It is very likely that the horse on these picture stones represents Óðinn's horse Sleipnir, not less than three centuries before it was recorded literally. At least, the stone carvings document the same concept of a mythological, miraculously fast horse. On Ardre VIII can be seen a smithy, two beheaded men behind the building, a bird-like creature and a woman (Fig. 1, in the lower part of the stone, beneath the ship). There is absolutely no doubt about the fact that this is a depiction of Wayland the Smith (Old Norse *Vǫlundr*) and his cruel revenge,[8] first recorded in the Eddic poem *Vǫlundarkviða*,[9] composed in Iceland in the 10th century or even earlier.[10] Examples like these clearly show that the picture stones from Gotland can bear mythological and heroic carvings and that using written sources in order to interpret them can be fruitful and reveals new information about the dating and distribution of certain narratives.

In addition, the iconography of these monuments can provide completely new insights into ancient Germanic and Viking religion, recording motifs that are not known from literally tradition. At this point I would like to present a hitherto unknown find from St. Valle in Rute Parish that I will publish and discuss in detail in my forthcoming book about Gotlandic picture stones.[11]

The fragment shows a man with horned headgear, hovering behind the stern of a ship, on the waves of the sea (Fig. 2), similar to the horned Eidolon figure who, on the Merovingian Period helmet plates (Fig. 3), assists the equestrian in throwing his spear, as a kind of divine helper in battle, a Germanic version of the *numen victoriae*.[12] In Old Norse literature there are no striking parallels to this depiction of a divine escort at sea. However, the motif on the Vendel plates can be connected to Old Norse written sources[13] such as the skaldic poem *Gráfeldardrápa* written

Figure 2. Unpublished fragment from Rute St. Valle (drawing S. Oehrl).
Copyright: Sigmund Oehrl, License: CC-BY-NC-ND

Figure 3. Helmet plate from Valsgärde 8 (drawing W. Lange, after Hauck
1981: fig. 26).

by Glúmr Geirason (after 974 AD), telling that the gods guide
or steer (*stýra*) the heroes on the battle field. In the Eddic poem
Hlǫðskviða stanza 28 (probably 9th century) the King of the Goths
invokes Óðinn, god of war and father of the fallen, to steer his
throwing spear (*láti svá Óðinn flein fliúga*).

As we have seen so far, the carved monuments from the isle
of Gotland are an important and unique source for Germanic
mythology and heroic legend. But there is a still unsolved problem that makes it almost impossible to make use of it entirely:
The depictions on the picture stones are often quite hard to identify. The low reliefs are quite primitive and the carved lines are
flat, almost invisible to the naked eye. In addition, they are often
degraded by weathering or by footsteps. This was the main problem faced by Sune Lindqvist and his forerunners who prepared
the edition of the Gotlandic monuments in 1941–1942 and it is
still a major – but regrettably rarely noted – problem of recent
picture stone research.[14] Lindqvist darkened the location in order
to use the light of an electric lamp which was placed in varying
positions. In preparation for the photographs for his picture stone
edition he then painted the grooves he regarded as having been
carved by the artist's hand (Fig. 4–5).

As a result, these images of the stones, which still provide the
main basis of research, reflect the individual view and estimation
of one single person. Even though Lindqvist was a specialist and
his work has unquestionably been of outstanding importance up
to the present day, subsequent research realized that certain parts
and details on the stones can be interpreted in several ways, while
Lindqvist's illustrations represent only one possible perception
(Fig. 6–7).[15]

There are different digital methods available today which can
be applied in order to improve the picture stone documentation
and to objectify our view of the depicted figures. That is what
I try to do in my current research project, which will result in
a monograph. One of these resources of digital archaeology is
3D-modelling.[16] I myself use the photogrammetry method, which
means creating 3D-models on the basis of photographs captured
from different angles. The advantages of using 3D-models for iconography are numerous: the surface model can be rotated and

Figure 4. Buttle Änge I, without paint. Photographer: Sune Lindqvist. Copyright: ATA, License: CC-BY-NC-ND.

Figure 5. Buttle Änge I, painted by S. Lindqvist. Photographer: H. Faith-Ell 1937. Copyright: ATA, License: CC-BY-NC-ND.

Figure 6. Klinte Hunninge I, drawing by O. Sörling (after Lindqvist 1941–1942 vol. II: fig. 428).

Figure 7. Klinte Hunninge I, painted by S. Lindqvist (after after Lindqvist 1941–1942 vol. I: fig. 128).

turned, natural stone colours as well as secondary painting can be deleted, different kinds of illumination can be simulated, details can be zoomed in on and observed from different angles and measurements can be taken.

The other technique I apply is called *Reflectance Transformation Imaging* (RTI).[17] It was invented by Hewlett Packard and developed for archaeological and cultural heritage conservation purposes by the non-profit corporation *Cultural Heritage Imaging* in California.[18] Basically, the image capture for obtaining the digital image data from which RTI files can be produced, is performed as follows (Fig. 8–9): A sequence of images of the monument is taken with a specific set of lighting angles. Thus, the flashlight changes its position step by step after every single shot while the camera does not move. A reflective sphere, like a billiard ball, is fixed on the monument. As a result, one obtains a set of images of the same subject with different shadow impacts and with a reflection on the sphere on different positions. On this basis the RTI software creates a single high-resolution image that can be analysed on the screen, applying different rendering modes and a virtual light beam which can be controlled with a trackball (Fig. 10–11). Ultimately, this is quite a simple but rather helpful tool when it comes to detecting and documenting single details and objectifying or disproving questionable readings.

In this paper I would like to present two examples for how new surface analysis with RTI can result in completely new viewpoints and iconographic interpretations. Both examples will be discussed in more detail in my forthcoming monograph. I would like to start with the 284 cm high picture stone No. I from Hunninge in Klinte Parish, on the middle west coast of the island, approximately 2km east of Klintehamn (type C) (Fig. 7). In the lower part of the monument a kind of rectangular enclosure is depicted (Fig. 12). Within the enclosure a man, characterized with a chin beard and typical tunic-like dress, is lying on his back, surrounded by serpents. A woman seems to reach into the enclosure.

This depiction is interpreted by most researchers as Gunnar in the snake pit.[19] The story of Gunnar, King of the Gjúkungar/ Niflungar and his heroic death is mainly recorded in *Vǫlsunga saga*, Snorri's *Skáldskaparmál* and Eddic heroic poetry, *Atlamál*,

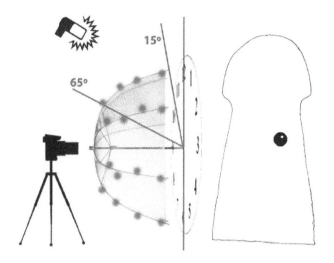

Figure 8. Image capture for RTI. Copyright: Sigmund Oehrl, License: CC-BY-NC-ND.

Figure 9. Image capture for RTI, Buttle Church, picture stone built into the floor in front of the altar. Photographer: P. Prestel. Copyright: Sigmund Oehrl, License: CC-BY-NC-ND.

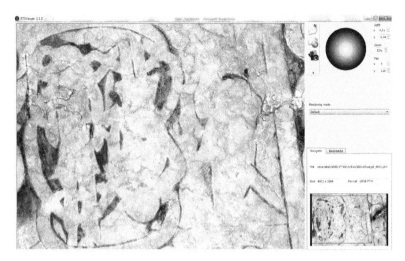

Figure 10. The RTI Viewer, showing a detail from Ardre Church VIII. Photographer: Sigmund Oehrl. Copyright: Sigmund Oehrl, License: CC-BY-NC-ND.

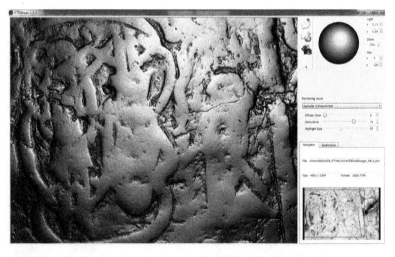

Figure 11. The RTI Viewer, showing a detail from Ardre Church VIII, analysed with rendering mode "Specular Enhancement". Photographer: Sigmund Oehrl. Copyright: Sigmund Oehrl, License: CC-BY-NC-ND.

Figure 12. Detail ("snake-pit") from Klinte Hunninge I, painted by S. Lindqvist (after spatium Lindqvist 1941–1942 vol. I: fig. 128).

Atlakviða, *Oddrúnargrátr* and *Dráp Niflunga*.[20] The oldest source is *Atlakviða*, which is dated to the ninth or tenth century. Atli, King of the Huns and husband of Guðrún, Gunnar's sister, invites Gunnar to a feast in order to get possession of the legendary hoard of gold that Sigurðr had won from the dragon Fáfnir. Gunnar refuses to surrender the treasure or to reveal where it is hidden. He is put in chains and thrown into an *ormgarðr*. There he plays the harp, brought by his sister Guðrún, in order to fend off or lull the serpents. Finally, he is killed by the animals. Although there is no harp depicted on Klinte Hunninge I, the image is interpreted on the background of this heroic narrative, the woman who reaches into the enclosure is considered to represent Guðrún, perhaps handing over the musical instrument.

As a matter of fact, the person in the enclosure depicted on Klinte Hunninge I cannot represent the Gunnar legend! By fading out Lindqvist's secondary painting of the carvings and illuminating it in the RTI Viewer, it becomes obvious that the figure has a pigtail/plait (Fig. 13–15, turned 90° to the right, so the figure is standing on its feet). According to Lindqvist's painting the figure's head, neck and back are formed by one single line. However, the RTI image clearly shows that there is another carved line, separating the figure's long hair from its body. In addition, the person's dress is a little longer and more curved than expected (train). The

Figure 13. Klinte Hunninge I, the figure in the "snake-pit", turned 90°
to the right, analysed with the RTI Viewer, rendering mode "Specular
Enhancement". Photographer: Sigmund Oehrl. Copyright: Sigmund Oehrl,
License: CC-BY-NC-ND.

Figure 14. Klinte Hunninge I, the figure in the "snake-pit", turned 90°
to the right, analysed with the RTI Viewer, rendering mode "Specular
Enhancement". Photographer: Sigmund Oehrl. Copyright: Sigmund Oehrl,
License: CC-BY-NC-ND.

Figure 15. Klinte Hunninge I, the figure in the "snake-pit", turned 90° to the right, analysed with the RTI Viewer, result. Photographer: Sigmund Oehrl. Copyright: Sigmund Oehrl, License: CC-BY-NC-ND.

upper body of the figure seems to be more slender. The supposed leg and foot cannot be verified.

Thus, the person lying in the enclosure has exactly the same gender characteristics as the female figures depicted on the same stone (Fig. 16). It is not a man but a woman in a snake pit we are dealing with. Incorrect re-painting from the early 20th century led generations of picture stone interpreters to follow a false trail. Now, we have a totally new set of facts to base an interpretation on.

One possible interpretation could be that the snake-filled enclosure on the picture stone is influenced by Christian eschatology. To make a long story short: Swarms of serpents torturing human souls has been a widespread motif in Christian visions of hell since the 9th century.[21] Iconographic records are also numerous, one of the earliest can be found in the *Utrecht Psalter*[22] from 820–835 AD (Fig. 17).[23] As an example from the 10th century the *Beatus-Apocalypse* from Girona[24] could be mentioned. Apparently, this

Figure 16. Klinte Hunninge I, women in and around the "snake-pit" (S. Oehrl, after Lindqvist 1941–1942 vol. I: fig. 128).

Figure 17. Utrecht Psalter, UB Utrecht Ms. 32, fol. 3v (after van der Horst et al. 1982–1984). Copyright: UB Utrecht.

Christian idea was also borrowed by Eddic poetry: The Eddic poem *Vǫluspá* (written in the 10th century or about the year 1000) contains, as most scholars agree,[25] certain Christian influences. One of them seems to be the hall (*salr*) formed by serpents, located on the shore of the dead (*Nástrǫndr*), in which the evildoers are punished with snake venom (stanza 38–39):[26]

Sal sá hon standa	*sólo fiarri*
Nástrǫndo á,	*norðr horfa dyrr;*
fello eitrdropar	*inn um lióra,*
sá er undinn salr	*orma hryggiom.*
Sá hon þar vaða	*þunga strauma*
menn meinsvara	*oc morðvarga,*
oc þannz annars glepr	*eyrarúno;*
þar saug Níðhǫggr	*nái framgengna,*
sleit vargr vera	[...].[27]

Such an influence, the Christian idea of a post-mortem place of punishment, can also be taken into account in the case of the woman in the snake pit depicted on the picture stone Klinte Hunninge I which probably dates to the 9th or 10th century. A second possible interpretation arises from a comparison of the iconography of Klinte Hunninge I (Fig. 7) with the images on the famous, already mentioned picture stone Ardre VIII (Fig. 1). Both monuments seem to be closely related.[28] The Viking ship is placed in the middle of their surface, below the head of the picture stone. This is quite unusual, normally the ship is placed on the lower part of the stone. On the lowest part of both picture stones a kind of enclosure or building is depicted. Inside the building, which seems to be a cattle barn, an ox can be seen. Finally, on *both* monuments a human lying in an *ormgarðr*, a rectangular enclosure filled with snakes, is depicted, along with two female figures standing next to it. In the case of Ardre VIII there is good reason to believe that the depiction represents the punishment of Loki, according to Snorri's *Gylfaginning* (ch. 50):

Þá tóku Æsir þarma hans ok bundu Loka með yfir þá þrjá steina – einn undir herðum, annarr undir lendum, þriði undir knésfótum – ok urðu þau bǫnd at járni. Þá tók Skaði eitrorm ok festi upp yfir hann svá at eitrit skyldi drjúpa ór orminum í andlit honom. En Sigyn kona hans stendr hjá honom ok heldr mundlaugu undir eitrdropa. En þá er full er mundlaugin þá gengr hon ok slær út eitrinu, en meðan drýpr eitrit í andlit honom. Þá kippisk hann svá hart við at jǫrð ǫll skelfr. Þat kallið þér landskjálpta. Þar liggr hann í bǫndum til ragnarøkrs.[29]

The gods capture Loki after he causes the death of Óðinn's son Baldr. He is brought into a cave and fettered by the gods. In the cavern the goddess Skaði takes a poisonous snake and affixes it above Loki's head in such a way that the serpent's venom drips onto his face. But Sigyn, Loki's wife, stands beside her husband and holds a bowl over his face, so the venom is caught in the bowl instead. However, when the bowl is full, Sigyn has to go and empty it. At that moment the venom can still drip onto Loki's face and the pain makes him flinch so violently that the entire earth shakes. The woman directly to the left of the serpent-filled enclosure on Ardre VIII holds the tail of one of the serpents in her hand (Fig. 18). This could be Skaði, taking one of the serpents in order to fix it above Loki's head.[30] The woman next to her is turning away from the scene holding a goblet- or bowl-like vessel in her uplifted hand. This seems to be Sigyn, emptying the bowl with the serpent's poison.[31]

If this interpretation is correct (which is not beyond doubt, of course), it is likely that, in the case of Klinte Hunninge I, the figure in the serpent-filled enclosure, surrounded by two women, also represents this very myth. But why should the god Loki be

Figure 18. Loki's punishment (?) on Ardre Church VIII, drawing on basis of RTI. Photographer: Sigmund Oehrl. Copyright: Sigmund Oehrl, License: CC-BY-NC-ND.

depicted with female attributes? Actually, according to Old Norse literary tradition, Loki features some crucial bisexual character-istics.[32] In Snorri's *Gylfaginning* (Ch. 42) he turns into a mare in order to give birth to the horse Sleipnir.[33] He also turns into a woman before he talks to Baldr's mother Frigg in order to find out, how Baldr can be injured (Ch. 49).[34] In the shape of a giantess he refuses to grieve for Baldr.[35] According to *Lokasenna* (stanza 23, 33)[36] Loki gave birth to children and according to *Hyndluljóð* (stanza 41)[37] he became pregnant after eating a roasted heart. Is it imaginable, against this very background, that in Viking art Loki can be depicted with female attributes? In fact, this actually seems to be the case on the famous Anglo-Scandinavian stone cross from Gosforth in Cumbria (Northumbria), erected in the first half of the 10th century (Fig. 19).[38] It depicts Loki lying on his back, his legs, arms and neck fettered, a serpent's head in front of his face and Sigyn sitting on a chair, holding a crescent-shaped bowl in her outstretched hand. There is absolutely no doubt, that this is a depiction of Loki's punishment (incorporated into a Christian

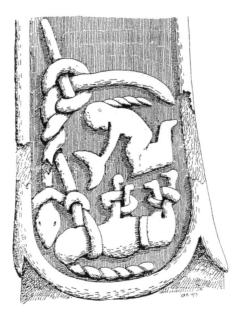

Figure 19 . Loki's punishment on the Gosforth Cross (West side), drawing by C. A. Parker (after Collingwood/Parker 1917: Fig 4).

Figure 20. Sanda Church IV, painted by Lindqvist (after Andersson 1968: Table 78).

context).[39] The fettered god is presented here with a braid, exactly the same hairstyle that characterizes his wife. No other male figure on the cross has a similar hairstyle. It is a reasonable assumption that the woman in the *ormgarðr* on Klinte Hunninge I also represents the god Loki in the snake-filled cavern. Thus, the two women surrounding the enclosure could also be interpreted. As suggested for the figures on Ardre VIII, they could be regarded as Skaði (below), holding a serpent in her hand and Sigyn (to the right), approaching with the bowl, handing it into the room.

The second monument I would like to present is picture stone No. IV from Sanda Church, about 4 km northeast of Klintehamn.[40] The 330 cm-high stone slab dates to the Migration Period, probably to the 6th century AD (type A). In Lindqvist's book only the upper half of the monument is shown,[41] the lower one was found in 1956, beneath the church floor. Lindqvist painted and published the entire stone in 1962 (Fig. 20–21).[42] According to the published painting, a carved horizontal line divides the stone into two halves. In the upper half a big disk with a whirl motif can be

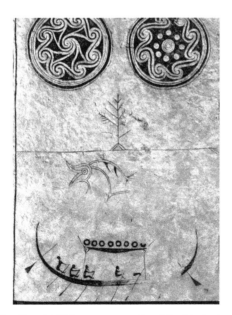

Figure 21. Sanda Church IV, lower part, painted by Lindqvist (after Andersson 1968: Table 79).

seen, as well as a pair of two smaller discs, encircled by serpents. A simplified tree is standing on the horizontal line. Beneath the line the forepart of an animal with open jaws can be seen, as well as a rowing boat with crew. However, my RTI analysis has revealed that there are remains of some more carvings on the stone, in particular in front of the animal. A relatively deep carved line can easily be seen. Some more grooves to the right of this line and a clearly carved plane beneath these grooves can be assembled into a horseman with a spear in his hand (Fig. 22–23). A very similar horseman with bent arm and a spear in his uplifted hand can be seen on picture stone No. I from Martebo Church (Fig. 24).[43]

Obviously, the Sanda horseman is fighting against the animal, probably a beast of prey, a lion-like creature or a kind of dragon. Against this background the depictions of a man in front of a millipede-like creature on Hangvar Austers I (Fig. 25)[44] and two armed horsemen flanking the serpent that encircles the whirl discs on Martebo Church I (Fig. 24) should also be interpreted

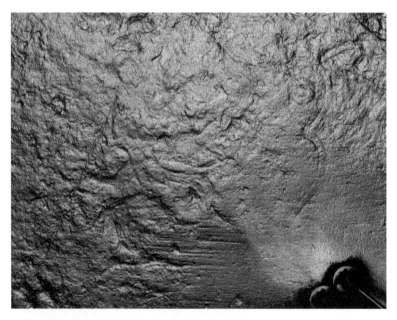

Figure 22. Sanda Church IV, equestrian, analyzed with the RTI Viewer, rendering mode "Specular Enhancement". Photographer: Sigmund Oehrl. Copyright: Sigmund Oehrl, License: CC-BY-NC-ND.

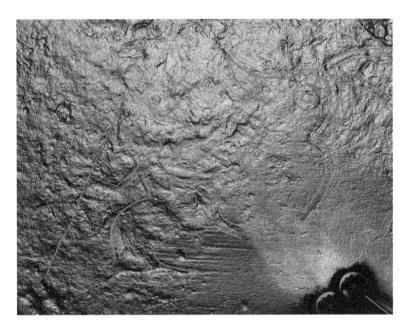

Figure 23. Sanda Church IV, equestrian, analysed with the RTI Viewer, result. Photographer: Sigmund Oehrl. Copyright: Sigmund Oehrl, License: CC-BY-NC-ND.

Figure 24. Martebo Church I (after Lindqvist 1941–1942 vol. I: Fig. 6).

Figure 25. Hangvar Austers I. Photographer: H. Faith-Ell 1937. Copyright: ATA, License: CC-BY-NC-ND.

as combat situations. Thus, a warrior fighting an animal seems to be one of the most important topics in the iconography of the Migration Period picture stones. Nevertheless, the equestrian defeating a serpent- or dragon-like enemy is a rarely documented motif in early Germanic art. Two parallels will be mentioned: the equestrian with spear and sword on the gold bracteate IK 65 Gudbrandsdalen-C (Fig. 26)[45] in Norway (Oppland) who seems to be struggling with a group of animals, defeating a kind of large reptile (late 5th century)[46] and the famous helmet plate from Vendel grave I (Fig. 27)[47] depicting a horseman with a spear, accompanied by two birds, riding down a snake (2nd half 7th century).[48]

As Wilhelm Holmqvist has already noted,[49] both images seem to be influenced by Christian rider motifs. The iconography of the Equestrian Saints arises from eastern Mediterranean art. Mainly Coptic depictions of mounted Warrior Saints, defeating lions or serpent-like demons were the models for a group of images of victorious equestrians from the Merovingian Period, in particular

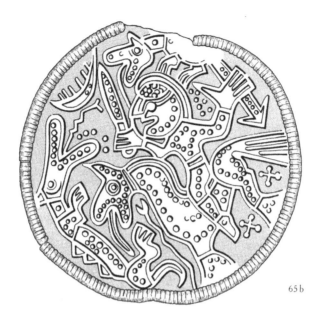

65 b

Figure 26. Gold bracteate IK 65 Gudbrandsdalen-C (after Hauck et al. 1985–1989: Taf. 78).

Figure 27. Helmet plate from Vendel I (drawing after Stolpe/Arne 1912: Taf. VI,I).

Figure 28. Equestrian Saint on a Mediterranean amulet found in Strasbourg (drawing after Fingerlin 2010: Abb. 16).

on press plate medallions (Fig. 28).[50] Roman coins with depictions of the Christian emperor, riding on horseback and killing a snake with a spear, should also be mentioned here (Fig. 29).[51] I assume that the warrior on horseback fighting the beast on Sanda Church IV (as well as Martebo Church I) is also influenced by Christian depictions like these. However, I do not believe that the Gotlandic stone carver intended to depict a Christian saint or the Roman emperor. It is more likely, following Holmqvist's view,[52] that he borrowed the motif from continental (or directly from Mediterranean) art and re-interpreted it, against the background of indigenous tradition.

Who the horseman and his enemy are, is difficult or even impossible to say. However, there are some observations to be made which give us more insight into the context of the combat. The figures are placed beneath the horizontal line with the tree. Thus, they are clearly located in an area under the earth. This interpretation is supported by the fact that the discs on the early Gotlandic picture stones, occasionally encircled by serpents, are commonly regarded as celestial bodies, representing cosmological concepts.[53] This interpretation is well reasoned: on the suggested models for the early Gotlandic picture stones, sepulchral stones from the Roman provinces, exactly the same whirl discs occur, among depictions of stars and the half moon.[54] The motif

Figure 29. Gold medallion of Constantius II. (337–361) (drawing after Vierck 1981: Abb. 5.5).

of a cosmic, world-encircling serpent is not only recorded in Old Norse religion (*Miðgarðsormr*) but likewise in Christian, first and foremost in eastern Mediterranean, Egyptian-Coptic tradition.[55] Last but not least the edges of many of these discs on Gotlandic picture stones are decorated with short lines or spikes looking like a kind of corona, possibly the rays of the sun.[56] As a result, the Sanda monument is divided into two cosmological spheres, the world above and the world below. The combat between the equestrian and the beast is located in an underworld. This observation goes well with the common interpretation of the rowing boat on the early picture stones of Gotland, which is regarded as the vessel that carries the dead to a transmarine world of death.[57]

Whether the tiny tree indicating the border between the two cosmological spheres could therefore be regarded as a kind of world tree and whether there is any connection to the world tree *Yggdrasill*, documented in Eddic poetry, remains uncertain. The beast directly beneath the roots of the tree could, against this background, be reminiscent of the dragon *Níðhǫggr* who, according to *Grímnismál* stanza 35,[58] is sitting under the world tree, gnawing at its roots. In *Vǫluspá* stanza 39 *Níðhǫggr* is devouring the corpses of the dead on the shore of the netherworld (*Nástrǫndr*).[59] Although there are four or even five centuries in between, it does not seem unlikely that the picture stone Sanda Church IV reflects ideas of the cosmos and the world of the dead comparable to those preserved in Old Norse literature. Nevertheless, the identity of the warrior who dares to compete against the demon of death remains enigmatic.[60]

As can be seen from the examples discussed above, the use of digital methods such as RTI and 3D-modelling permits a more objective documentation of the Gotland picture stones and allows re-readings that lead to entirely new interpretations, broadening our knowledge of Germanic religion and heroic legend. It should be the aim of future picture stone research to test and establish such more objective methods and, on this basis, provide a comprehensive re-edition of this unique and highly valuable source material.

Notes

1. The basic works are the edition Lindqvist 1941–1942, the little handbook Lamm & Nylén 2003 and the contributions in the conference volume Herlin Karnell et al. 2012, documenting the current state of research. See in addition Oehrl 2015; 2017b. A good overview about the status of research is also provided by Helmbrecht (2011:272–281). I would also like to mention the monographs Buisson (1976) about the prominent stone VIII from Ardre Church and Althaus (1993) as well as the unpublished works of Eshleman (1983) and Böttger-Niedenzu (1982). Guber's book (2011) about the early picture stones on Gotland (Type A and B) offers a helpful overview about the known material and common interpretations but does not lead to completely new insights (cf. Oehrl 2013a). The group of late Viking Rune stones (Type E) is investigated by Westphal (2004).

2. Lindqvist 1941–1942 vol. I:91–93 and Fig. 238, 239; Holmqvist 1952.

3. Lindqvist 1941–1942 vol. I:177ff.

4. Concerning this discussion see esp. Eshleman 1983:307–308; Hyenstrand 1989:31; Varenius 1992:52, 82; Wilson 1995:64; 1998; Imer 2001; 2012; Herlin Karnell et al. 2012:7, 14–15.

5. Lindqvist 1941–1942 vol. I: Fig. 137–138; vol. II:15–17, Fig. 305–306; Lamm & Nylén 2003: Nr. 4.

6. Lindqvist 1941–1942 vol. I: Fig. 139–140; vol. II:22–24, Fig. 311; Lamm & Nylén 2003: Nr. 16.

7. Esp. *Gylfaginning* ch. 42, in Faulkes 2005:34–35.

8. About the iconography of Wayland the Smith see esp. Nedoma 1988 (concerning Ardre VII see p. 27–31) and elaborately Oehrl 2012b (concerning Ardre VIII see p. 284–287) with bibliography. See also the relevant work Buisson 1976:70–80.

9. Neckel/Kuhn 1983:116–123.

10. Nedoma 1988:116.

11. The find was already published and discussed in *Zeitschrift für deutsches Altertum und deutsche Literatur* (Oehrl 2017a). For a preliminary report see Oehrl 2016.

12. Beck 1964:31–45; Hauck 1954:41–42; 1957:6–7; 1978:42–44; 1980:246–274; 1981:203–256; 1982:346–349; 1983a:595–599; 1983b:453–457; 1994:222–223. Concerning the concept of the divine helper in battle more generally, in biblical, antique and medieval tradition, see Graus 1977; Schreiner 2000; 2004.

13. See Beck 1964:31–45.

14. Concerning these basic problems see Oehrl 2012a, 2015 and 2017b with further literature and examples, as well as Kitzler Åhfeldt 2015:407–408.

15. Even Lindqvist himself was actually aware of this problem (1941–1942 vol. I:12–15).

16. Laila Kitzler Åhfeldt analyzed 3D-models of rune stones and picture stones, using a high-resolution portable optical 3D scanner (ATOS II from GOM), in order to investigate carving techniques and the use of templates (Kitzler Åhfeldt 2009; 2012; 2013; 2015); concerning the benefits of this method in terms of iconography see Oehrl 2012a:103–104; 2012b:302–303, Fig. 16; 2015:225, 232, Fig. 37–40.

17. I conducted my RTI analysis of picture stones on Gotland and in Stockholm between April and September 2013. The project was financed by DAAD, Fritz Thyssen Stiftung and Gerda Henkel Stiftung. Preliminary information about my research are published in Oehrl 2015:233 and Oehrl 2017b. See also Andreeff & Potter 2014.

18. http://culturalheritageimaging.org/Technologies/RTI/(19.10.2015). On the CHI web page there is also a list of publications about RTI.

19. To name only a few of them: von See 1981:118; Althaus 1993:204; Reichert 2003:33; Lamm & Nylén 2003:52; Oehrl 2006:109; Staecker 2006:365; Heinzle 2010:24; Aðalheiður Guðmundsdóttir 2012:1032ff. and 2015:359–360.

20. The written and the iconographic sources are gathered and discussed in Aðalheiður Guðmundsdóttir 2012 and 2015; Blindheim 1972–1973; 1973:21–23; Margeson 1980; von See et al. 2009:914, 928; Oehrl 2006:107–110.

21. See for instance Nordland 1949:93–100; Krappe 1940–1941:29–32.

22. UB Utrecht Ms. 32, fol. 3v and 59r.

23. Facsimile and commentary: van der Horst et al. 1982–1984.

24. Archivo Capitular de Girona ms. 7 olim 41, fol. 17v. Williams 1994–2003 vol. 1: pl. 23; vol. 2:56–57, Ill. 290.

25. Bang 1879; Bugge 1881–1889; Meyer 1889; Olrik 1922:131 and passim; Heusler 1941:190; Sigurður Nordal 1980:133–140; Hultgård 1990:353; Dronke 1992; McKinnell 1994:120–127; Dronke 1997:93–104; North 2003; McKinnell 2008; Horst 2010:239–249; concerning the current state of discussion see the contributions in the conference volume *The Nordic Apocalypse*: Steinsland 2013; Johansson 2013; Pétur Pétursson 2013; Samplonius 2013; Kure 2013.

26. See Kure 2013 with a critical point of view.

27. Neckel/Kuhn 1983:9. Cf. *Gylfaginning* ch. 52, in Faulkes 2005:53. Translation: "A hall she saw standing far from the sun, on Corpse-strand; its doors look north; poison-drops fall in through the roof-vents, the hall is woven of serpent's spines. There she saw wading in turbid streams false-oaths swearers and murderers, and the seducer of another man's close confidante; there Nidhogg sucks the corpses of the dead – a wolf tears at men [...]" (Larrington 2014:9).

28. Böttger-Niedenzu 1982:69; Oehrl 2009:548.

29. Faulkes 2005:49. Translation: "Then Skadi got a poisonous snake and fixed it up over him so that the poison would drip from the snake into his face. But his wife Sigyn stands next to him holding a basin

under the drops of poison. And when the basin is full she goes and pours away the poison, but in the meantime the poison drips into his face. Then he jerks away so hard that the whole earth shakes. That is what you call an earthquake. There he will lie in bonds until Ragnarok" (Faulkes 1989, 52).

30. Buisson 1976:65–66.

31. Lindqvist 1941–1942 vol. I:96. Lindqvist beliefs, however, that both women represent Sigyn, holding the vessel.

32. See for instance de Vries 1933:215–223; Ström 1956:69–73; Mundal 1998–2000; North 2001.

33. Faulkes 2005:34–35.

34. Faulkes 2005:45.

35. Faulkes 2005:48.

36. Neckel/Kuhn 1983:101, 103.

37. Neckel/Kuhn 1983:294.

38. Bailey & Cramp 1988:102–103, Ill. 288ff.

39. Calverley 1883:378–381; Stephens 1884:20–21; Bugge 1899:262; Olrik 1922:12; Reitzenstein 1924:46; Shetelig 1933:223; Ellis Davidson 1950:130; Bailey 1980:128; Lang 1989; Bailey 1996:87–88; Haavardsholm 1996:124–127 (critical); Bailey 2003:21; Fuglesang 2004:219–220; Bailey & Cramp 1988:102–103; Kopár 2012:90–101.

40. Lamm & Nylén 2003: Nr. 215.

41. Lindqvist 1941–1942 vol. II:110, Fig. 481.

42. Lindqvist 1962.

43. Lindqvist 1941–1942 vol. I: Fig. 6; vol. II:100–102, Fig. 462; Lamm & Nylén 2003: Nr. 194.

44. Lindqvist 1941–1942 vol. I: Fig. 27; vol. II:69, Fig. 403–404; Lamm & Nylén 2003: Nr. 126.

45. Hauck et al. 1985–1989:121, Taf. 77–78.

46. Concerning its interpretation see in particular Ellmers (1970:217ff.), who tries to connect the depiction with the battle of Ragnarøk, and Hauck (1983b:439), who regards the rider as a Dioscuric deity and divine helper against demons (see below en. 59).

47. Helmbrecht 2011: Kat. Nr. 1090, Abb. 6g, 11f–g, quoting the relevant literature.

48. The rider was often interpreted as Óðinn, accompanied by his two ravens. The snake, however, is difficult to include (see esp. Beck 1964:9–12, 19–31).

49. Holmqvist 1939:110ff., 270–271.

50. See esp. (with illustrations) Holmqvist 1939:110ff.; Böhner 1982:103ff.; Quast 2002:269, 275; 2009; Fingerlin 2010:42–46.

51. Holmqvist 1939:275; Beck 1964:23–25.

52. Holmqvist 1939:221 and passim.

53. The depictions on early Gotlandic picture stone, first and foremost on Sanda Church IV, were interpreted as cosmological concepts esp. by Ellmers (1981; 1986:342–350); Hauck (1983a); Ellis Davidsson (1969:140–145; 1988:168–170); Althaus (1993:77–84, 97–98, 147–149) and Andrén, who connects the images with the iconography of the Bronze Age (2012). Cf. already Lindqvist 1941–1942 vol. I:91–92.

54. Lindqvist 1941–1942 vol. I:91–93 and Fig. 238, 239; cf. Cumont 1942, esp. Fig. 54–59.

55. Oehrl 2013b; 2014; Ellmers (1981:36ff.; 1986:342ff.) interprets the two discs encircled by serpents as depictions of Miðgarðr and the netherworld (Hel), Hauck (1983a:546–547, 578–579) regards both of them as postmortem places of punishment.

56. Lamm & Nylén 2003:20; Guber 2011:44–47.

57. The literal, iconographic and archaeological references to the idea of a transmarine world of the dead and the afterlife journey by boat in Germanic tradition are collected and discussed in detail by Egeler 2015:113–180. Concerning the boat on the early picture stones of Gotland see in particular Hauck 1983a:546, 577.

58. Neckel/Kuhn 1983:64.

59. Neckel/Kuhn 1983:9.

60. The pairs of warriors and horses on the early Gotlandic picture stones are interpreted by Hauck (1983a) as Dioscuri, fighting against demons of death and protecting the dead on their way through the afterworld. Helmet plates of the Merovingian Period and Migration Period gold bracteates are also included in Hauck's comprehensive reconstruction of ancient Germanic Dioscuri (to name just a few more of his articles: Hauck 1980, esp. 264ff.; 1983b; 1984; 1994:208–242). The results of my re-analysis of Sanda Church IV could actually be interpreted against this very background. The equestrian could, following Hauck's idea, represent such a divine helper in need, struggling with a demon in the underworld. However, Hauck's results remain hypothetical to me. Nevertheless, his study has to be regarded as the most extensive and best-founded investigation of the iconography of early Gotlandic picture stones. Hauck's far-sighted consideration of Mediterranean parallels and his power of observation (as well as his imagination) are still unmatched.

References

Primary Sources

Gylfaginning. Faulkes, Anthony (ed.). 2005. *Edda 1. Prologue and Gylfaginning*. Second edition. Oxford: Viking Society for Northern Research.

———— Faulkes, Anthony. 1987. *Edda. Snorri Sturluson*. Translated from the Icelandic and introduced by Anthony Faulkes. Everyman's library, No. 499. London.

Edda. Neckel, Gustav & Kuhn, Hans (ed.). 1983. *Edda. Die Lieder des Codex Regius nebst verwandten Denkmälern I: Text*. Germanische Bibliothek. 4. Reihe: Texte. Fifth Edition. Heidelberg: Winter.

———— Larrington, Carolyne. 2014. *The Poetic Edda*. Second edition. Oxford World's Classics. Oxford: Oxford University Press.

Secondary Literature

Aðalheiður Guðmundsdóttir. 2012. Gunnar and the Snake Pit in Medieval Art and Legend. In *Speculum*, vol. 87:4, 1015–1049.

Aðalheiður Guðmundsdóttir. 2015. Gunnarr Gjúkason and Images of Snake-Pits. In W. Heizmann & S. Oehrl (eds.). *Bilddenkmäler zur germanischen Götter- und Heldensage.* RGA-E, 91. Berlin: Boston, 351–373.

Althaus, Sylvia. 1993. *Die gotländischen Bildsteine. Ein Programm.* Göppinger Arbeiten zur Germanistik 588. Göppingen: Kümmerle.

Andersson, Aaron. 1968. *L'art scandinave* 2. La nuit des temps 29. Saint-Léger-Vauban: Zodiaque.

Andreeff, Alexander & Potter, Rich. 2014. Imaging Picture Stones. Comparative Studies of Rendering Techniques. In H. Alexandersson et al. (eds.). *Med hjärta och hjärna. En vänbok till professor Elisabeth Arwill-Nordbladh.* GOTARC Series A, Gothenburg Archaeological Studies, vol. 5. Göteborg: Göteborgs universitet, 669–689.

Andrén, Anders. 2012. From Sunset to Sunset. An Interpretation of the Early Gotlandic Picture Stones. In *Gotländskt Arkiv* 2012, 49–58.

Andrén, Anders. 2014. *Tracing Old Norse Cosmology. The World Tree, Middle Earth, and the Sun from Archaeological Perspectives.* Vägar till Midgård 16. Lund: Nordic Academic Press.

Arne, Hjalmar & Stolpe, Ture J. 1912. *Graffältet vid Vendel.* Stockholm: Beckman.

Bailey, Richard. 1980. *Viking Age Sculpture in Northern England.* Collins Archaeology. London: Collins.

Bailey, Richard. 1996. *England's Earliest Sculptors.* Publications of the Dictionary of Old English, vol. 5. Toronto: Pontifical Inst. of Medieval Studies.

Bailey, Richard. 2003. Scandinavian Myth on Viking-period Stone Sculpture in England. In M. Clunies Ross (ed.), *Old Norse Myths, Literature and Society. Proceedings of the 11th International Saga Conference 2–7 July 2000.* Odense: University of Sidney, 15–23.

Bailey, Rosemary & Bailey, Richard N. 1988. *Corpus of Anglo-Saxon Stone Sculpture II: Cumberland, Westmorland and Lancashire North-of-the-Sands.* Oxford: Oxford University Press.

Bang, Anton Christian. 1879. *Vøluspaa og de Sibyllinske Orakler*. Christiania Videnskabsselskabs Forhandlinger 1879, No. 9. Christiania: Dybwad.

Beck, Heinrich. 1964. *Einige vendelzeitliche Bilddenkmäler und die literarische Überlieferung*. Bayerische Akademie der Wissenschaften. Philosophisch-Historische Klasse. Sitzungsberichte 1964:6. München: Verlag der Bayerischen Akademie der Wissenschaften.

Blindheim, Martin. 1972–1973. *Sigurds Saga i middelalderens billedkunst. Utstilling i Universitets Oldsaksamling 1972–1973*. Oslo: Universitet i Oslo.

Blindheim, Martin. 1973. Fra hedensk figur til kristent forbilde. Sigurdsdiktningen i middelalderens billedkunst. In *Iconografisk Post*, vol. 1973:3, 3–28.

Bugge, Sophus. 1881–1889. *Studier over de nordiske Gude- og Heltesagns Oprindelse*. Christiania: Cammermeyer.

Bugge, Sophus. 1899. Nordiske Runeindskrifter og billeder paa Øen Man. In *Aarbøger for Nordisk Oldkyndighed og Historie*, vol. 14, 247–262.

Buisson, Ludwig. 1976. *Der Bildstein Ardre VIII auf Gotland. Gottermythen, Heldensagen und Jenseitsglaube der Germanen im 8. Jahrhundert n. Chr*. Abhandlungen der Akademie der Wissenschaften in Göttingen. Philologisch-Historische Klasse, Dritte Folge, Nr. 102. Göttingen: Vandenhoeck Ruprecht.

Böhner, Kurt. 1982. Die Reliefplatten von Hornhausen. In *Festschrift Hans-Jürgen Hundt zum 65. Geburtstag, Teil 3: Frühes Mittelalter*. Jahrbuch des RGZM 23/24 (1976–1977). Mainz: Römisch-Germanischen Zentralmuseum Mainz, 89–129.

Böttger-Niedenzu, Beata. 1982. *Darstellungen auf gotländischen Bildsteinen, vor allem des Typs C und D, und die Frage ihres Zusammenhanges mit Stoffen der altnordischen Literatur*. Hausarbeit zur Erlangung des Magister Grades an der Ludwig-Maximilians-Universität München. München: Universität München.

Calverley, William Slater. 1883. The Sculptured Cross at Gosforth. In *Transactions of the Cumberland and Westmorland Antiquarian and Archaeological Society* 1883, 373–404.

De Vries, Jan. 1933. *The Problem of Loki*. FF Communications No. 110. Helsinki: Suomalainen Tiedeakatemia, Societas Scientiarum Fennica.

Cumont, Franz. 1942. *Recherches sur le Symbolisme Funéraire des Romains*. Paris: Geuthner.

Dronke, Ursula. 1992. Vǫluspá and Sibylline Traditions. In R. North & T. Hofstra (eds.). *Latin Culture and Medieval Germanic Europe. Germania Latina I*. Proceedings of the First Germania Latina Conference held at the University of Groningen, 26 May 1989. Groningen: University of Groningen, 3–21.

Dronke, Ursula. 1997. *The Poetic Edda, Volume II. Mythological Poems*. Edited with Translation, Introduction and Commentary by Ursula Dronke. Oxford: Clarendon.

Egeler, Matthias. 2015. *Avalon, 66° Nord. Frühgeschichte und Rezeption eines Mythos*. RGA-E 95. Berlin, Boston: de Gruyter.

Ellis Davidson, Hilda Roderick. 1950. Gods and Heroes in Stone. In Sir C. Fox & B. Dickins (eds.). *The Early Cultures of North-West Europe. H. M. Chadwick Memorial Studies*. Cambridge: Cambridge University Press, 123–139.

Ellis Davidson, Hilda Roderick & Gelling, Peter. 1969. *The Chariot of the Sun. And other Rites and Symbols of the Northern Bronze Age*. New York: Praeger.

Ellis Davidson, Hilda Roderick. 1988. *Myths and Symbols in Pagan Europe. Early Scandinavian and Celtic Religions*. Manchester: Manchester University Press.

Ellmers, Detlev. 1970. Zur Ikonographie Nordischer Goldbrakteaten. In *Jahrbuch des Römisch-Germanischen Zentralmuseums Mainz*, vol. 17, 201–284.

Ellmers, Detlev. 1981. Religiöse Vorstellungen der Germanen im Bildprogramm gotländischer Bildsteine und der Ostkrypta des Bremer Domes. In *Jahrbuch der Wittheit zu Bremen*, vol. XXV, 31–54.

Ellmers, Detlev. 1986. Schiffsdarstellungen auf skandinavischen Grabsteinen. In H. Roth (ed.). *Zum Problem der Deutung frühmittelalterlicher Bildinhalte. Akten des 1. Internationalen Kolloquiums in Marburg a. d. Lahn, 15. bis 19. Februar 1983.* Veröffentlichungen des Vorgeschichtlichen Seminars der Philipps-Universität Marburg a. d. Lahn, Sonderband 4. Sigmaringen: Philipps-Universität Marburg, 341–372.

Eshleman, Lori Elaine. 1983. *The Monumental Stones of Gotland. A Study in Style and Motif.* A Thesis submitted to the Faculty of the Graduate School of the University of Minnesota. Ann Arbor, Michigan: University Microfilms International.

Fingerlin, Gerhard. 2010. Die ältesten christlichen Bilder der Alamannia. Zu Herkunft und Ikonographie der drei silbernen Phalerae aus dem Kammergrab von der „Gierhalde" in Hüfingen, dem Hauptort der frühmittelalterlichen Baar. In V. Huth & J. Regnath (eds.). *Die Baar als Königslandschaft.* Sigmaringen: Jan Thorbecke Verlag, 25–46.

Fuglesang, Signe Horn. 2004. Dekor, bilder og bygninger i kristningstiden. In J. V. Sigurðsson et al. (eds.). *Religionsskiftet i Norden. Brytinger mellom nordisk og europeisk kultur 800–1200 e. Kr.* Oslo: Senter for Studier i Vikingtid og Nordisk Middelalder, 197–294.

Graus, František. 1977. Der Heilige als Schlachtenhelfer. Zur Nationalisierung einer Wundererzählung in der mittelalterlichen Chronistik. In K.-U. Jäschke & R. Wenskus (eds.). *Festschrift für Helmut Beumann zum 65. Geburtstag.* Sigmaringen: Jan Thorbecke Verlag, 330–348.

Guber, Sonja. 2011. *Die Bildsteine Gotlands der Völkerwanderungs- und Vendelzeit als Spiegel frühgeschichtlicher Lebenswelten.* BAR International Series 2257. Oxford: Archaeopress.

Haavardsholm, Jørgen. 1996. Gosforthkorset og dets kontekst. In M. Rindal (ed.). *Studier i kilder til vikingtid og nordisk middelalder.* KULTs skriftserie 46. Oslo: Norges forskningsråd, 117–146.

Hauck, Karl. 1954: Herrschaftszeichen eines wodanistischen Königtums. In *Jahrbuch für Fränkische Landesforschung*, vol. 14, 9–66.

Hauck, Karl. 1957. Alemannische Denkmäler der vorchristlichen Adelskultur. In *Zeitschrift für Württembergische Landesgeschichte*, vol. 16:1, 1–40.

Hauck, Karl. 1978. Bildforschung als historische Sachforschung. In
K. Hauck & H. Mordek (eds.). *Geschichtsschreibung und geistiges
Leben im Mittelalter*. Köln, Wien: Böhlau, 27–70.

Hauck, Karl. 1980. Die Veränderung der Missionsgeschichte durch
die Entdeckung der Ikonologie der germanischen Bilddenkmäler,
erhellt am Beispiel der Propagierung der Kampfhilfen des Mars-
Wodan in Altuppsala im 7. Jahrhundert. Zur Ikonologie der
Goldbrakteaten XX. In *Westfalen. Hefte für Geschichte, Kunst
und Volkskunde*, vol. 57, 227–307.

Hauck, Karl. 1981. Die bildliche Wiedergabe von Götter- und
Heldenwaffen im Norden seit der Völkerwanderungszeit. Zur
Ikonologie der Goldbrakteaten XVIII. In R. Schmidt-Wiegand (ed.).
Wörter und Sachen im Lichte der Bezeichnungsforschung. Arbeiten
zur Frühmittelalterforschung 1. Berlin, New York: de Gruyter,
168–269.

Hauck, Karl. 1982. Zum zweiten Band der Sutton Hoo-Edition. In
Frühmittelalterliche Studien, vol. 16, 319–362.

Hauck, Karl. 1983a. Text und Bild in einer oralen Kultur. Antworten
auf die zeugniskritische Frage nach der Erreichbarkeit mündlicher Überlieferung im frühen Mittelalter. Zur Ikonologie der
Goldbrakteaten XXV. In *Frühmittelalterliche Studien*, vol. 17,
510–599.

Hauck, Karl. 1983b. Dioskuren in Bildzeugnissen des Nordens vom
5. bis zum 7. Jahrhundert. Zur Ikonographie der Goldbrakteaten
XXVIII. In *Jahrbuch des RGZM*, vol. 30, 435–464.

Hauck, Karl. 1984. *Dioskuren*, §4–6. In RGA 5, 484–494.

Hauck, Karl. 1994. Altuppsalas Polytheismus exemplarisch erhellt
mit Bildzeugnissen des 5. – 7. Jahrhunderts. Zur Ikonologie der
Goldbrakteaten LIII. In H. Uecker (ed.). *Studien zum Altgermanischen*.
Festschrift für Heinrich Beck. RGA-E 11. Berlin, New York: de
Gruyter, 197–302.

Hauck, Karl et al. 1985–1989. *Die Goldbrakteaten der Völkerwanderungszeit. Ikonographischer Katalog 1–3*. Münstersche Mit-
telalter-Schriften 24, 1, 1–3, 2. München: Fink.

Heinzle, Joachim. 2010. *Die Nibelungen*. 2nd Edition. Darmstadt: Primus.

Helmbrecht, Michaela. 2011. *Wirkungsmächtige Kommunikationsmedien. Menschenbilder der Vendel- und Wikingerzeit und ihre Kontexte*. Acta Archaeologica Lundensia, Series Prima in 4° 30. Lund: Lunds Universitet.

Herlin Karnell, Maria et al. (ed.). 2012. *Gotland's Picture Stones. Bearers of an Enigmatic Legacy*. Gotländskt Arkiv 84. Visby: Fornsalen Publishing.

Heusler, Andreas. 1941. *Die altgermanische Dichtung*. 2nd Edition. Potsdam: Athenaion.

Holmqvist, Wilhelm. 1939. *Kunstprobleme der Merowingerzeit*. Stockholm: Wahlström & Widstrand.

Holmqvist Wilhelm. 1952. De äldsta gotländska bildstenarna och deras motivkrets. In *Fornvännen*, vol. 47, 1–20.

van der Horst, Koert et al. 1982–1984. *Utrecht-Psalter. Im Originalformat der Handschrift 32 aus dem Besitz der Bibliotheek der Rijksuniversiteit te Utrecht*. Codices selecti phototypice impressi 75–76. Bd. 1: Vollständige Faksimile-Ausgabe, Bd. 2: Kommentar von Koert van der Horst, übersetzt aus dem Holländischen von Johannes Rathofer. Graz: Akademische Druck- und Verlagsanstalt.

Horst, Simone. 2010. *Merlin und die Völva. Weissagungen im Altnordischen*. Münchner Nordistische Studien 5. München: Herbert Utz.

Hultgård, Anders. 1990. Old Scandinavian and Christian Eschatology. In T. Ahlbäck (ed.). *Old Norse and Finnish Religions and Cultic Place-Names. Based on Papers Read at the Symposium on Encounters Between Religions in Old Nordic Times and on Cultic Place-Names Held at Åbo, Finland, on the 19th–21st of August 1987*. Scripta Instituti Donneriani Aboensis XIII. Åbo: Donner Institute, 344–357.

Hyenstrand, Åke. 1989. *Socknar och stenstugor. Om det tidiga Gotland*. SAR, Nr. 22. Stockholm: Stockholm University.

Imer, Lisbeth. 2001. Gotlandske billedsten. Datering af Lindqvists gruppe C og D. In *Aarbøger for nordisk oldkyndighed og historie* 2001 (erschienen 2004), 47–111.

Imer, Lisbeth. 2012. The Viking Period Gotlandic Picture Stones. A Chronological Revision. In *Gotländskt Arkiv*, vol. 84, 115–118.

Johansson, Karl G. 2013. Vǫluspá, The Tiburtine Sibyl, and the Apocalypse in the North. In T. Gunnell & A. Lassen (eds.). *The Nordic Apocalypse. Approaches to Vǫluspá and Nordic Days of Judgement*. Acta Scandinavica. Aberdeen Studies in the Scandinavian World, vol. 2. Turnhout: Brepols, 161–184.

Kitzler Åhfeld, Laila. 2009. Keltiskt eller kontinentalt? Om mallanvändning på Gotlands bildstenar. In C. Hedenstierna-Jonson et al. (eds.). *Spaden och pennan. Minnesbok tillägnad Erik B. Lundberg och Bengt G. Söderberg*. Stockholm: Oeisspesis, 131–154.

Kitzler Åhfeld, Laila. 2012. Picture Stone Workshops and Handicraft Traditions. In *Gotländskt Arkiv* 84, 183–194.

Kitzler Åhfeld, Laila. 2013. 3D-scanning of Gotland Picture Stones. With Supplementary Material: Digital catalogue of 3D data. In *Journal of Nordic Archaeological Science, JONAS*, vol. 18 (2013), 55–65.

Kitzler Åhfeld, Laila. 2015. Picture-Stone Workshops on Viking Age Gotland. A Study of Craftworkers' Traces. In W. Heizmann & S. Oehrl (eds.). *Bilddenkmäler zur germanischen Götter- und Heldensage*. RGA-E 91. Berlin, Boston: de Gruyter, 397–431.

Kopár, Lilla. 2012. *Gods and Settlers. The Iconography of Norse Mythology in Anglo-Scandinavian Sculpture*. Studies in the Early Middle Ages, vol. 25. Turnhout: Brepols.

Krappe, Alexander H. 1940–1941. The Snake Tower. In *Scandinavian Studies*, vol. 16, 22–33.

Kure, Henning. 2013. Wading Heavy Currents. Snorri's use of Vǫluspá 39. In T. Gunnell & A. Lassen (eds.). *The Nordic Apocalypse. Approaches to Vǫluspá and Nordic Days of Judgement*. Acta Scandinavica. Aberdeen Studies in the Scandinavian World, vol. 2. Turnhout: Brepols, 79–91.

Lamm, Jan Peder & Nylén, Erik. 2003. *Bildstenar*. 3rd edition. Värnamo: Fälth & Hässler.

Lang, James. 1989. Pre-Conquest Sculpture in Eastern Yorkshire. In C. Wilson (ed.). *Medieval Art and Architecture in the East Riding of Yorkshire*. Conference Transactions for the year 1983. London: The British Archaeological Association, 1–8.

Lindqvist, Sune. 1941–1942. *Gotlands Bildsteine I–II*. Stockholm: Wahlström & Widstrand.

Lindqvist, Sune. 1962. Jättestenen från Sanda och andra nyfunna bildstenar. In *Gotländskt Arkiv*, vol. 34, 7–22.

Margeson, Sue. 1980. The Volsung Legend in Medieval Art. In F. G. Andersen et al. (eds.). *Medieval Iconography and Narrative. A Symposium*. Odense: Odense University Press, 183–211.

McKinnell, John. 1994. *Both One and Many. Essays on Change and Variety in Late Norse Heathenism*. Philologia 1. Rome: Il Calamo.

McKinnell, John. 2008. Vǫluspá and the Feast of Easter. In *Alvíssmál*, vol. 12, 3–28.

Meyer, Elard Hugo. 1889. *Völuspa. Eine Untersuchung*. Berlin: Mayer & Müller.

Mundal, Else. 1998–2000. Androgyny as an Image of Chaos in Old Norse Mythology. In *Maal och Minne* 1998–2000, 1–9.

Nedoma, Robert. 1988. *Die bildlichen und schriftlichen Denkmäler der Wielandsage*. Göppinger Arbeiten zur Germanistik Nr. 490. Göppingen: Kümmerle.

Nordland, Odd. 1949. Ormegarden. In *Viking. Tidskrift for norrøn arkeologi*, vol. 13, 77–126.

North, Richard. 2001. Loki's Gender. Or why Skaði Laughed. In K. E. Olsen & L. A. J. R. Houwen (eds.). *Monsters and the Monstrous in Medieval Northwest Europe*. Mediaevalia Groningana, New Series, Volume III. Leuven: Peeters, 141–151.

North, Richard. 2003. Vǫluspá and the Book of Revelation. In R. Simek & J. Meurer (eds.). *Scandinavia and Christian Europe in the Middle Ages. Papers of the 12ᵗʰ International Saga Conference,*

Bonn/Germany, 28ᵗʰ July – 2ⁿᵈ August 2003. Bonn: Universität Bonn, 403–412.

Oehrl, Sigmund. 2006. *Zur Deutung anthropomorpher und theriomorpher Bilddarstellungen auf den spätwikingerzeitlichen Runensteinen Schwedens.* Wiener Studien zur Skandinavistik 16. Wien: Praesens.

Oehrl, Sigmund. 2009. Wieland der Schmied auf dem Kistenstein von Alskog kyrka und dem Runenstein Ardre kyrka III. Zur partiellen Neulesung und Interpretation zweier gotländischer Bildsteine. In H. Beck et al. (eds.). *Analecta Septentrionalia. Beiträge zur nordgermanischen Kultur- und Literaturgeschichte.* RGA-E 65. Berlin, New York: de Gruyter, 540–566.

Oehrl, Sigmund. 2012a. New Iconographic Interpretations of Gotlandic Picture Stones Based on Surface Re-Analysis. In *Gotländskt Arkiv* 2012, 91–104.

Oehrl, Sigmund. 2012b. Bildliche Darstellungen vom Schmied Wieland und ein unerwarteter Auftritt in Walhall. In A. Pesch & R. Blankenfeldt (eds.). *Goldsmith Mysteries. The Elusive Gold Smithies of the North. Papers Presented at the Workshop Organized by the Centre for Baltic and Scandinavian Archaeology (ZBSA), Schleswig, June 20ᵗʰ and 21ᵗʰ, 2011.* Schriften des Archäologischen Landesmuseums. Ergänzungsreihe 8. Neumünster: ZBSA, 279–335.

Oehrl, Sigmund. 2013a. Review About Guber 2011. In *Zeitschrift für deutsches Altertum und deutsche Literatur*, vol. 142:2, 250–260.

Oehrl, Sigmund. 2013b. Das Uroboros-Motiv im germanischen Altertum und seine Kontexte. Eine Übersicht. In I. Heske et al. (eds.). *Landschaft, Besiedlung und Siedlung. Archäologische Studien im nordeuropäischen Kontext. Festschrift für Karl-Heinz Willroth zu seinem 65. Geburtstag.* Göttinger Schriften zur Vor- und Frühgeschichte 33. Neumünster, Hamburg: Wacholtz/Murmann, 455–468.

Oehrl, Sigmund. 2014. Uroboros. In *Germanische Altertumskunde Online* (GAO), Update 2/2014.

Oehrl, Sigmund. 2015. Möglichkeiten der Neulesung gotländischer Bildsteine und ihre ikonographische Auswertung. Ausgewählte

Beispiele und Perspektiven. In W. Heizmann & S. Oehrl (eds.). *Bilddenkmäler zur germanischen Götter- und Heldensage.* RGA-E 91. Berlin, Boston: de Gruyter, 219–259.

Oehrl, Sigmund. 2016. Horned Ship-Guide. An Unnoticed Picture Stone Fragment from Stora Valle, Gotland. In *Fornvännen*, vol. 111, 53–55.

Oehrl, Sigmund. 2017a. Der göttliche Schiffsbegleiter mit dem 'Hörnerhelm'. Ein bislang unbekanntes wikingerzeitliches Bildsteinfragment aus St. Valle im Kirchspiel Rute auf Gotland. In *Zeitschrift für deutsches Altertum und deutsche Literatur*, vol. 146:1, 1–40.

Oehrl, Sigmund. 2017b. Documenting and interpreting the picture stones of Gotland. Old problems and new approaches. In *Current Swedish Archaeology*, vol. 25, 87–122.

Olrik, Axel. 1922. *Ragnarök. Die Sagen vom Weltuntergang.* Übertragen von Wilhelm Ranisch. Berlin, Leipzig: de Gruyter.

Pétur Pétursson. 2013. Manifest and Latent Biblical Themes in Vǫluspá. In T. Gunnell & A. Lassen (eds.). *The Nordic Apocalypse. Approaches to Vǫluspá and Nordic Days of Judgement.* Acta Scandinavica. Aberdeen Studies in the Scandinavian World, vol. 2. Turnhout: Brepols, 185–202.

Quast, Dieter. 2002. Kriegerdarstellungen der Merowingerzeit aus der Alamannia. In *Archäologisches Korrespondenzblatt*, vol. 32, 267–280.

Quast, Dieter. 2009. Merovingian Period Equestrians in Figural Art. In A. Bliujiene (ed.). *The Horse and Man in European Antiquity. Worldview, Burial Rites, and Military and Everyday Life.* Archaeologia Baltica, vol. 11. Klaipeda: Klaipeda University, 330–342.

Reichert, Hermann. 2003. Die Nibelungensage im mittelalterlichen Skandinavien. In J. Heinzle et al. (eds.). *Die Nibelungen. Sage – Epos – Mythos.* Wien: Reichert, 29–88.

Reitzenstein, Richard. 1924. *Weltuntergangsvorstellungen. Eine Studie zur vergleichenden Religionsgeschichte.* Sonderabdruck aus Kyrkohistorisk Årsskrift 1924. Uppsala: Lundquistska Bokhandelen.

Samplonius, Kees. 2013. The Background and Scope of Vǫluspá. In T. Gunnell & A. Lassen (eds.). *The Nordic Apocalypse. Approaches to Vǫluspá and Nordic Days of Judgement.* Acta Scandinavica. Aberdeen Studies in the Scandinavian World, vol. 2. Turnhout: Brepols, 113–145.

Schreiner, Klaus. 2000. *Märtyrer, Schlachtenhelfer, Friedensstifter. Krieg und Frieden im Spiegel mittelalterlicher und frühneuzeitlicher Heiligenverehrung.* Otto-von-Freising-Vorlesungen der Katholischen Universität Eichstätt. Wiesbaden: Leske & Budrich.

Schreiner, Klaus. 2004. SIGNA VICTRICIA. Heilige Zeichen in kriegerischen Konflikten des Mittelalters. In G. Althoff (ed.). *Zeichen – Rituale – Werte. Internationales Kolloquium des Sonderforschungsbereichs 496 an der Westfälischen Wilhelms-Universität Münster.* Münster: Rhema, 259–300.

von See, Klaus. 1981. *Germanische Heldensage. Stoffe, Probleme, Methoden.* 2nd Edition. Frankfurt am Main: Athenaion.

von See, Klaus et al. 2009. *Kommentar zu den Liedern der Edda 6: Heldenlieder. Brot af Sigurðarkviðo, Guðrúnarkviða I, Sigurðarkviða in skamma, Helreið Brynhildar, Dráp Niflunga, Guðrúnarkviða II, Guðrúnarkviða III, Oddrúnargrátr, Strophenbruchstücke aus der Vǫlsunga saga.* Heidelberg: Winter.

Shetelig, Haakon. 1933. *Vikingeminner i Vest-Europa.* Instituttet for Sammenlignende Kulturforskning, Serie A: Forelesninger 16. Oslo, Leipzig: Aschenhoug, Harrassowitz.

Sigurður Nordal. 1980. *Völuspá.* Herausgegeben und kommentiert von Sigurður Nordal. Aus dem Isländischen übersetzt und mit einem Vorwort zur deutschen Ausgabe von Ommo Wilts. Texte zur Forschung 33. Darmstadt: Wissenschaftliche Buchgesellschaft.

Staecker, Jörn. 2006. Heroes, Kings and Gods. Discovering Sagas on Gotlandic Picture-Stones. In A. Andrén et al. (eds.). *Old Norse Religion in Long-Term Perspectives. Origins, Changes, and Interactions. An international Conference in Lund, Sweden, June 3–7, 2004.* Vägar till Midgård 8. Lund: Nordic Academic Press, 363–368.

Stephens, George. 1884. Prof. S. Bugge's Studier over nordisk mythologi. Supplement. In *Aarbøger for Nordisk Oldkyndighed og Historie 1884*, 1–47.

Steinsland, Gro. 2013. Vǫluspá and the Sibylline Oracles with a Focus on the *Myth of the Future*. In T. Gunnell & A. Lassen (eds.). *The Nordic Apocalypse. Approaches to Vǫluspá and Nordic Days of Judgement*. Acta Scandinavica. Aberdeen Studies in the Scandinavian World, vol. 2. Turnhout: Brepols, 147–160.

Ström, Folke. 1956. *Loki. Ein mythologisches Problem*. Acta Universitatis Gothoburgensis. Göteborgs Universitets Årsskrift Vol. LXII, 1956:8. Göteborg: Elander.

Varenius, Björn. 1992. *Det Nordiska Skeppet. Teknologi och samhällsstrategi i vikingatid och medeltid*. Stockholm Studies in Archaeology 10. Stockholm: Stockholms Universitet.

Vierck, Hayo. 1981. Imitatio imperii und interpretatio Germanica vor der Wikingerzeit. In R. Zeitler (ed.). *Les Pays du Nord et Byzance (Scandinavie et Byzance). Actes du colloque nordique et international de byzantinologie, tenu à Upsal 20–22 avril 1979*. Acta Universitatis Upsaliensis Figura, N. S. 19. Uppsala: Almqvist & Wiksell, 64–113.

Westphal, Florian. 2004. Untersuchungen zur späten Bildsteingruppe Gotlands. In M. Müller-Wille (ed.). *Zwischen Tier und Kreuz. Untersuchungen zur wikingerzeitlichen Ornamentik im Ostseeraum*. Studien zur Siedlungsgeschichte und Archäologie der Ostseegebiete, Bd. 4. Neumünster: Wachholtz, 377–454.

Williams, John. 1994–2003. *The Illustrated Beatus. A Corpus of Illustrations of the Commentary on the Apocalypse, Vol. 1–5*. London: Miller.

Wilson, David M. 1995. *Vikingatidens Konst*. Signums svenska konsthistoria 2. Lund: Bokförlag Signum.

Wilson, David. 1998. The Gotland Picture-Stones. A Chronological Re-Assessment. In A. Wesse (ed.). *Studien zur Archäologie des Ostseeraumes. Von der Eisenzeit zum Mittelalter. Festschrift für Michael Müller-Wille*. Neumünster: Wachholtz, 49–52.

Response

Anne-Sofie Gräslund
University of Uppsala

The RTI-method itself, together with some good examples of its benefits, was published by Oehrl after The Picture Stone Symposium in Visby 2011.[1] It seems to be a very useful tool for scholars to be able to see more details of the original carvings than you can with the naked eye. At the Mythology Conference in Stockholm 2015 Oehrl answered in the negative my question of whether the method is technically very difficult or expensive; that means that we probably can expect many more exciting results in the future. However, it is worth mentioning that, basically, Sune Lindqvist used the same technique with oblique light from different angles,[2] but of course, today's RTI-technique is much more elaborated, developed and powerful.

Sigmund Oehrl starts by showing that the iconography of the Gotlandic picture stones may provide new insights into ancient Germanic and Viking mythology, both regarding motifs that are totally unknown from literary tradition, such as the horned ship-guide on the stone from Stora Valle in Rute Parish recently published by him,[3] and motifs known from literature written down centuries later than the images in question.

The first example taken up in his current paper, the motif traditionally called Gunnarr in the snake pit is represented on the stone from Hunninge in Klinte parish. The RTI-picture shows that the person in the snake pit is not a man but a woman, having long hair, set up in a pigtail, and a long dress, both female characteristics. Oehrl's idea is either that there could be an influence from the Christian eschatology taken over into Old Norse mythology, expressed in *Vǫluspá*, stanzas 38–39 where the hall of the Sindre dynasty formed by snakes is described, or perhaps more likely, compared to the scene of the same motif on the picture stone Ardre VIII, the figure in the snake-filled enclosure may instead be interpreted as Loki, who is known for some bisexual characteristics. There Loki is depicted with a braid, the same hairstyle as his wife

Sigyn. The two women outside the enclosure may be interpreted as Sigyn with the bowl to collect the poison from the snake and Skaði holding a snake. However, it could be mentioned that the story about Sigurðr Fáfnisbani including that of Gunnarr in the snake pit were known in Scandinavia as seen from images on Late Viking Age rune stones. A good example of an image of Gunnarr comes from the Västerljung Stone (Sö 40) where Gunnarr plays the harp with his feet.

The second monument discussed by Oehrl is the large Migration Period stone IV from Sanda Church, dated to probably the 6th century. The upper part was found at the beginning of the 20th century. On the lower part, not discovered until 1956, the RTI-picture showed a rider with a spear in his hand, earlier totally unknown. A horizontal line carved over the stone surface is regarded as the border between the upper world and the underworld. Anders Andrén has connected the iconography of the Sanda Stone with a Bronze Age sun cult and the journey of the sun through the day and night.[4]

Regarding the rider, Oehrl mentions several parallels, mainly from the Merovingian Period, to this motif, from picture stones, gold bracteates and sheet foils from helmets, and he concludes with references to Wilhelm Holmqvist that its origin probably came from early Christian art on the continent and was re-interpreted against the background of indigenous tradition. This is a statement that I entirely agree with – so much of the Scandinavian iconography of the second half of the first millennium can be traced back to the early Christian art on the continent and then in its turn back to pre-Christian art in the Near East.[5]

Also, in this case there is interesting comparative material in the iconography of Late Viking Age rune stones. Images of riders occur on a number of Uppland rune stones and in my view several of them can be interpreted as holy riders, especially the one on stone U 691 from Söderby in Arnö Parish, where the centrally placed rider has a raised sword in one hand and a processional cross in the other. In Christian iconography riders, often armed, occur, generally interpreted as *Militia Christi*, representing the army of Christ.

However, for the rune stones in question I find another hypothesis more attractive, put forward by the Scottish archaeologist

Martin Goldberg in his work on the Pictish symbol stones. From the 8th century onwards, the Pictish symbol stones seem to have a mixture of pagan and Christian motifs, in the same way as pre-Christian and Christian representations are mixed on our picture stones and rune stones. It is easy to believe that, in a transition phase, motifs with a pagan as well as a Christian meaning were popular. There are many examples from various times and areas that, during conversion, customs from the old religion were accepted or tolerated, only given a new interpretation that fitted in with the new religion, the so-called *Interpretatio* (for example) *Scandinavica*. On some Pictish stones there are riders, and these are traditionally interpreted as hunting scenes. Goldberg's idea is that in this apparent motif there might be a hidden meaning – that the picture is an allusion of the so-called *Adventus* motif, the entry of Christ to Jerusalem on Palm Sunday, when he is welcomed as Messiah.[6] In my view this is supported by Maria Elena Ruggerini, who, in an article on the Anglo-Saxon liturgy of Easter including Palm Sunday, makes a comprehensive investigation of sources. She points out that the ninth-century hymn *Gloria laus et honor*, praising Christ as the pious and righteous king, redeemer of humankind, composed by Theodulph, Bishop of Orléans and based on Psalm 24 exists in a version *Canterbury Benedictional* with added verses. One of them asks: *Quis rex hic equitat, cui Gloria redditur ista?* (Who is this king who comes riding here, to whom glory is due?).[7] Obviously, the Sanda Stone is much earlier, probably from the 6th century, but as Oehrl argues in his article, it is more likely that the Gotlandic stone carver did not intend to depict a Christian saint or the Roman emperor – on the contrary, he borrowed the motif from continental or Mediterranean art and, as it was laden with symbolism in the Old Norse mythology, he re-interpreted it against the background of domestic tradition.

Notes

1. Oehrl 2012:91ff.

2. Nylén & Lamm 2003:3.

3. Oehrl 2016:55ff.

4. Andrén 2012:55ff.

5. Gräslund 2014:24ff.

6. Goldberg 2012:160ff.

7. Ruggerini 2011:213ff.

References

Andrén, Anders. 2012. From Sunset to Sunset. An Interpretation of the Early Gotlandic Picture Stones. In *Gotländskt Arkiv* 2012, 49–58.

Goldberg, Martin. 2012. Ideas and Ideologies. In D. Clarke et al. (eds.). *Early Medieval Scotland. Individuals, Communities and Ideas.* Edinburgh: National Museums Scotland Enterprises, 141–203.

Gräslund, Anne-Sofie. 2014. En påfågel i Odensala? Några reflexioner om ikonografin på runstenarna vid Harg. In *Situne Dei* 2014, 22–31.

Nylén, Erik & Lamm, Jan Peder. 2003. *Bildstenar.* 3:e upplagan. Stockholm: Gidlunds Förlag.

Oehrl, Sigmund. 2012. New Iconographic Interpretations of Gotlandic Picture Stones Based on Surface Re-analysis. In *Gotländskt Arkiv* 2012, 91–104.

Oehrl, Sigmund. 2016. Horned Ship-guide. An Unnoticed Picture Stone Fragment from Stora Valle in Rute, Gotland. In *Fornvännen* 111/2016, 53–55.

Ruggerini, Maria Elena. 2011. A Just and Riding God. Christ's Movement in the Descent into Hell. In D. Anlezark (ed.). *Myths, Legends, and Heroes. Essays on Old Norse and Old English Literature in Honour of John McKinnel.* Toronto, Buffalo, London: University of Toronto Press, 207–267.

Gold Foil Figures and Norse Mythology: Fact and Fiction?

Margrethe Watt

Bornholms Museum, Rønne

Gold foil figures (Swedish: *guldgubbar*) have been established as an archaeological "type" for nearly 300 years and are well known to Scandinavian archaeologists.[1] They have also attracted attention from historians and specialists in the history of religion.[2] As new finds appear from time to time, it seems appropriate to give a short update on some basic facts and to clarify the terminology used in the discussion.

The term "guldgubbe" is here applied to figures which are stamped with a bronze die (*patrix*) on thin sheets of gold or gold-silver alloys (Fig. 6a). The term "die" is used as a common denominator for figures embossed (stamped) on the same bronze die (die identity).

About 5 % out of a total of more than 3,000 figures are scratched on – or cut out of – thicker gold sheet. Three-dimensional figures are not included in this definition, but are relevant to the iconographic interpretation. In contrast to both bracteates and anthropomorphic figures, which, for example feature on objects decorated in the widespread animal Style I, they are a purely Scandinavian phenomenon.

Gold foil figures are first and foremost associated with large and important settlement sites.[3] Because the gold content is very variable and the value of the gold negligible, they are unlikely to have been part of a primary economy. Numerically, the vast majority of the figures are found on the island of Bornholm in the southern Baltic (several localities). Single figures dominate in south-eastern

How to cite this book chapter:
Watt, M. 2019. Gold Foil Figures and Norse Mythology: Fact and Fiction?. In: Wikström af Edholm, K., Jackson Rova, P., Nordberg, A., Sundqvist, O. & Zachrisson, T. (eds.) *Myth, Materiality, and Lived Religion: In Merovingian and Viking Scandinavia*. Pp. 191–221. Stockholm: Stockholm University Press. DOI: https://doi.org/10.16993/bay.h. License: CC-BY.

Scandinavia while gold foils showing two persons dominate on the Danish islands of Fyn and Sjælland as well as further north in Sweden in a stretch from Uppland across to Västra Götaland and in southern and western Norway.

The figures are difficult to date archaeologically as they are rarely found outside the wider context of settlement sites with long continuity; hence there is a considerable risk of chronological "contamination" due to a complex stratigraphy. Unlike many other artefact types, gold foil figures are almost completely absent from grave finds. Traditional dates range from the Late Migration Period to the early Viking Age – a span of 300–400 years. However, based on modern excavation methods, combined with iconographic as well as stylistic analyses, it has become increasingly difficult to uphold some of the late dates (Viking Age).[4] Stylistic as well as specific iconographic details point to dates in the 6th and 7th centuries for both single figures and man-woman pairs from southern Scandinavia. As an example, I am convinced that at least three of the figures from Borg in Lofoten off northern Norway may have been imported the long way by sea from places like Sorte Muld, Uppåkra or Lundeborg where stylistically very similar figures are found. The fact that two of the gold foils from Borg were found in a post hole of a large building, dated to the Viking Age,[5] does not preclude a connection to an earlier building phase. The reason for – or significance of – re-deposition in the Viking Age falls outside the scope of this paper. I have deliberately concentrated my effort on the iconographic aspects of the gold foils, and hence abstained from discussing the wider implication of their role in the pre-Christian cult (however important). This is in order to avoid over-simplification of this highly complex issue involving important sites like Helgö, Uppåkra, Sorte Muld and Guldhullet (Bornholm).[6]

Die-identical (or stylistically very similar) figures were almost certainly made within a short span of years. This, of course, does not rule out that some figures could have been handed down as "keepsakes" within a family. But it should be remembered that the majority of gold foil figures are *very* fragile – many of them with a weight of less than 0.1 g.

Only exceptionally do we see examples of gold foil figures mounted as pendants or showing wear, in which case the stamped figures always have a backing of a thicker bronze or gold sheet. Many figures – particularly from Sorte Muld – had been folded into small packages (possibly for re-melting) – a fact to remember when discussing their significance and use.

Misreading of iconographic details on the tiny gold foils is easy and has in some cases led to odd and even far-fetched interpretations.[7] Secondary folds or dents in the thin gold foil have not helped. It should be added that none of the gold foils bear inscriptions of any kind.

Die Families

In the same way Alexandra Pesch has defined a number of die-families for the Migration Period bracteates – based primarily on iconographic similarities,[8] this can also be done for the guld-gubbar (Fig. 1). At present, 63 such families are recognised, some

Figure 1. "Die-family" 9, represented at Sorte Muld and Uppåkra. The figures measure from 6 to 9 mm in height. Drawing: Eva Koch. Copyright: Bornholms Museum: License CC BY-NC-ND.

of which are very local while others have a wider distribution.⁹ Die links and/or family links as well as stylistic details indicate that some regional variations could be linked to "workshops" or to individual craftsmen.

Stylistic differences and regional variations in iconographic detail point to three major "provinces" (Fig. 2) that are believed to be relevant for the discussion of the political landscape and early state formation in Scandinavia.¹⁰

Iconographic Analysis

Based on the study of more than 750 different dies and close to 100 individually cut-out or engraved figures, I have registered a number of recurring elements: 1. the orientation of individual

Figure 2. Distribution of gold foil figures. Drawing: M. Watt Copyright: Margrethe Watt 2011, License: CC BY-NC-ND.

figures, 2. physiognomy (primary sexual markings), 3. hairstyle, 4. dress, 5. gesture and posture, and 6. attributes or "insignia" (staff/sceptre, drinking horn, etc.).

The considerable number of different dies allows for a statistical approach, and the combination of iconographic elements is the main key to understanding the gold foil figures. Details of dress and hairstyle are crucial for the determination of, for example, rank and sex. Gestures are important to understanding some of the less tangible "messages" conveyed by the figures.[11] I will not attempt to describe or explain all of these but will point to some examples that are – hopefully – relevant to the theme of the conference.

Motif Groups

The greatest variety is found within the group of single figures from southern Scandinavia, while the appearance and gestures of the widespread man-woman couples is more stereotyped despite numerous minor variations. Hence, the two are treated separately.

The statistical analyses have revealed that the die-families as well as individual dies form a number of motif groups consisting of figures with common iconographic features or a common theme. The most numerous motif-group among the single figures consists of approximately 180 different dies while some of the minor variations can be counted on one hand (Fig. 3a–c).[12]

Within the dominant single-figure motif group, the most detailed male figures display a dress of kaftan-type and a variety of insignia (e.g. staff, neck rings and arm rings) which have a bearing on social status and function in society. These figures have their closest parallels on the helmet plates found in the "royal" burials in Vendel, Valsgärde, Uppsala (Uppland) and Sutton Hoo (England).[13]

Similar "status indicators" are seen on many of the detailed female figures. Judging from fragments of textile and jewellery from contemporary burials, they depict a dress code that had become established among the Germanic elite from the 6th century onwards.[14] Despite the fact that each of the motif-groups also includes figures and figure types which are highly simplified, they still form recognisable stereotypes (Fig. 3c).

Figure 3a–c. Typical male figures from the motif-groups A1–A4, all carrying a long staff. Sorte Muld. Photographer: Kit Weiss (a–b); Lennart Larsen (c). Copyright: Bornholms Museum: License CC BY-NC-ND.

The man-woman pairs form one single motif group with small mostly regional variations in dress and gesture. Despite the fact that individual figures may measure only 6–8 mm, some still show a surprising amount of detail.

Discussion: Historical and Political Backdrop

Few written sources provide direct or indirect information about political or religious conditions in Scandinavia at the time of the production and use of the gold foil figures. Procopius (500–565) refers to kings who – allegedly – had contacts with Theoderic in Ravenna.[15] Both Jordanes (ca. 550) and the later *Origo gentes langobardorum* (643) – in their genealogies – also draw lines back to Scandinavia in an attempt to establish a divine origin for their royal lineage.[16]

Abundant archaeological material from both settlements and burials, not least on Bornholm, in Skåne and in Uppland, show that the Scandinavian "elite" was aware of the political developments in 6th and 7th century Continental Europe, and even appear to have imitated the Frankish concept of *Gefolgschaft*.[17]

Gregory of Tours (538–594), who is an important source for the relationship between Christians and pagans in the 6th century, makes no mention of the pre-Christian cult in southern Scandinavia. It also seems inevitable that news of the spreading Christianity and the ensuing religious conflicts should have filtered through to the pagan South Scandinavian elite.[18]

However, there are recent finds from a locality on Bornholm ("Guldhullet") of female figures, including gold statuettes, some of which have strong sexual connotations, suggesting the survival of an old fertility cult.[19] This combination of gold foils and small three-dimensional figurines forms a marked contrast to the ideals of the *Gefolgschaftskultur* with its warlords and petty kings seen in larger central places like Sorte Muld and Uppåkra.

Iconography and Myth

You may guess already from the title of this paper that I have certain reservations when it comes to identifying particular figures or motif groups with named mythological characters. Similar reservations have been expressed at intervals by others.[20] Archaeologists are trained to look at human beings through objects and faint structures in the soil, while colleagues who have studied history of religion are schooled to analyse the development of human relationships with the "otherworld".[21] When trying to interpret the pictorial content of the gold foils, you constantly find yourself in the challenging position of having to cross the boundaries into other specialist domains with different research traditions.

Understanding Late Antique pictorial language is one thing, but transferring this "understanding" to pre-Christian images is quite another. Here you are constantly faced with the dilemma of whether or not similar iconographic "language" reflects similar *meaning* when comparing the images of a pagan polytheistic cult on one side with 6th century Christianity on the other. In spite of this, I find contemporary written sources and traditions on the Continent – at least in principle – to be a safer point of departure for the interpretation of the imagery on the gold foils, than extrapolating "backwards" – sometimes several hundred years – from the Late Viking Age or the Middle Ages, however tempting this may be.

As an extension of his work on the Migration Period gold bracteates, the German historian Karl Hauck attempted to name certain types of gold foil figures as the natural extension of his work with the figures on the slightly older bracteates, some of which bear an unmistakable resemblance to the gold foils. Rather than entering into a complex discussion of specific gods or other named characters, I prefer, in this paper, just to look at the general *concept* as expressed in the iconographic details.

As indicated earlier all the different dies can be placed in one of the main motif groups – or alternatively in one of the groups of less common variants. In this paper, I have chosen four examples.

1. The Concept of "Warlord" or "King Among the Gods" (Fig. 3 a–c)

This numerically dominant group (with approximately 180 different dies) is first and foremost seen as a reflection of the 6th and 7th century continental *Gefolgschaftskultur* also represented in contemporary aristocratic and royal burials. The fact that many figures within this motif-group are extremely stylised (Fig. 3c) suggests that they represent a well-established iconographic concept. The main dilemma is that in both Late Antique and Early Medieval iconography renderings of "king" and "god" are almost indistinguishable. Hence, at present, I do not feel comfortable attaching names to specific figures within this group, although arguments *have* been put forward for identifying gold foils of this type with Þórr.[22]

The vast majority of figures belonging to this motif-group is concentrated at the two important central sites of Sorte Muld and Uppåkra, the latter associated with the "cult building". The combined archaeological material from both sites shows strong and widespread "international" connections. The figures in this motif group suggest the existence of some form of *Sakralkönigtum* in southern Scandinavia in the 6th and 7th centuries. But the issue is complex, as southern Scandinavia falls into the gap between Continental sources, linguistic evidence and later Norse tradition.[23]

2. "The Seer"

A small "family" of gold foils shows a male figure with a clearly accentuated thumb placed in the mouth (Fig. 4 a–b). This seemingly odd gesture has forerunners in the Late Migration Period

a   **b**

Figure 4a–b. "The seer's thumb" shown by two figures from Sorte Muld (a) and Uppåkra (b). "Die-family" 22. The figures measure 18–19 mm in height. Drawing: Eva Koch (a); M. Watt (b). Copyright: Bornholms Museum: License CC BY-NC-ND.

ornamentation "Style I" as well as on gold bracteates; as far as I am aware, it is unknown in either Roman or Byzantine iconography.

Hilda Ellis Davidsson has convincingly interpreted this gesture, which appears sporadically in parts of northern and western Europe, as illustrating the concept of "the seer's thumb", substantiated in Celtic Britain and Ireland in myths connected with Finn and Taliesin.[24]

I am only aware of a couple of examples where this particular gesture occurs in a clearly Christian context, namely a picture stone from Drumhallagh, Donegal (Ireland), dated to the 7th or 8th century and a 6th century belt buckle of Burgundian type (eastern France/Switzerland), belonging to a group known in the archaeological literature as "prophet buckles" (Fig. 5). In Viking Age Britain and Scandinavia, the gesture is associated with the Sigurd myth.

The gold foil figures belonging to this family also carry a (short) staff – or "wand" – and are shown with their legs crossed in the same manner as on certain gold bracteates.[25] The posture occurs sporadically throughout the Germanic area and may have supernatural and apotropaic undertones.[26]

The iconographic details on this small family of gold foil figures seem to point to someone with special powers – including the ability to see into the future. This ability is shared whether applied

Figure 5. Belt buckle of the so-called "prophet-type" from Eschallens-les-Condemines, Switzerland (6th century). The two figures, facing a large cross and flanked by "beasts", show the "seer's gesture". Drawn by M. Watt from a photograph in Haldimann & Steiner 1996. Licence: CC BY-ND.

to Christian prophets, pagan "soothsayers", Celtic heroes or powerful deities such as Óðinn in his capacity of "seer".

3. "The Seeress"

Attempting to identify the single female gold foil figures with named characters known from Norse mythology takes you into the sphere of the intangible and leaves you with different options, each of which has been discussed repeatedly in the literature: "Lady of the Mead Hall" (carrying a drinking vessel), Freyja who possessed magic, which she – according to the myths – brought with her from the Vanir gods, Valkyries – greeting the fallen heroes with a mead-horn on their arrival in Valhǫll (the latter obviously inspired by the popular interpretation of the so-called "*adventus*-motif" on the Gotland picture stones). Among other options are the Vǫlvir – and even nornir ("Women of Destiny").[27] No doubt, cases can be made for them all; so, we need to look for new details.

Within the group of single female figures, two dies, Uppåkra (U. 4469) and Bornholm ("Melle-1"), are equipped with an unusual combination of hand-held attributes (Fig. 6 a–b). The well preserved (possibly even unused) bronze die from Uppåkra (Fig. 6a) shows a woman who (besides the drinking horn) holds a short downward branching object *as well as* a short slender staff/"wand" (seen below the drinking horn).

Parallels to this combination of attributes are few and far between – and also staggered in time. Iconographically closest is a figure on the well-known picture stone from Gotland, Alskog-Tjängvide I. Here the woman holds – not just a drinking horn in one hand – but an additional branching object in the other. The stone belongs to Sune Lindqvist's groups C–D, now regarded as contemporary and dated to the 9th and 10th centuries.[28]

The gold foil figure "Melle-1" (Fig. 6b) holds what may be interpreted as a staff(?) with short downturned "side-twigs" (seen below the beaker or drinking horn). Though slightly different in appearance, it may well have the same symbolic content.[29] An example of the ambiguity that characterises many of the gold foil figures is a unique *en-face* figure (Sorte Muld-259) seen holding

a   b   c

Figure 6a–c. "Seeresses". a: Bronze die (patrix) from Uppåkra (Skåne). The figure carries a drinking horn, a downward-branching "staff" besides a short thin staff or "wand"(?); b: gold foil figure "Melle-1", Bornholm, with drinking vessel (beaker) and a "wand"(?) with short side branches; c: Gold foil figure from Sorte Muld (die 259), Bornholm, with an "empty" drinking horn, lying on its side. The figures measure from 18 to 23 mm in height. Photo: B. Almgren (a); Nationalmuseet, København (b). Drawing: Eva Koch (c). Copyright: Bornholms Museum: License CC BY-NC-ND.

an obviously empty(!) drinking horn – marked by the fact that it is lying on its side (Fig. 6c). Who drank the contents – the guests in the mead hall or the woman holding the empty horn (with a "magic" potion)?

The combination of the drinking horn with other "identification tags" (the "potion", the "wand" and branching staff) suggests that these figures could be associated, not just with supernatural powers, but more specifically with prophesy or magic.

It is well known that Tacitus refers to Germanic women with prophetic gifts or powers, and in his *Historiae* (IV:61, 65) makes specific mention of a woman Veleda who appears to have played an important part in the *Batavi*-war.[30] Several generations later, written sources also mention pagan seers and witches, who became a persistent "stone in the shoe" for the Christian Church.[31] According to the roughly contemporary Germanic *leges*, consulting such "infamous" women was punishable.[32] Even long after large parts of the Germanic area had converted to Christianity, it still seemed to have been necessary to legislate against "powerful women", who were obviously still regarded as a threat – not just to the church but to society as a whole.

Although few in numbers, I believe that this small group of gold foils is important for understanding the 6th century beliefs and cult in South Scandinavia, as token offerings connected with the wish to foretell (or maybe even influence) the future.[33] However, instead of naming the figures, I prefer to put the emphasis on the *concept of prophesy*.

Strangely common to the "seer" and "seeress" figures are the very small numbers in which they occur compared to the large number of other figures. Why this is so is a question I cannot answer.

4. "The Legally Binding Marriage"

The last motif-group that I wish to comment on shows a man and a woman facing each other. In contrast to the distribution of the single figures, this group occurs throughout Scandinavia and dominates the material in the Swedish and Norwegian "provinces" (Fig. 2). Common to all variations is some degree of physical contact, ranging from an embrace to a light touch (Fig. 7).

In several works Gro Steinsland has connected the motif with *hieros gamos*, and Gerðr and Freyr as the mythical founders of the Ynglinga dynasty, based on the story from *Skírnismál*. In a work from 1997 she similarly associates the man-woman pairs with Óðinn and Skaði as founders of the Ladejarl dynasty – tying it to the later Norwegian tradition surrounding the "Pillars of the High Seat".[34] She also points to the element of fate – in this case the conflict between gods and giants – affecting the future of the royal lineage. Her theories illustrate both the difficulties and complexity of deciphering a motif when stretching an archaeological/ iconographic material to the breaking point.

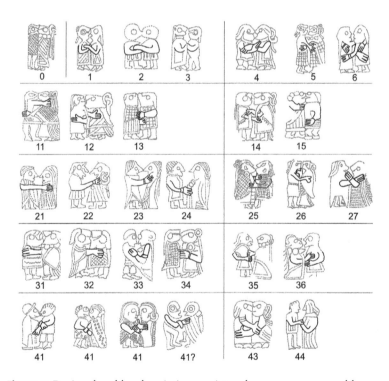

Figure 7. Regional and local variations registered on man-woman gold foil figures. Drawing: M. Watt. Copyright: Margrethe Watt, License: CC-BY-NC-ND.

Both Roman and not least "Germanic" legal practise mention rules for giving hands or touching each other.[35] Social, economic and political interests among the Germanic *elite* required legally binding marriages and betrothals. Rudolf Simek addressed this question some years ago in relation to the man-woman gold foils.[36] His view, with which I agree, is that the gestures shown by the well-dressed man-woman pairs represent the important visible sign of a formal and legally binding ceremony (the *Mundr*-marriage). Despite minor regional variations, I believe that the range (Fig. 7) reflects a widespread tradition, but will not attempt to identify the figure-type with named mythological characters – certainly not *Gerðr* and *Freyr* whose union (according to "Germanic law") would be regarded as an unacceptable common law marriage.

Conclusion

The aim of this paper is to give an impression of the complexity of the pictorial language shown on the tiny gold foil figures and point out possible pitfalls, whether you approach the material from the post-Roman European Continent or from later Norse literature and mythology. I realise that the few examples I have chosen leave many options which are impossible to discuss fully in a short paper.

Religion and cult practises are basically resilient, but must first and foremost be expected to echo socio-political changes at any given time. It is my belief that the gold foils reflect the establishment of petty kingdoms throughout the Germanic area towards the end of the Migration Period. This almost certainly resulted in a centralisation of the cult practise and introduction of new myths (including additions to the pantheon).[37]

Notes

1. Melle 1725; Sjöborg 1791; Mackeprang 1943; Watt 1992; 2004; 2015a, b.

2. E.g. Hauck 1992; Steinsland 1989.

3. Adamsen *et al.* 2008.

4. Lamm 2004; Watt 2015a:153; Watt *forthcoming.*

5. E.g. Stamsø Munch 2003.

6. Nielsen & Watt 2019.

7. Watt *forthcoming.*

8. Pesch 2007.

9. Watt *forthcoming.*

10. Cf. Høilund Nielsen 1991; Jørgensen 1991; Helgesson 2002.

11. Watt 2007; 2015a–b.

12. For diagrams showing all motif-groups see Watt 2015a or Watt 2015b.

13. Stolpe & Arne 1912; Bruce-Mitford 1978; Hauck 1981.

14. Watt 2011; Mannering 2006:213; Mannering 2017.

15. Künzl 2008:97.

16. Hedeager 1996; 1997.

17. Nørgård Jørgensen 1999:156.

18. von Padberg 2011:606.

19. Watt 2015b:188.

20. E.g. Price 2006.

21. E.g. Helmbrecht 2015.

22. Hauck 1993:420.

23. E.g. Sundqvist 2004:279.

24. Ellis Davidsson 1989; MacKillop 2005:225. The gesture should not be confused with the *dextera elata* – the raised right hand – seen on, for example, imperial coins and medals.

25. Hauck 1992, Fig. 60 & 61; Pesch 2007:135, "Formularfamilie B10".

26. Schmidt-Wiegand 1998:503.

27. E.g. Enright 1988; Simek 1993; 2002.

28. Lindqvist 1942, Taf. 57; Imer 2012.

29. Other examples of female figures holding a branching staff or are known from both barbarian imitations of 2nd century Roman coins (Bursche 2009) and from an imitation medallion from Aneby (Småland) (*Ikonographischer Katalog*, no. 14). On a Viking Age picture stone from Kirk Michael on the Isle of Man a woman dressed in a long garment is seen holding a staff with "leaves" at the upper end and a branching "root" at the other. The latter has been interpreted as a *Vǫlva* (Penz et al. 2009, Fig. 13).

30. Simek 1993:36; Reichert 1995:502.

31. Gregory of Tours: *Historia Francorum* V:14.

32. E.g. *Pactus Leges Salicae* (6th century):XIX, LIV; Lombard Laws of Luitprand (AD 727):84–85.

33. Watt, *forthcoming*.

34. Steinsland 1989; 1997.

35. Schmidt-Wiegand 1991; 1992.

36. Simek 2002.

37. Watt 2015b.

References

Primary sources

Gregory of Tours, *Historia Francorum*. Thorpe, L. 1974. *Gregory of Tours. The History of the Franks*. Translated by L. Thorpe. London: Penguin Classics.

Lombard Laws. Fischer Drew, Katherine. 1991. *Lombard Laws. Translated and Edited by Katherine Fischer Drew*. Philadelphia: University of Pennsylvania Press.

Pactus leges Salicae. Lex Salica. Fischer Drew, Katherine. 1991. *The Laws of the Salian Franks. Translated and with an Introduction by Katherine Fischer Drew*. Philadelphia: University of Pennsylvania Press.

Secondary literature

Adamsen, C. et al. (eds.). 2008. *Sorte Muld*. Wormianum, Kulturarvsstyrelsen. Kulturarvsstyrelsen (English language edition 2009 – *Sorte Muld*. *Wealth, Power and Religion at an Iron Age Central Settlement on Bornholm*). Rønne: Bornholms Museum.

Bruce-Mitford, R.L.S. 1978. *The Sutton Hoo Ship-Burial II. Arm and Armour and Regalia*. London: British Museum.

Bursche, A. 2009. Coins. In L. Boye & U. Lund Hansen (eds.). *Wealth and Prestige. An Analysis of Rich Graves from Late Roman Iron Age on Eastern Zealand*. Studier I Astronomi. Nyere Tid. Arkæologi 2. Denmark: Kroppedal, 185–192.

Ellis Davidsson, H. 1989. The Seer's Thumb. In H. E. Davidsson (ed.). *The Seer in Celtic and other Traditions*. Edinburgh: Donald, 66–78.

Enright, M. J. 1988. Lady with a Mead-Cup. Ritual, Group Cohesion and Hierarchy in the Germanic Warband. In *Frühmittelalterliche Studien* 22, 170–203.

Haldimann, M.-A. & Steiner, L. 1996. Les céramiques funéraires du haut Moyen Age en terre vaudoise. In *Jahrbuch der Schweizerischen Gesellschaft für Ur- und Frühgeschichte* 79, 143–193.

Hauck, K. 1981. Die bildliche Wiedergabe von Götter- und Heldenwaffen im Norden seit der Wölkerwanderungszeit. In R. Schmidt-Wiegand (ed.). *Arbeiten zur Frühmittelalterforschung 1. Wörter und Sachen im Licht der Bezeichnungsforschung*, Berlin & New York: Walter de Gruyter, 169–269.

Hauck, K. 1992. Frühmittelalterliche Bildüberlieferung und der organisierte Kult. In K. Hauck (ed.). *Der historische Horizont der Götterbild-Amulette aus der Übergangsepoche von der Spätantike zum frühen Mittelalter*. Abhandlungen der Akademie der Wissenschaften in Göttingen, Philologisch-Historische Klasse, Dritte Folge, 433–574.

Hauck, K. 1993. Die bremische Überlieferung zur Götter-Dreiheit Altuppsalas und die bornholmische Goldfolien aus Sorte Muld. In *Frühmittelalterliche Studien* 27 Berlin & New York, 409–479.

Hedeager, L. 1996. Myter og materiel kultur. Den nordiske oprindelsesmyte i det tidligt kristne Europa. In *TOR* 28, 217–234.

Hedeager, L. 1997. *Skygger af en anden virkelighed. Oldnordiske myter*. København: Samleren.

Helgesson, B. 2002. *Järnålderns Skåne. Samhälle, centra och regioner*. Uppåkrastudier 5. Acta Archaeologica Lundensia. Stockholm: Almqvist & Wiksell.

Helmbrecht, M. 2015. Bild und Bildträger während der Vendelzeit. Probleme und Möglichkeiten der Deutung von Bildern aus einer Kultur mit mündlicher Überlieferung. In Heizmann & S. Oehrl (eds). *Bilddenkmäler zur germanischen Götter- und Heldensage*. Ergänzungsbände zum Reallexikon der Germanischen Altertumskunde 91, 181–218.

Høilund Nielsen, K. 1991. Centrum og periferi i 6.–8. årh. Territoriale studier af dyrestil og kvindesmykker i yngre germansk jernalder i Syd- og Østskandinavien. In P. Mortensen & B. M. Rasmussen (eds). *Fra Stamme til Stat i Danmark. 2: Høvdingesamfund og Kongemagt*. Jysk Arkæologisk Selskabs Skrifter 22(2), 127–153.

Ikonographischer Katalog: Axboe M. et al. (eds). 1985–89. *Die Goldbrakteaten der Völkerwanderungszeit. Ikonographischer Katalog 1–3*. Münstersche Mittelalterschriften 24/1–3. München: Wilhelm Fink Verlag.

Imer, L.M. 2012. The Viking Period Gotlandic Picture Stones. A Chronological Revision. In *Gotländskt Arkiv* 84, 115–118.

Jørgensen, L. 1991. Våbengrave og krigeraristokrati. Etableringen af en centralmagt på Bornholm i det 6.–8. årh. e. Kr. In P. Mortensen & B. M. Rasmussen (eds). *Fra Stamme til stat i Danmark 2. Høvdingesamfund og Kongemagt*. Jysk Arkæologisk Selskabs Skrifter 22(2), 109–124.

Künzl, E. 2008. *Die Germanen. Geheimnisvolle Völker aus dem Norden*. Stuttgart: Theiss.

Lamm, J.P. 2004. Figural Gold Foils Found in Sweden. A Study Based on the Discoveries from Helgö. In H. Clarke & K. Lamm (eds). *Excavations at Helgö XVI. Exotic and Sacral Finds from*

Helgö. Stockholm: Kungl. Vitterhets Historie och Antikvitets Akademien, 41–142.

Lindqvist, S. 1942. *Gotlands Bildsteine II*. Stockholm.

Mackeprang, M.B. 1943. Om de såkaldte 'guldgubber'. In *Fra Nationalmuseets Arbejdsmark* 1943, 69–76.

MacKillop, J. 2005. *Myths and Legends of the Celts*. London: Penguin Books.

Mannering, U. 2006. *Billeder af dragt. En analyse af påklædte figurer fra yngre jernalder i Skandinavien*. Ph.D. diss. København: Københavns Universitet.

Mannering, U. 2017. *Iconic Costumes. Scandinavian Late Iron Age Costume Iconography*. Oxford: Oxbow Books.

Melle, I. A. 1725. *Commentatiuncula de simulacris aureis, quae in Boringholmia Maris Balthici insula, agris eruuntur*. Lübeck, Typis Io. Nicolai Thvnii.

Nielsen, F.O. & Watt, M. 2019. *Acta Archaeologica* 89, 77–89.

Nørgård Jørgensen, A. 1999. Waffen und Gräber. Typologische und chronologische Studien zu Skandinavische Waffengräbern 520/30 bis 900 n.Chr. In *Nordiske Fortidsminder*. Serie B 17.

Padberg, L. von 2011. Reaktionsformen des Polytheismus im Norden af die Expansion des Christentums im Spiegel der Goldbrakteaten. In W. Heizmann & M. Axboe (eds). *Die Goldbrakteaten der Völkerwanderungszeit. Auswertung und Neufunde*. Ergänzungsbände zum Reallexikon der Germanischen Altertumskunde 40. Berlin, New York: De Gruyter, 603–634.

Pentz, P. et al. 2009. Kong Haralds vølve. In *Nationalmuseets Arbejdsmark* 2009, 215–231.

Pesch, A. 2007. Die Goldbrakteaten der Völkerwanderungszeit. Thema und Variation. In *Ergänzungsbände zum Reallexikon der Germanischen Altertumskunde* 36. Berlin, New York: De Gruyter.

Price, N. 2006. What's in a Name? An Archaeological Identity Crisis for the Norse Gods (and Some of their Friends). In A. Andrén et al.

(eds.). *Old Norse Religion in Long-Term Perspectives. Origins, Changes, and Interactions. An international Conference in Lund, Sweden, June 3–7, 2004.* Vägar till Midgård 8. Lund: Nordic Academic Press, 179–183.

Reichert, H. 1995. Frau. In *Reallexikon der Germanischen Altertumskunde* 9. Berlin, New York: De Gruyter, 477–508.

Schmidt-Wiegand, R. 1991. Mit Hand und Mund. In *Frühmittelalterliche Studien* 25, 283–299.

Schmidt-Wiegand, R. 1992. Umarmung. In *Handwörterbuch zur deutschen Rechtsgeschichte* 34, 419–421.

Schmidt-Wiegand, R. 1998. Gebärde. Gebärdensprache im Recht. In *Reallexikon der Germanischen Altertumskunde* 10. Berlin, New York: De Gruyter, 500–504.

Simek, R. 1993. *Dictionary of Northern Mythology.* (English revised edition of *Lexikon der germanischen Mythologie* 1984. Stuttgart, Alfred Kröner Verlag). Cambridge: Brewer.

Simek, R. 2002. Goddesses, Mothers, Dísir. Iconography and Interpretation of the Female Deity in Scandinavia in the First Millenium. In R. Simek & W. Heizmann (eds).*Mythological Women. Studies in Memory of Lotte Motz (1922–1997).* Studia Medievalia Septentrionalia 7. Wien: Fassbaender, 93–123.

Sjöborg, N.H. 1791. *Topographia paroeciæ Raflunda et monumentorum quæ circæ sunt.* Lund.

Stamsø Munch, G. 2003. Borg as a Pagan Centre. In G. S. Munch et al. (eds). *Borg in Lofoten. A Chieftain's Farm in North Norway.* Arkeologisk Skriftserie 1.Trondheim: Tapir, 253–263.

Steinsland, G. 1989. *Det hellige bryllup og norrøn kongeideologi. En analyse af hierogami-myten i Skírnismál, Ynglingatal, Háleygjatal og Hyndluljóð.* Oslo: Solum.

Steinsland, G. 1997. Die mythologische Grundlage für die nordische Königsideologie. Germanische Religionsgeschichte. In *Ergänzungsband zum Reallexikon der Germanischen Altertumskunde* 5. Berlin, New York: De Gruyter, 736–751

Stolpe, H. & Arne, T.J. 1912. *Graffältet vid Vendel.* Stockholm: Kungl. Vitterhets historie och antikvitetsakademien.

Sundqvist, O. 2004. Sakralkönigtum. C. Skandinavische Quellen. In *Reallexikon der Germanischen Altertumskunde* 26. Berlin, New York: de Gruyter, 279–293.

Watt, M. 1992. Die Goldblechfiguren ('guldgubber') aus Sorte Muld, Bornholm. In K. Hauck (ed.). *Der historische Horizont der Götterbild-Amulette aus der Übergangsepoche von der Spätantike zum frühen Mittelalter.* Abhandlungen der Akademie der Wissenschaften in Göttingen, Philologische-Historische Klasse, Dritte Folge 200. Göttingen: Akademie der Wissenschaften in Göttingen, 195–227.

Watt, M. 2004. The Gold-Figure Foils (*"Guldgubbar"*) from Uppåkra. In L. Larsson (ed.). *Continuity for Centuries. A Ceremonial Building and its Context at Uppåkra, Southern Sweden.* Uppåkrastudier 10, Acta Archaeologica Lundensia. Stockholm: Almqvist & Wiksell, 167–221.

Watt, M. 2007. Kan man tyde guldgubbernes gestussprog? (Gold foil figures and gesture language). In I. Nordgren (ed.). *Kult, guld och makt. Ett tvärvetenskapligt symposium i Götene.* Skara: Historieforum Götaland, 133–148.

Watt, M. 2011. Images of the Female Elite in 6th–7th Century Scandinavia. In D. Quast (ed.). *Weibliche Eliten in der Frühgeschichte.* RGZM Tagungen 10. Mainz: Schnell & Steiner, 229–250.

Watt, M. 2015a. A Christian "Fingerprint" on 6th Century South Scandinavian Iconography? In Heizmann & Oehrl (eds). *Bilddenkmäler zur germanischen Götter- und Heldensage.* Ergänzungsbände zum Reallexikon der Germanischen Altertumskunde 91. Berlin, New York: de Gruyter, 153–180.

Watt, M. 2015b. "Christian" Gestures and Fertility Cult(?) Reflected in the Iconography of 6th Century Southern Scandinavia. In C. Rühmann & V. Brieske (eds). *Dying Gods – Religious Beliefs in Northern and Eastern Europe in the Time of Christianisation.*

Neue Studien zur Sachsenforschung. Band 5. Hannover: Niedersächsisches Landesmuseum, 177–190.

Watt *forthcoming*. (working title): Sorte Muld. Guldgubberne og Ibskerbygden. In *Nordiske Fortidsminder*. Købehavn: Kgl. nordiske oldskriftselskab.

Response

Olof Sundqvist
Stockholm University

Margrethe Watt is one of the world's leading experts on gold foil figures (Swedish "guldgubbar") with plenty of publications on this topic.[1] She has been working with this material for almost thirty years and she knows it in great detail. In the present article she focuses on the relationship between the gold foils and Old Norse mythology.

In what follows I will concentrate on the fourth group of foils, reflecting the concept of "The legally binding marriage". This refers to gold foils with a man and a woman facing each other. Common to all of these foils is some degree of physical contact between the male and the female, ranging from an embrace to a light touch. This motif is known from all three "provinces" (see Watt's text above). Gro Steinsland has connected it with ruler ideology and a hieros gamos between the god Freyr and the giantess Gerðr.[2] Her suggestion was based on Magnus Olsen's interpretation of the "double-figures" found at Klepp in Rogaland in western Norway as a reflection of the mythical "marriage" between Freyr and Gerðr as it appears in *Skírnismál*.[3] According to Snorri Sturluson's *Ynglinga saga* Ch. 10, this couple were the mythical founders of the Ynglinga dynasty. Their sexual union resulted namely in a son called Fjǫlnir, who was the first king in this family.[4] This strange hieros gamos between a god and a giantess thus has, according to Steinsland, ideological implications. She supported her argument with the fact that gold foils of this type often appear at aristocratic settlements, in halls and more precisely in the area of the high-seat.

Watt is sceptical to both Olsen's and Steinsland's mythical-ideological interpretations. Based on an argument originally presented by Rudolf Simek,[5] she argues that the gestures shown on these gold foils actually represent a formal and legally binding ceremony, the so called mundr-marriage, which is mentioned in legal texts and manuscript illustrations from later centuries, such as *Sachsenspiegel* and the medieval Swedish and Norwegian Provincial Laws from the 13th century or later. They mention and sometimes illustrate the rules for giving hands and touching each other when legally binding couples together in marriage. In this case, Watt accepts that medieval sources can be used when interpreting Merovingian Period iconography. Watt states, however, that she will not attempt to identify the figure-type appearing in this group with named mythological characters, "certainly not Gerðr and Freyr whose union (according to "Germanic law") would be regarded as an unacceptable common law marriage". In *Skírnismál* it seems as if Freyr took his bride with force and not in a legal way. The union between a god and a giantess could also be regarded as a misalliance against social norms.[6]

According to Watt, the myth about Freyr's courtship and unlawful marriage to the giantess Gerðr does not fit with the body language of "the double figures". Hence, both Watt and Simek[7] reject the possibility that these foils reflect cultic aspects related to Freyr. To a certain extent I must agree with them in this argument and I accept the idea that the foils may actually represent human couples too. I have, however, also some objections against Watt's (and Simek's) reasoning. When stating that the foils with the "double-figure" relate to the concept of "The legally binding marriage", the interpretation of the gestures and body language is dependent on legal sources written 500 years after the time when the foils were produced. The concept of "The legally binding marriage" used by Watt actually requires that there were laws or at least legal customs which were common in all Scandinavia during the Merovingian Period. "The double figures" appear namely in all three provinces where gold foils have been found, from Borg at Lofoten in the North to Gudme-Lundeborg on Fyn in the South. In order to understand the body language on these foils, the judicial rituals must have been uniform over this large area and stable over time for more than 500 years. In my opinion, we still cannot rule out that the couple embracing each other refers to a simpler expression of intimacy with no legal implications, or something else.

My second objection concerns Watt's (and Simek's) interpretations of the mythical beings in a more general sense. Should we ever expect that the god Freyr and the mythical being Gerðr were conceived in the same way during the 6th or 7th century as in the Eddic poems found in manuscripts from the 13th and 14th centuries written down in Christian contexts? The myths and the conception of mythical beings most likely changed over time. The poem *Skírnismál*, which contains the myth about Freyr and Gerðr, is usually regarded as a young lay and it has a literary character.[8] For instance, Daniel Sävborg[9] states that "*Skírnismál* should be interpreted as a high medieval poem, composed as pure entertainment by a person conscious of the literary fashion of his time". In a general sense, I agree with this statement, even if I think that it is possible that this "literary account" may be based on an older mythical tradition related to some type of hieros gamos and ruler ideology. It is likely that the union between the god Freyr and his bride (if it existed) had a different mythical context and was conceived in another way during the Merovingian Period and Viking Age compared to the one we may find in *Skírnismál*, *Gylfaginning* and *Ynglinga saga*.

We may actually partly follow this tradition back to Early Viking Age. The information in *Ynglinga saga* Ch. 10 that Freyr and his wife Gerðr had a son called Fjǫlnir can partly be supported by the 9th century poem *Ynglingatal*. In this poem it is mentioned that the kinsmen of Fjǫlnir were regarded as descendants of Freyr. In the stanza about Alrekr and Eiríkr the whole family is called *Freys afspringr*, 'Freyr's offspring', while Egill is *týsǫttungr*, 'descendant of the god'. The Uppsala king Aðils is described as *Freys ǫttungr*, 'Freyr's descendant' and Ingjaldr, finally, is designated *goðkynningr*, 'of divine descent'. In my opinion the reliable sources thus tell us that the Uppsala family reckoned its origin from Freyr, the *blótgoð svía*, who was praised as the Ynglingar's particular god. It is harder to identify the mother. The tradition found in *Ynglingatal* implicitly requires that Freyr had a wife, whoever she was.

There is actually an argument supporting the notion that some foils with the double figures may have represented Freyr and his bride during the Late Iron Age, at least in eastern Scandinavia. The distribution of theophoric place-names in the Lake Mälaren region indicates that the cult of the god Freyr was very important in the south-western part of the area, i.e. south Fjädrundaland, south Västmanland and Södermanland.[10] This area corresponds quite well to the places where gold foil figures have been found in this region, i.e. Husby (Glanshammar), Eskilstuna, Ultuna, Helgö, and Svintuna (Bodaviken). The phallic Rällinge statuette and the three phallic figures from Lunda, which most likely represent Freyr, may also be connected to this area. Adam of Bremen thus states in the 11th century about the image of Freyr in the Uppsala-temple: "His likeness, too, they fashion with an immense phallus" (*Cuius etiam simulacrum fingunt cum ingenti priapo*).[11] In my opinion, Steinsland's interpretation of the foils is thus possible, as long as we relate these objects to this geographic area. The mythical wedding on these foils may therefore sometimes be related to Freyr and his bride, perhaps a Merovingian Period conception of Gerðr. Moreover, Adam of Bremen states that sacrifices should be made to Freyr when celebrating wedding: "If plague and famine threaten, a libation is poured to the idol Thor; if war, to Wodan; if marriages are to be celebrated, to Fricco [Freyr]" (*Si pestis et fames imminet, Thor ydolo lybatur, si bellum, Wodani, si nuptiae celebrandae sunt, Fricconi*).[12] This indicates that Freyr in the 11th century Lake Mälaren area had a special relationship to marriages. Whether he had that 300 years earlier is, of course, uncertain.

It is possible, however, that the couple on the foils from Trøndelag represented another divine couple. Perhaps the couple on the foils from Mære could be related to Óðinn and Skaði, as suggested by Gro Steinsland,[13] since these mythical beings, according to *Háleygjatal*, were regarded as the divine parents of the Lade Earls. One could also relate the couple depicted on the gold foil figures to Þorgerðr Hǫlgabrúðr and Hǫlgi, who may have been considered to be the original mythical ancestors of the noble kin from Halogaland. This assumption presupposes that the Lade Earls had some influence on the sanctuary at Mære as early as the Merovingian Period. This idea must be considered somewhat uncertain. If gold foils were still used during the 8th century, this theory is at least possible. It is possible too that in an earlier period there may have been some other noble ruling families in Mære and Trøndelag, who regarded Freyr and his bride or another divine couple as their mythical ancestors. Later

Óðinn and Skaði were regarded as the mythical parents of the Haleygja kin. It should be noticed that these figures may have a double function, i.e. to memorize an aristocratic wedding between the ruling couple, and in the same time they could symbolize a divine spousal. I thus agree with Rudolf Simek when he states thus:

> Wir können die Funktion der Doppelgubber also als Opfer oder Memorialakt innerhalb einer dynastischen Hochzeit interpretieren, wobei die Identität der dargestellten Personen gleichzeitig als das irdische Fürstenpaar als auch ihrer mythologischen Vorbilder, also eines der Götterpaare wie Thor und Sif oder etwa Odin und Frigg ansehen.[14]

His next statement is however more uncertain and to a certain extent invalid when seen from the perspective of a historian of religions:

> Mit sicherheit auszuschließen sind als Vorbilder einer dynastischen Hochzeit inzestuöse Verbindungen wie Freyr und Freya oder gewaltsam herbeigeführte und unstandesgemäße Liaisons wie die von Freyr und Gerðr.[15]

In the history of religions, it is not odd that a mythical sister and brother, or a mother and son, had a sexual relationship. We meet several incestuous relationships in, for instance, the context of Greek myths.[16] The negative attitude to the incestuous relationship between Freyr and Freyja in the sources may thus be a consequence of a Christian impact on them.[17] In my opinion, moreover, we do not have to exclude that the union on the foils was between Freyr and his bride, perhaps the Merovingian Period conception of Gerðr, since this relation could have had another character during that period compared with the one we meet in the high medieval texts.

Even if I do not completely agree with Watt when interpreting the "double-figure", I must underline that her presentation above is probably the most solid and useful we have so far concerning these materials. Her interpretations of the foils are often balanced and convincing, and they are based on a great knowledge. Watt's scholarship is a very important contribution, not only to archaeology, but also to the history of religions.

Notes

1. See e.g. Watt 1992; 2004; 2007; 2011; 2015a; 2015b.

2. See e.g. Steinsland 1990; 1991; 2000.

3. Cf. Olsen 1909.

4. In *Ynglinga saga* Ch.10, Snorri states thus: "His wife was called Gerðr Gymisdóttir. Their son was called Fjǫlnir. (*Gerðr Gymisdóttir hét kona hans. Sonr þeira hét Fjǫlnir*)." This information does not appear elsewhere. *Hyndluljóð* st. 30 informs us, however, that Gerðr, Gymir's daughter, was married to Freyr (*Freyr átti Gerði*) and *Lokasenna* st. 42 mentions thus: "With gold you had Gymir's daughter bought (*Gulli keypta léztu Gymis dóttur*)".

5. Simek 2002.

6. Cf. Simek 2002; 2014:76

7. Simek 2002; 2014.

8. E.g. von See et al. 1997:64–65.

9. Sävborg 2006:339.

10. Sundqvist 2016.

11. Adam of Bremen IV, 26.

12. Adam of Bremen IV, 27.

13. Steinsland 1991.

14. Simek 2014:76.

15. Simek 2014:76.

16. See e.g. Burkert 1985:219–220.

17. This attitude can be seen in late texts such as *Ynglinga saga* Ch. 4 and *Lokasenna* st. 32 and 36.

References

Primary sources

Adam of Bremen. *Magistri Adam Bremensis Gesta Hammaburgensis Ecclesiae Pontificium*. Schmeidler, B. 1917. *Magistri Adam*

Bremensis Gesta Hammaburgensis Ecclesiae Pontificium. Scriptores
rerum germanicarum in usum scholarum. Ex Monumentis Germaniae Historicis. Editio Tertia. Hanover, Leipzig.

────── Tschan, F. J. 2002 (1959). *History of the Archbishops of
Hamburg-Bremen.* Trans. F. J. Tschan. New York: Columbia
University Press.

Edda. Neckel, Gustaf & Kuhn, Hans. 1983 (1914). *Die Lieder des
Codex Regius. Nebst verwandten Denkmälern.* Band 1. Text. (Ed.)
G. Neckel, 5. verbesserte Auflage von H. Kuhn. Heidelberg: Carl
Winter Universitätsverlag.

────── Larrington, Caroline. 1996. *The Poetic Edda.* A new translation by Carolyne Larrington. Oxford: Oxford University Press.

Hyndlolióð, see *Edda.*

Lokasenna, see *Edda.*

Snorri Sturluson, *Heimskringla.* Bjarni Aðalbjarnarson. 1979 (1941,
1945, 1951). *Heimskringla.* I–III. Íslenzk fornrit XXVI–XXVIII.
Reykjavík: Hið Íslenzka Fornritafélag.

────── Hollander, L. M. 1964. *Heimskringla. History of the Kings of
Norway.* Trans. L. M. Hollander. Austin: University of Texas.

Ynglinga saga, see Snorri Sturluson, *Heimskringla.*

Secondary literature

Burkert, W. 1985. *Greek Religion.* Orig. title *Griechische Religion der
archaischen und klassischen Epoche.* Trans. J. Raffan. Cambridge:
Harvard University Press.

Olsen, M. 1909. Fra gammalnorsk myte og kulthus. *Maal og minne,*
17–36.

See, Klaus von *et al.* 1997. *Edda: Kommentar zu den Liedern der
Edda,* 2. Heidelberg: Winter.

Simek, Rudolf. 2002. Goddesses, Mothers, Dísir. Iconography and
Interpretation of the Female Deity in Scandinavia in the First
Millenium. In R. Simek & W. Heizmann (eds). *Mythological*

Women. Studies in Memory of Lotte Motz (1922–1997). Studia Medievalia Septentrionalia 7. Wien: Fassbaender, 93–123.

Simek, Rudolf. 2014 (2003). *Religion und Mythologie der Germanen.* Darmstadt.

Steinsland, G. 1990. De nordiske gullblekk med parmotiv og norrøn fyrsteideologi. Et tolkningsforslag. In *Collegium Medievale* I. Vol. 3. Oslo, 73–94.

Steinsland, G. 1991. *Det hellige bryllup og norrøn kongeideologi. En analyse av hierogami-myten i Skírnismál, Ynglingatal, Háleygjatal og Hyndluljóð.* Oslo.

Steinsland, G. 2000. *Den hellige kongen. Om religion og herskermakt fra vikingtid til middelalder.* Oslo.

Sävborg, Daniel. 2006. Love among Gods and Men. Skírnismál and its Tradition. In Anders Andrén; Kristina Jennbert; Catharina Raudvere (eds.). *Old Norse Religion in Long-Term Perspectives. Origins, Changes, and Interactions: An International Conference in Lund, Sweden, June 3–7, 2004.* Vägar till Midgård, 8. Lund: Nordic Academic Press.

Watt, M. 1992. Die Goldblechfiguren ('guldgubber') aus Sorte Muld, Bornholm. In K. Hauck (ed.). *Der historische Horizont der Götterbild-Amulette aus der Übergangsepoche von der Spätantike zum frühen Mittelalter.* Abhandlungen der Akademie der Wissenschaften in Göttingen, Philologische-Historische Klasse, Dritte Folge 200. Göttingen: Akademie der Wissenschaften in Göttingen, 195–227.

Watt, M. 2004. The Gold-Figure Foils (Guldgubbar) from Uppåkra. In L. Larsson (ed.). *Continuity for Centuries – A Ceremonial Building and its Context at Uppåkra, Southern Sweden.* Acta Archaelogica Lundensia series in 8o, No. 48. Lund, 167–222.

Watt, M. 2007. Kan man tyde guldgubbernes gestussprog? In I. Nordgren (ed.). *Kult guld och makt, ett tvärvetenskapligt symposium i Götene.* Göteborg.

Watt, M. 2011. Images of the Female Elite in 6th–7th Century Scandinavia. In D. Quast (ed.). *Weibliche Eliten in der Frühgeschichte.* RGZM Tagungen 10. Mainz: Schnell & Steiner, 229–250.

Watt, M. 2015a. A Christian "Fingerprint" on 6th Century South Scandinavian Iconography? In Heizmann & Oehrl (eds). *Bilddenkmäler zur germanischen Götter- und Heldensage.* Ergänzungsbände zum Reallexikon der Germanischen Altertumskunde 91. Berlin, New York: de Gruyter, 153–180.

Watt, M. 2015b."Christian" Gestures and Fertility Cult(?) Reflected in the Iconography of 6th Century Southern Scandinavia. In C. Rühmann & V. Brieske (eds). *Dying Gods. Religious Beliefs in Northern and Eastern Europe in the Time of Christianisation.* Neue Studien zur Sachsenforschung. Band 5. Hannover: Niedersächsisches Landesmuseum, 177–190.

PART III:
MYTHS AND LIVED RELIGION

Finitude: Human and Animal Sacrifice in a Norse Setting

Christina Fredengren and Camilla Löfqvist
Stockholm University

Introduction

Most often, and traditionally, sacrifice is seen as being used in communication with the divine.[1] The practice of sacrifice may be a way of relating to the spirits of particular parts of the landscape and works to make selected places more holy. Sacrifice can also, for example, be understood as the process where some human and non-human others are selected, treated elsewise and rendered killable. Hence, this process deals with the management of relations between different bodies, but also with the exercise of power and control of the life/death boundary, where some bodies are given up in order for others to prosper. In this way, sacrifice is a technique that can be enrolled in what is called Necropolitics[2] i.e. in the exercise of political, social and religious powers that decides who should be killed and die. Also, Agamben[3] writes of how early Roman law regulated sacrifice and killability, and by othering some people, created states of exception.

As Brink has mentioned,[4] sacrifice of different kinds is evidenced in written sources such as the Guta Law. Sacrificial practices, or blót, were seemingly discussed as the church in the Middle Ages saw it necessary to ban them. Of particular importance in the Old Norse cognitive landscapes were lakes and springs that from time to time received depositions of artefacts even in Viking times and possibly in the Medieval Period.[5] However, the archaeological evidence for human and animal sacrifice has not always been forthcoming in a straightforward way and there is a need to

How to cite this book chapter:
Fredengren, C. & Löfqvist, C. 2019. Finitude: Human and Animal Sacrifice in a Norse Setting. In: Wikström af Edholm, K., Jackson Rova, P., Nordberg, A., Sundqvist, O. & Zachrisson, T. (eds.) *Myth, Materiality, and Lived Religion: In Merovingian and Viking Scandinavia*. Pp. 225–268. Stockholm: Stockholm University Press. DOI: https://doi.org/10.16993/bay.i. License: CC-BY.

discuss what types of deposition qualify as sacrifices. This paper publishes some of the results of the research project *The Water of the Times* that has mapped and radiocarbon dated human and animal remains depositions in wet contexts in Sweden. The aim of the project is to understand what effects these depositions had during the Late Bronze and Iron Ages and to investigate what entangled relationships between human, animals, environment and the divine that came into being at different times through these.

The project deals with the following questions:

- where and when the practice was common
- who was considered killable and deposited in different periods
- how they were treated in life and death
- what effects these depositions may have had on the transformation of society

The current paper focuses on depositions of human and animal remains in waters and wetlands in the wider Uppland region, where this archaeological material can feed into discussions of sacrifice and pre-Christian myth and religion (and possibly even have a bearing on post-conversion matters as indicated by some late radiocarbon dates). An overview of this material can be found in Fredengren 2015,[6] where the general occurrences of skeletal remains depositions and dates were published, thereby dealing mostly with the question of when and where the practice was common. Fredengren and Löfqvist[7] provide a case-study of the finds from Torresta in Uppland, where human and animal remains were deposited in the watery environment at a rock-art site during the Bronze Age and Roman Iron Age. The current paper adds a handful of new dates that have come in during the research process and focuses more on presenting evidence necessary for dealing with the questions of who was deposited. It also looks at how these depositions can fine-tune and add to the discussion of sacrifice in Old Norse religion and politics. Particularly, it centres on how such depositions create, change, or maintain particular

relations between humans, animals, the wetland environment and
possibly also the divine.

Research History

At least since Glob,[8] bog bodies have been understood through
Tacitus' writings. They have been interpreted either as slaves that
were killed and sacrificed after having attended to the goddess
Nerthus, or offenders executed and deposited in bogs after crimes
of shame. Hence, the written sources are used both to provide
information on their identity as well as reasons why these depositions took place. Furthermore, Tacitus portrays bogs as places
away from the public and that this location would make them
suitable for receiving the bodies of the disgraced. More recent
bog body research often concentrates on the deposited individuals with interesting results.[9] Classical bog bodies such as the
Grauballe Man come to us as individual icons, both due to the
quality of preservation and the way they are analysed and discussed. This current paper deals with skeletal remains from
watery places such as lakes, rivers, streams and bogs. It provides
a material that includes both human and animal remains from a
number of different places in Uppland. Instead of focusing on one
individual, the research deals with human and animal collections
of bodily remains.

Bog bodies are mainly associated with countries such as
Denmark, the Netherlands, Britain and Ireland. Ravn[10] has established that 145 out of Denmark's approximately 560 bog bodies date to the Late Bronze Age and Early Iron Age, where most
belong to the Pre-Roman Iron Age. Fabech's[11] reasoning about
the use of human, animal and food sacrifices (named fertility
sacrifices) in wetlands also underlines that depositions of human
remains in wetlands were carried out mainly during the earliest
Iron Age. In that paper it is argued that there would have been a
shift in religious manifestation between the Pre-Roman Iron Age
and the Migration/Merovingian Periods, and seemingly fertility
and war-booty sacrifices in wetlands ceased and the cult moved
into more formal settings in dryland environments. This in turn

was associated with the fall of the more hierarchical, West-Roman society. In Fredengren 2015[12] and below it is shown that depositions of human and animal remains in wetlands continued well after these time periods in areas such as Uppland. Also, this material suggests that there are rather complex patterns of depositional differences; in species composition, practices for handling the bodies as well as in temporal variation. It might even be so that there are differences between regions.

Overview of the Material

Bog bodies and depositions of skeletons in bogs are known in Denmark,[13] Norway[14] and Finland.[15] However, Sweden has been associated with only a few cases such as Bocksten Man or Dannike Woman. However, well known depositional locations are also Skedemosse and the sites around the country accounted for in Hagberg.[16] However, our project has, through surveys of archives and museum stores, been able to locate well over 100 places where human or animal remains have been found in wetlands, with concentrations in Skåne, Västergötland, Uppland, Öland and on Gotland. In Uppland, human and animal remains have been found in 17 water and wetland locations that together represent 117 human and animal individuals.

Not included in these numbers are finds from wells such as Apalle, Kyrsta or Gödåker, that together with the rather uncertain finds from Läby would bring the numbers up to 21 locations (as mentioned in Fredengren 2015). Of these, 55 human and animal individuals have been osteologically analysed by the current project. The other 62 have for various reasons been unavailable in the museum collections or remain in storage with the firms that excavated them. This group is accounted for in our analysis as paper bodies. There are 21 paper humans (PH) and 41 are paper animals (PA). Examples of these are the finds at River Örsundaån, that is noted in archaeological documentation, but where no corresponding collection can be found in the physical osteological archives in museums. These are bodily remains where there is only a paper record and within this category we have included bodies recorded by heritage institutions such as the Swedish National

Heritage Board or the Swedish History Museum. However, some of these paper bodies have been analysed by other osteologists and have therefore added in greater detail to our database. Others have been mentioned in museum or heritage board documentation where on occasion only species is mentioned and where there may be no information on sex, age, pathology or trauma type. Hence, the database consists of records with a somewhat uneven depth of information. This also means that numbers and percentages of, for example, pathologies and trauma may be somewhat uncertain and even underestimated, as a number of paper bodies have no information on these and other traits. The category of paper bodies could also be expanded by records from folklore collections[17] – however, that is not carried out in the current research compilation.

The radiocarbon dates from Uppland stretch from the Bronze to the Viking Age (see Fig. 1). The diagram shows a rise in the numbers during the Late Bronze Age and Pre-Roman Iron Age. Hence, there are similarities with the peak in dates of the Danish material. Also, the number of dates in the Viking Age is rather high. However, this diagram gives a somewhat skewed picture with regards to numbers, as excavated sites such as Riala with more dates get a heavier weight compared to other sites and affect the number of individuals from the Late Bronze Age. There are also a few dates in the Medieval Period as well as modern dates from two sites, Rickebasta and Riala. Also, many of the sites have

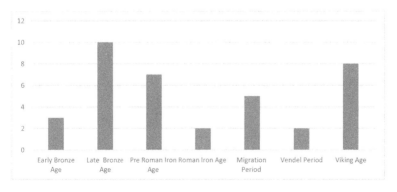

Figure 1. Diagram of radiocarbon dates of wetland bone material in Uppland. License: CC BY-NC-ND.

more skeletal remains than those that were radiocarbon dated; hence, these results may give a biased picture and can change when further dating takes place.

Who

The question of who was selected for deposition in watery places is here approached through osteology and rests on the osteological analysis carried out by Camilla Löfqvist.[18] The theoretical background for this discussion is dealt with in Fredengren 2013. The term figuration is used instead of identity in order to pay respect to the fact that the persons discussed consisted of, changed and came about through a variety of relations that cross-cut conceptualized identity borders. Here, the question of who was deposited is qualified by an investigation into what relations were woven together through sacrificial practices. However, such relations are narrowed down and abbreviated when they are captured in archaeological discourse and through the osteological nomenclature. Having said that, the following section makes use of standard osteological categories while bearing in mind the caveats of fixating the material in this way. It explores selection practices and what life-stories are evidenced in the human and animal remains in order to see whether there are any patterns in their bodily figurations that could explain their killability and deposition in waters away from burial grounds on land. This means to look at the composition of species in the material, at age and sex factors, but also health and life-style indicators. This is followed by a section on their death histories. When possible, the selection and treatment of animals is compared and contrasted to that of humans. In some cases, there is published information on selection processes in other material that is used as contrast material to the remains from Uppland.

Life – Species, Sex and Age

What is remarkable about the Uppland material, in comparison to collections from other parts of Sweden, is that it contains a high degree of human remains depositions from watery contexts. Of the 117 individuals, there are 52 (44%) human and 65 (56%) animals (MNI).

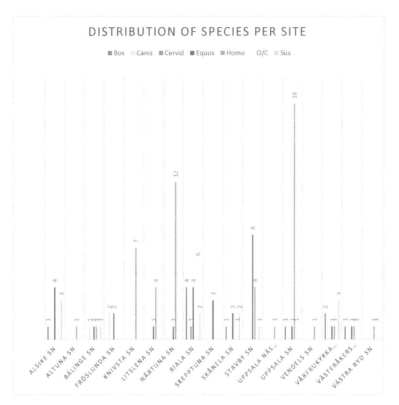

Figure 2. Species variation and MNI at different sites (sn=socken/parish). License: CC BY-NC-ND.

Some locations have more depositions than others. The location by and in the River Fyrisån in Uppsala Parish has yielded 21 human and animal individuals. This is followed by Hederviken in Närtuna Parish with 13 individuals and Lake Bokaren in Stavby Parish with 13 individuals each. The high numbers are due to the fact that they are in well-frequented areas or that they have been formally excavated. Many have both human and animal remains.

The animal remains consist of horses (24%), pigs (10%), cattle and sheep/goat (approx. 8.5% each). Dog and deer have a minor presence in the material.

Horses have often been associated with sacrifice.[19] This is further emphasized by the wetland material from Uppland presented here. However, there could be regional patterns in the species composition at sacrificial sites. The species in the Uppland

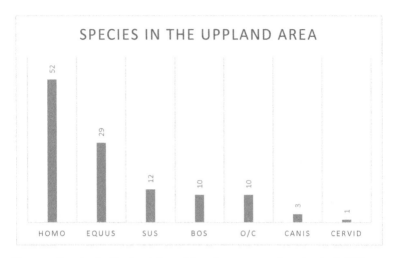

Figure 3. Species in Uppland depositions in waters and wetlands (MNI). License: CC BY-NC-ND.

depositions can, for example, be compared with the accumulation of bones at a selection of sites on and around Uppåkra in Skåne as accounted for by Magnell.[20] Here, the depositions around ceremonial house and weapon deposition at Uppåkra show an abundance of cattle (with percentages of 64 and 72%, calculated on NISP instead of MNI). In Magnell and Iregren's study around the island of Frösön,[21] located in the northern half of Sweden, other species patterns occurred. A deposition of animal bones beneath the church, considered to be a *blót* site, contained not only the bear bones that the site is best known for, but where pigs were the most common sacrificial animal, followed by sheep/goat and cattle. As mentioned by Magnell,[22] the ordinary relationship between species at a Mid-Swedish Iron Age farm would be a majority presence of cattle, followed by sheep/goat and pig.

While the focus on humans and horses in Uppland may indeed signal regional selection patterns, there might also be temporal differences within the material itself (hence it is a little problematical to group together and compare materials that could have accumulated at particular sites over time). Judging by the radiocarbon dates in Uppland, broadly speaking, it is more common to find animal bone depositions during the Bronze Age and human bone depositions from the Pre-Roman Iron Age and onwards. With more detail on species, it seems that the Bronze Age material mainly consists of cattle, but also pig, sheep/goat and horse are present. Hence, the focus is on domesticate animals that would have been present on farms and that people would have had more day-to-day relationships with. It is worth noting that cattle do not occur after Period 1 of the Pre-Roman Iron Age in these depositions. Instead, there is a marked shift through the periods from the Pre-Roman Iron Age, into the Roman Iron Age and the Migration Period where the variation of species lessens. There seems to be a particular focus on humans and horses, with a rare occurrence of dogs from one site at Fröslunda. Horses can be noted particularly in the Migration to Merovingian Periods. Whilst human remains in depositions increase during the Pre-Roman Iron Age, they more often date to the Merovingian and Viking Periods.

Age Distribution

Individual animals are generally determined as either juvenile or adult. Of the 65 animals, 23 were adults and 19 juvenile individuals. Horses were mainly adults, but young animals were also deposited. Both pigs and sheep/goat depositions mainly made use of juvenile individuals. Cattle, on the other hand, show the same

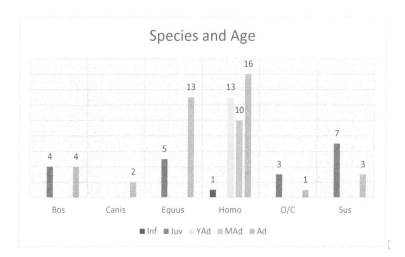

Figure 4. Species and age distribution. License: CC BY-NC-ND.

percentage of juvenile and adult animals, suggesting equal importance between meat (young animals) and dairy (older animals) producing animals.

The deposited humans are with one exception adults. Out of the 40 aged human individuals, 32.5 % were young adults followed by mature adults (25%). In the human group 40% could be determined as adults only. This is due to the preservation and fragmentation of the bones. One vertebra fragment of an infant was found at Lake Bokaren, Stavby Parish.

The age profile for bodies of humans and animals in the depositions differs somewhat, where juvenile humans seem to have been avoided, but both juvenile and adult animals were eligible for deposition in watery places.

Sex and Age of Humans

Out of the 33 humans with osteological sex determinations, there were 19 males (57.5%), 12 females (36.5%) and two individuals (6%) of indeterminate sex (Fig. 5).

Some animal remains have skeletal sexual markers; teeth show that two pigs are females and one male, while the pelvis from a sheep/goat indicates a female.

Figure 5. Sex determinations humans. License: CC BY-NC-ND.

Figure 6. Humans, age and sex. License: CC BY-NC-ND.

When bringing in the variables of sex and different age groups, a divergence between the males and females becomes obvious. Of the 31 human individuals that could be determined as to both age and sex (Fig. 6), the pattern shows that males are distributed rather evenly between age groups. However, there are mainly young adult females (MNI 6) and only one individual in the mature adult age group. The pattern suggests that its particularly young adult females that were being deposited in these watery places.

Disease, Malnutrition and Ante Mortem Trauma

Parts of these persons' life-styles and relations to others can be detected in the skeleton. For example, bone can carry the imprint of a variety of diseases such as tumours, arthritis, caries, of a deteriorated health condition and/or malnutrition, as can be evidenced in pitting of the skull (cribra, porotic hyperiotis or other cranial pitting) and alterations in the teeth enamel (enamel hypoplasia). There could also be evidence for bone trauma during life (described as occurring ante-mortem) accrued through accidents or violent relations with others. However, it should be noted that there are a range of diseases and trauma that will not leave any traces on the bone.

Pathologies

Evidence of pathologies were detected on a total of 20 human individuals out of the total number of 52 (i.e. 38.5%) and one animal (1.5%). In the group of humans with pathologies there were 10 males, 7 females and 3 indeterminate. One animal, an adult horse from Knyllinge, Fröslunda Parish, had pathologies on the shoulder blade resulting from repeated stress or a single traumatic event.

The most common pathology on humans was endo- and ectocranial pitting and periostitis. In the majority of cases these were associated with ante-mortem trauma to the head. This suggest that the ante-mortem trauma to the head might have caused infections, but that the trauma and infection has healed, indicating that the people had some means of treating wounds and injuries. The individuals with such pathologies are, for example, skeleton (Sk) 93, a male from Torresta that dates to the Roman Iron Age. This person displayed multiple pathologies and trauma during their life. The cranial and postcranial remains of this male, aged 35–45 years, for example reveal mild degenerative changes to the spine and joints of the long bones as well as ectocranial pitting on the skull, possibly indicating iron or nutritional deficiencies, but also healed ante-mortem injuries such as a possible fractured fibula. Apart from the mild joint condition in several bone elements, this was also found to be more severe on some of the metatarsals expressed through pitting and deformation of parts of the skull.[23]

Cranial pitting can be found on both male and female skeletons. However, cranial pitting in combination with trauma were found on Sk 57 from Knivsta, Sk 66 from Hederviken, Sk 72 from Bokaren. These are all males that date to the end of the Viking Period. The last one, Sk 77, a male from the River Fyrisån remains undated.

Six individuals might have suffered malnutrition or disease in early childhood. There are three individuals with enamel hypoplasia. One of these, a female from Gryteby, Sk 79, dates to the

Early Bronze Age, while the others belong to the Early and Later Iron Age (Sk 72 Bokaren (as above), Sk 75 a male from the River Fyrisån Rudan). A further three individuals (5,8%) showed traces of cribra orbitalia (Sk 56 a male from Knivsta, Sk 73 of indeterminate sex and Sk 74, a male, both from the River Fyrisån).

As can be seen in Table 1 all sites with human remains depositions also have individuals with some sort of pathology and/or ante-mortem trauma.

Ante-mortem Trauma Pattern on the Animal and Human Bone

Trauma, such as for example fractures, is together with dental and joint disease regarded as one of the most common pathologies in the archaeological material.[24]

Taken together, evidence for trauma could be found on a total of 55 bone elements divided between 36 individuals, whereof 17 were humans and 19 were animals, and had occurred ante-, peri- and postmortem (Fig. 7). Some individuals displayed several

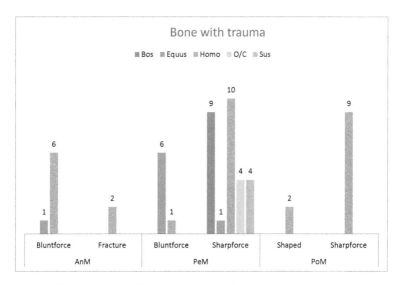

Figure 7. Total number of bone elements with trauma type and the time it occurred AnM= ante mortem, PeM= peri mortem and PoM= postmortem. License: CC BY-NC-ND.

Table 1. Human individuals with osteological pathologies and ante-mortem trauma. License: CC BY-NC-ND.

Site	Sk no	Anatomical unit	Age	Sex	Cribra	PH Por hyp	Endo/ Ecto cr pitting	Periostitis	Tumour	OA	Schmorls	Misc& Nonmetric	Dental path	Caries	Enamel hyp	Calculus	AnM Trauma/ fracture	Comment
Knivsta Parish, Knivsta bog	56	Cranium	MAd	M	I				I			I						
	57	Cranium	YAd	M			I			I		I					I	Healed
Närtuna Parish, Hederviken	60	Humerus	YAd	F								I						
	60	Tibia															I	Healed
	65	Femur	Ad					I										
	66	Cranium	YAd	F			I	I									I	Healed
	67	Cranium	YAd	M		I	I											
Uppsala-Näs Parish, Lake Sätra	70	Cranium	Ad	F			I	I				I						
Stavby Parish, Lake Bokaren	72	Cranium	YAd	M			I	I				I					I	Healed
	72	Dens/ Dentes											I		I	I		

Site	No.	Element	Age	Sex								Notes
	94	Cranium	YAd	M					1			
	94	Dens/Dentes				1	1					
Uppsala Town, in/by River Fyrisån	73	Cranium	MAd	Indet	1							
	74	Cranium	MAd	M	1	1					1	
	75	Cranium	MAd	M	1							
	75	Dens/Dentes				1	1			1		
	77	Cranium	YAd	M	1	1	1		1		1	Healed
	77	Dens/Dentes				1						
	78	Cranium	YAd	F	1	1						
	79	Cranium	YAd	F	1							
Vendels Parish, Gryteby in bog	79	Dens/Dentes				1	1					
Västra Ryd Parish, Granhammar Lake	19PH	Costae	MAd	M	1						1	Healed fracture
Torresta Parish, Häljebolsta, bog	93	Cranium	MAd	M	1						1	Healed

(Continued)

Table 1. *Continued*

Site	Sk no	Anatomical unit	Age	Sex	Cribra	PH Por hyp	Endo/Ecto cr pitting	Periostitis	Tumour	OA	Schmorls	Misc& Nonmetric	Dental path	Caries	Enamel hyp	Calculus	AnM Trauma/fracture	Comment
	93	Dens/Dentes											I			I		
	93	Vert thor								I	I							
	93	Humerus										I						
	93	Femur										I						
	93	Fibula															I	Healed fracture
	93	Tibia										I						
	93	Mt								I								
Litslena Parish, Lake Hallarby	96	Cranium	Ad	F				I				I						
	97	Cranium	Ad	F								I						
	99	Cranium	Yad									I						

trauma types, for example two human individuals (Sk 72 & 93) who displayed both AnM and PoM trauma while a further one human individual (Sk19PH from Granhammar) had records both of AnM and PeM trauma. Sk 60 and Sk 93 had been exposed to AnM, PeM and PoM trauma. Seven humans (13.5%) and one animal (1.5%) display ante-mortem trauma on a total of 9 bone elements. These are dealt with in the section below, while PeM and PoM are discussed under the following heading.

Looking at the seven human individuals displaying AnM traumas, it can be noticed that blunt force trauma to the head was most frequent. One mature adult male exhibited both a well-healed trauma to the lower fibula as well as a blunt force, now healed, trauma to the head (Sk 93, Torresta). The changes to the fibula are most likely due to a fracture or possibly a sprain. A second mature adult male, from Granhammar, 19PH, had fractured a rib, which was well healed by time of death.

Individuals Sk 57, 66, 72 and 77 had all been exposed to a blunt force trauma to the head which were all healed. The injuries were caused by blows to the head or possibly a fall. Besides Sk 66, a female from Hederviken, these were all males. Also, Sk 60, a female from Hederviken, seems to have received at blow to the lower leg (tibia) which was well healed at the time of her death. The majority were young adults, possibly indicating that they had fought and survived the injuries they received.

As mentioned above, the shoulder blade of a horse showed traces of a well-healed trauma, possibly caused by one single traumatic event or by a repeat stress to the bone. The injury may have caused the horse to go lame. The fact that the injury seems healed suggests that the horse had been cared for and would have been given time to recuperate, indicating that the individual was valued as working animal and/or as a pet.

Death – Killing, Selection of Body parts, Handling and Deposition

This section follows the death histories evidenced in the material and of particular interest is investigating trauma that could help in the discussion of sacrifice but also throw light on the handling of bodies and the selection of body parts for deposition.

Table 2. Antemortem (AnM) trauma. License: CC BY-NC-ND.

Site	Animal or Sk no	Species	Anatomical unit	Age	Sex	Trauma	Trauma Time	Trauma type	Trauma type specified
Knivsta bog	57	Homo	Head	YAd	M	1	AnM	Bluntforce	BluntForce/Fall
Hederviken	60	Homo	Tibia	YAd	F	1	AnM	Bluntforce	Blow
	66	Homo	Head	YAd	F	1	AnM	Bluntforce	BluntForce/Fall
Lake Bokaren	72	Homo	Head	YAd	M	1	AnM	Bluntforce	BluntForce/Fall
In/by River Fyrisån	77	Homo	Head	YAd	M	1	AnM	Bluntforce	Blow
Torresta, Häljebolsta, bog	93	Homo	Head	MAd	M	1	AnM	Bluntforce	Blow
	93	Homo	Fibula			1	AnM	Fracture	Healed fracture
Knyllinge, wetland	19A	Equus	Scapula	Ad	–	1	AnM	Bluntforce	Blow/repeat stress
Granhammar, Lake	19PH	Homo	Costae	MAd	M	1	AnM	Fracture	BluntForce/Fall
Total						9			

Death can occur due to disease, accidents or drowning that does not necessarily leave traces on the skeleton. The skeletal remains presented here show the injuries that have resulted in imprints on the skeleton. As will be shown, there are both traumas to the bodies that occurred perimortem (PeM) – i.e. associated with the time of death and postmortem (PoM) some time after death and when the bones had lost most of their plasticity. There seems to have been a particular selection of body parts for deposition and some bones were also handled and altered/shaped before their deposition in wetlands.

Perimortem Trauma

Out of the 117 individuals in this study, there were a total of 23 human and animal individuals that displayed perimortem trauma, 18 animals (27.7%) and five humans (9.6%).

The material suggests that these have been exposed to a slightly higher degree of trauma when compared to, for example, Medieval Sigtuna where 5.5% (or 2.6% if the mass grave is excluded) of the adult population displayed sharp force trauma. Other sites to compare with are Medieval Lund (0.6%), St. Stefan (7.3%) and Westerhus (2.9%).[25]

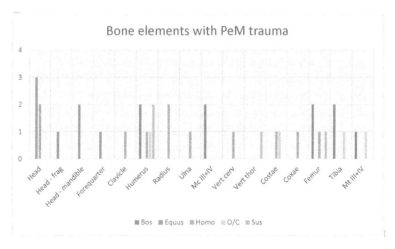

Figure 8. Bone elements with perimortem trauma. License: CC BY-NC-ND.

Table 3. Peri- and postmortem trauma. License: CC BY-NC-ND.

Site	Animal or Sk no	Species	Anatomical unit	Age	Sex	PeM trauma	PoM trauma	Trauma Time	Trauma type	Trauma type specif	Comment
Stavby Parish, Lake Bokaren	71	Homo	Head	MAd	F	1		PeM	Bluntforce	Blow	
	72	Homo	Vert cerv	YAd	M	1		PeM	Sharpforce	Beheading	
	5PA	Equus	Head - mand	Ad		1		PeM	Bluntforce	Blow	
	6PA	Equus	Head - frag	Ad		1		PeM	Bluntforce	Blow	
	7PA	Equus	Head - mand	Ad		1		PeM	Bluntforce	Blow	
	7PA	Equus	Forequarter	Ad		1		PeM	Sharpforce	Chopped up	
	8PA	Equus	Head	Juv		1		PeM	Bluntforce	Blow	
	98A	Equus	Head	Ad		1		PeM	Bluntforce	Blow	
	9PA	Equus	Head	Ad		1		PeM	Bluntforce	Blow	
Västra RydParish, Granhammar Lake	15PA	O/C	Mt III+IV			1		PeM	Sharpforce	Splitt	

Site	ID	Taxon	Element	Age	Sex		Mod	Fracture	Alteration	Notes
Litslena Parish, Lake Hallarby	19PH	Homo	Head	MAd	M	1	PeM	Sharpforce	PeM cuts	Also AnM
	19PH	Homo	Humerus			1	PeM	Sharpforce	PeM cuts	
	19PH	Homo	Radius			1	PeM	Sharpforce	PeM cuts	
	19PH	Homo	Ulna			1	PeM	Sharpforce	PeM cuts	
	99	Homo	Head	YAd			PoM	Sharpforce	Cutm	
Närtuna Parish, Hederviken	58	Homo	Head	MAd	M	1	PoM	Shaped	Alter	
	60	Homo	Radius	YAd	F	1	PeM	Sharpforce	Alter	Also AnM
	60	Homo	Femur				PoM	Sharpforce	Alter	
	61	Homo	Humerus	Ad		1	PoM	Sharpforce	Alter	
	61	Homo	Femur			1	PoM	Sharpforce	Alter	
	64	Homo	Head	MAd	M	1	PoM	Shaped	Alter	
	67	Homo	Head	YAd	M	1	PoM	Sharpforce	Alter	
Vårfrukyrka Parish, Hjältängarna	1A	Bos	Femur	Ad		1	Pem	Sharpforce	Chopped up	
	2A	Bos	Tibia	Juv		1	Pem	Sharpforce	Chopped up	

(Continued)

Table 3. *Continued*

Site	Animal or Sk no	Species	Anatomical unit	Age	Sex	PeM trauma	PoM trauma	Trauma Time	Trauma type	Trauma type specif	Comment
	2A	Bos	Mt III+IV	Juv		1		Pem	Sharpforce	Chopped up	
	5A	Sus	Vert thor	Juv		1		Pem	Sharpforce	Chopped up	
	5A	Sus	Humerus	Ad		1		Pem	Sharpforce	Chopped up	
	6A	Sus	Humerus	Juv		1		Pem	Sharpforce	Chopped up	
Knivsta Parish, Knivsta bog	56	Homo	Head	MAd	M		1	PoM	Sharpforce	Cutm	
Riala Parish, Burehäll	33PA	Bos	Humerus	Ad		1		Pem	Sharpforce	Cutm	
	33PA	Bos	Mc III+IV			1		Pem	Sharpforce	Chopped up	
	33PA	Bos	Mc III+IV			1		Pem	Sharpforce	Chopped up	
	33PA	Bos	Humerus			1		Pem	Sharpforce	Cutm	
	34PA	Bos	Femur	Juv		1		Pem	Sharpforce	Chopped up	
	38PA	O/C	Tibia	Juv		1		Pem	Sharpforce	Cutm	
Alsike Parish, Rickebasta	16A	Sus	Femur	Juv	F	1		PeM	Sharpforce	Chopped up	

Uppsala Näs Parish, Lake Sätra	70	Homo	Head	Ad	F	1	PoM	Sharpforce	Alter
Tadem	?	O/C	Costae			1	PeM	Sharpforce	Cutm
Torresta Parish, Häljebolsta	93	Homo	Head	MAd	M	1	PeM	Sharpforce	Cutm
	93	Homo	Clavicle			1	PeM	Sharpforce	Cutm
	93	Homo	Costae			1	PeM	Sharpforce	Cutm
	93	Homo	Coxae			1	PeM	Sharpforce	Cutm
	93	Homo	Femur			1	PeM	Sharpforce	Cutm
	7A	Bos	Tibia	Juv		1	Pem	Sharpforce	Chopped up
	9A	O/C	Humerus	Ad	F	1	Pem	Sharpforce	Cutm
Uppsala Parish, in/by Fyrisån	73	Homo	Head	MAd	Indet	1	PoM	Sharpforce	Alter
	75	Homo	Head	MAd	M	1	PoM	Sharpforce	Alter
Total						36	14		

The bone assemblage can crudely be divided into two groups, one where the perimortem trauma indicates killing practices such as a blow to the head or beheading, and another group where the trauma suggests that the bodies were dismembered (mainly animal bone material).

The first group contains both human and animal material. Parts of this group consist of horses from a wetland site at Bokaren in Stavby Parish.[26] Six of these were mentioned by Lundholm[27] and a further two horses (one juvenile) were discovered during excavations in 2015. Out of these eight individuals, five had been exposed to a blunt force trauma, most likely a killing blow, to the head. One of these individuals also had their front legs cut off at the knees. Furthermore, a vertebra from the tail of this individual suggests the skull, feet and tail, so the inedible parts, had been deposited. It seems likely that these individuals had been killed by a forceful blow to the head whereby the head and possible lower extremities has been deposited at the site.

From Bokaren, there are also remains of four humans, of whom two had most likely received perimortem blows to the head before they were placed in the watery deposit. A mature adult female (Sk 71) from this site had received a PeM blunt force trauma to the head. The location at the forehead, above the left eye, suggest that this blow was dealt by someone facing her. The shape and outline of the depression in the skull suggest that she was hit by something large and heavy, possibly an oblong oval-shaped stone club or something similar. Though the blow was hard, it did not completely penetrate the skull as with the above-mentioned horses. However, it would most likely have stunned and immobilized the individual and, considering the heavy blow, it might have resulted in death. The bone showed no traces of healing.

A second individual from Bokaren, the young adult male (Sk 72) with ante-mortem traumas to the head also had perimortem trauma. A cervical vertebra displayed two parallel cuts which suggest a possible case of cutting of the throat or a beheading (Fig. 9). The third human individual from Bokaren, Sk 94 has no skeletal evidence of trauma.

However, Sk 19PH, a mature adult male from Granhammar, displayed cuts to more than one bone element. Several cuts were

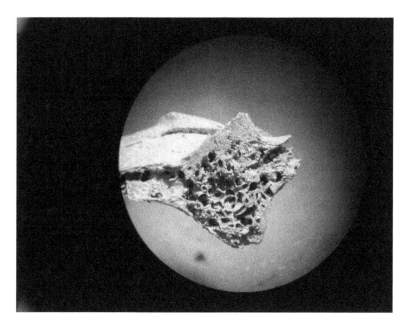

Figure 9. Cervical vertebra fragment from Sk 72, Bokaren. License: CC BY-NC-ND.

detected on the skull but also on the humerus, radius and ulna of the left arm. Perhaps they indicate defensive injuries.

Sk93 from Torresta displayed several perimortem cranial and postcranial injuries caused by sharp force trauma. As there is no sign of healing, it is likely that these injuries were received at around the time of death. Injuries to the skull included several cuts to the back of the head, likely caused by a sharp, probably metal implement, and possibly indicating the intention of decapitating this individual. Further sharp trauma has been recorded on the right clavicle, the ribs, left coxae and both femurs, where cuts were into still soft bone and were likely received around the time of death.[28]

The second group consist of animals considered to produce, for example, meat, milk etc. such as cattle, sheep/goat and pigs. The bones as well as traumas mainly indicate a deliberate, selective process which, together with the location of the cut marks and the helical fractures to high marrow-bearing elements, suggest these animal individuals were butchered i.e. their bodies were dismembered to become meals. This would fit with the number of piglets and lambs in the depositions. Hence, it is likely that these animals were used for food before their bones were left in the water environment. These animals were from sites such as Granhammar, Hjältängarna, Riala, Rickebasta, Tadem and Torresta. Here, the osteological material provides no particular information on how the animals were killed. Strikingly, there is also evidence that human bodies were divided up at the time of death. The left distal radius of Sk60, a young adult female from Hederviken, showed clear evidence of the bone being cut up. This is suggested first by a possible "false" start followed by a cut through the bone. The edge is very straight and is parallel to the "false" start cut. It is also possible that the proximal diaphysis has been cut. This type of appearance on an animal bone would likely be interpreted as a butchery mark.

Postmortem Trauma

There is evidence that some of the bodies were not deposited in the wet contexts directly upon death, but that they were curated

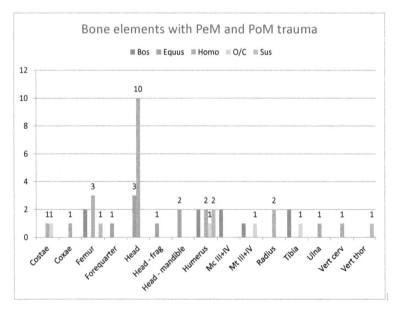

Figure 10. Bone elements with PeM and PoM trauma. License: CC BY-NC-ND.

and modified before deposition. Seemingly some of the bodies were exposed to violence after death.

In all 11 human individuals had been exposed to mainly sharp force postmortem trauma. Of these, the majority, a total of nine, had cuts to the skulls. In six of the cases it seems as if the intention has been to shape the skull. This can be seen as straight and clear cuts through part of the skull bone that is very hard and thus would not easily break naturally. A crude bowl-shaped appearance, as well as polished surfaces possibly from being handled might suggest occasional postmortem alterations and shaping of bone. Examples of this are Sk 58, 64 (Fig. 11) and possibly 67 from Hederviken, Sk 56 from Knivsta bog and Sk 70 from Lake Sätra. Such traces were possibly also Sk 99 from Lake Hallarby.

Two individuals (Sk 60 & 61, Hederviken) had cuts to long bones such as the femur and humerus indication the bodies had been dismembered before deposition. One femur (Sk 61, Hederviken) also had traces of possible gnawing, showing that

Figure 11. Possible shaped skull of Sk 64, Hederviken. License: CC BY-NC-ND.

scavengers had access to the bone at some stage. The last individual had perimortem cuts to several bone elements, but also a few cuts to rib, pelvis and femur which possibly might be postmortem.

What these examples show is both that the bodies, in order to have been available for being dismembered or shaped, most likely were killed and decomposed elsewhere than in their wetland depositional locations.

Bone Elements

It is quite rare to find full body depositions in the Uppland material. Instead, it seems that there is further evidence for that there was a selection of body parts that were suitable for deposition. It is worth noting that bones can also become detached from each other due to taphonomic processes and that skulls are easier to identify and retrieve.

Bone elements from all anatomical units were present in the material. On meat-producing animals these can be divided into regions where the meaty parts are considered to be: the spine and ribs, the front quarter (shoulder and front legs) and the hindquarter

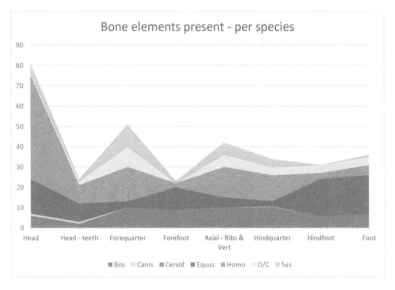

Figure 12. Bone elements and anatomical units. License: CC BY-NC-ND.

(pelvis and hind leg). The less meaty regions are the head including the lower jaw, the fore- and hindfoot (metapodials, carpals and tarsals) and the foot (the phalanges). The least meaty region includes teeth, horn core and antler. It has been argued elsewhere that it is mainly the less rich body parts that were deposited in wetlands.[29]

The material presented here suggests a modification to this view, which seems to be species-dependent. It is clear that sheep/goat and pig follow have a majority of the bone elements from the meat rich areas such as fore- and hindquarter as well as from the spine and ribs. The horse, on the other hand, shows a reverse pattern, with a higher percentage of skull fragments, fore- and hind foot together with feet present and hence confirms this pattern. Cattle showed the most even distribution, but with an inclination toward the less meat-rich elements being present. The low number of bone elements from dog were all from the skull while the few deer bones were all from the hindquarters.

Humans stood out through the high frequency of skulls and skull fragments present adding up to 44% of the human bones analysed (52% including the teeth). Rarer were those individuals that were represented by their full bodies in the depositions. Here Sk 19PH from Granhammar, Sk 93 Torresta and Bokaren Sk 94 indicate depositions of the corpse directly after death in wet ground.

Depositions in the Bronze Age and Pre-Roman Iron Age

The general traits of this material are that the sites established during the Bronze Age and Pre-Roman Iron Age can be found around the rock-art rich areas of Enköping, but some are also found further afield. At Hjältängarna the survey inventory describes that this is a wetland area located on both sides of parish boundaries of Härnevi and Vårfrukyrka. While this area is situated to the south of the larger waterways that today form River Örsundaån, the area drains into present-day River Enköpingsån. Here, the inventory text mentions how both human and animal remains have been retrieved in the locality from time to time. The site seems to be spread out across a 100 m area, where human, horse, cattle and pig bones have been found. Of these bones, only a small number of cattle and pig bones have been retrieved in museum storage that could be dated by the project. These have overlapping radiocarbon dates in Periods III and IV of the Bronze Age. However, this seems to have been a more extensive depositional site and the presence of human and horse bones may suggest that it was also used in other periods. The depositional area is surrounded by rock-art sites. There are numerous cup-marked boulders, but also some cross-formed pieces.

This site resembles that of Torresta, situated to the north of River Örsundaån.[30] Here, animal bones from cattle, horse and sheep/goat were found. These can be dated to the Bronze Age and Periods II, IV and V. There was also a male human skeleton that belongs to the Roman Iron Age. These were retrieved from a wading place across what now is a drain – but what would have been much wetter ground in the past. This wading place is flanked by cup-marked boulders, one on each side of the water. On higher ground there is also rock-art with ship-carvings. Similarly, the contract excavations at wetlands in Riala have produced cattle, pig and horse bones that can be dated to the end of the Late Bronze Age and the beginning of the Pre-Roman Iron Age. Rock-art is also present here. Near the depositional spot is a vertical cliff. Here a composition of a cross, surrounded by nine concentric circles faces out over the depositional area. Several cup-marked rocks and a rock-slide are located in the vicinity of the site. There are structural similarities between this rock art and the depositions in water. The cutting into the stone can also be understood as a material practice that penetrates beyond the surface, into the inner parts of the rock. The deposition of items in watery places also penetrates the surface and reach into the elements of wetlands and waters. Both practices can be said to work to perforate two different membranes of the world and stretch into and make physical contact with the underworld.

Approximately 12 km to the east of Hjältängarna is another depositional place with associated rock-art that has human remains that can be dated to the Pre-Roman Iron Age and the Migration Period. Here, at Lake Hallarbysjön other items have also been deposited. An amber bead has been retrieved from the area where the skeletal remains were retrieved. Furthermore, what may be parts of a Late Bronze Age twisted torque was found in this general area during farming. There is a need for further field-work in this location to investigate whether it was a part of a larger hoard of similar items and the connection to the bone-finds by the lake. During the Pre-Roman Iron Age there is evidence for more depositions in mid-Uppland at sites as Lake Sätrasjön, Tadem and possibly also Stora Ullentuna.

Depositions During Roman Iron Age and Later Periods

There are sites with dates that overlap the Bronze and Iron Ages, such as Torresta. Other sites such as Bokaren have the earliest dates in the Roman Iron Age (a period of few depositions). During the Migration Period, sites that were used for depositions in ear-lier periods seem to have been re-activated by the deposition of the remains particularly of horses. This is exemplified by the finds from Lake Hallarbysjön, Tadem, Bokaren and Rickebasta. It is worth noting that Rickebasta is situated next to Tuna in Alsike, which would be considered as a centre at least on the borders between the Migration and Merovingian Periods. Other site such as Hederviken and Knivsta seem to have been used mainly during the Viking Age, where the depositions in the River Fyrisån uphold a middle position. The role of these sites in the politics of Iron Age Uppland has been dealt with elsewhere.[31]

Discussion

Sacrifice is a particular way of dealing with the end of life. It can, for example, be understood as a management of human and ani-mal finitude, sometimes used for communication with the divine, but also as a way of transforming inter-species relationships as well as the relationships between humans. Furthermore, sacri-fice can be used to alter the relationship with the divine and the landscape.

This paper publishes some of the results of the research project *The Water of the Times* and traces what bodies were used for depositions and sacrifices and how they, with all their network connections, can be understood as sacrificial figurations. The content of the depositions indicates shifting species relations with regard to which bodies were rendered as killable in order to be sacrificed and possible to deposit in wetland places in Uppland. As mentioned earlier, during the Bronze and earliest Iron Ages the depositions mainly contained domesticated animals such as cattle, sheep/goat, pig and horses. Most likely, people would have had quite close relationships with and tended these domesticated animals on a next day-to-day basis. There is not much indication of the welfare of these animals in these skeletal remains. Besides the trauma to the shoulder of the horse from Knyllinge, there is no clear evidence in this material that violence was inflicted on these animals when they were still alive or if they were treated with care during their life. However, more studies are needed that pay attention to issues of animal welfare in the past.

The content of the depositions shifted considerably over the Iron Age when humans and horses dominate the material. This suggests that the relationship to these animals as well as that towards humans seems to have altered considerably over time. The human bone material presented here has supplied a number of cases where both the life and death histories of the individuals have been rather troubled. One example is the person from Torresta who was exposed to violence both during life and death. There seems to be evidence for a path-dependency in this, but also in other cases for that a violent and neglected life also ended in a traumatized way, as if the sacrifice played a role in other politics of exclusion. What is particularly striking is the number of individuals with challenged health status that were deposited in the Viking Age and the fact that many males also were exposed to violence during their lives. Hence, these depositions can be read as examples of changing relationships in the practice of Necropolitics, where those in focus for these altered over time in the Uppland area, where some deaths were managed and possibly became a part of public display and later deposition in wetlands.

Throughout this paper the term *depositions in wetlands* has been favoured over the term sacrifice and as flagged for at the beginning there is a need to discuss what is actually counted as sacrifice. At a broad level, all depositions in wetlands can be understood as sacrifices, but the issue is more complex than this. As shown above, there are indeed cases in this material that qualify for a narrower archaeological definition of sacrifice, where there is evidence of lethal perimortal violence, with no evidence for defensive injuries on the skeleton and where the deposition was carried out in a particular selected part of the archaeological landscape. One example of this is Torresta, where human remains were deposited in a wetland location at a fording place that had been marked by rock-art. What is more, earlier animal remains depositions were retrieved from this place, which attests to a placing of the bones at a traditional depositional location. At the same time, the skeletal evidence points to a life history of neglect. Another example is the site of Bokaren with a depositional tradition that stretch over a span of some 1,000 years and where there are both human and animal remains with evidence of perimortal, lethal violence.

When it comes to how the dead bodies were handled, there are only a few examples of full bodies having been retrieved from the wetlands. On many occasions, however, only certain body parts were deposited (sites like Bokaren have received both full bodies and body parts). Seemingly, in these cases when only body parts are present, both the actual killing as well as the decomposition and handling of the bodies must have taken place away from the wet areas. There are examples of when the more meat-rich parts of bodies were deposited – hence, such depositions can possibly be interpreted as providing food for the divine. There are other examples of depositions of less meat-rich parts being used in the depositions and where possibly the meat-rich parts were used as food for the living, who possibly shared the meals with the divine or the spirits. Adding to the variation in practice is the evidence that points to the fact that certain bodies, after their death and decomposition, must have been curated, handled and carved into before being deposited at a particular wetland location. However, these may also under certain circumstances be understood as sacrifices as they could have been a part of a practice centred on the giving up of some bodies or body parts in exchange for something else to prosper.

Traditionally, sacrifice is understood as a way of communicating and carrying out an exchange with the divine or with spirits of various locations in the environment. Besides that, sacrifice may be connected to a wish for good crops, for status or for a society to prosper, and these practices may also indicate particular types of relationships with the landscape. As focused on in this paper, the depositions have been retrieved in watery environments and may, as shown in the material above, have worked to weave together the faith of humans, animals and these parts of the landscape, albeit in constellations that changed over time. These depositions form a part of a multi-species history, that may have worked to alter the relationship with the environment. As discussed elsewhere,[32] depositions in water may have been understood to work not only to fulfil wishes – but also to draw out sacred power and holiness onto particular places in the landscape. In this way the landscape may have been understood as if it were perforated where the deposition of sacrifices of different kinds would work to channel holy water from the underworld and attract it into the world of the living, thereby making the sacred immanent in the world.

Depositions in wetlands, understood as sacrifices or not, may have worked to indicate, activate and set up a variety of inter-species, age-related and landscape relationships that changed over time. What has been accounted for here is a rather complex material that indicates a variety of inter-species relations, value scales and practices that need to be kept in mind when discussing issues around sacrifice.

Notes

1. Hubert & Mauss 1964 (1891).

2. See also Mbembe 2003.

3. Agamben 1998.

4. Brink 2013:40–41.

5. See Lund 2010; Zachrisson 1998; Fredengren 2015.

6. Fredengren 2015.

7. Fredengren & Löfqvist 2015.

8. Glob 2004 (1969):153, 159–163.

9. Cf. Asingh 2009.

10. Ravn 2010:113.
11. Fabech 1991:284.
12. Fredengren 2015.
13. See Ravn 2010.
14. Henriksen & Sylvester 2005.
15. Wessman 2009.
16. Hagberg 1967.
17. See Kama 2015.
18. See appendix for catalogue and method.
19. Nilsson 2009; Monikander 2010.
20. Magnell 2011.
21. Magnell & Iregren 2010.
22. Magnell & Iregren 2010:233.
23. Fredengren & Löfqvist 2015.
24. Roberts & Manchester 1999:65.
25. Kjellström 2005:82, tab. 5.4
26. See Fredengren 2015; Eklund & Hennius (*forthcoming*).
27. Lundholm 1947.
28. Fredengren & Löfquist 2015.
29. Hagberg 1967.
30. See Fredengren 2015.
31. Fredengren 2015.
32. Fredengren 2016.

References

Asingh, P. 2009. *Grauballe Man. Portrait of a Bog Body.* Aarhus: Aarhus University Press.

Brink, S. 2013. Myth and Ritual in Pre-Christian Scandinavian Landscape. In S. Walaker, & S. Brink (eds.). *Sacred Sites and Holy Places*. Brepols: Turnhout, 33–52.

Eklund, S. & Hennius, A. (*forthcoming*). *Våtmarksoffer i Bokaren. Avrapportering av gamla undersökningar. Rasbo 137:1, Rasbo socken, Uppsala kommun, Uppland, Uppsala län.* SAU rapport 2014:20. Uppsala: SAU.

Fabech, C. 1991. Samfundsorganisation, religiøse ceremonier og regional variation. In C. Fabech & J. Ringtved (eds.). *Samfundsorganisation og regional variation. Norden i romersk jernalder og folkevandringstid.* Aarhus: Aarhus universitetsforlag.

Fredengren, C. 2013. Posthumanism, the Transcorporeal and Biomolecular Archaeology. In *Current Swedish Archaeology* 21, 53–71.

Fredengren, C. 2015. Water Politics. Wetland Deposition of Human and Animal Remains in Uppland, Sweden. In *Fornvännen, Journal of Swedish Antiquarian Research* 11, 161–183.

Fredengren, C. & Löfqvist, C. 2015. Food for Thor. The Deposition of Human and Animal Remains in a Swedish Wetland Area. In *Journal of Wetland Archaeology* 15.

Fredengren, C. 2016. Unexpected Encounters with Deep Time Enchantment. Bog Bodies, Crannogs and 'Otherwordly' Sites. The Materializing Powers of Disjunctures in Time. In *World Archaeology* 48:4.

Glob, P. V. 2004 (1969). *The Bog People.* London: Faber and Faber.

Green, M. 1998. Humans as Ritual Victims in the Later Prehistory of Western Europe. In *Oxford Journal of Archaeology* 17(2), 169–189.

Hagberg, U. E. 1967. *The Archaeology of Skedemosse II.* Stockholm: Vitterhetsakademin.

Henriksen, M. M. & Sylvester, M. 2005. Boat and Human Remains from Bogs in Central Norway. In *Archaeology from the Wetlands. Recent Perspectives Proceedings of the 11th Annual WARP conference,* 343–347.

Hubert, H. & Mauss, M. 1964 (1891). *Sacrifice. Its Nature and Function.* Chicago: University of Chicago Press. Midway reprint 1981.

Kjellström, A. 2005. *The Urban Farmer. Osteoarchaeological Analysis of Skeletons from Medieval Sigtuna Interpreted in a Socioeconomic Perspective.* Theses and Papers in Osteoarchaeology No 2. Stockholm: Stockholm University.

Liebe-Harkort, C. 2010. *Oral Disease and Health Patterns. Dental and Cranial Paleopathology of the Early Iron Age Population at Smörkullen in Alvastra, Sweden.* Theses and Papers in Osteoarchaeology No 6. Stockholm: Stockholm University.

Lindström. J. 2009. *Bronsåldersmordet.* Stockholm: Norstedt.

Lund, J. 2010. At the Water's Edge. In M. Carver et al. (eds.). *Signals of Belief in Early England. Anglo-Saxon Paganism Revisited.* Oxford: Oxbow Books.

Lundholm, B. 1947. *Abstammung und Domestikation des Hauspferdes.* Zoologiska Bidrag från Uppsala 27. Uppsala: Almqvist & Wiksell.

Magnell, O. & Iregren, E. 2010. Veistu hvé blóta skal? The Old Norse Blót in the Light of Osteological Remains from Frösö Church, Jämtland, Sweden. In *Current Swedish Archaeology* 18, 223–250.

Magnell, O. 2011. Sacred Cows or Old Beasts? A Taphonomic Approach to Studying Ritual Killing with an Example from Iron Age Uppåkra, Sweden. In: *The Ritual Killing and Burial of Animals. European Perspectives.* Oxford: Oxbow Books, 192–204.

Mbembe, A. 2003. Necropolitics. In *Public Culture* 15(1), 11–40.

Monikander, A. 2010. *Våld och vatten. Våtmarkskult vid Skedemosse under järnåldern.* Stockholm Studies in Archaeology 52. Stockholm: Stockholm University.

Nilsson, L. 2009. Häst och hund i fruktbarhetskult och blot. In A. Carlie (ed.). *Järnålderns rituella platser.* Halmstad: Kulturmiljö Halland, 81–99.

Sundqvist, O. 2004. Uppsala och Asgård. Makt, offer och kosmos i forntida Skandinavien. In A. Andrén et al. (eds.). *Ordning mot kaos – studier av nordisk förkristen kosmologi.* Vägar till Midgård 4. Lund: Nordic Academic Press.

Ravn, M. 2010. Burials in Bogs. Bronze and Early Iron Age Bog Bodies from Denmark. In *Acta Archaeologica* 81, 112–123.

Roberts, C. & Manchester, K. 1999. *The Archaeology of Disease.* New York: Cornell University Press.

Wessman, A. 2009. Levänluhta – A Place of Punishment, Sacrifice or Just a Common Cemetery? In *Fennoscandia Archaeologica* 26.

Zachrisson, T. 1998. *Gård, gräns, gravfält.* Stockholm Studies in Archaeology 16. Stockholm: Stockholm University.

Response

Klas Wikström af Edholm
Stockholm University

Christina Fredengren and Camilla Löfqvist present the preliminary results of the research project *The Water of the Times*. From
the analysis of human and animal deposits in wet contexts in
the wider Uppland area, they discuss what effects these depositions may have had during the Late Bronze Age and Iron Age and
investigate how these indicate, activate and set up inter-species,
age-related and landscape relations. One of the most important
contributions from an interdisciplinary perspective is that the project proposes a starting point of an alternative basis for the study
of sacrifice.

Henri Hubert and Marcel Mauss presented a definition of sacrifice already in their study in 1898, which has often been used
in the comparative study of history of religions.[1] The word *sacrifice* is derived from the Latin *sacer* 'sacred' and *facere* 'to make',
meaning 'to make sacred', signifying the establishing of a means
of communication between the sacred and the profane worlds
through the mediation of a victim (which in the course of the
ceremony is destroyed). As for example Caroline Humphrey and
James Laidlaw also make clear, sacrifice means the killing of a living being, by a sacrificer, as a gift to a divine/supernatural receiver.[2]
I find the definition proposed by Hubert & Mauss as well as
Humphrey & Laidlaw useful in the interdisciplinary study of, for
example, human sacrifice, since the intention as a gift, the divine
receiver, as well as the constructive element (i.e. creating a communication) makes us able to distinguish a sacrifice from other kinds
of ritual killing. Fredengren and Löfqvist use this definition as a
basis when they propose an alternative and widened definition
of sacrifice. In their analysis, sacrifice also works as the process
where some human and non-human others are selected, treated
elsewise and rendered as killable, i.e. a management of relations
between different bodies and the exercising of power and control
over life and death; with the intention of altering the relationship

to the landscape and drawing sacred power and holiness onto particular places. From the perspective of archaeology, sacrifice is a very problematic term, but as Fredengren and Löfqvist mention already at the beginning of their paper, the problem of identifying what depositions qualify as evidence of sacrifice, within an archaeological material, is both crucial and difficult. This question raises a fundamental theoretical issue, namely the different spheres of study of the disciplines of Archaeology and History of Religions. The study pinpoints one of the areas where the disciplines may have a great mutual impact on each other.

The archaeological material can of course only show us the results of the sacrifice, since the premises for the interpretation are limited to the actions themselves, and lack the intention behind the actions. In the definitions of sacrifice propounded above, the intention behind the action is crucial for the interpretation as a sacrifice. For this reason, I find it a strength that the abovementioned archaeological application of sacrifice is focusing on the action that makes the site sacred and how a sacred site is created, but a precondition for this is the occurrence of something holy or divine that could be connected to the site. We still need something that the action relates to; what power is the sacrifice a communication with? Who is the receiver? The archaeological finds show us the remains of (ritual) killings of animals and humans. In line with the archaeological use of the category sacrifice, these killings (or rather the traces of them) can be interpreted as performative actions that mark or make the site into a communication node (with the divine); the place is (re)established as "holy". The killings/sacrifices constitute, confirm, or intensify the site as "special", and possibly sacred, or holy.

The issue of the potential occurrence of human sacrifices in Old Norse religion has encouraged a long debate. Several written sources mention the sacrifice of humans among the Germanic tribes, some of them in watery areas, others on dry land. The archaeological finds, such as bog bodies, have already from their very discovery been used as an important evidence of such practices. One central argument for denying the occurrence of the practice of human sacrifice in the Iron Age has been the lack of relevant and indisputable archaeological finds.[3] As Fredengren and Löfqvist have showed, the research project *The Water of the Times* may have the potential to create new source material for the discussion of human sacrifices in an Old Norse tradition. The depositions from the area of Uppland show a large representation of human and horse in the analyzed material. At the former Lake Bokaren in Stavby Parish, the similarity of ante-mortal trauma on both horses and humans may be an important aspect for the interpretation of the material as the remains of sacrifice. Both species have been subject to similar treatment, including violence to the head. The horses are deposited in parts, and then only the less meaty parts; humans are represented by both single skulls and whole bodies. As the horse seems to have been a frequently represented species in wetland depositions, an interpretation as a preferred sacrificial animal can at least be considered probable. Can we make the same conclusions about the human remains?

As Fredengren and Löfqvist do, we ought to ask *who* were sacrificed. The written sources speak of sacrifices of prisoners of war. The Roman descriptions of Germanic tribes, sacrificing their vanquished enemies to Mars or Mercury, have a certain similarity with the customs connected to the cult of Óðinn in Old Norse religion. The Icelandic skald Helgi Trausti mentions his killing of an enemy as a sacrifice to Óðinn;[4] *Egils saga einhendar ok Ásmundar berserkjabana* (Ch. 8) and *Orkneyinga saga* (Ch. 8) describe the sacrificing of the captive enemies to Óðinn.[5] In the depositions in the Uppland area, we find the majority of the human bodies to be young men with healed bone trauma, possibly the results of fighting and surviving battles? In this we find an intriguing congruence with the written sources' sacrificed captives of war. It also poses the question of who received these sacrifices? Were they devoted to a god of war, such as Týr or Óðinn? The archaeological material in itself does not allow us to answer that question, but an interdisciplinary perspective may give us at least a hint. In almost all cases, the human sacrifices in the context of the Old Norse texts are connected to Óðinn.

The study by Fredengren and Löfqvist also gives us a basis for a discussion of the difference between (human) sacrifice and offering of (human) bodies or body parts in a Scandinavian setting. As in some cases the animal and human bodies have apparently been killed and disjointed (perhaps even decomposed), or in the case of animals slaughtered and butchered (likely also eaten) somewhere other than the site that they were later deposited, we are dealing with a secondary offering. From a perspective of phenomenology of religion, the sacrifice is constricted to the destruction of the object, and killing of the living being. The secondary post-mortem handling of the body, be it preparing a meal or decapitating the corpse, is separated from the act of sacrifice in a narrow sense. The deposition in water may in itself be an act of devotion by offering the body parts to a divine being. In both cases (sacrifice and offering) the result is a communication with the divine, and may be the establishing of a certain relationship with the landscape, to "draw out sacred power and holiness onto particular places in the landscape".[6]

There is need for a continued interdisciplinary research of wetland depositions and identification of human and animal sacrifices. One of the most important points of Fredengren and Löfqvist's study is that the prolonged practice of wetland depositing and sacrifice continued up to the end of the Viking Age, and the study of the practice must be considering a more complex pattern of chronological and regional variations.

Notes

1. Hubert & Mauss 1898.

2. Humphrey & Laidlaw 2007:263–264.

3. Hultgård 2001.

4. Finnur Jónsson 1912:99; Beck 1970:254.

5. A connected custom is the dedicating of the enemy army to the god even before the battle begins, as seen in *Þáttr Styrbjarnar svíakappa*, *Sǫgubrot af fornkonungum*, *Eyrbyggjasaga* and *Hlǫðskviða* (Nordberg 2003:108–112). To this we may add the archaeological finds of large quantities of weapons in bogs and other wet sites, often interpreted as deposited spoils of war (Ilkjær 2000).

6. See Fredengren & Löfqvist in this volume.

References

Primary Sources

Egils saga einhendar ok Ásmundar berserkjabana. Guðni Jónsson. 1944. *Fornaldar sögur Norðurlanda.* Band III. Reykjavik: Bókaútgáfan Forni.

Eyrbyggjasaga. Einar Ól. Sveinsson. 1935. *Eyrbyggjasaga, Einar Ól. Sveinsson gaf út.* Íslenzk fornrit IV. Reykjavik: Hið Íslenzka fornritafélag.

Hlǫðskvíða. Jónas Kristjánsson & Vésteinn Ólason. 2014. *Eddukvæði II.* Íslenzk fornrit XXXII. Reykjavik: Hið Íslenzka fornritafélag.

Orkneyinga saga. Finnbogi Guðmundsson. 1983. *Orkneyinga saga.* Íslenzk Fornrit XXXIV. Reykjavik: Hið Íslenzka fornritafélag.

Sǫgubrot af fornkonungum. Bjarni Guðnason. 1982. *Danakonunga sǫgur.* Ízlensk Fornrit XXXV. Reykjavik: Hið Íslenzka fornritafélag.

Þáttr Styrbjarnar svíakappa. Vilhjálmur Bjarnar; Finnbogi Guðmundsson & Sigurður Nordal. 1944. *Flateyjarbók I–IV.* Flateyjarútgáfan. Akraness: Printverk Akraness.

Secondary Literature

Beck, Heinrich. 1970. Germanische Menschenopfer in der literarischen Überlieferung. In H. Jankuhn (ed.). *Vorgeschichtlische Heiligtümer und Opferplätze in Mittel- und Nordeuropa.* Göttingen: Göttingen Universität, 240–258.

Finnur Jónsson. 1912. *Den norsk-islandske skjaldedigtning.* Udgiven av Finnur Jónsson. 2 vol. København: Nordisk forlag.

Fredengren, Christina & Löfqvist, Camilla. 2019. Finitude. Human and Animal Sacrifice in a Norse Setting. In K. Wikström Edholm Edholm, et al. (eds.). *Myth, Materiality, and Lived Religion in Merovingian and Viking Scandinavia.* Stockholm: Stockholm University Press, 225–268.

Hubert, Henri. & Mauss, Marcel. (1898) 1964. *Sacrifice. Its Nature and Function.* Chicago: University of Chicago Press.

Hultgård, Anders. 2001. Menschenopfer. In *Reallexikon der germanischen Altertumskunde.* Band 19. Berlin: Walter de Gruyter, 533–546.

Humphrey, Caroline & Laidlaw, James. 2007. Sacrifice and Ritualization. In E. Kyriakidis (ed.). *The Archaeology of Ritual.* Cotsen Institute of Archaeology. New Mexico: University of New Mexico Press, 255–276.

Nordberg, Andreas. 2003. *Krigarna i Odens sal. Dödsföreställningar och krigarkult i fornnordisk religion.* Stockholm: Stockholm University.

Ilkjær, Jørgen. 2000. *Illerup Ådal. Ein archäologischer Zauberspiegel.* Moesgård: Moesgård Museum.

Understanding Embodiment Through Lived Religion: A Look at Vernacular Physiologies in an Old Norse Milieu

Frog
University of Helsinki

Ero vǫlor allar	*frá Viðólfi,*
vitcar allir	*frá Vilmeiði,*
enn seiðberendr	*frá Svarthǫfða,*
iotnar allir	*frá Ymi komnir.*[1]
All *vǫlva*s are	from Viðólfr,
all sorcerers	from Vilmeiðr,
yet *seiðr*-workers	from Svarthǫfði,
all giants	from Ýmir come.

The materiality of lived religion manifests itself in countless ways. These include fundamental understandings of embodied experience. Understandings of bodies are socially constructed and result in what is called a *body image* – i.e. a symbolic and iconic model of what our body is (and is not).[2] The resulting body image can be thought of as an imaginal understanding of the body's physiology. In Western cultures today, medical science is fundamental to people's understandings of the body and how it works. The internalization of the body image occurs in the dynamic dialectic between our empirical experiences and imaginal perceptions on the one hand and, on the other, a full spectrum of circulating discourses[3] about health, fitness, illnesses, pains, nutrition, muscles, organs, joints, emotions, souls, death, ghosts, psychics, and so on and so forth. As we negotiate these discourses, encounters with

How to cite this book chapter:
Frog. 2019. Understanding Embodiment Through Lived Religion: A Look at Vernacular Physiologies in an Old Norse Milieu. In: Wikström af Edholm, K., Jackson Rova, P., Nordberg, A., Sundqvist, O. & Zachrisson, T. (eds.) *Myth, Materiality, and Lived Religion: In Merovingian and Viking Scandinavia.* Pp. 269–301. Stockholm: Stockholm University Press. DOI: https://doi.org/10.16993/bay.j. License: CC-BY.

medical specialists, with their dazzling technologies, scientific descriptions, diagnoses, remedies and models of health, provide authoritative frames of reference for developing our understanding. The outcome might vary from person to person, but at a social level it results in a biologically defined *hegemonic body image*, or an image that is the predominantly-shared frame of reference of people in society. In pre-modern cultures, body images were also internalized through the dialectic between perceived experiences and authoritative specialists, but the specialists had very different technologies. We tend to think about technologies in terms of mechanical and electronic devices. However, technologies are basically tools, techniques and strategies for accomplishing tasks. It is thus reasonable to talk about *ritual technologies* and associated specialists in those technologies. The development of understandings of the materiality of the body and vernacular physiologies can be considered in relation to those technologies and the specialists who use them. On the other hand, there seem to have been multiple technologies associated with different specialists in the Old Norse world. It is not clear that all of these specialists shared a single body image. Consequently, it is reasonable to consider that lived religion may have resulted in different body images for people aligned with different practices and specialists.

The present chapter considers whether there may have been multiple body images co-existing in an Old Norse milieu. This is explored by interrogating the relationship between ritual specialists, the technologies of their practices, and the body image with which the technologies interface. The institutions taken as examples for comparison are *berserkir*, *vǫlur* and what will be described as deep-trance specialists. This chapter does not seek to offer a full account of each institution and its sources, which is not possible in a short article. The aim here is to open the question of whether these practices may have been interfaced with different body images. This possibility is not unlike the technology of classic Chinese acupuncture existing alongside Western medicine although the former is interfaced with an incompatible body image based on the movement of life energy along bodily meridians.[4] However, the Chinese and Western body images are today engaged as alternatives for our biologically defined hegemonic understanding of all 'humans'. In the epigraph above, *vǫlur* and other types of specialists are each defined in terms of a common origin alongside *jǫtnar* 'giants'. When 'human' is not defined biologically on the basis of the empirical materiality of the body, it pulls the rug out from under our basic ontologies of social identities and our fundamental modern distinction between 'real' and 'not real'. In its place, we find an ethnocentric construct of 'people like us' from which 'others' can be fractionally differentiated – i.e. by potentially subtle increments of individual features – both physically and at an imaginal level. As a consequence, sameness or difference that we would class as supernatural may be equally or more important than empirically observable bodily features.[5] Our own ontologies incline us to interpret the origin of all *vǫlur* from Viðólfr in terms of an origin of characteristic practices that are taught and learned and thereby of the social role of a *vǫlva*. However, when this origin is presented as comparable to the origin of *jǫtnar* from Ýmir, it becomes necessary to question whether *vǫlur* are being distinguished as somehow physiologically different from the hegemonic norm of 'people like us', and, if so, how such differentiation relates to the ritual technologies on which this social identity relies.

Background

There has been a great deal of discussion surrounding conceptions of 'souls' and 'spirits' connected with vernacular religion, magic and ritual in an Old Norse milieu.[6] The conclusions of these studies vary in relation both to the material foregrounded and to the scholar's focus and methodology. Scholars tend to focus on the term and concept of *seiðr*, which gets connected to the *vǫlva*, deep-trance specialists, as well as being linked to a variety of other magic and ritual practices. The orientation of these studies is customarily to reconstruct and generalize a more or less hegemonic model of the supernatural for the Old Norse world, a model often compared and contrasted with neighbouring and historically related cultures. *Berserkir* are sometimes addressed in these discussions[7] but they are not usually seen as performers of *seiðr* and have generally been at the centre of a separate debate.[8]

272 Myth, Materiality, and Lived Religion

The present discussion differs from earlier research on the following key points: *a*) the focus is on relationships between embodied experience and ritual technologies; *b*) ritual practices are approached in terms of technologies that are not assumed to be the same or even necessarily compatible for all varieties of ritual specialist; *c*) ritual technologies are considered to interface with body images and understandings of the unseen world, *d*) which are reciprocally accessed and internalized through practices and behaviours and the discourse surrounding them; and *e*) individuals are considered to relate to specific practices in different ways and to different degrees according to, for example, social role, age, status, occupation, interest and their relationships and interactions with authoritative individuals.

The ethnocentric image of 'people like us' can be assumed to include a hegemonic body image. In his massive comparative study, Clive Tolley argues with a linguistic and philological emphasis that there is a lack of evidence for a Norse conception that 'people like us' had a free-soul. In other words, Tolley argues that an individual's consciousness or 'soul' was not generally conceived as able to leave the body and travel independently of it; he attributes cases that would appear to represent shamanic soul-journeys to Sámi contacts and narrative strategies of 'othering'.[9] A body image based on a penetrable body boundary without a free-soul appears to have entered North Finnic cultures with an incantation-based ritual technology during the Iron Age.[10] This body image allowed an individual to affect things at a distance through will, intention and perception, but consciousness could not be active independent of the body.[11] As I have sought to show elsewhere, the relevant technology was strategically contrasted with, and gradually displaced, inherited forms of shamanism,[12] and also shamanism among Sámi populations that eventually were linguistically assimilated.[13] Later Scandinavian and Finno-Karelian legend traditions similarly seem to identify the separable soul with the Sámi as 'other'.[14] In contrast, supernatural journeys by non-Sámi appear to be conceived of in terms of transformations of the physical body.[15] Norse emotions and illness seem to have been similarly conceived of in terms of forces and influences (including via perception or awareness as a form of interaction) that penetrate the boundary of the body image; that boundary became more open in relation to fear and passivity, or more resilient in relation to strength of will and aggression.[16] The penetrable body will be tentatively taken as a hegemonic body image of 'people like us' in relation to which a body image with a free-soul was considered 'other'. Importantly, both Scandinavian and Finno-Karelian traditions nevertheless reveal an awareness of multiple body images.

Source Materials and Approach

Medieval Scandinavian written sources present a rich variety of apparently relevant information ranging from simple vocabulary to elaborate descriptions of magical and ritual practices. The practices are represented from non-specialist perspectives, and they were in all likelihood seen as historically, religiously and culturally 'other' (i.e. belonging to a pre-Christian cultural milieu). Such sources are here inferred to draw on a) contemporary circulating discourse, and potentially also on b) other written texts that developed in an evolving dialogue with that discourse. The sources thus reflect the individual and social imagination of the past. The authors are Christians – at least in their own eyes.[17] They were writing for Christian audiences in a form of heritage construction, representing the past as relevant to the present and its social order.[18] An implicit principle *What we say about them, we say about ourselves*, can be assumed. The representations of magic and ritual in historically remote contexts can be contrasted with their absence from the so-called contemporary sagas, which should equally be viewed as self-representation. The sources discussed here are Icelandic, where it is doubtful that the *vǫlva* institution became rooted in the emergence of the insular culture,[19] where *berserkir* became emblems of paganism in conversion discourse,[20] and where, in contrast, what appears to be a deep-trance ritual is described as deciding the legal conversion of Iceland.[21]

Culture is here viewed as "localized in concrete, [socially] accessible signs, the most important of which are actually occurring instances of discourse."[22] Mythology is approached in the broad sense of systems of symbols and structures that are emotionally invested (if potentially contested) models for interpreting experience and understanding seen and unseen worlds with which people interact in the present, past and/or future. From this perspective, the model of a supernaturally empowered agent such as a *vǫlva* or a *berserkr* is viewed as a symbol of mythology. Body images are equally viewed as symbolic models for understanding one's own or others' bodies. Such symbols are analysed and interpreted in terms of *mythic discourse*. Mythic discourse refers to mythology as it is engaged, used, manipulated and communicated by individuals in societies.[23] It is characterized by the ongoing negotiation of these symbols, their interpretations and significance, which vary like a "kaleidoscope, in perpetual motion" as they are used from different perspectives, in different contexts, and in different combinations.[24] Although interpretations, valuations and uses may vary, they must remain recognizable in order to function. For example, FIRE DOES NOT BURN BERSERKR (small capitals indicate a symbolic unit) appears to be a motif historically connected with *berserkr*.[25] This motif was also taken up in conversion narratives, where it was used in a narrative pattern that asserts the superior power of Christianity: FIRE DOES NOT BURN BERSERKR is affirmed as valid for normal fires, but not for fires consecrated by Christians.[26] The motif maintains formal continuity as a symbolic, meaning-bearing unit of narration, while the action and the *berserkr* performing it are interpreted and evaluated from a Christian perspective with a variation that shows the *berserkr*'s inferiority to the power of Christianity.

Methodologically, the present study identifies traditional units of narration related to practices and outcomes of practices that are attached to each type of specialist. Mythic symbols are distinguished according to formal types that are used in structural combinations: an *image* is a static unit equivalent to the grammatical category of a noun (e.g. VǪLVA, FREE-SOUL, etc.); a *motif* is a minimal unit that entails the equivalent to the grammatical category of a verb and in which one or more images participate (e.g. VǪLVA PERFORMS RITUAL); a *narrative pattern* is a complex conventional sequence of images and motifs that forms a recognizable unit of narration.[27] Symbolic units are considered to be distinguishable from the language that mediates them, so the word *vǫlva* may in some cases be used as a general word for 'witch' whereas the image VǪLVA may be recognizable through description or in relation to a motif or narrative pattern without the term *vǫlva*. Units of narration are compared and analysed in order to extract information with which they are encoded about practices and practitioners. For example, the motif FIRE DOES NOT BURN BERSERKR indicates that *berserkir* were thought to remain unburned by fire; the narrative pattern discussed below includes information on a performance situation considered emblematic of a *vǫlva*. The relevance of this information for historical perspectives is conditional on the units of narration having continuity from the corresponding social institution. The features discussed below do not seem to be adapted from foreign literature and Christian discourse, and they are considered more likely to be rooted in historical phenomena than to be spontaneous inventions without models.

The examples of traditional units of narration discussed below have the characteristics of *legends*, which conditions them as sources of information. A legend can be described as a short story about a specific encounter that is developed on a traditional plot or motif and engages contestable beliefs about history or the supernatural. Legends are built around concrete elements in an event and/or its outcomes as they would appear to an observer. Scandinavian and Finno-Karelian legends of Sámi shamanism are instructive: their core is simply 'the man lay there as if he were dead and when he woke up he possessed/knew something that was impossible to explain except by magic'; and this core is situated in a framing situation (which may itself be established in the tradition).[28] The shaman's performance activity tends to remain unmentioned except insofar as it is directly relevant to the plot. Information about performance was (to varying degrees) in circulation, but it was not essential to telling these stories. Instead, it provided a resource for prolongation, for the creation of verisimilitude and for other rhetorical effects (e.g. underscoring "otherness"). In the legends, a shaman's practices are not only reduced to a single, emblematic activity: traditionalization generally excludes the ethnographic information that would be of interest here. Performances by the types of specialists brought into focus below exhibit the same sort of reduction to minimal elements of what an onlooker might observe.

Berserkir *and* Berserksgangr

A *berserkr* is represented as a supernaturally empowered warrior. *Berserkir* appear in Old Norse sources as a king's elite guard, the soldiers leading a battle charge, as valorised ancestors of Icelanders, and as exceptionally dangerous vikings.[29] They often appear as adversaries against whom heroes prove themselves. Presumably by extension, they also appear in conversion narratives as supernatural agents in local communities whose power can be overcome by Christianity. Corresponding ritual and magical performances are not attributed to *berserkir*, but they are distinguished by *berserksgangr* 'the going of a *berserkr*' – wild behaviour characterized by howling and biting on a shield.[30] The activity state of *berserksgangr* seems to have manifested a supernatural empowerment linked to the motifs of imperviousness to iron and fire.[31] The conception of burning has not been investigated in terms of vernacular physiology, although it clearly relates to the ability of fire to affect the body. The motif IRON DOES NOT CUT was linked to a broad range of battle magic, including protective objects[32] and incantations.[33] Sources may account for this imperviousness with the motif GAZE BLUNTS IRON, relating it to will and magical agency (not specific to *berserkir*). However, imperviousness to iron may also simply appear as a "fact" that the protagonist must circumvent, suggesting an inherent quality of the *berserkr* or *berserksgangr*.[34] The body image is emphasized by reference to *berserkir* as *hamrammr*. *Hamr* means 'embodied form' and *rammr* means '(supernaturally) powerful'. *Berserkir* are also described as *eigi einhamr* 'not single-formed', although written sources do not characterize *berserkir* as shapeshifters *per se*.[35] The motif IRON DOES NOT CUT "leads to many a *berserkr* being clubbed to death,"[36] which underscores that *berserkir* are not impervious to injury *per se* but rather to penetration of the body's boundary.

If the *berserkr* is accepted as a historical type of supernaturally empowered warrior who performed *berserksgangr*, it can be inferred that *berserksgangr* did not occur randomly in society and could be initiated by *berserkir* when the situation required (e.g. for a duel). It was thus a trained behaviour of heightened (but directionally controlled) aggression that could be strategically incited by the *berserkr*, even if it might also be incited through situational stimuli. Performance practices can then be inferred for both training the behaviour and self-incitement. The emblematic howling and shield-biting can be interpreted as a performance of posturing to build confidence and intimidate adversaries.[37] These behaviours are also directly comparable to the performance of Finno-Karelian ritual specialists who, through such behaviour, manifest a hyperactive trance that they conceived in terms of "raised" supernatural power which secured the body's boundary.[38] The heightened aggressive behaviour appears directly linked to supernatural empowerment[39] that correlates with the motif IRON DOES NOT CUT. Viewed in relation to the hegemonic body image postulated above, this state of raised aggression can thus be viewed as an extension of that physiological model to seal the body's boundary also against weapons, which is directly paralleled in Finno-Karelian battle magic.[40] Reference to *berserkir* as *hamrammr* and *eigi einhamr* has been interpreted as a change in the body's form e.g. into that of a bear or wolf. The approach outlined here suggests that these terms centrally referred to a conception of *berserksgangr* as a supernatural change in *hamr* that made the body impenetrable without necessarily affecting its outward appearance.[41] This model is accepted here for the sake of argument.

Vǫlur

The term *vǫlva* is commonly associated with supernaturally empowered women who have the power to prophesy, although the term and corresponding image do not invariably co-occur.[42] Nevertheless, the term *vǫlva* is particularly associated with a distinct performance situation. Such performances will here be considered as emblematic of the specialist and as central to maintaining the distinct image VǪLVA.[43] The performance situation is encoded as the central scene in the complex narrative pattern that John McKinnell identifies as *The hostile young man*: a *vǫlva* is hosted by a patriarch at a feast where she publicly performs prophesies; the young hero disapproves of the event; he does not want to hear his own fortune after others have been told;

the seeress makes her prophesy anyway and the hero is resent-
ful or aggressively hostile.[44] The social performance situation is
interfaced with the narrative pattern and cannot be significantly
altered without changing the narrative pattern itself. This interface would stabilize the social transmission of the performance
situation in cultural memory.[45] When used in the narrative pattern, no additional information about performance is normally
included except that the *vǫlva*'s activity was an itinerant practice: she moved from feast to feast in her role. When the performance situation is presented in other contexts, more information
appears. In *Eiríks saga rauða* 4, the elaboration of detail yields a
deceptive verisimilitude that raises a flag of caution about taking it at face value.[46] In *Hrólfs saga kraka* 3, minimal additional
details are mentioned but do not seem of interest as such to the
author.[47] Saxo's *Gesta Danorum* VII.1.5 also gives a description
of this episode in *Hrólfs saga*, but the description is problematic
because it seems to conflate the *vǫlva*'s performance with a ritual
performed by *galdramenn* 'incantation men' according to *Hrólfs
saga* 1.[48] The basic performance situation also seems to be the setting of the *vǫlva*'s speech in *Vǫluspá*, presented before the patriarch Óðinn and a broader audience.[49] However, in dialogues with
vǫlur in the mythology, the *vǫlur* seem to be raised from the dead
and compelled to speak; they should thus not be assumed to accu-
rately reflect the practices of *vǫlur* in society.

These accounts suggest that a *vǫlva* performed prophesies and
perhaps imparted other knowledge[50] at social events where she
was hosted. The performance appears structured and may have
been elaborate, including supporting roles.[51] The specific performance activities of a *vǫlva* are uncertain.[52] However, the *vǫlva* is
represented as responding to questions in verse,[53] which suggests
that *a)* she was conscious, *b)* she mediated knowledge in direct
interaction with others present, and *c)* she formulated responses in
a form of aesthetically distinct verbal art. (N.B. – the Eddic form
of the *vǫlva*'s responses may be a convention of the representation of verbal art in epic/saga genres rather than being historically accurate to a *vǫlva*'s mode of ritual speech.) Verse responses
are introduced with the formulaic expression *varð henni þá ljóð
á munni* 'then a song came into her mouth', which is linked to

women's spontaneous verse speech.[54] This formula situates agency and the source of information spoken outside of the woman, which could relate to the *vǫlva* switching between first and third person in verses of *Vǫluspá* and *Ǫrvar-Odds saga*.[55] The *vǫlva* nevertheless appears able to orchestrate inspired speech in a controlled way within the interactive framework of the ritual event. The mythic image VǪLVA would thus be characterized by a body image that is opened to external power or knowledge in contrast to the supernaturally closed body image of a *berserkr*. The wider use of the *verðr e-m ljóð á munni* formula suggests an extension of the hegemonic body model that may be related to conceptions of gendered difference in open/closed, weak/strong or soft/hard bodies (as in Finno-Karelian tradition[56]). However, rather than the body image of a *vǫlva* being a hegemonic body image at an extreme of openness, it was presumably supernaturally opened in a controlled and strategic way. The distinction of a *berserkr* from other people in terms of his *hamr* presents the possibility that the *vǫlva*'s body image was also considered fractionally differentiated from the hegemonic norm. Such differentiation could account for *vǫlur* being categorically distinguished according to descent from a primal origin alongside *jǫtnar* as if *vǫlur* were a type of supernatural being. This interpretation remains conjectural, but it is not inherently improbable; it will be accepted here for the sake of argument.

Deep-Trance Specialists

There are a number of accounts of individuals who conceal their bodies under a covering or in a closed space during which an animal appears and acts on the performer's behalf or following which the performer possesses knowledge from remote locations.[57] The performers are not identified with any single noun. Clive Tolley observes that the motif of covering the face or body in shamanic rituals exhibits an isogloss including Norse, Sámi and, to the east across the White Sea, Nenets,[58] not to mention Irish to the west.[59] This isogloss appears indicative of cross-cultural contacts. The Norse sources do not seem to distinguish between performances by *Finnar*[60] and those by Norsemen. Treating practices as categorically equivalent across an otherwise socially significant Norse-*Finnr* ethnic divide suggests that they were completely "other" from the hegemonic perspective of the sources. Analysis is further complicated by the possibility that circulating discourse has homogenized diverse practices of both Norsemen and *Finnar*. As a result, traditionalization has subordinated practices that were historically distinct. Nevertheless, the model of practice in circulating discourse is fairly well represented and offers at least some perspective on formal aspects of a ritual practice.

The ritual separated the performer(s) physically or symbolically from others: the performer covered their body or head, or one or more performers enclosed themselves in a space so that the performance is completely concealed. As in later legends of Sámi shamanic rituals, there is no indication of performative activity *per se*. Nor is there any indication that it was orchestrated before an audience. The activity is distinct from murmuring into a cloak or skin and gaining access to knowledge while in a conscious state.[61] The performer is closed off from communication for the duration of the event, which is emphasized by a prohibition against speaking the performer's name until the performance is concluded. If an animal or monster appears and acts on the behalf of the performer, the length of the performance seems to correlate with the period during which the animal is active; when the performance concerns the acquisition of knowledge, it may last one or more days.

The description is consistent with a shamanic ritual involving a deep-trance state[62] and journey of a free-soul and/or spirit helpers. Descriptions of animal agents acting on behalf of the performing individuals in sagas strikingly suggests that images of helping spirits or free-souls had advanced in circulating discourse from legends of encounters and conflicts in the supernatural world to interaction with heroes and their adversaries as agents physically present. In later legends, naming can disrupt magical transformations,[63] which could potentially be linked to the naming prohibition. The *Finnar* maintained shamanic practices, as is evident from the exceptional account in the *Historia Norwegiae*.[64] The trans-ethnic homogenization of representations in circulating discourse suggests that the ritual behaviour was not ethnically marked as it appears to be in later legends, with several implications: *a*) certain Norse practices were considered to be equivalent to the shamanic rituals of *Finnar*; *b*) the Norse practices may have been more prominent in shaping the representation in Norse circulating discourse than their counterpart(s) among *Finnar*; *c*) some sources may identify such practices with *Finnar* in narration as a strategy of "othering" rather than representing knowledge of the ethnicity of the specialists concerned;[65] *d*) some sources may disregard supernatural aspects in order to minimize the "othering" of the performer.[66]

The homogenization of practices makes it possible that several different technologies may have been conformed to this model of representation. It is not clear whether this practice was *útisetja* 'sitting out'[67] or if *útisetja* may have been a term for a range of practices subordinated to this convention of representation. The descriptions could equally reflect the *vǫlva*'s technology orchestrated in private practice activity (and such practice by *vǫlur* is not improbable). They could also reflect a vigil-like practice for summoning supernatural agents to mediate knowledge.[68] Rituals for strategic and structured "dreaming" are also quite possible[69] and would conform to dreams as an established venue in Norse culture for direct communication with supernatural agents,[70] whose visitation could follow from being called on.[71] Nevertheless, the trans-ethnic homogenization with *Finnar* rituals indicates that, not only did the performances exhibit some formal parallels, but that at least some of the practices were marked as at an extreme of "otherness": they were not viewed as belonging to the society of "people like us". Moreover, the prohibition against naming the performer seems most likely to relate somehow to the performer's consciousness – some form of free-soul – being active as a goal-oriented agent while their body remained in one place.[72] Vernacular ritual technologies dependent on a free-soul would thus depend on a body image very different from the Norse hegemonic model but consistent with that of *Finnar*. Whatever the rituals might have been, a physiological equivalence in "otherness" could account for the trans-ethnic homogenization of what were most likely ethnically distinct practices.

Perspectives

Traditional motifs and narrative patterns in circulating discourse remain encoded with information about different types of specialist ritual performers and emblematic features of their abilities, of their practices, and of the outcomes of their practices. This information can be triangulated to hypothetically model understandings of the body image associated with these practitioners. The body image of the particular type of practitioner can then be viewed in relation to a probable Norse hegemonic norm of "people like us". In the case of *berserkir*, tentatively, performance appears to have sealed the body's boundary through aggression; this involved a process that was considered to exceed the capacities of a hegemonic body image and thus qualified as a change in *hamr*. In contrast, *vǫlur* seem more likely to have strategically opened their bodies in performance in a controlled way that would allow them to mediate inspired speech from supernatural sources outside of themselves (however this may have been imagined). This opening of the body should not be misconstrued as passivity: *vǫlur* are presented as respected supernaturally empowered agents. They are represented as being able to control what was or was not predicted, able to shape their predictions and even to construct fates through their performance. The body images of *berserkir* and *vǫlur* appear most likely to reflect gendered difference in body images carried to supernaturally empowered extremes or ideals that simultaneously set them apart from other members of society. The deep-trance specialist is in some respects more ambiguous to approach. The conventional representation of this practice in circulating discourse suggests its central referent was a practice involving activity of a free-soul, and that this was perceived as wholly "other". This view reciprocally supports the theory that the hegemonic body image excluded the free-soul (as in Finno-Karelian cultures), or at least excluded a free-soul that could operate independently of the empirically perceivable body through the individual's conscious agency. Each of these three categories of practitioner appears to be characterized by a body image distinguished from the hegemonic norm.

The verses of the epigraph to this chapter seem to suggest that different types of ritual performers were categorically distinguished by common origins like varieties of supernatural beings. The sources do not foreground this. *Eiríks saga* mentions that Þórbjǫrg *lítilvǫlva*'s nine sisters had all been *spákonur* 'prophesy-women'.[73] The term *hálf-berserkr* 'half-*berserkr*'[74] treats *berserkr* as an ethnic category,[75] and *Skalla*-Grímr seems to inherit a changeable *hamr* from his father, although he is not called a *berserkr*,[76] while his son Egill exhibits a corresponding personality profile.[77] At least in some sources, it appears that the "otherness" of these categorical identities was seen as inheritable, of which it seems body image was a likely part.

Each of the three cases above appears to be a practice-based institution. Although their ritual technologies are beyond reconstruction, it is clear that these practices depended on competence and could be strategically initiated with predictable outcomes. Each can thus be assumed to have relied on a ritual technology which could be used to situationally initiate the supernaturally empowered state. That technology would have been linked to social perceptions of competence and specialization, but it would also have been fundamental to training the presumably ecstatic behaviour as a response to performance and as essential to structuring and controlling the performer's experience.[78] In each case, the ritual technology can be assumed to be interfaced with the corresponding body image with which it engages. At the same time, the hegemonic body image can be assumed to have been interfaced with ritual technologies for healing, sex appeal and potency, protection from forces and agents in the environment, and so forth. In other words, "people like us" who were not specialized in ritual technologies would have internalized their body images in large part through practices related to their own bodies and the authorities who engaged those body image models in ritual and discourse. Such ritual practices might be described as "mainstream" technologies. The Finno-Karelian traditions suggest by analogy that *berserkir* could have or did employ (some of) the same "mainstream" technologies in *berserksgangr*. This is much less certain with *vǫlur*, whose emblematic performance practices differed in complex ways. They appear to have used distinct genres of verbal art also in dialogic situational interaction. Attested Eddic poetry does not exhibit the flexibility and formulaic infrastructure conducive to appropriate situational improvisation.[79] This women's poetry may have been in a separate poetic system equipped for this type of use.[80] In this case, the mythology interfaced with the poetic system may have differed in significant ways from the mythology known through the *Edda*s and skaldic verse.[81] Their ritual practices may equally have operated through technologies markedly different from "mainstream" technologies, and the minimal variation from a hegemonic body image suggested here could be grossly oversimplified. Leaving aside the potential variety of practices that may be concealed behind representations of deep-trance specialists, central (though not necessarily all) technologies employed in these practices seem to have been interfaced with a body image marked as "other". They are likely to have not only been different from those of other specialists addressed here; they were potentially no less inconsistent with the technology of *berserkir* than Chinese acupuncture is with modern Western medicine (which does not prevent one person from using both). When considering the potential diversity of body images in an Old Norse milieu, it should be born in mind that these body images are not arbitrarily identified with different types of people; they are internalized and understood through practices, the ritual technologies on which these practices rely, and the broader range of circulating discourse. Identifying marked difference in body image between types of specialists thus becomes a crucial symptom of difference in the technologies on which their respective practices rely.

Notes

1. *Vǫluspá inn skamma* (*Hyndluljóð* 33).

2. See e.g. Stark 2006:146–162 and works there cited.

3. On circulating discourse, see Urban 1991:1–28 *et passim*; see also Urban 1996:249–253. I use discourses in the plural because discourse is linked to social situations and to the groups and networks participating in those situations. As a consequence, not all discourse is

uniformly accessible to everyone in a society and the different groups and networks can maintain multiple discourses in parallel.

4. In her research on mainly eighteenth-century Swedish vernacular religion, Van Gent (2009:12) refers to this type of phenomenon as a "plurality of discourses of the self".

5. See also Lévi-Strauss 1952:11–16; de Castro 1998:474–477; in Old Norse, see also Lindow 1995:*passim*.

6. These discussions are often integrated into broader treatments of magic, ritual and religious practices, e.g. Strömbäck 2000 (1935):150–190 but see also 220–236; Price 2002:224–227 *et passim*; Dillmann 2006:238–308; Heide 2006:*passim*; for extensive chapters devoted to the topic, see Tolley 2009 I:167–271.

7. Price 2002:366–388; Dillmann 2006:261–268; Tolley 2009 I:563–579.

8. Recent monographs devoted to the topic of *bersirkir* are Samson 2011 and Dale 2014.

9. Tolley 2009 I:463–517 and see also 176–199, esp. 193, 199, and 589.

10. For discussion and references see Frog 2013, esp. 59–68.

11. See Stark 2006:146–162, 254–356, 451–458.

12. The term 'shamanism' has a problematic history of use (for an extreme view, see Rydving 2011). It is here used in the narrow sense of Central and Northern Eurasian traditions or 'classic shamanism' (Siikala 1978:14–15), which are characterized by a system of features that take culture-specific forms within local religious and mythological frameworks. Problems in applying classic shamanism to Proto-Sámi (on which see Frog 2017:61) do not extend to features relevant to the present discussion.

13. Frog 2013:59–68, 73–74, 80–84, 87–91.

14. Christiansen 1958: type 3080; Jauhiainen 1998: types D1031–1040; af Klintberg 2010: types M151–160.

15. E.g. af Klintberg 2010:Q11–20. A notable exception is a migratory legend-type and its variations in which the image of a free-soul

is structurally interfaced with the plot (Q1–3). Already Lauri Honko (1960) observed that these models vary by genre: motifs of 'soul loss' could appear in Finno-Karelian genres that do not seek full verisimilitude with social life, such as folktales and epic, while remaining absent from illness diagnostics and healing practices. Note that the distinction foregrounded here has often been overlooked or not considered significant: the Cartesian model of the mind/spirit as separate from the body seems to have led the interpretation of the vernacular traditions, and also earlier led me to view such stories through the lens of 'soul journeys'. Emphasis heré is also on models circulating in narrative traditions and ritual practices and does not exclude the idea that individual accounts referring to separation of mind/soul and body might be found, for example, in court records (cf. Van Gent 2009:79–85), where this remains unclear.

16. Kanerva 2015:93–94, 135–144. Van Gent (2009, esp. Ch. 3) discusses the penetrable body interfaced with Swedish vernacular magic and ritual but her focus is the "semantics" of the magical body as reflecting social tensions without exploring how the dynamics of penetrability or forces affecting it were conceived.

17. Lotman 1990:130.

18. See also Tulinius 2002, esp. 65–68.

19. The emblematic ritual context of a *vǫlva*'s performance is described as an itinerant practice in which the *vǫlva* would move from location to location as a guest of honour at feasts that were presumably costly to each in the series of hosts. If any *vǫlur* immigrated to Iceland, there is no reason to assume that the practice would be embraced locally or regionally, or even that it persisted on a single farm across generations.

20. E.g. *Kristni saga* 2, 9; *Grágás* 7; Dale 2014:140–141, 314–319; in contrast, translation literature from Norway includes Christian *berserkir* and historical records show *berserkr* as an epithet of Christians as late as the 14th century (Samson 2011:225–226; Dale 2014:180–183; 200–202).

21. On this ritual, see Jón Hnefill Aðalsteinsson 1978:esp. Ch.13.

22. Urban 1991:1; I edit Urban's "publicly" to "socially" to accommodate cultural elements transmitted in contexts closed to some

members or perhaps the majority of a society and that may thus be socially but not publicly accessible.

23. The approach to mythic discourse used here is introduced more fully in Frog 2015.

24. Siikala 2012:19.

25. Samson 2011:238–240 and Dale 2014:139–142.

26. E.g. *Kristni saga* 2, 9.

27. See further Frog 2015:38–41.

28. Christiansen 1958:3080; Jauhiainen 1998:D1031–1040; af Klintberg 2010:M151–160.

29. See Samson 2011:151–156, 198–225; Dale 2014:111–114.

30. Samson 2011:227–232; Dale 2014:71–98, 147–162; *Gesta Danorum* VII.2.7:185 correlates sorcery directly with this performance behaviour.

31. Samson 2011:236–240; Dale 2014:139–145.

32. E.g. *Hálfdanar saga Eysteinssonar* 16, 20.

33. Cf. *Hávamál* 148.

34. Dale 2014:142–146.

35. Dale 2014:120–127; for a view linking this vocabulary to transformation, see Samson 2011:244–260; see also Bourns 2017:215–225.

36. Dale 2014:142.

37. Dale 2014:162–163.

38. On the specialist's trance techniques, see Siikala 2002:242–250; on increased 'hardness' of the body in this state, see Stark 2006:310–314.

39. See also Price 2002, Ch. 6.

40. The incantation tradition is generally informed by the semiotics of Iron Age warfare and so ritual defences against physical and supernatural harm converge, noting that with modernization such rituals also provided protection against bullets (see e.g. Siikala 2002:281–294; Stark 2006:279–281).

41. Bourns similarly stresses that the verb *hamask*, related to *hamr*, can mean either to change appearance or, as he puts it, "to change temperament and enter a wild frenzy, like a *berserkr*" (2017:219; cf. Cleasby & Vigfusson 1896, *s.v. hamask*; ONP, *s.v. hama*).

42. See McKinnell 2003:118–119.

43. Cf. Sámi being identified as supernaturally empowered agents in a variety of legend-types (e.g. af Klintberg 2010:M32, 43, 61–65, 107, 135) but remaining the only agents in legends of deep trance rituals.

44. McKinnell 2003:122–125. This narrative pattern appears with a full performance context in *Ǫrvar-Odds saga* 2, *Orms þáttr Stórólfssonar* 5, *Vatnsdœla saga* 10, and with the role of the *vǫlva* filled by the mother of the king (not called a *vǫlva*) in *Flateyjarbók*'s *Óláfs saga Tryggvasonar* 50; cf. also *Flateyjarbók*'s *Óláfs saga helga* 25. The production of written accounts of the performance context in these and other sources no doubt played a part in its evolution in circulating discourse, but the body of sources suggests a vital position in ultimately oral discourse rather than a literary invention.

45. See also Frog 2014, esp.128.

46. Tolley 2009 I:487–498; see also Egeler 2015:88.

47. See also Egeler 2015:87–88.

48. Saxo's *vǫlva* tries to acquire objects from a remote location (children!), falls unconscious, and, whereas she interrupts her visionary performance in *Hrólfs saga* 3 when a physically present person throws gold into her lap, the people in the physically remote location threw gold into her lap according to Saxo.

49. *Vǫluspá* 1.

50. *Hrólfs saga* 3 (paralleled in *Gesta Danorum*; cf. also *Vǫluspá*) may suggest that a *vǫlva* could also find lost and stolen objects, but this might simply be the result of subordinating the ritual to the saga's plot.

51. *Eiríks saga* links the event to the saga through a supportive singer in the ritual. Within the narrative, the *vǫlva*'s prophesy for this individual equates to a reward for assistance, which makes it seem more

likely to reflect circulating discourse of supporting singing than an authorial invention to motivate the reward. Saxo also mentions the *vǫlva*'s assistants where these are structurally relevant to narration. If the *vǫlva* was an itinerant specialist hosted at a feast of any magnitude, a correspondingly elaborate performance can be expected.

52. *Eiríks saga* and *Hrólfs saga* mention that performance is on a *seiðhjallr* 'scaffold for performing magic (*seiðr*)'. However, in narrative discourse, a *seiðhjallr* was a characteristic location for a formalized pagan ritual performance (see also Sundqvist 2012:281–283). The writers or redactors of these two sagas (or their informants) may have independently added this detail as an elaboration with a commonplace from the discourse on pagan practices without a historical link to a *vǫlva*'s performance *per se*. In *Lokasenna* 24, Loki insults Óðinn for 'tapping on a *vétt* like a *vǫlva*' (*draptu á vétt sem vǫlor*), but alliteration between *vétt* and *vǫlva* presents the possibility that either word could be a poetic alternative for another noun and thus may not refer to the activity of a *vǫlva* as a type of specialist.

53. *Ǫrvar-Odds saga* 2; *Orms þáttr* 5; *Hrólfs saga* 3; Saxo also stresses her *carmina* 'songs; oracular responses', but his account is problematic.

54. For a survey and discussion of this formula, see Quinn 1998.

55. *Hrólfs saga* mentions that the *vǫlva* yawns a great deal before her first prophetic speech. This has been interpreted as taking spirits into her body (Tolley 1995:58; Price 2002:209), but motifs of yawning and becoming drowsy are generally associated with supernatural contact (Strömbäck 2000 (1935):152–159; *Njáls saga* 13:37 n.7; Jón Hnefill Aðalsteinsson 1978:109–121. This motif could have been linked to the *vǫlva*'s performance as an elaboration with no connection to historical practices.

56. See Stark 2006:264–265.

57. E.g. Strömbäck 2000 (1935):160–206; Jón Hnefill Aðalsteinsson 1978:113–123; Price 2002:361–362.

58. Tolley 2009 I:260.

59. Jón Hnefill Aðalsteinsson 1978:116–117.

60. Most likely speakers of Southwest Proto-Sámi.

61. Jón Hnefill Aðalsteinsson 1978:110–113; cf. *Njáls saga* 13:37 n. 9.

62. My thanks to Jens Peter Schjødt for pointing out that "unconscious trance" is a problematic overgeneralization. On different depths of trance in relation to types of performance, see Siikala 1978:338–339.

63. E.g. af Klintberg 2010:Q42–43, 45–46.

64. On this account, see Tolley 2009 I:258–268.

65. Cf. the *vǫlva* as a *Finna* in *Vatnsdæla saga* 10; for discussions of how magic is used and manipulated in discourse, see e.g. Stark 2006; Van Gent 2009; Meylan 2014.

66. E.g. Þorgeirr Þorkelsson's performance.

67. E.g. Strömbäck 2000 (1935):126–129; Dillmann 2006:42–44; Tolley 2009 II:133–134.

68. Cf. Jón Árnason 1862:436–438.

69. Ef. Jón Hnefill Aðalsteinsson 1978:116–117.

70. See e.g. Kelchner 1935:66–72.

71. E.g. *Þorláks saga biskups* 28, 65–67, 69, 81.

72. Cf. also Siikala 1978:339 on deep trance and interaction with non-performers.

73. *Eiríks saga* 4.

74. *Svarfdæla saga* 7.

75. With the exception of *hálf-troll* 'half-troll', it is characteristic of such 'half-breed' terms that they appear as *hapax legomena* – e.g. *hálf-bergrisi* 'half-mountain-giant', *hálf-risi* 'half-giant', *hálf-Finnr* 'half-*Finnr*', *hálf-Karell* 'half-Karelian'.

76. *Eigils saga* 40.

77. See also Samson 2011:151–156.

78. See also Siikala 1978, esp. 49–52 and 339 on shamans' performances.

79. Frog 2011:19–28 and works there cited.

80. This has been suggested by Eila Stepanova for women's lament poetry (2011:140; cf. also Mundal 2013:368–379).

81. Cf. the differences between the mythology of Karelian lament poetry and the Kalevalaic epic and incantation poetry with which it co-existed for centuries, discussed in Stepanova 2012:265–281.

References
Primary sources

Egils saga. Íslenzk Fornrít II. Reykjavík: Hið Íslenzka Fornritafélag.

Eiríks saga rauða. Íslenzk Fornrít IV. Reykjavík: Hið Íslenzka Fornritafélag.

Flateyjarbók. Guðbrandur Vigfússon & Carl Rikard Unger (eds.) 1860–1868. *Flateyjarbók: En samling af norske konge-sagaer I–III.* Christiania: P.T. Mallings Forlagsboghandel.

Gesta Danorum. Olrik, J. & H. Ræder (eds.) 1931. *Saxonis Gesta Danorum.* Hauniæ: Levin & Munksgaard.

Grágás. Vilhjálmur Finsen (ed. & trans.). 1852. *Grágás. Islændernes lovbog i fristatens tid, udg. efter det kongelige Bibliotheks haanskrift I–II.* Copenhagen: Berling.

Hálfdanar saga Eysteinssonar. Guðni Jónsson & Bjarni Vihjálmsson (eds.). 1943–1944. *Fornaldarsögur Norðurlanda III.* Reykjavik: Bókaútgáfan Forni, 285–319.

Hávamál. Neckel, Gustav & Kuhn, Hans. 1963. *Edda. Die Lieder des Codex Regius nebst vewandten Denkmälern I: Text.* 4th Edition. Heidelberg: Carl Winters Universitätsbuchhandlung, 17–44.

Historia Norwegie. Ekrem, Inger & Boje Mortensen, Lars (eds.). 2006. *Historia Norwegie.* Trans. Peter Fisher. Copenhagen: Museum Tusculanum Press.

Hrólfs saga kraka. Guðni Jónsson & Bjarni Vihjálmsson (eds.). 1943–1944. *Fornaldarsögur Norðurlanda II.* Reykjavik: Bókaútgáfan Forni, 3–93.

Hyndluljóð. Neckel, Gustav & Kuhn, Hans 1963. *Edda. Die Lieder des Codex Regius nebst vewandten Denkmälern I: Text*. 4th Edition. Heidelberg: Carl Winters Universitätsbuchhandlung, 288–296.

Kristni saga. Hannes Finnsson (ed.). 1773. *Kristni-saga, sive Historia Religionis Christianæ in Islandiam introductæ; nec non Þattr af Isleifi Biskupi, sive Narratio de Isleifo Episcopo: Ex Manuscriptis Legati Magnæani*. Hafnia: Frid. Christian Godiche.

Lokasenna. Neckel, Gustav & Kuhn, Hans. 1963. *Edda: Die Lieder des Codex Regius nebst vewandten Denkmälern I: Text*. 4th Edition. Heidelberg: Carl Winters Universitätsbuchhandlung, 96–110.

Njáls saga. Íslenzk Fornrít XII. Reykjavík: Hið Íslenzka Fornritafélag.

Óláfs saga helga, see *Flateyjarbók*.

Óláfs saga Tryggvasonar, see *Flateyjarbók*.

Orms þáttr Stórólfssonar. Íslenzk Fornrít XIII. Reykjavík: Hið Íslenzka Fornritafélag.

Ǫrvar-Odds saga. Íslenzk Fornrít I. Reykjavík: Hið Íslenzka Fornritafélag, 283–399.

Svarfdæla saga. Íslenzk Fornrít IX. Reykjavík: Hið Íslenzka Fornritafélag.

Þorláks saga biskups. Íslenzk Fornrít XVI. Reykjavík: Hið Íslenzka Fornritafélag.

Vatnsdæla saga. Íslenzk Fornrít VIII. Reykjavík: Hið Íslenzka Fornritafélag.

Vǫluspá. Neckel, Gustav & Kuhn, Hans. 1963. *Edda. Die Lieder des Codex Regius nebst vewandten Denkmälern I: Text*. 4th Edition. Heidelberg: Carl Winters Universitätsbuchhandlung, 1–16.

Secondary literature

Bourns, Timothy J. S. 2017. *Between Nature and Culture. Animals and Humans in Old Norse Literature*. Unpublished PhD dissertation. Oxford: University of Oxford.

de Castro, Eduardo Viveiros. 1998. Cosmological Deixis and Amerindian Perspectivism. In *Journal of the Royal Anthropological Institute*, vol. 4, no. 3, 469–488.

Christiansen, Reidar Th. 1958. *The Migratory Legends. A Proposed List of Types with a Systematic Catalogue of the Norwegian Variants*. Folklore Fellows' Communications 175. Helsinki: Academia Scientiarum Fennica.

Cleasby, Richard & Gudbrand Vigfusson 1896. *An Icelandic English Dictionary Chiefly Founded on the Collections made from Prose Works of the 12th–14th Centuries*. Oxford: Clarendon Press.

Dale, Roderick Thomas Duncan. 2014. *Berserkir. A Re-Examination of the Phenomenon in Literature and Life*. PhD dissertation, University of Nottingham. Available at: http://eprints.nottingham. ac.uk/28819/.

Dillmann, François-Xavier. 2006. *Les magiciens dans l'Islande ancienne. Etudes sur la representation de la magie islandaise et de ses agents dans les sources litteraires norroises*. Acta Academiae Regiae Gustavi Adolphi, 92. Uppsala: Kungl. Gustav Adolfs Akademien för Svensk Folkkultur.

Egeler, Matthias. 2015. A Retrospective Methodology for Using *Landnámabók* as a Source for the Religious History of Iceland? Some Questions. In *RMN Newsletter*, vol. 10, 78–92.

Frog. 2011. *Alvíssmál* and Orality I: Formula, Alliteration and Categories of Mythic Being. In *Arkiv för Nordisk Filologi*, vol. 126, 17–71.

Frog. 2013. Shamans, Christians, and Things in Between. From Finnic-Germanic Contacts to the Conversion of Karelia. In L. Słupecki & R. Simek (eds.). *Conversions. Looking for Ideological Change in the Early Middle Ages*. Studia Mediaevalia Septentrionalia, 23. Vienna: Fassbaender, 53–98.

Frog. 2014. Germanic Traditions of the Theft of the Thunder-Instrument (ATU 1148b). An Approach to *Þrymskviða* and Þórr's Adventure with Geirrøðr in Circum-Baltic Perspective. In E. Heide & K. Bek-Petersen (eds.). *New Focus on Retrospective Methods. Resuming Methodological Discussions. Case Studies from Northern Europe*. Folklore Fellows' Communications 307. Helsinki: Academia Scientiarum Fennica, 118–160.

Frog. 2015. Mythology in Cultural Practice. A Methodological Framework for Historical Analysis. In *RMN Newsletter*, vol.

10 (special issue: Frog & Karina Lukin (eds.) *Between Text and Practice: Mythology, Religion and Research*), 33–57.

Frog. 2017. Sámi Religion Formations and Proto-Sámi Language Spread. Reassessing a Fundamental Assumption. In *RMN Newsletter*, vol 12–13, 36–69.

Heide, Eldar. 2006. *Gand, seid og åndevind*. PhD dissertation. Bergen: Universitetet i Bergen.

Honko, Lauri. 1960. Varhaiskantaiset taudinselitykset ja parantamisnöytelmä. In J. Hautala (ed.). *Jumin keko. Tutkielmia kansanrunoustieteen alalta*. Helsinki: Suomaliasen Kirjallisuuden Seura, 41–111.

Jauhiainen, Marjatta. 1998. *The Type and Motif Index of Finnish Belief Legends and Memorates*. Folklore Fellows' Communications 267. Helsinki: Academia Scientiarum Fennica.

Jón Árnason 1862. *Íslenzkar þjóðsögur og æfintýri I*. Leipzig: J.C. Hinrichs.

Jón Hnefill Aðalsteinsson. 1978. *Under the Cloak. A Pagan Ritual Turning Point in the Conversion of Iceland*. Studia Ethnologica Upsaliensia, 4. Uppsala: Almqvist & Wiksell International.

Kanerva, Kirsi. 2015. *Porous Bodies, Porous Minds. Emotions and the Supernatural in the Íslendingasögur (ca. 1200–1400)*. Annales Universitatis Turkuensis, B, 398. Turku: University of Turku.

Kelchner, Georgia Dunham. 1935. *Dreams in Old Norse Literature and Their Affinities in Folklore*. Cambridge: Cambridge University Press.

af Klintberg, Bengt. 2010. *The Types of the Swedish Folk Legend*. Folklore Fellows' Communications 300. Helsinki: Academia Scientiarum Fennica.

Lévi-Strauss, Claude. 1952. *Race and History*. Paris: UNESCO.

Lindow, John. 1995. Supernatural Others and Ethnic Others. A Millennium of World View. In *Scandinavian Studies*, vol. 67, no. 1 (special issue: John Lindow & Timothy R. Tangherlini (eds.). *Nordic Legends and the Question of Identity*), 8–31.

Lotman, Yuri M. 1990. *Universe of the Mind. A Semiotic Theory of Culture*. Bloomington: Indiana University Press.

McKinnell, John. 2003. Encounters with *Völur*. In M. Clunies Ross (ed.). *Old Norse Myths, Literature and Society*. Viking Collection, 14. Viborg: University Press of Southern Denmark, 110–131.

Meylan, Nicolas. 2014. *Magic and Kingship in Medieval Iceland. The Construction of a Discourse of Political Resistance*. Studies in Viking and Medieval Scandinavia 3. Turnhout: Brepols.

Mundal, Else. 2013. Female Mourning Songs and Other Lost Oral Poetry in Pre-Christian Nordic Culture. In L. Boje Mortensen et al. (eds.). *The Performance of Christian and Pagan Storyworlds. Non-Canonical Chapters of the History of Nordic Medieval Literature*. Turnhout: Brepols, 367–388.

ONP = Ordbog over det norrøne prosasprog – The Dictionary of Old Norse Prose. Available at: https://onp.ku.dk.

Price, Neil S. 2002. *The Viking Way. Religion and War in Late Iron Age Scandinavia*. Uppsala: University of Uppsala.

Quinn, Judy. 1998. 'Ok verðr henni ljóð á munni'. Eddic Prophecy in the *Fornaldarsögur*. In *Alvíssmál*, vol. 8, 29–50.

Rydving, Håkan. 2011. Le chamanisme aujord'hui. Constructions et déconstructions d'une illusion scientifique. In *Études mongoles et sibériennes, centrasiatiques et tibétaines*, vol. 42, 1–13.

Samson, Vincent. 2011. *Les Berserkir. Les guerriers-fauves dans la Scandinavie ancienne, de l'Âge de Vendel aux Vikings (VIe–XIe siècle)*. Lille: Presses Universitaires du Septentrion.

Siikala, Anna-Leena. 1978. *The Rite Technique of the Siberian Shaman*. Folklore Fellows' Communications 220. Helsinki: Academia Scientiarum Fennica.

Siikala, Anna-Leena. 2002. *Mythic Images and Shamanism. A Perspective on Kalevala Poetry*. Folklore Fellows' Communications 280. Helsinki: Academia Scientiarum Fennica.

Siikala, Anna-Leena. 2012. Myths as Multivalent Poetry. Three Complementary Approaches. In Frog et al. (eds.). *Mythic*

Discourses. Studies in Uralic Traditions. Studia Fennica Folkloristica, 20. Helsinki: Finnish Literature Society, 17–39.

Stark, Laura. 2006. *The Magical Self. Body, Society and the Supernatural in Early Modern Rural Finland.* Folklore Fellows' Communications 290. Helsinki: Academia Scientiarum Fennica.

Stepanova, Eila. 2011. Reflections of Belief Systems in Karelian and Lithuanian Laments. Shared Systems of Traditional Referentiality? In *Archaeologia Baltica*, vol. 15 (special issue: D. Vaitkevičienė & V. Vaitkevičius (eds.). *Archaeology, Religion and Folklore in the Baltic Sea Region*), 128–143.

Stepanova, Eila. 2012. Mythic Elements of Karelian Laments. The Case of *syndyzet* and *spuassuzet*. In Frog et al. (eds.). *Mythic Discourses. Studies in Uralic Oral Traditions.* Studia Fennica Folkloristica, 20. Helsinki: Finnish Literature Society, 257–287.

Strömbäck, Dag. 2000 (1935). *Sejd och andra studier i nordisk själsuppfattning.* Acta Academiae Regiae Gustavi Adolphi, 72. Hedemora: Gidlunds Förlag.

Sundqvist, Olof. 2012. Var sejdhjällen (fvn. *seiðhjallr, hjallr*) en permanent konstruktion vid kultplatser och i kultbyggnader? In *Fornvännen* 107, 280–285.

Tolley, Clive. 1995. *Vǫrðr* and *Gandr*. Helping Spirits in Norse Magic. In *Arkiv för Nordisk Filologi*, vol. 110, 57–75.

Tolley, Clive. 2009. *Shamanism in Norse Myth and Magic I–II.* Folklore Fellows' Communications 296–297. Helsinki: Academia Scientiarum Fennica.

Tulinius, Torfi H. 2002. *The Matter of the North. The Rise of Literary Fiction in Thirteenth-Century Iceland.* Trans. Randi C. Eldevik. Viking Collection, 13. Odense: Odense University Press.

Urban, Greg. 1991. *A Discourse-Centered Approach to Culture. Native South American Myths and Rituals.* Austin: University of Texas Press.

Urban, Greg. 1996. *Metaculture. How Culture Moves through the World.* Minneapolis: University of Minnesota Press.

Van Gent, Jacqueline. 2009. *Magic, Body and the Self in Eighteenth-Century.* Leiden: Brill.

Response

Margaret Clunies Ross
University of Sydney

The Approach

In this chapter Frog looks for Old Norse-Icelandic textual evidence for the relationship between embodied experience and the ritual technologies assumed to have been practised in "the Old Norse world". The time period covered by his enquiry is not precisely defined, but the source material he uses dates mostly from the medieval period and is mostly Icelandic, at least in the form we have received it. He also looks to identify different types of ritual specialist evidenced in Old Norse sources, as well as evidence for the interface between ritual technologies, body images and understandings of the unseen world. He frequently backs up his findings by comparisons with Finno-Karelian legendary traditions. Some of his remarks suggest that concepts of the penetrable body and the free-soul may have entered the Scandinavian tradition from North Finnic cultures, but his position on this does not emerge clearly. What he does credibly argue is that the three case studies he analyses in this chapter establish the body images of the various practitioners based on an ethnocentric norm of "people like us" which includes a hegemonic body image of a penetrable body as a frame of reference.

Methodology

Although Frog recognises that most of the surviving texts at our disposal were written by Christians "writing for Christian audiences in a form of heritage construction", his approach to the sources assembled to support his description of three different types of ritual practitioner (*berserkr*, *vǫlva*, deep-trance specialist) does not discriminate clearly between these sources in terms of their likely source value to a mythographer and the likely intellectual background to their articulation. This leads to a picture of a type of ritual practitioner in which more or less equal weight is given to the different kinds of evidence assembled, and this may be misleading in the context of research into the underlying conceptual world of early Scandinavians.

The *Berserkr*

The methodological difficulty mentioned above is particularly apparent in Frog's treatment of the category of *berserkr* (if indeed berserks were *ritual specialists*, something for which there is little evidence). The *berserkr* is presented as "a supernaturally empowered warrior", and yet there is no unquestionable evidence in the sources to support this view. If berserks were supernaturally empowered, what force empowered them? Where berserks first appear in Old Norse texts, in the late ninth- or early tenth-century poem *Haraldskvæði* by Þorbjǫrn hornklofi (stanzas 8 and 21), they are not attributed with supernatural powers but rather with ferocious physical strength; they are called "wolf-skins", they howl and brandish iron spears; they are Haraldr Fine-hair's crack troops. Their name has suggested to many that they wore animal skins over their armour (or, on an alternative etymology, that they wore no body armour). Some saga texts of later date, where berserks appear as highly conventionalised, often pagan, trouble-makers, associate berserks with being impervious to iron weapons, a motif not exclusive to them alone, however. There are also some places where they are reported as claiming to be able to resist fire, but in most cases of the latter type, the fire motif should likely be understood as influenced by, and possibly generated by, Christian concepts of the ordeal as a test of a person's merit, whether physical or spiritual or both. It is also notable that in the examples of berserks claiming imperviousness to fire (*Kristni saga* and related texts), they are represented as doing so in the context of trials of strength with Christian authorities, and they fail the fire test miserably, thus demonstrating the superiority of their Christian opponents.

Whether the association with imperviousness to fire points to a once active pre-Christian belief in supernatural powers possessed by such warriors is a matter for speculation. This possibility is, however, enhanced by the fact that the Christian Laws section of *Grágás*[1] lists falling into a berserk frenzy among the magical practices that attract a penalty of lesser outlawry. The fact that the *berserksgangr* 'berserk frenzy' (literally 'berserk's rush') is mentioned in the context of magical practices that people ought to control or discontinue suggests that in medieval times it was considered to be a learned human behaviour, and in that respect, I agree with Frog that it must have been "a trained behaviour of heightened (but directionally controlled) aggression". Whether this also implied a closed body image, as he maintains, is a little more dubious: the associations of the *berserkr* with invulnerability to iron and fire are very general motifs, and may not have been unique to the berserk's image, whereas the *berserksgangr*, which implies an outward flow or passage (*gangr*) of aggression, seems to require the body to allow its powers to surge forth beyond its confines.

Oddly enough, Frog does not adduce the one piece of textual evidence that might support his case for the berserk as supernaturally empowered, and possibly being associated with a cult of Óðinn. This is the passage in *Ynglinga saga* Chapter 6[2] that is also one of the main sources of our information about the *berserksgangr*. In this source berserks are warriors firmly associated with the euhemerised Óðinn as his men who went without armour, crazed as dogs or wolves, biting their shields, killing men and being affected by neither fire nor iron while in the berserk state. In the following chapter,[3] Óðinn is revealed as a shape-changer par excellence (*Óðinn skipti hǫmum*) and a master of out-of-body experiences, taking the form of a bird, animal, fish or snake, while his body lies as if asleep or dead (*lá þá búkrinn sem sofinn eða dauðr*). As John Lindow has observed,[4] Óðinn is here presented, not as a deity, but as a human shaman, imbued with the powers that Snorri knew Saami sorcerers possessed, and, in the euhemerised context of *Ynglinga saga*, as teaching this technology to the native Scandinavians, who came to regard him as a god. This context suggests that berserk behaviour was also something the pre-Christian Scandinavians thought came from the euhemerised Óðinn.

The *Vǫlva* and the Deep-Trance Specialist

The remaining two categories of ritual practitioner identified in Frog's chapter, the *vǫlva* and the deep-trance specialist, are more readily acceptable as such than the *berserkr*. In general, Frog's descriptions of these practitioner types seem valid, though there are a good number of questions arising, as he admits, because of our lack of evidence. Many of the inferences he draws from the available sources are speculative and cannot be verified, even with his frequent recourse to Finno-Karelian traditions of post-medieval date and provenance. In the case of the *vǫlva*, a body image gendered female, what is the connection between the *vǫlur* depicted in saga literature, itinerant soothsayers performing their rites for a fee before audiences of farm communities, and the *vǫlur* of mythological poetry raised involuntarily from a death-like state by Óðinn to inform him of the fates of the gods, the cosmos and his own dead son, which, perhaps, he already knows? And what of the gods' killing of Gullveig or Heiðr in *Vǫluspá* 21–22 (the latter a name commonly applied to the *vǫlur* of saga literature)? It seems that there may be a bridge between the human and the divine in this case, though Frog does not mention this enigmatic passage.

He is certainly right that, whereas the *vǫlva* requires an audience, whether of one or many, the deep-trance specialist is separated from society by virtue of the nature of the ritual he performs. What is interesting but perhaps controversial in Frog's presentation here is not so much his identification of this ritual type as shamanic, involving an unconscious trance-like state and journey of a free-soul and/or spirit helpers, as in *Ynglinga saga*'s description of the euhemerised Óðinn, but his contention that there is "trans-ethnic homogenization of representations in circulating discourse suggest[ing] that the ritual behaviour was not ethnically marked as it appears in later legends". In other words, such practices associated with ethnic Scandinavians are not differentiated in Old Norse-Icelandic sources in terms of their presentation of the ritual itself or its performer from those associated with '*Finnar*' 'Saami', except where the practitioners are identified as Saami in order to mark the behaviour as 'other'. Unfortunately,

Frog does not give any examples to support this contention, except for an allusion to the episode recorded by Ari Þorgilsson in *Íslendingabók* in which the then law-speaker Þorgeirr Þorkelsson lay down under his cloak for a day and a night, in order to decide whether Iceland should adopt Christianity or not. Although this episode has been interpreted as shamanic,[5] not everyone accepts this understanding of Þorgeirr's behaviour, for which Ari himself gives no explanation.

Notes

1. K 7; '*Grágás*' I a:23; Dennis *et al.* 1980:39.

2. *Íslenzk Fornrít* XXVI:17.

3. *Íslenzk Fornrít* XXVI:18.

4. Lindow 2003:97–106.

5. Jón Hnefill Aðalsteinsson 1999:103–123.

References

Andrew, Dennis et al. (trans.). 1980. *Laws of Early Iceland. Grágás I.* Winnipeg: University of Manitoba Press.

Vilhjálmur Finsen (ed.). 1852. *Grágás. Islændernes lovbog i fristatens tid, udgivet efter det Kongelige Bibliotheks haandskrift.* Copenhagen: Berling. Rpt 1974 Odense: Odense University Press.

Bjarni Aðalbjarnarson (ed.). 1941. *Snorri Sturluson. Heimskringla I.* Íslenzk fornrit XXVI. Reykjavík: Hið Íslenzka Fornritafélag.

Jón Hnefill Aðalsteinsson. 1999. *Under the Cloak. A Pagan Ritual Turning Point in the Conversion of Iceland.* Second ed. Reykjavík: Félagsvísindastofnun, Háskólaútgáfan.

Lindow, John. 2003. Cultures in Contact. In M. Clunies Ross (ed.). *Old Norse Myths, Literature and Society.* The Viking Collection 14. Odense: University Press of Southern Denmark, 89–109.

Animals of Sacrifice: Animals and the *Blót* in the Old Norse Sources and Ritual Depositions of Bones from Archaeological Sites

Ola Magnell
Arkeologerna, National Historical Museums

Introduction

In the practice of Old Norse religion, animals seem to have played an important role.[1] Both the written sources and the archaeological record indicate that the sacrifice of animals played a significant part in the *blót*, the Old Norse act of sacrifice. At the *blót*, the ritual killing of animals was followed by consumption and feasts on the meat, which is described in the Eddic and scaldic poetry, Icelandic sagas, in Early Medieval laws, rune stones, and foreign sources by bishops and Arabic travellers.[2]

Sacrifices of animals seem to have been a significant part of various religious practices on different occasions and in different contexts. *Blót* was a seasonal occurring communal sacrificial feast, which can be described as a ritual to ensure fertility and a "good year" – a thanksgiving to the gods.[3] Sacrifices of animals were also included in family rituals at the farm-houses, such as the *álfablót*.[4] In Viking Age funeral rites, the killing of animals was also important.[5] *Blót* appears to have been a natural part of the assembly meeting at the thing (*þing*).[6] Furthermore, there are sources indicating the sacrifice of animals in order to ensure good luck in sailing, trading, at single combat (*hólmganga*), and in sorcery aiming to cause misfortune to enemies.[7] The ritual

---

How to cite this book chapter:
Magnell, O. 2019. Animals of Sacrifice: Animals and the *Blót* in the Old Norse Sources and Ritual Depositions of Bones from Archaeological Sites. In: Wikström af Edholm, K., Jackson Rova, P., Nordberg, A., Sundqvist, O. & Zachrisson, T. (eds.) *Myth, Materiality, and Lived Religion: In Merovingian and Viking Scandinavia.* Pp. 303–337. Stockholm: Stockholm University Press. DOI: https://doi.org/10.16993/bay.k. License: CC-BY.

practice of *níðstǫng* and the raising of a horse's head on a pole in order to cast bad luck (*níð*) on enemies also include the killing of a horse.[8]

The problem of using written sources in order to understand Old Norse religion and especially the practice of the religion is well known and has been an important issue in the studies of Old Norse religion.[9] The source criticism involves several different aspects concerning translation and linguistic interpretation and the fact that most texts written down in the 12th–14th centuries describe events that took place centuries earlier. Furthermore, the authenticity of texts was probably affected by the writer's agenda, which in most cases was written from a Christian perspective and the literary genre may also have affected the texts.[10]

The aim of this study is a comparative analysis of the sacrifice of animals in written sources about Old Norse religion and the archaeological record with animal bones interpreted to represent ritual depositions. To restrict the study, funeral rites and killing of animals from burials have not been included.

The use of the archaeological record and animal bones to study sacrifices and rituals is associated with at least as many problems as with interpreting texts, but the problems are different. They involve issues about taphonomy and preservation, dating, and how to identify the remains of ritually killed animals. In archaeology, interpretation and definition of ritual depositions have often been relatively arbitrary, but how to identify ritual depositions and how to differentiate them from common waste have been widely discussed and debated.[11] This study is based on a compilation of several different excavations, so criteria and definitions for ritual depositions have varied between different archaeological studies. In general, it is based on finds of animal bones in specific contexts such as cult houses and stone packings, often associated with ritual objects such as amulet rings. Also, the arrangement of bones in archaeological structures and the placing of specific bones, such as skulls or whole mandibles, have been interpreted as ritual bone depositions.

In the study of Old Norse religion, the archaeological finds have in many cases been used as a kind of "illustration" to the texts, and finds of ritual deposition have often been used to verify the written sources. When ritual depositions are to be interpreted in archaeology, there is sometimes a desperate and almost futile search for written sources from the Icelandic sagas via Tacitus to Celtic folklore so as to verify interpretations rather than basing them on the archaeological record and methodology. This is not necessarily a bad thing to do and is partly the purpose of this paper, but the most important aim in archaeological studies of ritual depositions must be to consider and reveal new aspects of the Old Norse religion that we do not find in the written sources. One of the advantages of using the archaeological record for the understanding of the Old Norse religion is the extensive material which is constantly increasing with new excavations and the development of methods that makes it possibly to study archaeological finds from older excavations with new perspectives. One of the purposes of this study is to show how the archaeological record, and especially animal bones, can be used to study the sacrifices of animals.

The Animals

The importance of different kinds of animals in the *blót* has been quantified by the number of citations of animals in various written sources. In a total of 17 texts describing Old Norse religious practice, it is evident that cattle are the animals that occur most frequently (in eleven of the sources). Horse is also common and occurs in nine cases (Table 1). Other animals such as pig, sheep, goat and dog occur more rarely and are mentioned in two sources.

Even though the authenticity of several of the written sources and especially the sagas can be questioned, the significance of sacrifices of cattle is of interest. It has often been stated that horse had a special position as the sacrificial animal in the Old Norse religion.[12] This claim is mainly based on the most detailed descriptions of the animal sacrifices from the *blót* in Hlade in *Hákonar saga góða,* Adam of Bremen's and Thietmar of Merseburg's

Table 1. The number of times different animals occur in written sources of Old Norse religion. n= *níðstǫng*.

	Horse	Cattle	Pig	Sheep	Goat	Dog
Adam of Bremen, *Gesta Hammaburgensis* Ch. 27[13]	1					1
Al-Tartuschi's visit to Haithabu[14]		1	1	1	1	
Egil saga Skallagrímsonar Ch. 56, Ch. 66[15]	1^n	1				
Þiðranda þáttr ok Þórhalls, Flateyjarbók[16]		1				
Guta Saga[17]		1				
Hákonar saga góða Ch. 14, Ch. 17, *Heimskringla*[18]	2					
Hervarar saga ok Heidreks Ch. 8 and 11[19]	1		1			
Hyndluljóð Ch. 10, Poetic Edda[20]		1				
Ibn Fadlan's meeting with the *Rûs*[21]		1		1		
Kormáks saga Ch. 22[22]		1				
Stentoften rune stone[23]	1				1	
Thietmar of Merseburg, *Cronicon* I:17[24]	1					1
Ùlfljót Landnámabók I[25]		1				
Vatnsdæla saga, Ch. 34[26]	1^n					
Víga-Glúms saga Ch. 9[27]		1				
Völsa þáttr, Flateyjarbók[28]	1					
Ynglingatal Ch. 15, 26, *Heimskringla*[29]		2				
total	9	11	2	2	2	2

descriptions of sacrifices from Uppsala and Lejre, respectively. The reliability of these sources has also been debated, but to some extent has been considered to be authentic by several scholars.[30] In the *blót* in *Hlade* it is stated that "they also killed small livestock and also horse...",[31] and Adam of Bremen also states "that of every living thing that is male, they offer nine heads..."[32] This indicates that not only horse was sacrificed at these *blót*, but rather different kinds of animals. Further, the Arabic sources describing sacrifices mention cattle, sheep, goat and pigs, but no horses. It has also been discussed whether these sources describe actual Old Norse rituals or other groups of people rather than Scandinavians.[33]

An analysis of 104 different depositions of animal bones from 53 archaeological sites in Scandinavia and Iceland[34] indeed shows that horse occurs commonly in 52 % of these, but cattle, pigs, sheep and goat occur almost as often (Figure 1). Dogs are less common and appear in 20 % of the depositions. Based on bone morphology, it is often difficult to differentiate sheep from goat. In the cases identification has been carried out sheep is confirmed in 16 depositions and goat in six. Since sheep is most common in bone assemblages from settlements, this rather reflects the fact that sheep was more available and not specifically chosen to be sacrificed.

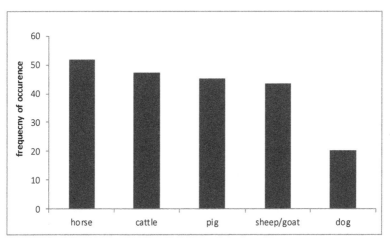

Figure 1. Frequency of occurrences of animals in 104 ritual depositions of bones from Scandinavia and Iceland. Copyright: Ola Magnell.

This compilation is based on sites dating from the Merovingian Period and Viking Age (approx. 7th–11th Centuries). It could be questioned how relevant ritual bone depositions from the 7–8th century is to written sources of which many are written down in the 12–14th Centuries. Because of this, chronological differences in the occurrence of animals in ritual depositions have been studied. There seems to be a change over time in the relative occurrence of different kinds of animals between the two periods. Cattle are the most occurring animals in ritual depositions from the Merovingian Period while, during the Viking Age, cattle are only the third most common animals. In ritual depositions from the Viking Age, horse is the most occurring animal, but the increase is relatively small. Pigs increase distinctly, while for sheep and goat no change in occurrence can be noticed. On settlements from the Viking Age the frequencies of pigs are generally higher than on sites from the Merovingian Period.[35] The increase of pigs in ritual depositions corresponds with the increase of pigs in the subsistence and preference for pork during the Viking Age. However, the most significant chronological difference is the high frequency of dogs in the ritual depositions from the Viking Age (Figure 2).

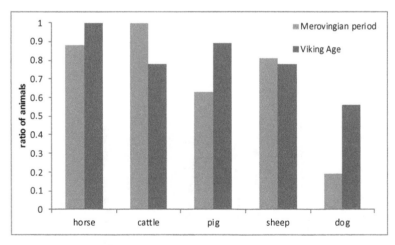

Figure 2. The ratios of animals present in ritual bone depositions from Merovingian Period (550–800 AD) and Viking Age (800–1050 AD). To enable comparison ratios of the occurrence of different animals in ritual depositions have been calculated in relation to the most frequently occurring animal species from each period. Copyright: Ola Magnell.

Ritual depositions from the two regions Uppland and Skåne have also been examined in order to study regional differences in the occurrence of animals in ritual depositions. The comparison reveals some regional differences. In both regions horse is the animal most frequently found in ritual depositions, but sheep, pigs and especially dogs seem to occur relatively more often in depositions from Uppland (Figure 3).

At the Viking Age cult site Frösö Church in the Province of Jämtland, in the northern part of Sweden, bones from brown bear and elk occur frequently.[36] These are animals which are not found on ritual sites in the southern parts of Sweden. This can partly be explained by ecological differences, but it has also been interpreted to be the result of a Sami influence in the ritual practice at this site.[37] Anyhow, this indicates regional variations of animals in ritual depositions between different regions.

This study is based on ritual depositions from various archaeological contexts. The written sources mention sacrifices in different places and structures. Several sources mention *blót* associated with places called *hǫrgr*, which seems to have had a kind of stone

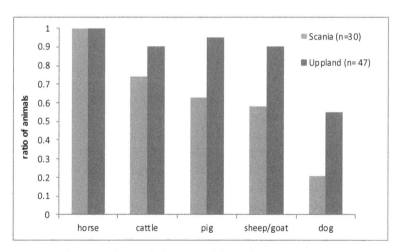

Figure 3. The ratio of animals from ritual bone depositions from Uppland, Sweden and South Scandinavia (Skåne, Sjælland, Fyn). To enable comparison ratios of the occurrence of different animals in ritual depositions have been calculated in relation to the most frequently occurring animal species from each geographic region. Copyright: Ola Magnell.

structure.[38] Several archaeological finds of stone structures from places such as Lilla Ullevi, Slavsta and Kättsta have been interpreted to be the remains cult places corresponding to *hǫrgr*.[39] It is also mentioned in Old Norse sources that *blót* took place at house structures called *hov* and *blóthús*.[40] At several places, such as Borg in Östergötland, Uppåkra, Tissø and Lejre, archaeological finds of house structures interpreted to be cult houses have been found.[41] Furthermore, there are written sources mentioning sacrificial trees or groves and the depositions of bones around the remains of a birch tree in Frösö Church and the site at Lunda are archaeological examples which have been interpreted as ritual depositions by trees or groves.[42]

The analysis shows some interesting patterns in the frequencies of animals from different types of contexts which have been divided into different categories. In depositions from wetlands, it is horse that is the most frequently occurring animal (Figure 4). These kinds of rituals can possibly represent the continuation of a long tradition of the ritual depositions in bogs from the Early Iron Age where horses occur frequently.[43] The depositions in wells also have a frequent occurrence of horse. Smaller livestock, such as pigs, sheep and goats occur less frequently, but rather regularly in the depositions in wells (Figure 4). The animal bones from sites in open-air cult places with stone constructions interpreted as *hǫrgr*, depositions of weapons or amulet rings as well as within cult houses or halls show a similar pattern with relatively few finds of horse and dog, but with a large proportion of the common livestock; cattle, pigs and sheep (Figure 4). Most of these kinds of depositions consist of food remains and in certain cases and sites it can be discussed to what extent the bones from some of these sites represent remains from ritual meals or ordinary consumption at the settlements.

The house depositions have more equal occurrence of different kind of animals and a high occurrence of cattle and pigs as for cult houses, but also a relatively large proportion of horse and dog as for the wells. The depositions in houses probably represents family rituals and cult activities on household level involving sacrifices of various kinds of animals at the farmhouses.[44]

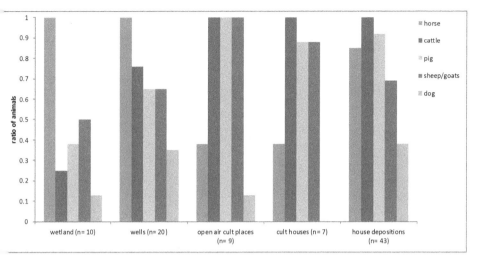

Figure 4. The ratios of animals present in ritual bone depositions from different types of archaeological contexts. To enable comparison ratios of the occurrence of different animals in ritual depositions have been calculated in relation to the most frequently occurring animal species from each type of context. Copyright: Ola Magnell.

Sacrifices of Bulls and Stallions?

Whenever the written sources mention the sex of the sacrificed animals, it is in almost all cases male. The number of cases mentioned is four stallions, five bulls or oxen, one he-goat and two boar.[45] In the description of the *niðstǫng* in *Vatnsdœla saga* a mare is killed and this is the only example of a female animal.[46]

For horses and cattle there are few bones from ritual depositions where the sex has been determined, but it is quite clear that not only males were sacrificed, which has been noticed in earlier studies[47] (Figure 5). There are more stallions than mares in the ritual depositions, but the sample size is small. The sex distribution of cattle shows that bulls/oxen are somewhat more common than cows. In faunal remains from the Viking Age settlements, there is almost always a larger proportion of cows (about 60–70 %).[48] Even though the sample sizes are small from ritual depositions, the higher proportion of males may indicate that bulls were preferred in sacrifices in relation to cows. In ritual deposition, boars are also more frequently found than sows. However, this is often

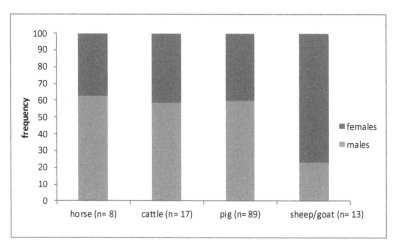

Figure 5. Sex distribution of different animals found in ritual depositions. Copyright: Ola Magnell.

also the case at settlements, so it cannot be concluded that boars were preferred over sows in the sacrifices. Few sheep and goats have been sexed, but bones of females occur more frequently than those of males. Also, this rather seems to reflect what is found among animal bones from settlements.[49]

Feasting and Handling of Body Parts

The sacrifices of animals seem in almost all cases to have been followed by feasting with the cooking and consumption of meat. This is mentioned in many of the written sources about the *blót*[50] and is also confirmed by the animal bones from ritual depositions which to a large extent consist of food refuse. Butchering marks show that the meat of the slaughtered animals was taken care of and eaten. It does not seem as though whole animals were killed and given to the gods, but rather that the consumption was an important part of the *blót*. At several cult houses from Borg and Uppåkra large amounts of animal bones have been found indicating large scale feasting.[51] Several scholars have also discussed the significance of ceremonial feasts at the *blót*.[52]

However, there are exceptions such as depositions of an entire he-goat, dogs, large parts of a cow and the hind limb of a horse in the sacrificial wells in Trelleborg.[53] In a well in Old Uppsala, a find of a whole neck and the hind limb from a horse is another example of a deposition of larger body parts.[54] What these kinds of depositions represent is a little unclear, but possibly it is not from the "ordinary" annual *blót*. Rather, it may represent sacrifices with a more specific purpose such as promises to a deity that a specific animal would be sacrificed if a particular event, such as a safe return from warfare or travel.

Besides the slaughtering, cooking and consumption, there are few descriptions in the written sources of how different parts of the animals were treated and whether certain body parts were dedicated to the gods. However, there may have been rituals with blood performed at the *blót*, which some sources mention.[55] This has been widely debated – some scholars will see this as pure fiction based on biblical inspiration by the authors, while others have stated that even the word *blót* means "the sprinkling of sacrificial blood".[56] At the Viking Age cult place Götavi in Närke, Sweden, an analysis of lipids from a stone paving has indicating that blood has frequently been left and decayed at the site.[57] If rituals actually involved the handling of blood, it most likely played a significant part in the *blót*.[58]

However, some written sources mention further rituals with the heads of the sacrificed animals. The Arabic sources, i.e. Ibn Fadlan's meeting with the *Rûs* and Al-Tartuschi's travels to Haithabu, tell us that the heads of the sacrificed animals were placed on poles.[59] The description of the sacrifices at Uppsala by Adam of Bremen can be interpreted as the heads of the killed animals being given to the gods by hanging them in the trees.[60]

Whether the heads of the sacrificed animals were placed on posts or in trees is difficult to verify from the archaeological record. However, there are a lot of examples of depositions of skulls in various contexts such as wetlands, wells and pit houses indicating rituals with skulls and mandibles. From the wooden monument in Old Uppsala there are several examples of depositions of skulls and mandibles of horse, cattle and pigs in the postholes of the pillars.[61] Finds of 23 cattle skulls at the Hofstaðir settlement on Iceland indicate that the heads of sacrificed animals have probably been placed on the roof of a house.[62] If this was a common practice, it would only in exceptional conditions be preserved in the archaeological record.

Furthermore, there is evidence from several sites indicating rituals and depositions of mandibles. From a pit at Norra Gärdet and postholes from the hall on the Kungsgården plateau in Old Uppsala, depositions of cattle mandibles have been found.[63] Also, from a weapon deposition in Uppåkra of mainly lance heads similar depositions of cattle mandibles have been found.[64] The deposition at Frösö Church consists to a large part of mandibles and in several pit houses from Old Uppsala depositions of whole mandibles have been found.[65]

Conclusions

The written sources emphasize the significance of horse and cattle in the *blót*, while archaeological finds of ritual depositions indicate that pigs, sheep and goats were almost as important in the sacrifices. Even though the choice of animal for killing and slaughter at the *blót* probably has varied depending on the purpose of the sacrifice and the socio-economic setting; it often seems to be the case that several different types of animals were sacrificed. Partly, this could have been affected by the availability of animals, but possibly it could also have been of significance to include the different animals that were important in the everyday-life in the rituals.

The chronological differences in the occurrence of animals in ritual depositions can be noticed, with a decrease of cattle while pigs and dogs occuring more commonly in the Viking Age. This indicates a shift in preference of sacrificial animals. The regional differences of animals in ritual depositions indicate that the killing of smaller animals, such as pigs, sheep and dogs, was more frequent in Uppland than in Skåne.

The frequency of sacrificed animal species varies between ritual contexts. Horse seems to have been associated with depositions in water, such as wetlands and wells, while at open air-cult places and cult houses cattle, pigs and sheep played a more significant part in the sacrifices. There also seems to have been differences in the ritual practices in different social context. At Old Uppsala cattle and horse occur relatively more frequently in communal ritual areas, such as the wooden monument and cult area by burials, while smaller livestock and dogs are relatively more frequently found in ritual depositions on the farms.[66] This possibly indicates the preference of large prestigious animals at communal sacrifices and feasts at cult places, while smaller animals were more commonly sacrificed in the family rituals on the household level.

No obvious selection of males in sacrifices can be noticed in the ritual depositions, as stated in written sources. Skulls and mandibles are shown to have been of major significance in the rituals, both in the texts and in the depositions of bones.

Several aspects of the sacrifices of animals in the Old Norse religion mentioned in the written sources and the ritual depositions of bones are in accord, but there are also clear discrepancies. The interpretations of ritual depositions of animal bones, and how representative they are as source to sacrifices, must be considered and discussed, but it can also be concluded that the ritual depositions of bones represents an important source, which contributes to a more complex and detailed picture of the animal sacrifices. In particular, it is important to consider and study the chronological, regional and contextual aspects of animal sacrifices and other ritual depositions to gain a deeper understanding of the religious practice of the Old Norse religion.

Notes

1. Jennbert 2002; Jennbert 2011; DuBois 2012.

2. Näsström 2002; Steinsland 2007:300–327; Aðalsteinsson 1997:222–226.

3. Näsström 2002; Steinsland 2007:300–302; Hultgård 2011:215.

4. Dillmann 1997:62.

5. Iregren 1998; Price 2010:135–136; Jennbert 2011:102–105.

6. Aðalsteinsson 1997:223.

7. Aðalsteinsson 1996:14–17; Ibn Fadlan, translation by Wikander 1978:65; *Egils saga Skallagrímsonar* Ch. 66, in Jóhannesson et al. 2014a.

8. Steinsland 2007:395.

9. Hultgård 1993; Steinsland 2007:35–38.

10. Hultgård 1993, Sundqvist 2000:36–37.

11. Grant 1991; Hill 1995; Berggren 2006; Thilderkvist 2013:27–42.

12. Carlie 2002:124; Nilsson 2003:89–90.

13. Adam of Bremen, *Gesta Hammaburgensis*, translation by Svenberg 1984.

14. Birkeland 1954:103–104.

15. *Egils saga Skallagrímsonar*, in Jóhannesson et al. (eds.) 2014a.

16. *Flateyjarbók*, in Vigfússon & Unger (eds.) 1860–1868.

17. *Guta Saga*, in Herlin Karnell 2012 (ed.) 2012.

18. *Heimskringla*, translation by Johansson 1994.

19. *Hervar saga ok Heidreks*, translation by Tolkien 1960.

20. *Eddukvæði I, Godakvæði*, in Kristjánsson & Ólason (eds.) 2014a.

21. Ibn Fadlan, translation by Wikander 1978:65.

22. *Kormáks saga*, in Jóhannesson et al. (eds.) 2014a.

23. Santesson 1989:221–229.

24. Thietmar of Merseburg, *Cronicon*, translation by Trillmich 1957.

25. *Landnámabók*, translation by Ohlmarks 1962:123.

26. *Vatnsdæla saga*, in Jóhannesson et al. (eds.) 2014c.

27. *Víga-Glúms saga*, in Jóhannesson et al. (eds.) 2014b.

28. *Flateyjarbók*, in Vigfússon & Unger (eds.) 1860–1868.

29. *Heimskringla*, translation by Johansson 1994.

30. Hultgård 1997:43; Sundqvist 2016:113–120.

31. *Hákonar saga góða* Ch. 14, *Heimskringla*, translation by Johansson 1994.

32. Adam of Bremen, *Gesta Hammaburgensis* Ch. 27, translation by Svenberg 1984.

33. Birkeland 1954; Montgomory 2000.

34. Lindqvist 1910; Christensen 1991; Ambrosiani & Ericsson 1993; Backe et al. 1993; Thörn 1995; Lindeblad & Nielsen 1997; Ljungkvist 2000; Carlie 2002; Nilsson 2003; Carlie 2004; Olson 2004; Björhem et al. 2005; Lindkvist 2005; Seiler 2005; Stensköld 2006; Lucas & McGovern 2007; Nordström & Evanni 2007; Olsson 2007; Andersson & Skyllberg 2008; Bäck et al. 2008; Fagerlund & Lucas 2009; Friman & Skoglund 2009; Magnell & Iregren 2010; Monikander 2010; Beronius & Seiler 2011; Gotfredsen & Thomsen 2011; Jennbert 2011; Sköld 2012; Lucas & Lucas 2013; Magnell et al. 2013; Björck 2014; Carlie & Lagergren 2014; Jørgensen et al. 2014; Strömberg et al. 2014; Zachrisson 2014; Fredengren 2015; Gotfredsen et al. 2015; Eklund & Wikborg 2016; Lagerås & Magnell 2016; Magnell 2016; Frölund et al. 2017; Seiler & Magnell 2017; Wikborg & Magnell 2017.

35. Bergman et al. 2017.

36. Magnell & Iregren 2010

37. Näsström 1996:77; Welinder 2008:90–91.

38. Näsström 2002:126–128; Steinsland 2007:311.

39. Olsson 2007; Bäck et al. 2008; Fagerlund & Lucas 2009.

40. Näsström 2002:128–130; Steinsland 2007:311–312; Sundqvist 2016:95–96.

41. Gräslund 2011:250–252; Kaliff & Mattes 2017; Sundqvist 2016:97–102.

42. Hultgård 1997:38–39; Andersson & Skyllberg 2008; Magnell & Iregren 2010; Gräslund 2011:253; Sundqvist 2016:212–255.

43. Nilsson 2009; Monikander 2010, Fredengren 2015.

44. Seiler & Magnell 2017.

45. Adam of Bremen, *Gesta Hammaburgensis* Ch. 27, translation by Svenberg 1984; *Egils saga Skallagrímsonar* Ch. 66, in Jóhannesson et al. (eds.) 2014a; *Helgakviða Hiǫrvarðssonar, Eddukvæði II, Hetjukvæði* in Kristjánsson & Ólason (eds.) 2014b; *Hervar saga ok Heidreks* Ch. 8 and 11, translation by Tolkien 1960; *Kormáks*

saga Ch. 22, in Jóhannesson et al. (eds.) 2014a; Stentofte runestone, translation by Santesson 1989:221–229; Thietmar of Merseburg, *Cronicon* I:17, translation by Trillmich 1957; *Víga-Glúms saga* Ch. 9, in Jóhannesson et al. (eds.) 2014b; *Völsa þáttr, Flateyjarbók*, in Vigfússon & Unger (eds.) 1860–1868; *Ynglingatál* Ch. 15 & 26, *Heimskringla*, translation by Johansson 1994.

46. *Vatnsdæla saga*, in Jóhannesson et al. 2014c.

47. Hultgård 1997:37.

48. Wigh 2001; Magnell 2017.

49. Wigh 2001; Magnell 2017.

50. Dillmann 1997:61–62; Näsström 2002:182–185.

51. Lindeblad & Nielsen 1997; Magnell 2011; Magnell et al. 2013.

52. Dillmann 1997; Sundqvist 2000:170–173; Hultgård 2011:215–216; Sundqvist 2016:344–351.

53. Gotfredsen et al. 2015.

54. Seiler & Magnell 2017

55. *Hyndluljóð* ch. 10, *Eddukvæði I, Godakvæði* in Kristjánsson & Ólason (eds.) 2014a; *Hervar saga ok Heidreks* Ch.20, translation by Tolkien 1960; *Hákonar saga góða* Ch. 14, *Heimskringla*, translation by Johannson 1994; *Kormáks saga* Ch. 22, in Jóhannesson et al. (eds.) 2014a

56. Aðalsteinsson 1997:233–236.

57. Svensson 2010:72.

58. Sundqvist 2016:341–343.

59. Birkeland 1954:103–104; Ibn Fadlan, translation by Wikander 1978:65.

60. Hultgård 1997:32.

61. Wikborg & Magnell 2017.

62. Lucas & McGovern 2007.

63. Lindkvist 2005; Frölund *et al.* 2017.

64. Magnell 2011; Magnell et al. 2013.

65. Magnell & Iregren 2011; Seiler & Magnell 2017.

66. Seiler & Magnell 2017.

References

Primary sources

Adam av Bremen. Svenberg, Emanuel. 1984. *Historien om Hamburg-stiftet och dess biskopar.* Translation Emanuel Svenberg. Stockholm: Proprius.

De isländska sagorna. Ohlmarks, Åke. 1962. *De isländska sagorna. Första bandet. Landssagor, Upptäckssagor, Sydvästlandssagor.* Translation Åke Ohlmarks. Stockholm: Steinsviks bokförlag. 1962.

Edda. J. Kristjánsson & V. Ólason (eds.). 2014a. *Eddukvæði I, Godakvæði.* Íslenzk fornrit. Reykjavík: Hið íslenzka fornritafélag.

—— J. Kristjánsson & V. Ólason (eds.). 2014b. *Eddukvæði II, Hetjukvæði.* Íslenzk fornrit. Reykjavík: Hið íslenzka fornritafélag.

Flateyjarbók. G. Vigfússon & C. R. Unger (eds.). 1860–1868. *En samling af norske konge-sager med indskudte mindre fortællinger om begivenheder i og udenfor Norge.* Band 1–3. Christiania: Maling.

Guta saga. M. Herlin Karnell (ed.). 2012. *Gutasagan. en gotländsk krönika.* Visby, Gotlands museum.

Ibn Fadlan. Wikander, Stig. 1978. *Araber Vikingar Väringar.* Translation Stig Wikander. Lund: Svenska Humanistiska Förbundet.

Islänningasagorna. Jóhannesson, Gunnar D Hansson & Karl G Johansson (eds.). 2014a. *Islänningasagorna. Samtliga släktsagor och fyrtionio tåtar.* I. Skalder, Grönland, Vinland. Reykjavik: Saga förlag.

—— Jóhannesson, Gunnar D Hansson & Karl G Johansson (eds.). 2014b. *Islänningasagorna. Samtliga släktsagor och fyrtionio tåtar.* II. Fredlösa, skalder och kämpar. Reykjavik: Saga förlag.

—— Jóhannesson, Gunnar D Hansson & Karl G Johansson (eds.). 2014c. *Islänningasagorna. Samtliga släktsagor och fyrtionio tåtar.* IV. Lokala fejder. Reykjavik: Saga förlag.

Saga of King Heidrek the wise. Tolkien, Christopher. 1960. *Saga of King Heidrek the wise.* Translation Christopher Tolkien. London: Thomans Nelson and Sons Ltd.

Snorri Sturluson, *Heimskringla.* Johansson, Karl G. 1994. *Nordiska kungasagor I. Från Ynglingasagan till Olav Tryggvasons saga.* Translation Karl G. Johansson. Stockholm: Fabel.

Thietmar of Merseburg. *Chronicon.* Trillmich, Werner. 1957. *Thietmar of Merseburg. Chronicon.* Translation Werner Trillmich. Darmstadt: Ausgewählte Quellen zur deutschen Geschichte des Mittelalters.

Secondary literature

Aðalsteinsson, Jón, Hnefil. 1996. Blot in forna skrifter. *Scripta Islandica* vol. 47, 11–32.

Aðalsteinsson, Jón, Hnefil. 1997. *Blót í Norrænum Sið. Rýnt í forn trúarbrögð með Þjóðfræðilegri aðferð.* Reykjavik: Háskólaútgáfan.

Ambrosiani, Björn & Erikson, Bo G. 1993. *Birka vikingastaden.* Volym 3. Höganäs: Wiken.

Andersson, Gunnar & Skyllberg, Eva. 2008. *Gestalter och gestaltningar. Om tid, rum och händelser på Lunda.* Stockholm: Riksantikvarieämbetet.

Backe, Margareta, et al. 1993. Bones Thrown into a Water-Hole. In G. Arvidsson, et al. (eds.). *Sources and Resources. Studies in honour of Birgit Arrhenius.* PACT 38. Rixensart: Pact Belgium, 327–342.

Berggren, Åsa. 2006. Archaeology and Sacrifice. A Discussion of Interpretations. In A. Andrén, et al. (eds.). *Old Norse religion in a Long-Term Perspective. Origins, Changes, and Interactions.* Lund: Nordic Academic Press, 303–307.

Bergman, Jonas, et al. 2017. Med landet i centrum. Boskap, åkerbruk och landskap i Gamla

Uppsala. In L. Beronius Jörpeland et al. (eds.). *at Upsalum – människor och landskapande. Utbyggnad av Ostkustbanan genom Gamla*

Uppsala. Arkeologerna Rapport 2017:1:1. Stockholm: Arkeologerna, Statens Historiska Museer, 129–152.

Beronius Jörpeland, Lena & Seiler, Anton. 2011. Mälbys många ansikten. En tidigmedeltida sätesgård, förhistorisk och historisk gårdsbebyggelse. Uppland, Tillinge socken, Tillinge-Mälby 1:20 och 5:1, RAÄ 327. In *UV Rapport* 2011:57. Hägersten: Riksantikvarieämbetet.

Birkeland, Harris. 1954. *Nordens historie i middelalderen etter arabiske kilder.* Oslo: Det Norske Videnskaps-Akademi.

Björhem, Berit, et al. 2005. Fredriksberg 13A–D. Öresundsförbindelsen. In *Malmö Kulturmiljö Rapport* Nr. 23/24. Malmö: Malmö Kulturmiljö.

Björck, Niclas. 2014. Björkgärdet. Aspekter på vikingarna och deras förfäder. Gårdar och rituella komplex från yngre bronsålder och järnålder. In *UV Rapport* 2014:125. Hägersten: Riksantikvarieämbetet.

Bäck, Matthias, et al. 2008. Lilla Ullevi. Historien om det fridlysta rummet. In *UV Mitt Rapport* 2008:39. Hägersten: Riksantikvarieämbetet.

Carlie, Anne. 2002. Gård och kultplats. Om bruket av offerhandlingar på en yngre järnåldersgård i Hjärup, sydvästra Skåne. In A. Carlie (ed.). *Skånska regioner. Tusen år av kultur och samhälle i förändring.* Stockholm: Riksantikvarieämbetet, 653–679.

Carlie, Anne. 2004. *Forntida byggnadskult. Traditioner och regionalitet i södra Skandinavien.* Stockholm: Riksantikvarieämbetet.

Carlie, Anne & Lagergren, Anna. 2014. Lindängelund 1. Bebyggelse och offerplats från yngre stenålder, bronsålder, järnålder samt vikingatid/tidig medeltid. In *UV Rapport* 2014:36. Lund: Riksantikvarieämbetet.

Christiensen, Tom. 1991. Lejre beyond Legend. The Archaeological Evidence. In *Journal of Danish Archaeology*, vol. 10, 163–185.

Dillmann, François-Xavier. 1997. Kring de rituella gästabuden i fornskandinavisk religion. In A. Hultgård (ed.). *Uppsala och Adam av Bremen.* Nora: Nya Doxa, 51–73.

DuBois, Thomas Andrew. 2012. Diet and deities. Contrastive liveli-
hoods and animal symbolism in Nordic Pre-Christian religions.
In C. Raudvere & J. P. Schjødt (eds.). *More than mythology.
Narratives, ritual practices and regional distribution in Pre-Christian
Scandinavian religions*. Lund: Nordic Academic Press, 65–96.

Eklund, Susanna & Wikborg, Jonas. 2016. Malma. Mellan grophus
och hall. Arkeologisk undersökning. Uppsala 490:1, Valsätra 1:9,
Uppsala, socken, Uppland, Uppsala län. In *SAU Rapport* 2016:15.
Uppsala: Societas Archaeologica Upsaliensis.

Fagerlund, Dan & Lucas, Robin. 2009. Slavsta. Romartida bebyggelse och vikingatida kult. In *Upplandsmuseets rapporter* 2009:1.
Uppsala: Upplandsmuseet.

Fredengren, Christina. 2015. Waterpolitics. The Wetland Depositions
of Human and Animal Remains in Uppland, Sweden. In
Fornvännen, vol. 110, 161–183.

Friman, Bo & Skoglund, Peter. 2009. Gårdsknutna ritualer. En disk-
ussion om föremål och depositionsmönster. In A. Högberg et al.
(eds.). *Gården i landskapet. Tre bebyggelsearkeologiska studier*.
Malmö: Malmö Museer, 233–268.

Frölund, Per, et al. Kungsgården i Gamla Uppsala: Hall, hantverk och
hus från yngre järnålder och medeltid. Arkeologisk undersökning
Uppsala 263:1, Uppsala, Uppland. Gamla Uppsala – framväxten
av ett mytiskt centrum. Rapport 8. *Upplandsmuseets rapporter*
2017:27. Uppsala: Upplandsmuseet.

Gotfredsen, Anne Birgitte & Gebauer Thomsen, Lone. 2011. Three Pit-
Houses of the Magnate's Residence at Lake Tissø. In L. Boye (ed.).
The Iron Age on Zealand. Status and Perspectives. Copenhagen:
The Royal Society of Northern Antiquaries, 211–220.

Gotfredsen, Anne Birgitte, et al. 2015. A Ritual Site with Sacrificial
Wells from the Viking Age at Trelleborg, Denmark. In *Danish
Journal of Archaeology*, vol. 3, Nr. 2, 1–19.

Grant, Annie. 1991. Economic or Symbolic? Animals and Ritual
Behavior. In P. Garwood (ed.). *Sacred and Profane. Proceedings of
a Conference on Archaeology, Ritual and Religion Oxford, 1989*.
Oxford: Oxford University, 109–114.

Gräslund, Anne-Sofie. 2011. The Material Culture of Old Norse Religion.
In S. Brink (ed.). *The Viking World*. London: Routledge, 249–256.

Hill, J.D. 1995. *Ritual and Rubbish in the Iron Age of Wessex. A Study of the Formation of a Specific Archaeological Record.* Oxford: Tempus Reparatum.

Hultgård, Anders. 1993 Altskandinavische opferrituale und das problem der quellen. In T. Ahlbäck (ed.). *The Problem of Ritual.* Based on Papers Read at the Symposium on Religious Rites Held at Åbo, Finland on the 13th–16th of August 1991. Åbo: Donner Institute, 221–259.

Hultgård, Anders. 1997. Från ögonvittnesskildring till retorik. Adam av Bremens notiser om Uppsalakulten i religionshistorisk belysning. In A. Hultgård (ed.). *Uppsala och Adam av Bremen.* Nora: Nya Doxa, 9–50.

Hultgård, Anders. 2011. The Religion of the Vikings. In S. Brink (ed.). *The Viking World*. London: Routledge, 212–218.

Iregren, Elisabeth. 1998. Why Animal bones in Human Graves? An Attempt to Interpret Animals Present in Iron Age Cremations in Sweden. In: E. Smits, et al. (eds.). Cremation Studies in Archaeology. Amsterdam: Logos, 9–32.

Jennbert, Kristina. 2002. Djuren i nordisk förkristen ritual och myt. In K. Jennbert et al. (eds.). *Plats och praxis. Studier av nordisk förkristen ritual.* Vägar till Midgård 2. Lund: Nordic Academic Press, 105–133.

Jennbert, Kristina. 2011. *Animals and Humans. Recurrent Symbiosis in Archaeology and Old Norse Religion.* Lund: Nordic Academic Press.

Jørgensen, Lars et al. 2014. Førkristne kultpladser. Ritualer og tro i yngre jernalder og vikingetid. In *Nationalmuseets Arbejdsmark* 2014, 186–199.

Kaliff, Anders & Mattes, Julia. 2017. Tempel och kulthus i det forna Skandinavien. Myter och arkeologiska fakta. Stockholm: Carlson Bokförlag.

Lagerås, Per & Magnell, Ola. Arkeobotanisk och osteologisk analys. In A. Bolander. Östra Grevie 9:30 och 12:14. Där backe möter

slätt – mellan mosse och lund. Skåne, Vellinge kommun, Östra
Grevie socken, fastighet 9:30 och 12:14, fornlämning Östra
Grevie 40 och 41. *Arkeologerna Rapport* 2017: 18. Stockholm:
Arkeologerna, Statens Historiska Museer.

Lindeblad, Karin & Nielsen, Ann-Lili. 1997. *Kungens gods i Borg.
Om utgrävningarna vid Borgs säteri i Östergötland. UV Linköping
Rapport* 1997:12. Linköping: Riksantikvarieämbetet.

Lindkvist, Ann. 2005. Kring ett dike på Norra Gärdet. Arkeologisk
undersökning av boplatslämningar från yngre järnålder i Gamla
Uppsala. In *SAU Skrifter* 11. Uppsala: Societas Archaeologica
Upsaliensis.

Lindqvist, Sune. 1910. Ett "Frös-Vi" i Närke. In *Fornvännen*, Vol. 5,
119–138.

Ljungkvist, John. 2000. *I maktens närhet. Två boplatsundersökningar
i Gamla Uppsala: Raä 285, Norra Gärdet, Raä 547 Mattsgården,
Gamla Uppsala socken, Uppland*. Uppsala: Societas Archaeologica
Upsaliensis.

Lucas, Gavin & McGovern, Thomas. 2007. Bloody Slaughter.
Ritual Decapitation and Display at the Viking Settlement of
Hofstadir, Iceland. In *European Journal of Archaeology*, vol. 10,
nr. 1, 7–30.

Lucas, Malin & Lucas, Robin. 2013. Gårdar och hästoffer. Järnålder
och tidig medeltid i Fyrislund. In *Upplandsmuseets Rapporter*
2013:2. Uppsala: Upplandsmuseet.

Magnell, Ola. 2011. Sacred Cows or Old Beasts? A Taphonomic
Approach to Studying Ritual Killing with an Example from Iron
Age Uppåkra, Sweden. In A. Pluskowski (ed.). *The Ritual Killing
and Burial of Animals. European Perspectives*. Oxbow Books:
Oxford, 192–204.

Magnell, Ola. 2016. Animalosteologisk analys. In K. Brink & S. Larsson
(eds.). *Arkeologisk undersökning 2013. Östra Odarslöv13:5, ESS-
området. Forntid möter framtid. Volym 3 – Analyser och bilagor.
Skåne, Lunds kommun, Odarslövs socken, fornlämningarna*

Odarslöv 46, 49, 51 och 52. Arkeologerna Rapport 2017:11. Stockholm: Arkeologerna, Statens Historiska Museer, 47–67

Magnell, O. 2017. Gårdarnas djur. Osteologisk analys. Utbyggnad av Ostkustbanan genom Gamla Uppsala. Arkeologisk undersökning, Uppsala län; Uppland; Uppsala kommun; Uppsala socken; Gamla Uppsala 20:1, 21:13, 21:27 m.fl.; Uppsala 134:4, 240:1, 284:2, 586:1, 597:1, 603:1, 604:1, 605:1 och 606:1. *Arkeologerna Rapport* 2017:1:12. Stockholm: Arkeologerna, Statens Historiska Museer.

Magnell, Ola & Iregren, Elisabeth. 2010. Veitstu Hvé Blóta Skal. The Old Norse Blót in the Light of Osteological Remains from Frösö Church, Jämtland, Sweden. In *Current Swedish Archaeology*, Vol. 18, 223–250.

Magnell, Ola, et al. 2013. Fest i Uppåkra. En studie av konsumtion och djurhållning baserad på djurben från ceremonihus och vapendeposition. In: B. Hårdh & L. Larsson (eds.). *Folk, fä och fynd. Uppåkrastudier* 12. Lund: Lund University, 85–132.

Monikander, Anne. 2010. *Våld och vatten. Våtmarkskult vid Skedemosse under järnåldern.* Stockholm: Institutionen för arkeologi och antikens kultur, Stockholms universitet.

Montgomory, James, E. 2000. Ibn Fadlan and the Rūsiyyah. In *Journal of Arabic and Islamic Studies*, vol. 3, 1–25.

Nilsson, Lena. 2003, Blóta, Sóa, Senda. Analys av djurben. In B. Söderberg (ed.). *Järrestad. Huvudgård i centralbygd.* Stockholm: Riksantikvarieämbetet, 287–308.

Nilsson, L. 2009. Häst och hund i fruktbarhetskult och blot. In A. Carlie (ed.). Järnålderns rituella platser. Halmstad: Hallands länsmuseer, 81–99.

Nordström, Annika & Evanni, Louise. 2007. Hämringe. Boplatslämningar från järnålder till nyare tid. Väg E4, sträckan Uppsala–Mehedeby: Uppland, Uppsala socken, Fullerö 18:6, 18:13, 18:22, 18:33, 18:35, 18:36; Gamla Uppsala 79:2, RAÄ 600. In *UV GAL Rapport* 2007:2. Uppsala: Riksantikvarieämbetet.

Näsström, Britt-Mari. 1996. Offerlunden under Frösö kyrka. In S. Brink (ed.). *Jämtlands kristnande. Projekten Sveriges kristnande.* Uppsala: Lunne böcker, 65–85.

Näsström, Britt-Mari. 2002. *Blot. Tro och offer i det förkristna Norden.* Stockholm: Norstedts.

Olson, A. 2004. *Till fest och vardag. En osteologisk analys av djurben från terrass 4, husgrupp II på Helgö. Seminarieuppsats i osteologi.* Stockholm: Institutionen för arkeologi och antikens kultur, Stockholms universitet.

Olsson, Robin. 2007. Det rituella kontraktet. Kultiskt återutnyttjande av ett äldre gravfält under vikingatid och medeltid. In M. Notelid (ed.). *Att nå den andra sidan. Om begravning och ritual i Uppland. Arkeologi E4 Uppland – Studier, volym 2.* Uppsala: Societas Archaeologica Upsaliensis, Riksantikvarieämbetet och Upplandsmuseet, 445–460.

Price, Neil. 2010. Passing into poetry: Viking Age mortuary drama and the origins of Norse mythology. *Medieval Archaeology* vol. 54, 123–156.

Santesson, Lillemor. 1989. En blekingsk blotinskrift. En nytolkning av inledningsraderna på Stentoftenstenen. In *Fornvännen*, vol. 84, 221–229.

Seiler, Anton. 2005. Vallby norra. En boplats från yngre bronsålder, yngre järnålder och tidig medeltid i Tämnaråns dalgång. Väg E4, sträckan Uppsala–Mehedeby, Uppland, Tierps socken, Fäcklinge 2:10, Vallby 1:3 och 2:4, RAÄ 231. Arkeologi E4 Uppland. Riksantikvarieämbetet. In *UV GAL, Rapport* 2005:1. Uppsala: Riksantikvarieämbetet.

Seiler, Anton & Magnell, Ola. 2017. *Til Ars og Friðar*, gårdsnära rituella depositioner i östra

Gamla Uppsala. In L. Beronius Jörpeland et al. (eds.). *at Upsalum – människor och landskapande. Utbyggnad av Ostkustbanan genom Gamla Uppsala. Arkeologerna Rapport* 2017:1.1. Stockholm: Arkeologerna, Statens Historiska Museer, 189–208.

Sköld, Katarina. 2012. En gård från yngre järnålder i Valla, Östergötland. In *UV Rapport* 2012:73. Linköping: Riksantikvarieämbetet.

Steinsland, Gro. 2007. *Fornnordisk religion*. Stockholm: Natur & Kultur.

Stensköld, Eva. 2006. Flying Daggers, Horse Whispers and a Midwinter Sacrifice. Creating the Past during the Viking Age and Early Middle ages. In *Current Swedish Archaeology*, vol. 14, 199–219.

Strömberg, Bo et al. 2014. Lockarp 24:1, 42:1 och 43:1. Lindängelund 4. In *UV Rapport* 2014:83. Lund: Riksantikvarieämbetet.

Sundqvist, Olof. 2000. *Freyr's offspring. Rulers and Religion in Ancient Svea society*. Uppsala: Department of Theology, Uppsala University.

Sundqvist, Olof. 2016. *An Arena for Higher Powers. Ceremonial Buildings and Religious Strategies for Rulership in Late Iron Age Scandinavia*. Leiden: Brill.

Svensson, Kenneth. 2010. Götavi, en vikingatida kultplats i Närke. In P. Bratt & G: Grönwall (eds.). *Makt, kult och plats: högstatusmiljöer under äldre järnåldern: kultplatser*. Stockholm: Stockholms länsmuseum, 68–77.

Thilderqvist, Johan. 2013. *Ritual Bones or Common Waste? A Study of Bone Deposits in Northern Europe*. Groningen: Barhuis & University of Groningen Library.

Thörn, Raimond. 1995. Vikingatida hästoffer i Oxie by. In *Elbogen. Malmö Fornminnesförenings årskrift*, vol. 1995, 11–36.

Welinder, Stig. 2008. *Jämtarna och samerna kom först*. Östersund: Jamtli.

Wigh, Bengt. 2001. *Animal husbandry in the Viking Age Town of Birka and its hinterland*. Stockholm: Birka Project, Riksantikvarieämbetet.

Wikborg, Jonas & Magnell, Ola. 2017. Händelser kring stolpar. En analys av stolpfundamentens fyndinnehåll. In L. Beronius Jörpeland et al. (eds.). *at Upsalum – människor och landskapande. Utbyggnad av Ostkustbanan genom Gamla Uppsala. Arkeologerna Rapport* 2017:1:1. Stockholm: Arkeologerna, Statens Historiska Museer, 292–312.

Zachrisson, Torun. 2014. De heliga platsernas arkeologi. Materiell kultur och miljöer i järnålderns Mellansverige. In E. Nyman et al. (eds.). *Den heliga platsen. Handlingar från symposiet Den heliga platsen. Härnösand 15–18 september 2011*. Härnösand: Mittuniversitetet, 87–126.

Response

Kristin Armstrong Oma
University of Stavanger

Bare Bones and Slippery Myths – Questions that Arise from the Place where Myth Meets the Material

Ola Magnell's contribution raises several interesting issues that bring to the fore new questions, many of them rhetorical and they cannot be expected to be answered in a straightforward manner. My questions are mostly related to the nature of materialisation and are meant as starting points for further reflection. Magnell's chapter, a meeting between zooarchaeology and Norse mythology, is very important, considering the question: what does the materialisation of myths entail? This, again, raises further questions, such as: how should we expect to see the living out of a myth in a material record? What does the materiality mean? How do we identify importance? For example, the zooarchaeologist identifies bone remains according to species, sex, age, skeletal elements, butchery methods and so on. But how do these lists translate into a lived religion and past world views? How does it correspond to the archaeological record? As Magnell demonstrates, there is some overlap; cattle and horses are two of the main animals found in both the written sources and also mostly in the archaeological record. But what do the faunal remains, one by one – bone by bone, represent? As opposed to the different species outweighing one another when all the bones are identified? So what I am getting at: is materiality as mass – sheer numbers – equivalent to mythological significance? The more the merrier? Or is mythological significance much stronger in those infrequent occurrences when we find the rare and the exotic?

Another important question is how we understand *blót* as a category in relation to the categories normally used in archaeology: on the one hand settlement sites considered as mundane and everyday, and on the other hand ritual deposition thought to reflect the sphere of myths and religion? When trying to bridge this gap, we can wonder if we got the categories right.

One common assumption is that faunal remains from settlements mostly equal the remains of meals, understood as being within the realm of mundane household activities, where eating and sharing food was a daily occurrence, and maybe occasionally also the remains of feasting. But, in essence, food and eating in relation to animal flesh is understood as sustenance and not of mythological significance. But is this a valid separation? Today's meat consumption, in which meat is consumed by many at almost every meal of the day, is unprecedented in historical terms, as is the lack of knowledge in the general public of where the food stems from and the processes involved in bringing it from the soil or from the womb of an animal into the supermarket. In the Iron Age, porridge was the everyday norm, whereas meat was presumably eaten only rarely, at specific times of the year, presumably mostly in late autumn and winter, when feeding the animals would have been a stretch throughout winter. This leads me to the suggestion: could not every meal of animal flesh, (or even every meal regardless of its contents) have been a sacred action, in which the procurement of the food was honoured? In a life world where – that is, if we accept the mythological significance of animals as a structuring principle – animals were sacred, was every meal not an embodiment of the sacred?

Magnell states that, regarding the contribution of archaeology to such questions, the "most important aim must be to consider and reveal new aspects of the Old Norse religion we do not find in the written sources". Thus, archaeology is not a handmaiden to history, and should not be seen merely as a supplement to what the written sources can say. Rather, archaeology reveals the kinds of stories, narratives, even mundane things little and big about life that no medieval monk, bard or jester considered sufficiently important to write down, or sing and dance about. The true nature of the everyday consumption of food could be one such mundane action in which the consumption of animal flesh held some sacred significance.

The Muddy Nature of Materialisations

Magnell's contribution can be read as an unmasking of the difficulties of working interdisciplinary inbetween myth and materiality.

Partly this springs from the slipperiness of interdisciplinarity, and the necessity of appreciating the full picture of the data as well as its contextual situation prior to drawing conclusions based on data from disciplines outside of one's own. Magnell presents the whole of his dataset and it does not show a clear and straightforward pattern. The animal bones appear in a variety of contexts and in a variety of ways. There are regional variations, there are variations through the cycle of the year, and although there is a predominance of skulls there are also other skeletal elements. This muddled image is in contrast to how archaeology is normally used by scholars from other disciplines, historians, linguists, historians of religion, folklore and so on. Very often, archaeology is used for cherry-picking the neatest sites, the ones that fit with our conclusions, the most spectacular, the ones that are easiest to understand within the context we want them to explain. Or, we want them to "prove" that the written sources were correct. As Magnell correctly suggests, sometimes there is "a desperate and almost futile search for written sources". We all do it from time to time. But of course, archaeologists also cherry-pick from, for example, the written sources, which can be problematic in its own ways.

One interesting result from Magnell's research is that the archaeological record varies across regions – which gives us a more finely-grained image of how myths became materially manifested in different ways in different parts of Scandinavia. Why is this? Is the "core symbol" and its meaning the same across regions? Or are there regional variations concerning religious beliefs and adherence to myths? This could be compared for example with place names, as has been done in the Nordic countries, which indicates that there are regional variations in the way names of deities are used in place names in different regions.

Another question that arises is, in the myths, what do the animals signify? The faunal remains that Magnell identified are almost only farm animals, horses, pigs, sheep/goat – this goes for both settlement contexts and ritual depositions. All of them are somewhat present in myths or in references to sacrifice, some more so than others. At the end of the day, the animals butchered for sustenance and those butchered for ritual deposition came from the same place – the farm. What about those animals? Was a pig a pig a pig? Did every pig represent the idea of pig-ness in a mythological sense? Or was there something special about the pig that came to be deposited in what we understand as a ritual deposition?

What then, of the importance of Nidhoggr, Ratatosk, Fenrir, Hugin and Munin? We find them only very rarely in the faunal remains – and if so, mostly in graves, like the princely graves from the Merovingian Period with several unusual species of animals[1] and not in scatterings left over from meals. We know they were mythologically significant, not just from their role in the written sources, but also because they are found in the iconography, on jewellery, rune stones, carved wood, etc.[2]

One of the most interesting finds in Magnell's study is the depositional patterns of the faunal remains from horses. In Magnell's data set the horses are frequently found in wetland sacrifices, and seldom on settlement sites and even not frequently in buildings associated with cult and sacrifice. The conclusion that Magnell draws from this is that horses are less important in *blót* than is often made out. However, horses were clearly exceptionally important in materialisations of myths, regarding their frequent occurrence in graves, on iconography and the way they are portrayed in the Eddas and the Icelandic sagas. Magnell mentions the *níðstǫng* as one practice in which horses were slaughtered to use the head to cast a curse. For example, during the conference Carolyne Larrington pointed out that horses were "slaughterhorses" – *Valglaumr* – and guides that were leading the dead. I have argued similarly on many occasions, also because horses and horse equipment are frequently found in graves, especially in the Viking Period.[3] In the following, I want to expand upon the symbolic role of horses in the *blót* and how this came to play an important role in the troubled time that ended up as the conversion to Christianity.

Blót at the Cusp of a New Time – Materialisation between Old and New Myths

A common criticism against using written sources is that is must be acknowledged that they do not give a one-to-one representation of the societies they describe, rather, they are riddled with ulterior motives. One example of this is the famous *blót* described in *Hákonar saga*. What is this event meant to portray? It is a clash of the old, the traditions, with the new, Chrisitanity and a more "civilised" world that would not practice heathen customs. It is meant to describe a political situation, and is as such a forerunner for events to come. Does this mean that we should disregard it entirely as a framework of knowledge that can be used to contextualise archaeological situations? Preben Meulengracht Sørensen[4] suggested that the written sources can be read at three different levels. The most obvious level being the narrative itself, then follows the ulterior motives, or intentions that underlie the angle given to the text, and finally, as an underlying current that runs through those aspects of society, belief systems and world view that the maker of the story is so embedded in that s/he cannot escape them. This level is referred to as the structural level,[5] although it also relates to the ontological aspects of the writer as locked in a certain situation. With this in mind, let us take a closer look at the story of the *blót* at *Hlade*:

The English king Aethelstan fostered Håkon the Good. Håkon's foster father converted him to Christianity and taught him how to be a good Christian. When Håkon returned to Norway, he found himself in a religious minefield. His saga relates how Håkon was frustrated by the practice of *blót* and its frequency, and he wanted no part in it. Rather, he observed the Christian customs, such as keeping the Sunday and fasting on Fridays. At the same time, he attempted to keep his head down so as to not get involved with the battle between the pagan religion and Christianity. But he did not always succeed in staying out of trouble. One of the earls, Sigurd Ladejarl, held great *blót*s, gathering all of the farmers from wide and far. Horses and cattle were butchered and the blood was gathered up in large cauldrons. A sort of wisp was used to sprinkle the blood on the walls of the shrine, and also of the stables, leaving the walls red with blood. One winter Håkon the Good arrived during such a *blót*. Håkon would normally try to sneak off and eat in another house, but the men refused him this – eating together was an act of social recognition. The men made Håkon sit in the high seat and demanded that he join the party. The first

334 Myth, Materiality, and Lived Religion

day the king was bound to drink to Óðinn, but got away with it by marking his cup with a cross. The following day was trickier:

> The next day, when the people sat down to table, the farmers pressed the king strongly to eat of horseflesh; and as he would on no account do so, they wanted him to drink of the soup; and as he would not do this, they insisted he should at least taste the gravy; and on his refusal they were going to lay hands on him. Earl Sigurd came and made peace among them, by asking the king to hold his mouth over the handle of the kettle, upon which the fat smoke of the boiled horse-flesh had settled itself; and the king first laid a linen cloth over the handle, and then gaped over it, and returned to the high seat; but neither party was satisfied with this.

This conflict between Håkon the Good and the farmers escalated until Håkon was bound to desert his mission of Christianisation. The text recounts the great resistance to Christianity amongst the Norwegians. Yet in the long run, Christianity was victorious. This story about Håkon the Good serves as an example of how horses and horseflesh came to represent and embody the pagan practices in this conflict between religions.[6] To Håkon, horseflesh was the pinnacle of everything pagan, and he did not want to contaminate his body by allowing horseflesh to pass his lips.

After the conversion to Christianity, any kind of *blót* was forbidden. As mentioned above, this prohibition is set down in the Gulathing Law. This law is the oldest that is known from Norway, it dates back to the Viking Age and is thus originally a pagan law (the final part of the Iron Age, approx. 800–1030 AD), but the version we know dates from the early Middle Ages, from the fledgling Christian state. It clearly has a Christian orientation, and refers to deeply embedded Christian institutions. It acts as a counter-weight to the pagan religion, as to how paganism is narrated in the saga of Håkon the Good.

Blót and Feasting as Political Manoeuvres in Troubled Times

This reading adds an extra layer to the zooarchaeology of feasting that Magnell lays out in his article. The story from the saga demonstrates how the consumption of meat was perceived as a deeply political act. Though the prohibition of consumption of certain types of flesh at certain times is referred to as a ban given by the new religion, it seems like politics in disguise. It might have been deeply felt, but the ulterior motive of the kings who banned these types of consumption were doing so to break the hold of the pagan, fragmented powers ("one king on each hill"), in their quest to forge larger political units and ultimately a kingdom. Thus, an attempt at "mythocide" was part of the ulterior motive, the local kings on the hills lost their justification for the material manifestiation of the myths – bound as they were to particular historical situations and locales.

Did they succeed in their attempt at "mythocide"? The rewriting of festivals – yule to the birth of Christ, midsummer to St. John's feast, acted as a two-egged sword. On the one hand it assured a continuity between old and new traditions, thus taking away potential mourning of, and later reinstatement of, the old pagan traditions, and on the other hand it allowed remnants of the pagan tradition to go under ground and live on in disguise. Thus, laws had to be made to ensure that the people did not use these new feasts as a "carte blanche" to carry on as per usual. Therefore, the Norwegian Gulathing law strictly forbade the custom of *blót* and consumption of horse meat. But does this mean that the people obeyed? According to osteoarchaeologist Marianna Betti, one archaeological find supports the practice of horse cults post the conversion. Faunal remains from Kaupang dating to the early Medieval Period have cut marks consistent with butchering, these bones are clearly the remains of meals.[7]

Onwards – Concluding Remarks

As I hope to have demonstrated in my comment, many interesting questions spring from Magnell's work, and several avenues of new projects are gleaned. For me, one of the most interesting one is the slippery gap between sacrificial *blót* and everyday consumption. Magnell states that: "Most of these kinds of depositions consist of food remains and to a certain extent it can be discussed to which degree the bones represent remains from ritual meals or ordinary consumption at the settlements." As I mentioned earlier, it is hard to separate the ordinary from the sacred, and possibly these events were not as categorically defined as we tend to imagine.

This leads me to the question of scale. Surely *blót* and ritual consumption played important roles both in small-scale and large-scale events, but how would they look, and how would they differ, archaeologically? Probable levels of scale that could all facilitate *blót* and be identified as an archaeological context are: the local – the household of the farm, the regional level – larger regional gatherings like the thing, and the superregional level like described in the gathering at Uppsala. Is it plausible to think of *blót* as a category that fit these different levels? What would these differences mean in terms of archaeological context and character of deposition? Is this really what Magnell is identifying, with his different contexts?

A further avenue for understanding *blót* and consumption in ritual contexts would be to compare the occurrence of animal bones in graves and look for correlations and discrepancies compared with faunal remains from ritual meals. This might substantiate or refute claims frequently made about faunal remains in graves as remains of meals for the dead. What does the presence of animal bones in graves signify – the remains of a funeral feast for the mourners, or food for the afterlife? Or does the presence of animals reflect a desire to harness their powers – or simply the animals as themselves, as companions?

Notes

1. E.g. Jennbert 2011.

2. E.g. Hedeager 2011; Jennbert 2011.

3. Oma 2001; 2004; 2005; Armstrong Oma 2011; 2015; 2016.

4. Meulengracht Sørensen 1991.

5. Meulengracht Sørensen 1991; Herschend 1997.

6. Armstrong Oma 2016.

7. Betti 2007.

References

Armstrong Oma, Kristin. 2016. From Horses to Jesus. Saving Souls in the Transition from Pagan to Christian Scandinavia. In D. Davis & A. Maurstad (eds.). *The Meaning of Horses. Biosocial Encounters.* London, New York: Routledge, 24–38.

Armstrong Oma, Kristin. 2015. "… det treet, som ingen veit kvar det av rotom renn". Religion i førkristen tid. In *Viking* LXXVIII, 189–206.

Armstrong Oma, Kristin. 2011. *Hesten. En magisk følgesvenn i nordisk forhistorie.* Oslo: Cappelen Damm.

Betti, Marianna. 2007. *Animals and the Christianisation of Norway.* Conference Paper Presented at Nordic Theoretical Archaeology Group in Aarhus, on May 11th 2007.

Hedeager, Lotte. 2011. *Iron Age Myth and Materiality. An Archaeology of Scandinavia AD 400–1000.* London, New York: Routledge.

Herschend, Frands. 1997. *Livet i hallen.* Opia 14. Institutionen för arkeologi och antik historia. Uppsala: Uppsala universitet.

Jennbert, Kristina. 2011. *Animals and Humans. Recurrent Symbiosis in Archaeology and Old Norse Religion.* Lund: Nordic Academic Press.

Meulengracht Sørensen, Preben. 1991. Om Eddadigtenes alder. In G. Steinsland, et al. (eds.). *Nordisk Hedendom. Et symposium.* Odense: Odense Universitetsforlag, 217–228.

Oma, Kristin. 2005. Hestetenner i kokegroper. På sporet av blot? Eit perspektiv frå Veien. In L. Gustafson et al. (eds.). *De gåtefulle kokegroper.* KHM Varia 58, 243–259.

Oma, Kristin. 2004. Hesten og det heilage. Materialiseringa av eit symbol. In L. Melheim et al. (eds.). *Mellom himmel og jord. Foredrag fra et seminar om religionsarkeologi. Isegran 31. januar – 2. februar 2002.* Oslo Arkeologiske Serie 2. Oslo: Universitetet i Oslo, 68–81.

Oma, Kristin. 2001. Hesten i jernalderen. I brytningspunktet mellom seige strukturar og endring i den materielle kulturen. In *Primitive tider* 4, 38–50.

Configurations of Religion in Late Iron Age and Viking Age Scandinavia

Andreas Nordberg[1]
Stockholm University

Over the last two or three decades, chronological, spatial and social religious variation has been an increasingly significant area of study in the research into pre-Christian Scandinavia among archaeologists, historians of religion, folklorists and researchers in sacred place-names. One important aspect of religious variation, which however has rarely been emphasized in Old Norse studies, is that even individual people usually lack a uniform system of religious beliefs and practices, alternating instead between certain more or less incongruent or even inconsistent subsystems or configurations of religious thought, behaviour and references of experience. Such forms of personal alternation between complexes of religious beliefs and behaviour usually occur spontaneously and instinctively. Often, the parallel frames of experience are closely associated with corresponding socio-cultural spheres in the person's own life world, relating, for example, to varying types of subsistence and cultural-ecological milieus, or memberships and activities within different social groups.

Anthropological researchers of religion have for a long time emphasized such forms of individual alternation between different religious identities. For students of Old Norse religion, however, observing similar variations is much more difficult. While anthropologists may gain detailed personal data from their informants by a variety of means and methods, the researcher into Old Norse religion lacks such possibilities. Does this mean that this aspect of religious variation is in fact impossible to study for the researcher

How to cite this book chapter:
Nordberg, A. 2019. Configurations of Religion in Late Iron Age and Viking Age Scandinavia. In: Wikström af Edholm, K., Jackson Rova, P., Nordberg, A., Sundqvist, O. & Zachrisson, T. (eds.) *Myth, Materiality, and Lived Religion: In Merovingian and Viking Scandinavia*. Pp. 339–373. Stockholm: Stockholm University Press. DOI: https://doi.org/10.16993/bay.l. License: CC-BY.

into Old Norse religion? Maybe not. In the present paper, I suggest that existing sources on Old Norse religion may actually indicate that people shifted between certain partly parallel patterns of religious experience, beliefs and behaviour. Below, I refer to these patterns as *religious configurations*.

Religious Configurations – A Suggested Framework

I understand a socio-cultural *configuration* to be a relative and functionally dynamic arrangement of socio-cultural parts or elements that make up a whole. It is a pattern of thought, behaviour, emotions, and sometimes spatial movement, which reflects cultural values, norms and perception of reality, and as such defines a framework for action. By *religious configurations* then, I mean concurrent complexes of religious beliefs, religious practices and frames of experience which are related to certain corresponding socio-cultural settings, forms of subsistence and spatial cultural-ecological milieus.

As far as I know, the first researcher to study this phenomenon focusing particularly on religion was Åke Hultkrantz, who identified three parallel "coherent systems of religious elements", or "configurations of religious beliefs", in the lived religion of the Wind River Shoshoni in Wyoming, USA. These configurations were related to the hunter's vision quest, the Sun dance, and the telling of myth. When one of these concurrent configurations dominated over the other two, it momentarily displaced these in the area of active belief. The decisive factor triggering this domination was each configuration's functional association with a dominant social situation.[2] Since Hultkrantz was particularly interested in the cognitive and intellectual attitude among the Shoshoni to the incoherent relationship between their in a strictly logical sense incompatible religious configurations, it might be worth relating his study in some detail.

The Shoshoni were fundamentally a hunting community, and, as in so many other hunting cultures, the individualism of the hunter was a prominent feature. The core of the hunter's configuration of religious belief consisted of the vision quest, associated with a category of nature and animal spirits called *puha*. The most significant of these were Lightning, Thunderbird and Eagle. The vision quest took place in isolated locations that were often associated with mythical stories and decorated with rock carvings of animals, in whose forms the spirits could make themselves known. During the visionary trance, the spirits transferred their powers to the hunter and guaranteed him hunting luck. As the Shoshoni increasingly became a warrior community that lived off hunting buffalo on the prairies, their needs for cohesion and social organisation grew. This was manifested in the Sun Dance, which took place within the community and actualised a different configuration of religious belief. At its centre stood the Supreme Being Tam Apö, who was identified with both the sky and a power behind the sky. Tam Apö was the creator of the universe, the upholder of cosmic order and a guarantor of the prosperity of the tribe. The Sun Dance also involved Mother Earth, the personification of the living earth itself, and the Buffalo, which presided over the buffalo herds of the prairies and provided people with food and hides for clothes.

The Sun Dance and the vision quest brought two religious configurations to the fore that were largely logically incongruent. In the hunter configuration, Lightning and Thunderbird were ranked the highest in the hierarchy of spirits. In the Sun Dance configuration, the highest in rank was the Supreme Being Tam Apö. The Sun Dance did not concern the *puha* spirits, while the Supreme Being and Mother Earth played no part in the vision quest. According to Hultkrantz, there appears to have been no attempt to relate or compare the highest beings from each religious configuration to each other.

Mythical storytelling further increased this incoherence. The mythical configuration was brought to the fore mainly during the winter months when the Shoshoni spent a large part of their time together indoors. Although the mythical stories were often entertaining and full of humour and epic embellishment adapted to the audience at the time, most story-tellers maintained that the myths were, as they called them, "true stories". These stories were set long ago in a legendary time, when a series of supernatural beings, the foremost of which were Wolf and Coyote, inhabited the world. Assisted by Coyote, Wolf was the creator of animals and humans, the order of nature and the prerequisites for life, but he was also the instigator of death. However, even in this case there were no established ideas about, for example, how Wolf in the mythical configuration related to Tam Apö of the Sun Dance configuration, or Lightning and Thunderbird of the hunter configuration. The Shoshoni people perceived these three parallel belief complexes separately as equally true and logically cohesive, as they were related to different social and cultural-ecological settings.

Analogous phenomena have also been observed elsewhere. For example, Stanley Tambiah has emphasized that villagers in rural Thailand switch between what he viewed as four distinct "ritual complexes" of both Buddhist and indigenous traditions, which are nevertheless linked together in "a single total field".[3] An example from closer to home is given by Matti Sarmela, who claims that Finnish pre-Modern popular culture and popular religion consisted of three major tradition-ecological segments or "cultural systems", historically linked to hunting, slash-and-burn cultivation and agricultural farming.[4] Similarly, during his anthropological fieldwork among the Bambara and Mandinka in Mali, the historian of religion Tord Olsson observed that the lived religion of these peoples is structured into three overall "ritual and mythical fields", linked to farming, hunting and spirit possession, and that "people, in many cases the same individuals, are moving between these fields". The ritual field related to farming is centred on the village and its surrounding arable land and is characterised by ancestor worship, secret societies and a complex cosmological tradition linked to the farmer's activities, life cycles, marriage, as well as a body of conceptions about the Supreme Being and Creator, and other beings created by him. The hunter's ritual field, by contrast, primarily uses the bush as its arena. Here the cult is mainly focused on certain spirits called Djinns, believed to live in the bush and roam around near villages and farmland, as well as a pantheon of deities that has no direct significance in the ritual field of farming. The Djinns, finally, are also at the centre of the third ritual field related to spirit possession.[5]

The concepts *religious configuration*, *complex*, *system*, and *field* used in the referred studies, are semantically synonymous.

The limited scope of this paper restrains me from referring to further parallels from around the world (although it should be noted that such phenomena are by no means exceptional). Instead, on the basis of the examples already given, it is possible to outline the contours of a more general framework of the alternation between *religious configurations*, for example:

- That religion is not a uniform or homogeneous system, either in a society as a whole, or in the arrangement of religious beliefs and behaviour of individual people or groups.
- That the lived religion is an integrated part of everyday life, and is consequently formed (and transformed) by people's day-to-day livelihoods, subsistence and affiliation to social groups.[6]
- That religious beliefs and behaviour relating to corresponding forms of subsistence and social and cultural-ecological milieus, may form into parallel religious configurations.
- That people, both individually and as social groups, may alternate between these different religious configurations, and that a decisive factor in these alternations is the person's or the group's movement between the corresponding social and cultural-ecological settings.
- That the beliefs and practices of the religious configuration that temporarily dominate a person's active belief, may momentarily displace the beliefs and behaviour of other religious configurations.

Religious Configurations in Late Iron Age and Viking Age Scandinavia

Can the general framework of religious configurations, as outlined above, be applied as a form of lens or raster through which we may study Old Norse religion? And if so, may this lens reveal some sort of parallel religious configurations even in Late Iron Age and Viking Age Scandinavia? In my opinion, it can and it does. I suggest that there existed at least three major religious configurations in Scandinavia during this period: the religious

configuration of the farmstead community, the religious configuration of the hunting and fishing grounds, and the religious
configuration of the warband institution. In addition to this, one
could argue for the existence of a fourth mythological configuration as well, although this would partly coincide with the religious
configurations of the farmer and of the warrior.

There is, of course, an obvious chronological layering between
these suggested religious configurations. Hunting and fishing are
much older livelihoods than farming, which in turn spread to
Scandinavia several thousands of years before the rise of the
aristocratic warband institution during the Early Iron Age.
However, since this cultural historical development involves
an unmanageably large timescale,[7] I will settle for the observation that the suggested three or four religious configurations
existed in parallel in Scandinavia during the Late Iron Age and
the Viking Age.

Furthermore, Scandinavia constitutes a very large geographical area, and encompasses natural environments which vary
from region to region. Since these shifting ecological conditions
affected people's day-to-day subsistence, and since religion was an
integrated part of everyday life, obviously Scandinavia's shifting
cultural-ecological milieus indirectly allowed considerable religious variation. Hence, although I maintain that the suggested
religious configurations were common throughout the Germanic
parts of Scandinavia, there must have existed extensive regional
variations, both within each religious configuration, and in the
significance of one religious configuration in proportion to the
other.

Finally, each of the religious configurations encompassed
numerous beliefs and traditions of varying origin, and any effort
to summarize all of their aspects and characteristics in only a few
pages will inevitably lead to an all too simplified result. However,
since the primary objective and motivation of this paper is to
introduce an alternative theoretical and methodological perspective of religious variation into the research of Old Norse religion,
and since I for the sake of this argument nevertheless need to present such summaries below, I will focus only on the core or semantic centre of each of the religious configurations.

The Religious Configuration of the Farmstead Community

The most basic social foundations in Late Iron Age society in Scandinavia were the communities of the family and lineage, the farmstead, and the local settlement area. The households of both the aristocracy and the peasants were fundamentally self-sufficient through farming, animal husbandry, hunting and fishing. Livelihoods and the annual agricultural cycles constituted a shared dominating interest[8] for the whole community, and this common ground was also reinforced by the fact that many peasants lived directly adjacent to the large aristocrats' farms and were linked to them through work and possibly tenancies, etc.

The religious configuration of the farmstead community involved more or less all people, i.e. women and men of all ages and social classes. It encompassed much of what in a broad sense related to the maintenance of a good life, such as cosmic order and regeneration, societal stability and peace, agriculture and stock raising, prosperity, pregnancy and birth, puberty rituals, marriage, and other phases of the life-cycle, health, illness and remedies, death and burial, the relationship to the dead, as well as all of the religious beliefs and daily ritual behaviour associated with the many aspects of the domestic household, the farmstead and its infields. Unfortunately, due to the lack of sources our knowledge of the domestic side of the configuration of the farmer is rather scant. But it should be noticed that the evidence that we do have on the domestic religion for the most part does relate to the areas just mentioned.[9]

Fortunately, there is more information about the public dimension of the religious configuration of the farmstead community. The hope and aspiration for cosmic order, prosperity and the regeneration of the crop and animal stock, as well as the well-being of land and people, obviously comprised the semantic centre of this religious configuration. This is apparent for example in the common pre-Christian ritual formula *til árs ok friðar*. The word *friðr* primarily refers to 'peace, unity', but the term also had certain sexual connotations that strengthened the ritual formula's associations with regeneration and fertility. The term *ár* means 'year, annual yield/harvest, yield from crops and livestock'. Semantically *ár ok friðr* therefore expresses the hope of a new year, annual yield/harvest, fertility and peace.[10] This was also an explicit purpose of the seasonal festivals of the agricultural year, which according to several sources were celebrated *til árs* 'for the harvest, annual yield,' *til árbótar* 'for better annual yield', *til gróðrar* 'for the crops', etc.[11]

In addition to a variety of local deities[12] and spirits related to the household, the farmstead and the arable lands (which might actually have played a more prominent part in everyday religion than did the higher gods), it is evident from both theophoric place names and literary depictions, that the public cult relating to the religious configuration of the farmstead community was above all devoted to uranic and chthonic gods such as, for example, Þórr, Ullr, Freyr, Freyja and Njǫrðr.[13] The worship of Þórr and Freyr may have partly overlapped, although, judging from the distribution of the theophoric place names, at least in some areas of Scandinavia the significance of one over the other may also have varied regionally.[14] In the Norse mythological sources, Þórr appears to have a special position as the protector of the cosmos and the people,[15] whereas Freyr and Freyja in particular were assumed to guarantee regeneration and fertility.[16] Freyr was therefore called *inn fróði* 'the prolific one',[17] and bore epithets such as *árguð* 'god of the year's crop', and *fégjafi* 'the bestower of *fé* [= cattle or riches]'.[18] According to Adam of Bremen, *Thor* (ON. Þórr) reigned in the air and controlled thunder, lightning, wind, rain, sunshine and crops, while *Fricco* (i.e. OSw. Frø, ON. Freyr) "bestows peace and pleasure on mortals" (*pacem voluptatemque largiens mortalibus*).[19] Adam's choice of words may allude to the formula *til árs ok friðar*, which according to some scholars appears to have been particularly linked to the worship of Freyr and Njǫrðr.[20]

The fact that prosperity and regeneration constituted a dominating interest within the religious configuration of the farmstead community is also indicated by terms such as *ármaðr, árguð* and *ársæll*. The *ármaðr* 'the year man, the harvest man', was according to an Icelandic family saga a ruling spirit who ensured good yields from grain fields and livestock.[21] The name *árguð* was, as already mentioned, an epithet for Freyr. The adjective *ársæll* described certain kings and noblemen, who through their inherent luck and good relationship with the gods guaranteed good years of prosperity for the land and its people.[22] In this role, the *ársæll* ruler and Freyr the *árguð* carried similar functions.[23] The latter is related to the fact that aristocrats were expected to manage the public sanctuaries and uphold the public worship on behalf of the people and the land. Several Old Norse sources even state that the gods were deemed able to turn against the people and punish them with bad years and crop failure if the nobles did not fulfil their duties.[24]

Probably, the inscription on a 7th-century rune stone in Stentoften in Blekinge province, Sweden, relates to this cultic task of the aristocracy. An extract from the text reads:

niuhAborumRniuhagestumRhAþuwolAfRgafj

niu habrumR, niu hangistumR, HaþuwulfR gaf j

[With] nine goats, nine stallions, HaþuwulfR gave year [= a good annual yield].[25]

The final rune **j** in the quotation is an ideograph, referring to the word Proto-Norse *jára* = ON. *ár* 'year, annual yield, harvest'. Thus, at some point in the 7th century, a man HaþuwulfR in Blekinge ensured a new year with a good annual yield for the land and people by sacrificing nine goats and nine horses.

The rune stone from Stentoften is, however, interesting for additional reasons. Alongside HaþuwulfR, the inscription also mentions the name HariwulfR. It is highly likely that the men carrying these names were *úlfheðnar*, elite warriors dedicated to the god Óðinn. The names thus remind us of a different religious configuration in Late Iron Age and Viking Age Scandinavia.

The Religious Configuration of the Warband Institution

The aristocratic warband or *comitatus* is very prominent in archaeological, literary and onomastic sources about Scandinavia during the Late Iron Age and the Viking Age. The embryo of this institution appears to have developed as early as in the Late European Bronze Age. Subsequently it was affected by the Celtic culture and by Roman civilisation. A central arena of the warband was the aristocratic hall, which was introduced in Scandinavia onto certain large farms in the 4th and 5th centuries AD, while in the 7th century grander halls started to appear in central-place complexes, consisting of, for example, assembly sites, marketplaces, craft sites, public sanctuaries and monumental burial mounds. In the European Migration Period the warband was a central institution among all Germanic peoples, and in Scandinavia it retained this position during the Viking Age.[26]

Ideologically, the most prominent arena for the warband community was the hall, where the warlord and his wife convened their retinue with feasts and rewarded the men with exchanges of gifts, in return for their promises to fight and possibly die for their lord and lady. In this respect, the ceremonial gathering in the hall constituted a social foundation of the retinue, although it was also a highly formalised religious communion, which appears to have been expressed most strongly during the fellowships of the ritual meal and especially of drinking.[27]

When a warrior was admitted into a warlord's retinue, he entered into a relationship with his lord and lady that resembled adoption.[28] This relationship is even reflected in the complex of myths and heroic sagas about Óðinn, who in several semi-mythical heroic poems and *fornaldar* sagas is portrayed as an adviser, companion or foster-father to his chosen warriors. When his warriors die, Óðinn brings them to Valhǫll, where he acknowledges them as his *óskasynir* 'wish-sons', i.e. foster-sons,[29] and invites them to endless feasting and drinking in the company of his female valkyries. These epic motifs thus fundamentally reflect the communion in the aristocratic hall between the warlord, his wife, and the "adopted" men of the retinue.[30]

But actually the motifs may even hint at a deeper religious relationship between the warrior god and the members of the warband community. Ideally, young men had to undergo certain initiation rites before they were admitted into the warband. Even though such rites are often secret, it is evident from several sources that a vital part of the warrior initiation centred on a ritual drama during which the initiate assumed the shape of a wolf or bear, and received a new name that alluded to this therianthropic transformation.[31] It is, for example, in this cultural historical context that the names HaþuwulfR and HariwulfR on the Stentoften Stone must be viewed. These two names also appear on a contemporary rune stone in Istaby, Blekinge, together with yet a third analogous name HeruwulfR. The three names correspond to a broader group of similar names testified to in a range of sources from different parts of the Germanic area, all have the final element PN. *-wulfR*, ON. m. *úlfr* 'wolf'. The first element PN. *haþu-* in HaþuwulfR corresponds to ON. *hǫð* f. 'battle', and the name therefore means 'Battle Wolf'. In HariwulfR, the first element is PN. *hari-*, ON. *herr* m. 'war-host', and the name therefore means 'War-Host Wolf'. Lastly, HeruwulfR means 'Sword Wolf', as the first element is PN. *heru-*, ON. *hiǫrr* m. 'sword'. Most likely these men were given their names when undergoing initiations to become *úlfheðnar* and admitted into a warband.[32] The *úlfheðnar* 'wolf-skins' along with the *berserkir* 'bear-shirts' were the elite warriors with strong personal relations to Óðinn.

Óðinn, of course, was the god *par preference* of the royal and aristocratic warband institution, and he represented all the characteristics of the at times capricious life in the warband community. On the one hand, he personified all the abilities that were regarded as virtuous and coveted within the warrior aristocratic hall culture. For example, Óðinn was the god of wisdom and the god of death, because he acquired his in-depth knowledge by voluntarily dying in order to be initiated into the mysteries of the Other World, conquering the finality of death and thus being able to consult the dead for advice. He was the god of poetry, which was a highly respected art form in the aristocratic hall culture. Ideally, each warlord had at least one skald in his retinue. He was the god of the mead, the most preferable beverage in the ceremonial drinking in the hall.[33] On the other hand, he was also the terrifying, erratic and deceitful god of war and as such he personified the unpredictability of violence and battle, as well as the warrior's ecstatic rage. The latter is even reflected in his name, ON. *Óðinn* > PrGmc *Wōðanaz*, from *Óð-*, *Wōð-* 'rage, fury'.[34] Adam of Bremen, who in 1076 described an idol of Óðinn in the central holy place in (Old) Uppsala, emphasised this central aspect of Óðinn, relating that "Wodan, that is fury" (*Wodan, id est furor*).[35]

According to the Eddic poem *Vǫluspá*, Óðinn initiated the first war in the world between the two tribes of gods: the Æsir and the Vanir. From a mythical perspective this was a prototypical action.[36] When battles between aristocratic warlords are depicted in Old Norse skaldic poetry, the fallen, bloodied warriors on the battlefields are often described using concepts that also occur in religious sacrificial terminology, indicating a religious aspect of the violence.[37] On the one hand, slaying enemies on the battlefield could be conceived of as making sacrificial offerings to the god of war. On the other hand, death on the battlefield could be perceived as the warrior's final reward. Through a violent death in battle, Óðinn's initiated warriors ultimately achieved complete communion with their god.

Spatial and Mental Alternation between the Religious Configurations of the Farmstead Community and of the Warband Institution

In my opinion, the most prominent aspects of the cult of Óðinn mainly belonged to the religious configuration of the royal and aristocratic warband institution, while the cult of gods such as Þórr, Freyr, Freyja and Njǫrðr instead belonged to the religious configuration of the farmstead community, which was of major importance for everyone. Even the kings' and the warlords' residences were basically large farmsteads, and kings, warlords and warriors were in this sense, if not farmers themselves, at least directly dependent on the agricultural and pastoral community's prosperity and good fortune. Cosmic and societal order, the cohesion of the family and lineage, general prosperity, regeneration and a good annual yield from crops and livestock – all these things were dominating interests for all members of the community. It was with such hopes that the kings and aristocrats represented the entire community and all its inhabitants to the gods, as they bore the cost of and even led the public cult *til árs ok friðar* at the communities' common sanctuaries. And it was probably because of these social and religious functions that certain royal dynasties such as the *Ynglingar* of central Sweden (and later of southern Norway) claimed to be descendants of the fertility god Freyr.

The religious configuration of the farmstead community was thus of major importance for all people. But the warlords and their warriors also shifted to the religious configuration of the warband institution, which differed radically, both socially and religiously, from the farmstead's religious configuration. Unfortunately, we know little about the attitudes of common people to the religious configuration of the warband, since the preserved Norse literary sources primarily originate from the royal and aristocratic socio-cultural milieus. Probably the set of religious traditions that constituted the semantic centre of the warband institution was of little interest outside this exclusive social stratum. Óðinn was the god of war *par preference* in the skaldic and mythic poetry, yet it is still possible (or even probable) that commoners also, or even rather, invoked Þórr and maybe Freyr even in case of occasional personal violent conflicts.[38] When ordinary people did invoke Óðinn, they still lacked any profound personal ties to the god equivalent to those between Óðinn and the elite warriors of the aristocratic retinues. The socio-cultural centre of the most prominent aspects of the cult of Óðinn was certainly the warband institution, from which most people were excluded.

A decisive factor for the aristocrats' and the elite warriors' alternation between the religious configurations of the farmstead community and of the warband institution, was the functional association of each religious configuration with a corresponding dominant socio-cultural context. But these social situations did not only determine which of the religious configurations dominated and momentarily displaced the other in the area of active religious belief,[39] it seems as if the alternation also activated two partly parallel social and even existential configurations of values.

For example, while the farmstead community depended on the cohesion of the family, lineage, local district and region, the aristocratic warband institution was based on the social foundations of an exclusive, initiated society which was built not on biological family ties, but instead on a pact between the warlord and lady and the warriors of the retinue. Within the religious configuration of this exclusive social framework, the members of the aristocratic warbands seem to have revered Óðinn as the only god of significance, or at least as the highest god of the pantheon, as *Hávi* 'the

High One',[40] *Hár* 'High',[41] and *Alfaðir* 'All-Father',[42] etc. Yet, in parallel with this, within the religious configuration of the farmstead community the aristocrats also led the common worship of life-affirming deities such as Þórr, Freyr, Freyja and Njǫrðr at the public sanctuaries, and in this context they honoured not Óðinn but rather Þórr or Freyr as the foremost of the gods,[43] in the latter case for example as *Veraldar goð* 'god of the world',[44] *fólkvaldi goða* 'ruler of the gods',[45] and *ása iaðarr* 'protector of the Æsir'.[46] And while the worship of the gods within the religious configuration of the farmstead community was based on a need and desire for cosmic order, peace, regeneration, good health, and prosperity in this life, the semantic centre of the religious configuration of the warband institution was instead related to the constantly ongoing small-scale endemic warfare – sometimes within the warrior aristocrats' own lineages – which ideally would end in an honourable death in battle, subsequently rewarded by a glorious existence in the afterlife.

Yet, despite these sharp contrasts – which strictly logically speaking are conflicting and inconsistent – there is no indication that these two parallel sets of religious beliefs and behaviour appear to have been perceived as contradictory, either by the warrior aristocrats themselves, or among other people of the peasant communities (to the extent that the latter were familiar with the religious configuration of the warband institution). This, I argue, was because the decisive factor for the alternation between the two parallel religious configurations was the functional association of each configuration to its corresponding social situation and socio-cultural milieu.

The Religious Configuration of the Hunting and Fishing Grounds

As suggested above, the religious configuration of the warband institution mainly belonged to the religious life of those within the higher strata of society. Most people in Late Iron Age and Viking Age Scandinavia did not usually shift to this religious configuration, since they were not a part of the warband institution's corresponding socio-cultural milieu. I do suggest, however, that most peasants could alternate between the religious configuration of the farmstead and that of the hunting and fishing grounds.

It is not totally clear who were engaged in hunting and fishing. Probably it concerned most people in one way or the other. Some Norse sagas mention men involved in big-game hunting and deep-sea fishing in Norway and Iceland, but it is quite probable that also women and even children were engaged in small-game hunting and freshwater fishing. Admittedly, textual and archaeological sources especially relating to religious traditions associated with hunting and fishing in pre-Christian times are actually on the whole so few,[47] so that the suggestion of a particular pre-Christian religious configuration associated with hunting and fishing of course is but a hypothesis. Yet, it is still absolutely reasonable to assume that a wealth of such pre-Christian religious traditions did exist. The lived religion in pre-Christian Scandinavia was an integrated part of everyday life and as such strongly associated with day-to-day sustenance. Since most people were partly dependent on the hunting and fishing economy (in the coastal regions more so than in the inland areas), this livelihood may well have been a dominating interest that could trigger a certain configuration of beliefs and practices in the lived religion. At least, this would certainly have uncountable ethnographic parallels, both in for example the religious traditions among neighbouring Baltic, Finno-Ugrian and Sámi peoples,[48] and in later Scandinavian folklore and popular customs.

In all of these contexts we meet complexes of religious beliefs and ritualistic behaviour associated with hunting and fishing, that centred around ideas of, for example, omens, forewarnings and taboos, traditions concerning envy and limited goods, magical practices and ritual regulations on how to handle weapons and hunting tools, how to kill and cut up the game, and so forth. Of greatest importance is the hunter's or fisherman's good relationship with the supernatural lord, ruler or owner of the fish and prey of the hunting grounds and fishing waters. Corresponding notions are well documented in later Scandinavian folklore and folk customs,[49] not least regarding the complex of traditions relating to the owner of nature,[50] who is known in Scandinavian folklore for example as the Swedish *skogsrå* 'ruler of the woods' and *sjörå* 'ruler of the lake, or fishing waters', or *havsfrun* 'the mermaid', etc.,[51] and the Norwegian *huldra* 'hulder' (ie. *huld-ra* 'hidden ruler').[52] In Nordic traditions lucky hunters and fishermen were often believed to be blessed with a good relationship with the *rå* or the *huldra*. Even impersonal collectives of supernatural beings are mentioned in similar contexts,[53] corresponding with the information in the Icelandic *Landnámabók*, from the early 13th century, that people who were blessed with hunting and fishing luck had a good relationship with the *landvættir* (the spirits of the land) that ruled over the hunting and fishing grounds.[54]

Thus, what is almost completely missing in the early sources on Old Norse religion is, interestingly enough, instead common in mediaeval and later Scandinavian folk traditions. Whatever the explanation for this might be,[55] the most urgent question relating to the scope of this paper is what relevance the late evidences may have for our understanding of earlier cultural historical periods. In my view, at least it should not be totally dismissed. In his outline of a tradition-ecological and tradition-historical perspective on folk traditions, the Finnish folklorist Lauri Honko stresses that stabile social institutions, group identities, and economic utilization of the cultural-ecological milieu are of fundamental importance for the continuity of cultural traditions.[56] This actually corresponds fairly well with the relative stable social and culture-ecological settings associated with hunting and fishing activities during the last millennium before the major urbanization process in the 19th and 20th centuries in Scandinavia. Thus, without in any way disregarding the many complex problems concerning the relation between pre-Christian religion and Mediaeval and pre-Modern folk customs, it seems more likely in my view that the later popular traditions associated with hunting and fishing at least to some extent are related to an earlier complex of ideas, rather than solely being a product of cultural inventions and influx during Catholic or Protestant times. This certainly does not mean that these late folk traditions constituted some sort of frozen, stagnated cultural survivals from pre-Christian times, in the sense early evolutionistic scholars may have understood them. Rather, I suggest that it opens up for the possibility of the existence of a similar configuration also in pre-Christian times, as this form of tradition complex was an adaptable part of the lived religion even in the medieval and late pre-Modern eras.

The latter is emphasized for example by the Swedish ethnologist Orvar Löfgren in a study of local fishing communities in Sweden and Norway in the 19th and early 20th centuries. According to Löfgren, these communities constituted "a milieu in which belief in supernatural powers associated with fishing was a living reality, and where the learning of ritual techniques and magical rules formed part of the natural socialisation process in the fishing profession".[57] The fishing milieus and fishing activities thus were related to a corresponding cognitive belief system, parallel with the Christian worldview. Löfgren continues:

> Our cultural world of experience can therefore be full of inner contradictions and inconsistencies, and in addition, individuals can switch between different cultural repertoires or value systems depending on their current situation. This is the type of problem that we have encountered in the earlier discussion of how fishermen were able to be converted from sceptics to active believers following an appalling fishing season, or how Jesus and the mermaid [Sw. *havsfrun*] could exist side by side in the lives of fishing communities. For most fishermen, their belief in supernatural powers probably constituted a religious system that was clearly separated from the Christian worldview. These two cosmologies existed side by side as autonomous and largely contradictory moral systems, although some integration (syncretism) did occur between them.[58]

What Löfgren refers to as a separate, autonomous religious system relating to the fishing milieu, existing in parallel with the Christian worldview is actually more or less identical with what I am conceptualizing as parallel religious configurations. Of course, this autonomous system associated with fishing in late pre-Modern Scandinavia is not evidence of far earlier conditions. It does not prove a religious configuration associated with hunting and fishing in the Viking Age. Yet, I do propose that it does at least strengthen the possibility of a corresponding religious configuration even in pre-Christian Scandinavia. And again, what triggered this religious configuration relating to hunting and fishing in active belief – in late pre-Modern times as well as in pre-Christian periods – was its functional association with the corresponding cultural-ecological milieus of the hunting and fishing grounds, and the social situations of the lone hunter/fisher or the small hunting/fishing party.

A Mythological Configuration?

It is paradoxical that so much of our knowledge of Old Norse religion is based on mythical sources at the same time as we remain largely in the dark about who the narrators of the myths were and in what context the myths were narrated.[59] We do know, however, that sagas were told at major official events, feasts and in the aristocratic hall assemblies,[60] and probably also in more private everyday contexts, although the latter is much more difficult to demonstrate due to the nature of the sources. Mythical storytelling probably followed roughly the same pattern. There are many indications that the mythical traditions were well known among both commoners and the elite.[61] Myths were probably retold in many different contexts, in public and in the private sphere of the family, in poetic and prose forms, by professional storytellers and lay people (such as the tradition bearers of the Finnish Kalevala poetry). Through mythical associations, poetic allusions and kennings, prominent storytellers and poets linked mythical tales together in a way that in some contexts almost resembled an independent mythical dimension.

Could this be apprehended as a separate mythological configuration? Admittedly, there are many relevant objections to such a suggestion. Mythical storytelling was important in the religious configurations of the farmstead community and of the warband institution (but apparently not in that of the hunting and fishing grounds). A mythical configuration would therefore partly coincide with these. Conversely, mythology does display important aspects that are not expressed in the other religious configurations, and there is intrinsic value in highlighting these distinctive characteristics in their own right. For consistency, although there may possibly be better ways of conceptualising this, I am therefore opting to talk of a loosely formed and partly overlapping mythological configuration, with boundaries that admittedly are difficult to define.

The Old Norse myths display all the characteristics of the mythical genre in general. Through a combination of religious notions and epic motifs, a mythical universe emerges which partly resembles human society, but is also part of a totally different world. The pre-Christian gods appear in anthropomorphic form, with human traits, characteristics and emotions. In certain myths, the deities' adventures are set in an unspecified ancient age, before humans walked the earth. In others, the gods instead interact with humans, often with the intention of confirming social norms or affecting humans' existence in certain ways. Here the Old Norse myths are also sometimes interwoven with certain motifs from the Scandinavian-Germanic heroic tradition, in which human heroes interact with gods (usually Óðinn) and other supernatural beings in a partly mythical and partly semi-historical context. Many myths recount stories that had no or few parallels in religious practice, the central aspect instead being the actual consequences of what happened in the myth, as these occurrences shaped the world and therefore were continuously affecting people's life worlds. Furthermore, many of the gods and supernatural beings occurring in the myths were not the subject of actual worship. These included some probably purely epic figures, such as Loki,[62] as well as gods and other beings that were deemed to exist but without being the subject of active veneration. For example, the enigmatic god Heimdallr may be a representative of the latter.

Common to the world of myth is further that the gods are organised into family systems and internal relationships that are not expressed in the corresponding cult. The Greek deities, to make a comparative analogy, were systematised in mythology into a joint Olympic family pantheon, led by Zeus. But, in the lived religion of ancient Greece, the gods were generally worshipped separately, usually in separate sanctuaries and within the framework of separate feasts led by separate ritual specialists. Admittedly, sometimes several deities were worshiped collectively, but in general, neither the myths' epic dramas nor their systematised family pantheons had parallels in actual cult. The same pattern is also seen in pre-Christian Scandinavia. Although a great variety of gods, lesser deities and other beings appear in the myths, only some of them seem to have been objects of actual worship.[63]

Additionally, in the Old Norse myths the gods are characterised by their degree of anthropomorphic concretion, features that probably become even more accentuated by the narrators' use of, for example, enactments, gestures, facial expressions and masks.[64] Such epic motifs with the gods must not, however, be confused with a general conception (or even perception) of the gods' essential nature. While the epic anthropomorphic form is a distinctive characteristic of the mythic genre (which was also reproduced in iconography), the same conceptions of the gods may have been expressed differently in, for example, prayers and hymns, and to an even greater extent in everyday speech, in which the gods sometimes seem to have been spoken of as an impersonal ruling collective (compare for example designations such as *regin* pl. 'the rulers, leaders', *bǫnd* pl. and *hǫpt* pl. 'the obligators, decision makers', etc.).[65] Yet another distinctive characteristic of the mythical genre appears to be that some beings were given a higher status in the mythical world than in daily religion. One example of this is that elves and giants were portrayed in a much more elaborated and elevated manner in the myths than in medieval and later folklore. There might be several reasons for this, but in my view, the differences could be old and dependent on the various genres of lore.[66]

The conceptualisation of the mythical dimension of religion as an overlapping and loosely formed mythical configuration does not preclude mythical storytelling, poetry and pictorial art from featuring in other parts of religion (which also contributed to making the mythology more varied and superficially contradictory). But it does accentuate the mythical dimension's many specific and uniting characteristics, which often differentiated mythology and mythical storytelling from other aspects of the lived religion. It also highlights the considerable significance of the situational and contextual framing of the mythical storytelling as such.

Configurations of Religion in Late Iron Age and Viking Age Scandinavia – A Conclusion

As stated in the introduction to this paper, the aim of this study is to contribute an additional theoretical perspective to the ongoing discussion about religious variation, in research into Old Norse religion. My suggestion is, that the polytheistic lived religion in Late Iron Age and Viking Age Scandinavia was not a uniform or homogeneous system, either in the society as a whole or in the individual people's cognitive arrangement of religious beliefs and behaviour. Rather, religion was an integrated part of people's daily life, and thus to a great extent formed (and transformed) by their day-to-day livelihoods, subsistence and affiliation to social groups. Since these fundamental social and cultural-ecological conditions were not homogeneous, the religious beliefs and behaviour formed parallel religious configurations corresponding with these variations. Above, I have proposed three such major religious configurations, that of the farmstead community, that of the warband institution, and that of the hunting and fishing grounds. In addition, I have suggested that even mythic storytelling might in part have formed a similar mythological configuration.

When people moved between different social and cultural-ecological milieus, they also alternated between the corresponding religious configurations. The decisive factor in this alternation was the functional association between the social situation and the corresponding religious beliefs and behaviour. Consequently, most people did alternate between the religious configurations of the farmstead community and those of the hunting and fishing grounds, since both of these religious configurations related to two parallel cultural ecological milieus with major importance for their day-to-day subsistence. However, while the religious configuration of the warband institution was of central importance to the aristocratic warrior elite, it did not usually engage ordinary people, because they were not a part of this social institution. The warrior aristocrats, for their part, probably alternated between all of the religious configurations.

Of course, structuring the lived religion in accordance with this theoretical framework is but a tentative approach to gain a deeper understanding of people and life ways in pre-Christian Scandinavia. Yet, I believe that the model has its advantages. It makes our view of the polytheistic lived religion more strongly contextualised and situated, and in addition it even helps us identify areas of the lived religion which for various reasons we still know little about.

The model of "religious configurations" offers an additional way of understanding socio-religious variation in Late Iron Age and Viking Age Scandinavia. What have sometimes been emphasised as signs of incoherence and contradictions in the preserved sources of Old Norse religion gain a logical explanation in this context. They exemplify the polytheistic lived religion's expected natural variations.

Notes

1. This study is sponsored by Riksbankens Jubileumsfond / The Swedish Foundation for Humanities and Social Sciences.

2. Hultkrantz 1956.

3. Tambiah 1970, especially p. 370.

4. Sarmela 2009; similarly Honko 1993.

5. Olsson 2000, quote p. 29, translated from Swedish: "I själva verket illustrerar det religiösa livet [...] tre rituella och mytiska fält [...] och att människor, i flera fall samma individer, rör sig mellan dessa fält."

6. Compare the tradition-ecological and tradition-historical perspectives advocated for by for example Lauri Honko 1993:51–60.

7. Compare Sarmela 2009, who does weight in a time scale of several millennia.

8. The concept of *dominant* or *dominating interests* was first coined by the ethnologist Albert Eskeröd, who defined it as "the foundation for the growth of ideas of the supernatural relationships between the different needs of human beings grouped together and the environment" (1964:85).

9. Compare for example DuBois 1999; Steinsland 2005:327–356; Carlie 2004; Murphy 2018.

10. Hultgård 2003; Nordberg 2006:84–86.

11. Cf. Beck 1967:48–57, 89–90; Nordberg 2006:76–77 with references.

12. Cf. Hultgård 2001.

13. Vikstrand 2001; Brink 2007. For simplicity I use the Old Icelandic forms of the gods' names for the entire Nordic region.

14. Sundqvist 2016:516–519.

15. Bertell 2003.

16. Steinsland 2005:143–164, 195–207.

17. *Skírnismál* st. 1, in Neckel/Kuhn 1983:69.

18. *Skáldskaparmál* Ch. 7, in Faulkes 1998:18.

19. *Gesta Hammaburgensis* IV, 26, in Schmeidler 1917.

20. Wessén 1924:126–130, 177–183.

21. *Krístni saga* Ch. 2, in Guðni Jónsson 1968.

22. Sundqvist 2016:462–464.

23. Sundqvist 2014.

24. Sundqvist 2016:241–258.

25. Interpretation and translation following Santesson 1989, supported by e.g. McKinnell & Simek & Düwel 2004:54–56; Schulte 2006.

26. Enright 1996; Herschend 1998:14–49; Brink 1999.

27. Brady 1983; Enright 1996:69–96; Nordberg 2004:177–198.

28. Brady 1983:215–216; Enright 1996:74–77.

29. *Gylfaginning* Ch. 20, in Faulkes 1988:21.

30. Nordberg 2004:153–223.

31. Blaney 1972:64–129.

32. Sundqvist & Hultgård 2004.

33. For surveys of Óðinn's many aspects, cf. Turville-Petre 1964:35–74; Steinsland 2005:165–194. For the significant connection between Óðinn and the ruler ideology among kings and aristocrats, cf. Schjødt 2007.

34. de Vries 1962:416.

35. *Gesta Hammaburgensis* IV, 26, in Schmeidler 1917.

36. Nordberg 2004:92–120.

37. Beck 1967:117–177.

38. Compare Schjødt 2012; Sundqvist 2014.

39. Compare Hultkrantz 1956:211.

40. *Hávamál* st. 109, 111, 164, in Neckel/Kuhn 1983:34, 44.

41. *Vǫluspá* st. 21, in Neckel/Kuhn 1983:5.

42. *Grímnismál* st. 48, in Neckel/Kuhn 1983:67.

43. Many researchers into Old Norse religion have emphasized this foremost position of especially the god Þórr, and to some extent Freyr (for example Turville-Petre 1964). It is also indicated in the Scandinavian theophoric place names. Although the name *Óðinn* does occur in some place names, it is virtually never found in the names of central places, which instead include gods' names such as *Freyr/Frø*, *Þórr* and *Njǫrðr/*Niærdh-* (Vikstrand 2001:412–414 with references). In my opinion the most reasonable explanation for this pattern is that the cult of Óðinn, and that of Þórr, Freyr, Freyja and Njǫrðr, above all belonged to two different religious configurations that were related to different social contexts. This is also supported by the fact that the worship of Þórr, Freyr and Freyja, but not Óðinn, played prominent parts in the religion of the Icelanders during the Viking Age. According to Gabriel Turville-Petre (1972) this was because Óðinn was above all revered by a Scandinavian warrior aristocracy, which was not represented among those who immigrated to Iceland.

44. *Ynglinga saga* Ch. 10, in Aðalbjarnarson 1979:25.

45. *Skírnismál* 3, in Neckel/Kuhn 1983:69.

46. *Lokasenna* 35, in Neckel/Kuhn 1983:103.

47. Snorri states in *Gylfaginning* Ch. 23 (Faulkes 1988:23), that Njǫrðr could calm the sea, give good wind for navigation, and was invoked for a good catch when fishing (*til veiða*). Snorri, however, is the only source of this brief information. Again in *Skáldskaparmál* Ch. 14 (Faulkes1998:19), Snorri claims that Ullr was characterized as *veiði-áss* 'hunting/fishing god'. However, this kenning does not prove

that Ullr was invoked by hunters and fishermen. It may just as well be associated with a lost myth, in which Ullr himself went hunting or fishing (Nordberg 2006:406–407). Similarly, the myth that relates Þórr's fishing expedition and the Midgarðr's serpent primarily had a cosmologic function, and cannot in my view be regarded as evidence that fishermen generally invoked Þórr for a good catch.

48. Cf. Hultkrantz (ed.) 1961a; Honko 1993:63–71,117–189; Sarmela 2009.

49. Joensen 1975, 1981; Löfgren 1981; Tillhagen 1985; Hodne 1997.

50. In the introduction to the anthology *The Supernatural Owners of Nature*, Åke Hultkrantz (1961b:7) sententiously summarizes the tradition complex of the Owner: "One of the key conceptions in primitive hunting ideology is precisely the notion of the 'owner' of Nature. The owner – or, as he may also be called, the master, lord, ruler, guardian – rules over a certain region or over a certain animal species. As soon as man sets foot upon and exploits this region or hunts these animals, he risks feuding with the owner unless contact with the latter is established before or after the encroachment. This contact finds expression in rites calculated to secure the owner's permission or to conciliate him for an action already performed. The owner is also frequently the subject of legends and, where he is identified with higher divine beings, as is the case in e.g. South America, also in myths."

51. Cf. Granberg 1935; Gambo 1965; Häll 2013.

52. Georges Dumézil (1973:213–230) has suggested that Njǫrðr might be identified with the ruler of the sea (Sw. *havsrå* and *sjörå*) in later folk traditions. This hypothesis has not gained support from other scholars, yet we should not rule out the possibility that some of Njǫrðr's functions may have locally coincided with those of the *havsrå* and *sjörå* in communities that were particularly dependent on marine livelihoods.

53. Joensen 1975.

54. *Landnámabók* Ch. S329, in Benediktsson 1986:330.

55. Possibly, these ethnographic and folkloric analogies may hint at why information about religious traditions linked to hunting and

fishing is missing in the earliest sources. These types of traditions were often expressed in folk beliefs, folk legends, and immaterial ritualistic behaviours, while the sources on Late Iron Age and Viking Age religion in Scandinavia are mostly of other genres and types, comprising for example written and pictorial mythological material, religious place names, ancient monuments and archaeological finds.

56. Honko 1993:51–60.

57. Löfgren 1981:80, my translation "… en miljö, där tron på övernaturliga krafter i fisket var en levande realitet och där inlärningen av rituella tekniker och magiska regler ingick som en naturlig del av socialisationen till fiskaryrket".

58. Löfgren 1981:82, my translation "Vår kulturella erfarenhetsvärld kan alltså vara fylld av inre motsättningar och inkonsistenser, och till detta kommer att individer kan växla mellan olika kulturella repertoarer eller värdesystem beroende på den handlingssituation de befinner sig i. Det är denna typ av problem vi mött i den tidigare diskussionen av hur fiskare kunde förvandlas från skeptiker till trosutövare efter en usel fiskesäsong, eller hur Jesus och havsfrun kunde existera sida vid sida i fiskarbefolkningens liv. För de flesta fiskare var säkerligen tron på övernaturliga krafter ett religiöst system som klart avgränsades från den kristna världsbilden. Dessa två kosmologier existerade sida vid sida som autonoma och till stor del motstridiga moralsystem, även om det förekom en viss integration (synkretism) dem emellan."

59. Although cf. e.g. Gunnell 1995; 2011.

60. Cf. Andersson 2006.

61. At least judging, for instance, by the mythical allusions in West Norse skaldic poetry and the religious iconography from all over Scandinavia.

62. Drobin 1968.

63. This is, for example, implied by Scandinavia's theophoric place names, which mainly indicate public cult sites dedicated to Óðinn, Þórr, Freyr, Ullr/Ullinn, Njǫrðr, Týr and probably Freyja. To quote Stefan Brink, the toponymic sources "does not indicate that there

was an actual cult of all the gods and goddesses in the pantheon mentioned in *Snorra Edda*, the *Poetic Edda*, skaldic poetry, and by Saxo" (Brink 2007:124–125).

64. Cf. Gunnell 1995; 2011.

65. Compare Olsson 1985; Nordberg 2004:60–65, 121–151.

66. Compare for example how the *tomte* or *nisse* was portrayed in much different ways in folk legends and folk beliefs in pre-Modern Scandinavia (Ejdestam 1943).

References

Primary Sources

Adam of Bremen. Schmeidler, Bernhard. 1917. *Hamburgische Kirchengeschichte*. Scriptores Rerum Germanicarum in usum scholarum ex monumentis germaniae historicis separatim editi. Magistri Adam Bremensis Gesta Hammaburgensis ecclesiae pontificum. Hannover: Hahnsche Buchhandlung.

Edda. Neckel, Gustav & Kuhn, Hans (eds.). 1983. *Edda. Die Lieder des Codex Regius nebst verwandten Denkmälern*. 5. verbesserte Auflage. Vol. I. Text. Heidelberg: Carl Winter Universitätsverlag.

Edda Snorri Sturlusonar. Faulkes, Anthony (ed.). 1988. *Snorri Sturluson. Edda. Prologue and Gylfaginning*. London: Viking Society for Northern Research.

Faulkes, Anthony. 1998. *Snorri Sturluson. Edda. Skáldskaparmál 1. Introduction, Text and Notes*. London: Viking Society for Northern Research.

Heimskringla. Bjarni Aðalbjarnarson (ed.). 1979. *Heimskringla I*. Íslenzk fornrit 26. Reykjavík: Hið íslenzka Fornritafélag.

Íslendingabók, Landnámabók. Jacob Benediktsson (ed.). 1986. *Íslendingabók Landnámabók*. Íslenzk fornrit 1. Reykjavík: Hið íslenzka Fornritafélag.

Krístni saga. Guðni Jónsson (ed.). 1968. *Íslendinga sögur I*. Reykjavík: Íslendingasagnaútgáfan.

Secondary Literature

Andersson, Theodore M. 2006. *The Growth of the Medieval Icelandic Sagas (1180–1280)*. London: Cornell University Press.

Beck, Inge. 1967. *Studien zur Erscheinungsform des heidnischen Opfers nach altnordischen Quellen*. München. (Diss).

Bertell, Maths. 2003. *Tor och den nordiska åskan. Föreställningar kring världsaxeln*. Stockholm: Stockholms universitet. (Diss).

Blaney, Benjamin. 1972. The Berserker. His Origin and Development in Old Norse Literature. (Unprinted Diss). University of Colorado: Department of Languages and Literature.

Brady, Caroline. 1983. Warriors' in *Beowulf*. An Analysis of the Nominal Compounds and an Evaluation of the Poet's Use of Them. In *Anglo-Saxon England II*, 199–246.

Brink, Stefan. 1999. Social Order in Early Scandinavian Landscape. In *Settlement and Landscape. Proceedings of a Conference in Århus, Denmark, May 4–7 1998*. C. Fabech, J. Ringtved (eds.). Høbjerg. Jysk Arkæologisk Selskabs skrifter, 423–439.

Brink, Stefan. 2007. How Uniform was the Old Norse Religion? In *Learning and Understanding in the Old Norse World. Essays in Honour of Margaret Clunies Ross*. J. Quinn & K. Heslop & T. Wills (eds.). Turnhout: Brepols Publishers. 105–136.

Carlie, Anne. 2004. *Forntida byggnadskult. Tradition och regionalitet i södra Skandinavien*. Stockholm: Riksantikvarieämbetets förlag.

Drobin, Ulf. 1968. Myth and Epical Motifs in the Loki-Research. In *Temenos* 3, 19–39.

DuBois, Thomas. 1999. *Nordic Religions in the Viking Age*. Philadelphia: University of Pennsylvania Press.

Dumézil, Georges. 1973. Njörðr, Nerthus and the Scandinavian Folklore of Sea Spirits. In *From Myth to Fiction. The saga of Hadingus*. Chicago: The University of Chicago Press, 213–230

Ejdestam, Julius. 1943. Är tomten ett dragväsen? In *Folkminnen och folktankar* 30, 8–17.

Enright, Michael. 1996. *Lady with a Mead Cup. Ritual, Prophecy and Lordship in the European Warband from La Tène to the Viking Age.* Portland: Four Courts Press.

Eskeröd, Albert. 1964. Needs, Interests, Values, and the Supernatural. In *Lapponica. Studia Ethnographica Upsaliensia* XXI, 81–98.

Gambo, Ronald. 1965. The Lord of Forest and Mountain Game in the More Recent Folk Traditions of Norway. In *Fabula* 7:1, 33–52.

Granberg, Gunnar. 1935. *Skogsrået i yngre nordisk folktradition.* Skrifter utg. av Kungl. Gustav Adolfs Akademien för folklivsforskning, 3. Uppsala.

Gunnell, Terry. 1995. *The Origins of Drama in Scandinavia.* Cambridge: Brewer.

Gunnell, Terry. 2011. The Drama of the Poetic Edda. Performance as a Means of Transformation. In *Pogranicza teatralnosci. Poetzja, poetyka, praktyka.* A. Dąbrówski (ed.). Institut Badán literackich polskiej akademii nauk, 13–40.

Herschend, Frands. 1998. *The Idea of the Good in Late Iron Age Society.* Uppsala: OPIA 15.

Hodne, Ørnulf. 1997. *Fiske og jakt. Norske folketraditioner.* J. W. Cappelens forlag.

Honko, Lauri. 1993. *The Great Bear. A Thematic Anthology of Oral Poetry in the Finno-Ugrian Languages.* Helsinki: Suomalaisen kirjallisuuden seura.

Hultgård, Anders. 2001. Lokalgottheiten. In *Reallexikon der germanischen Altertumskunde* 18. Berlin & New York: De Gruyter, 476–479.

Hultgård, Anders. 2003. Ár – "gutes Jahr und Ernteglück" – ein Motivkomplex in der altnordischen Literatur und sein religionsgeschichtlicher Hintergrund. In *Runica – Germanica – Mediaevalia.* W. Heizmann, A. van Nahl (eds.). Berlin/New York. 282–308.

Hultgård, Anders. 2007. Wotan-Odin. In *Reallexikon der Germanische Altertumskunde* 35. Berlin & New York: De Gruyter, 750–785

Hultkrantz, Åke. 1956 Configurations of Religious Belief among the Wind River Shoshoni. In *Ethnos* 1956:3–4, 194–215.

Hultkrantz, Åke. (ed.) 1961a. *The Supernatural Owners of Nature. Nordic Symposium on the Religious Conceptions of Ruling Spirits (genii loci, genii speciei) and allied Concepts.* Stockholm Studies in Comparative Religion 1. Stockholm: Almqvist & Wiksell.

Hultkrantz, Åke. 1961b. Preface. In Hultkrantz 1961a, 7–8.

Häll, Mikael. 2013. *Skogsrået, näcken och djävulen. Erotiska naturväsen och demonisk sexualitet i 1600- och 1700-talens Sverige.* Stockholm: Malört.

Joensen, Jóan Pauli. 1975. *Færøske sluppfiskere. Etnologisk undersøgelse af en erhvervsgruppes liv.* Skrifter från Folklivsarkivet i Lund nr 17. Lund: Liber Läromedel.

Joensen, Jóan Pauli. 1981. Tradition och miljö i färöiskt fiske. In *Tradition och miljö. Ett kulturekologiskt perspektiv.* L. Honko & o. Löfgren (eds). Lund: Liber läromedel. 95–134.

Löfgren, Orvar. 1981 De vidskepliga fångstmännen – magi, ekologi och ekonomi i svenska fiskarmiljöer. In *Tradition och miljö. Ett kulturekologiskt perspektiv.* L. Honko, O. Löfgren (eds.). Lund: Liber läromedel, 64–94.

McKinnell, John & Simek, Rudolf & Düwel, Klaus. 2004. *Runes, Magic and Religion. A Sourcebook.* Studia Medievalia Septentrionalia 10. Wien: Fassbender.

Murphy, John Luke. 2018. Paganism at Home: Pre-Christian Private Praxis and Household Religion in the Iron-Age North. In *Scripta Islandica* 2018.

Nordberg, Andreas. 2004. *Krigarna i Odins sal. Dödsföreställningar och krigarkult i fornnordisk religion.* Stockholm: Stockholms universitet (Diss. 2003).

Nordberg, Andreas. 2006 *Jul, disting och förkyrklig tideräkning. Kalendrar och kalendariska riter i det förkristna Norden.* Acta Academiae Regiae Gustavi Adolphi 91. Uppsala: Swedish Science Press.

Nordberg, Andreas. 2006. Ull und Ullin. In *Reallexikon der Germanischen Altertumskunde* 31. Berlin & New York: De Gruyter, 406–407.

Olsson, Tord. 1985. Gudsbildens gestaltning. Litterära kategorier och religiös tro. In *Svensk religionshistorisk årsskrift* 1, 42–63.

Olsson, Tord. 2000 De rituella fälten i Gwanyebugu. In *Svensk religionshistorisk årsskrift* 9, 9–63.

Santesson, Lillemor. 1989. En blekings blotinskrift. En nytolkning av inledningsraderna på Stentoftenstenen. In *Fornvännen* 84, 221–229.

Sarmela, Matti. 2009. *Finnish Folklore Atlas. Ethnic Culture of Finland* 2. Helsinki: Matti Sarmela.

Schjødt, Jens Peter. 2007. Óðinn, Warriors, and Death. In *Learning and Understanding in the Old Norse World. Essays in Honour of Margaret Clunies Ross.* J. Quinn et al. (eds.). Turnhout: Brepols, 137–152.

Schjødt, Jens Peter. 2012. Óðinn, Þórr and Freyr. Functions and Relations. In *News from the Other World. Studies in Nordic Folklore, Mythology and Culture. In Honor of John F. Lindow.* M. Kaplan & T. R. Tangherlini (eds.). Berkley: North Pinehurst Press, 61–91.

Schulte, Michael. 2006. Ein kritischer Kommentar zum Erkenntnisstand der Blekinger Inschriften. In *Zeitschrift für deutsches Altertum und deutsches Literatur* 135, 399–412.

Steinsland, Gro. 2005. *Norrøn religion. myter, riter, samfunn.* Oslo: Pax forlag A/S.

Sundqvist, Olof. 2014. Frö – mer än en fruktbarhetsgud? *Saga och sed* 2014, 43–67.

Sundqvist, Olof. 2016. *An Arena for Higher Powers. Ceremonial Buildings and Religious Strategies for Rulership in Late Iron Age Scandinavia.* Leiden: Brill.

Sundqvist, Olof & Hultgård, Anders. 2004. The Lycophoric Names of the 6th to 7th Century Blekinge Rune Stones and the Problem of their Ideological Background. In *Namenwelten. Orts- und Personennamen in historischer Sicht*. Berlin & New York: de Gruyter, 583–602.

Tambiah, Stanley J. 1970. *Buddhism and the Spirit Cults in North-East Thailand*. London: Cambridge University Press.

Tillhagen, Carl-Herman. 1985. *Jaktskrock*. Stockholm: LTs förlag.

Turville-Petre, Gabriel. 1964. *Myth and Religion of the North. The Religion of Ancient Scandinavia*. London: Weidenfeld and Nicolson.

Turville-Petre, Gabriel. 1972. The Cult of Óðinn in Iceland. In *Nine Norse Studies*. London: Viking Society for Northern Research, 1–19.

Vikstrand, Per. 2001. *Gudarnas platser. Förkristna sakrala ortnamn i Mälarlandskapen*. Acta Academiae Regiae Gustavi Adolphi, 77. Uppsala.

de Vries, Jan. 1962. *Altnordisches Etymologisches Wörterbuch*. Leiden: Brill.

Wessén, Elias. 1924. *Studier till Sveriges hedna mytologi och fornhistoria*. Uppsala universitets årsskrift 1924. Uppsala: A.-B. Lundequistska bokhandeln.

Response
Maths Bertell
Mid-Sweden University

Nordberg adds a comparative religion perspective to the study of Old Norse religion, a field that in many ways has been insular in its approach to religious diversity during the Viking Age. Usually, religious diversity has meant the coming of Christianity or Sámi contacts, and on travels, encounters with Muslims such as Ahmad Ibn Fadlan. The written sources from Iceland give us little to work with and the text provided by Adam is short, and Adam never visited Uppsala. However, Nordberg points out that the Old Norse religion should be considered an umbrella, where different scenarios and milieus shaped different religious expressions, and that individuals and groups could move between those. He introduces the idea of religious configurations and suggests three: the warband, the farmstead and the hunting/fishing configuration. Nordberg uses a comparative method, suggesting Wind River Shoshoni of Wyoming, and in short rural Thailand and pre-industrial Finland. In these contexts, the believers/worshippers could move between different systems, without considering them contradictory.

Even though several researchers has pointed out over the years that the Old Norse religion must have had regional variation, there is also a tendency among scholars of the field to describe a pan-Scandinavian religion, unified and where all sources offer pieces of the same puzzle. This is highly unlikely, even considering that the Icelandic sources mainly stem from a ruling Óðinn-worshipping tradition, there are cracks in the image. The creation is depicted in very different ways in *Vǫluspá*, *Vafþrúþnismál* and Snorri's *Edda*, as is the role of Loki.

This is not, however, what Nordberg points out, and I am not entirely sure whether the suggested parallels really adds to our understanding of the Old Norse religion. The Wind River Shoshoni situation is a different kind of society and moving in between Missionary religions such as Buddhism and Christianity and folk religion is also something else. The division of the Scandinavian religious configurations is problematic and I would suggest that what we see here is something different. The hall/ war band configuration is more likely to be a religiolect,[1] a social/ regional variation, with its own inner universe, but using the same material. As Nordberg points out, the people of the hall/warband may leave the hall and enter the farmstead/fertility sphere, but the people of the farmstead/fertility may not enter the hall. There is little suggesting that the hall/warband people were actually leaving their religious configuration/religiolect when entering the fertility sphere; they may as well still be in their own context and interpretation. I would suggest that the hall/warband is its own religiolect and if there are any different religious configurations to move in between, these are to be found within that universe. What remain are the hunter/fishing and farmstead religious configurations. Here is another problem, the lack of sources. It is entirely possible that there have been two sets of powers and mythological motifs; however, we do not know how different these would be from each other or how groups moved between them. Instead, Nordberg uses sources from very different time periods; 7th century, 13th century and 19th century, but not really addressing any difficulties in doing so. Furthermore, the groups described by Nordberg are also predominantly male and traditionally represent male culture. How would women and feminine religion fit into the description? Are there female configurations, distinct from the male or female/ male subdivisions of each configuration?

As suggested by Terry Gunnell,[2] the idea of a pantheon may very well be something introduced by Snorri and also the idea of Óðinn as the high one, and mainly reflecting Norwegian aristocracy. As I understand Hultkrantz, the systems within the Wind River Shoshoni are separate and offer contradictions, while what may be seen in the Old Norse source material are of dialects or sociolects, in other words different religiolects, using the same material. A comparative approach is very much lacking in Old Norse religion studies, but questions raised by other material needs to resonate within the sources we have, written or archaeological. If they do not, the parallels do not apply.

Notes

1. Wiktorin 2011:25–31.

2. Gunnell 2015.

References

Gunnell, Terry. 2015. Pantheon? What pantheon? Concepts of a Family of Gods in Pre-Christian Scandinavian Religions. *Scripta Islandica, Isländska sällskapets årsbok 2015*, 55–76.

Wiktorin, Pierre. 2011. *Religion och populärkultur* [Elektronic resource]. *Från Harry Potter till Left Behind*. Lund: Sekel. Access: http://lup.lub.lu.se/luur/download?func=downloadFile&recordOId=2175016&fileOId=2175017

Tangible Religion: Amulets, Illnesses, and the Demonic Seven Sisters

Rudolf Simek
University of Bonn

It is a well-known fact within Medieval studies that in Western Europe in the Middle Ages there existed, side by side, three major strategies of coming to terms with illnesses:

Firstly, what we today would consider proper medical therapy, in its many variants from traditional monastic medicine (by the *infirmarii*) to itinerant barber surgeons (*medici*) to academic medical science (*phisici*) as practised within and without the Salernitan school. Medical handbooks in manuscript form, containing collections of active ingredients (*simplicia*) and prescriptions for particular ailments (*indicationes*) as well as rules on dietetics and prognostics testify to this tradition even in Old Norse vernacular texts.

Secondly, by taking recourse to miraculous divine help, usually in the form of asking the saints for intercession on the behalf of the patient or his kin, whether by prayer alone or the promise of votive gifts, resulting in the miraculous recovery of the patient – at least in the many successful cases reported and handed down in hagiographic literature, usually in the miracle collections tied to the lives of particular saints, certainly not as case histories on the recovery of particular patients and even less connected with particular illnesses – unless the saint in question was known to "specialise" in certain medical problems, such as St. Margaret for difficult births and St. Blaise for throat illnesses, to name but two of many.

Thirdly, by taking resort to religio-magical practises, such as magical charms, amulets, and rituals. Although all of these were

How to cite this book chapter:
Simek, R. 2019. Tangible Religion: Amulets, Illnesses, and the Demonic Seven Sisters. In: Wikström af Edholm, K., Jackson Rova, P., Nordberg, A., Sundqvist, O. & Zachrisson, T. (eds.) *Myth, Materiality, and Lived Religion: In Merovingian and Viking Scandinavia.* Pp. 375–395. Stockholm: Stockholm University Press. DOI: https://doi.org/10.16993/bay.m. License: CC-BY.

expressly condemned not only in the ecclesiastical writings of the missionary period – which considered them to be remnants of the heathen past – but also in penitential handbooks throughout the Middle Ages. Many of these practises may indeed have their roots in the pagan pre-Christian Germanic religion, but there is also much interference from much older Mediterranean and Near Eastern magical methods, that merged into what we now term typical Medieval Popular Religion.

The present paper only concerns itself with the third method of fighting illnesses, and within this group only with apotropaic measures to be found on amulets (*ligamina, ligamenta, obligamenta, ligaturae*).

When, in previous papers,[1] I was trying to work out what role the *álfar* had in the Scandinavian medieval popular religion (– who were occasionally, but rarely seen as having medical powers in the Icelandic sagas),[2] and had to come to the conclusion that by the 11th–14th centuries, *álfar* (called *elvos, elvas* or similar in their Latinized form) were considered demons of illness, and the charms which preserve such identifications are found on lead amulets meant to conjure and thus avert the doings of these demons, thus removing the source of the illness. This throws light on an instance in *Kormáks saga*: the magical practise suggested here by an old witch thus did not attempt to call on the *álfar*/demons to *heal* the person in question, but rather tempt/bribe the demons to remove themselves as being the source of the illness. In this particular instance, the passage implies that: *álfar* are subterranean, that they live in (grave?)-mounds and have supernatural powers related to illnesses and that they can be influenced through rituals / magic practices.

But this is the only text I know of this particular type, although there may be others in hagiographic sagas. In other Old Norse sources, especially in Eddic poetry, the *álfar* were not primarily considered to be demonic at first sight. They are to the largest extent found in alliterative formulae, such in *álfar ok æsir*, or *álfar ok æsir ok vísir vanir*, and unless one would like to claim that the demonization of the old Scandinavian gods had progressed quite far at the time of the composition of Eddic poetry, we have to assume that the *álfar* stood for a mythological race whose exact identification is no longer possible, but was not synonymous with that of the *æsir*.

However, it is not unlikely that they were considered to be connected with the world of spirits, and perhaps also directly connected
with the dead, but in any case, to be one of the subterranean races.

In the present paper, I am not concerned with the identification
and the nature of the *álfar*, but rather with the connection of *álfar*
and other spirits to illnesses in popular religion, and mainly on
medieval amulets.

Of these, an increasing number of textual amulets have been
found in recent years, most of them made from thin lead sheets,
although a few silver and copper ones are known, too.[3] Imer[4] is
able to list 30 amulets with text for Norway, 20 for Sweden and
over a 100 for Denmark. In addition to that, a steadily increasing
number of amulets are found in Germany, especially in the eastern part of the country.[5] As far as I can make out, the majority of
Danish amulets are executed in runes, the German ones mainly in
Latin or cryptography. To these we may add some 18 Norwegian
and two Swedish lead mortuary crosses,[6] of which those with text
on them seem always to be scratched in runes rather than Roman
letters.[7] Despite the fact that most of the Danish amulets are either
illegible, fragmentary, or cannot be opened without damage to the
object, it is noticeably that those with longer texts tend to be executed in Roman letters (the exceptions being the Odense and the
Blæsinge amulets), whilst the shorter and/or unintelligible ones
are predominantly in runes.

Apart from those amulets which carry an explicitly apotropaic
text, conjuring spirits to prevent an illness, the amulets which
carry either the full text of the beginning of the gospel according to John,[8] such as the Randers amulet,[9] or else reference to
that Gospel and the very first word of it,[10] such as the one from
Schleswig, can also be considered to carry apotropaic messages, as
is confirmed by the *Codex Upsaliensis* C 222 from c. 1300, which
preserves a conjuration beginning

> *Jnitium sancti euangelij secundum iohannem. Jn principio erat uer-
> bum [...] hoc erat in principio apud deum etc. Adiuro uos elphos
> elphorum gordin. ingordin. Cord'i et ingordin. gord'I.*[11]

However, only the Schleswig lead tablet[12] seems to combine the
Gospel with a conjuration as in the Uppsala manuscript, and I

shall not consider the amulets with the beginning of John's Gospel in the following paper, although the connection between this text and particular ailments has to date not been fully investigated. But, as Steenholt Olesen[13] points out correctly: "In general, the evidence from late medieval medical books makes it clear that specific Latin phrases were used in rituals of protection and for the healing of fevers, eye diseases, boils, and so on."

Only a small number of Scandinavian Medieval amulets actually contain a direct invocation of spirits, either as *álfar* or demons,[14] but, as this identification is beyond doubt in these cases, the use of the terms *elvos*, *elvas* and similar may simply be seen as an attempt to produce the vernacular term for demon in the otherwise Latin texts – perhaps to ensure that the demons which were being conjured understood in any case. Therefore, I shall include all texts concerned with demonic conjurations, whatever term for demons is used, and whether written in Latin letters or (very occasionally) in runes; whichever script is used, the language is Latin throughout, with only a few vernacular words interspersed and several names of mixed, but mainly Latin, Greek, or even Near Eastern provenance. Despite the above-mentioned fact that a majority of lead amulets seems to be written in runes, those relatively few that contain a legible coherent text are predominantly written in Latin. This is a point that needs stressing, because "Lead tablets with Latin inscriptions in roman letters are also known from the Danish area, but unfortunately they have not been systematically registered."[15] Why this is so, and why archaeologists in Scandinavia seem to be more interested in amulets in runic script than those with Roman script one can only guess at. One may also speculate on the reasons why there are more *meaningful* amulets preserved in Roman script although the total number of runic ones is greater, especially as several of the shorter runic inscriptions do not seem to make sense at all or are even written in pseudo runes.[16]

Nearly all the amulets with longer texts I have studied not only conjure some supernatural beings, but also specify in some detail how or where the conjuration should protect the person in question, who I would like to call "the patient", as it can be assumed that these amulets were not issued primarily to healthy persons to protect from all eventualities – the conjurations are somewhat too specific for that – but as a means to (further) protect a sick person from further suffering, if proper medical help had either proven ineffective or else was unavailable. To gain further insight into the methods used for these apotropaic measures I shall firstly look into the types of protection from illnesses named on the amulets and secondly try to ascertain whether there is any relation between the protection requested and the types of demons conjured.

In the current investigation, I have used the following amulets:

1. The lead amulet from Blæsinge (Zealand, Sj 50), dating from any time between the 13th and the 15th century, is executed in Latin in runes and is, with roughly 500 runes, in fact the longest runic inscription found in Denmark to date.
2. The lead amulet from Viborg (Jutland, MJy 32), from 1050–1300, with a short Latin text in runes which are difficult to read, but also preserves a type of Latin conjuration or prayer.
3. The lead amulet from Romdrup (near Aalborg, Jutland), dating to around 1200, executed in Latin script like all the following texts.
4. A newly found and not as yet properly published lead amulet from Møllergarde, Svendborg, also roughly dated to the High Middle Ages, in Latin letters.
5. The lead amulet from Schleswig from either the 11th or early 12th century containing the longest of the texts with just under 600 letters.
6. The lead amulet cross from Halberstadt (Saxony-Anhalt, Germany, dated to 1142), with a Latin text only fractionally shorter than the Schleswig amulet.

Of these, the following amulets name or define the spirits that are conjured: The Blæsinge amulet names them *septem sorores ... Elffrica (?), Affricea, Soria, Affoca, Affricala*, the one from Romdrup *eluos uel eluas aut demones*, the one from Svendborg apparently more or less the same formula, the long Schleswig amulet the more comprehensive *demones siue albes ac omnes pestes omnium infirmitatum* and the one from Halberstadt the somewhat different *alb(er) qui [u]ocaberis diabolus v(e)l satanas,* i.e. the Devil himself.

As all the amulets mentioned are conjurations, and the rest of the texts on them have much in common between them,[17] it can be assumed that the terms for the spirits conjured on these amulets were, at least to some extent, interchangeable, so that we have a list of spirits called, in the latinized forms used:

Demones (pl.)
Elvae (pl. f.)
Elves (pl. m.)
Albes (pl. f. and m.?)
Pestes (*omnium infirmitatum*) (pl., obviously as a personification of *pestis* "plague": "you plagues of all illnesses")
Septem sorores (with five out of seven names)
Alber (sg. m.)
Diabolus (sg. m.)
Satanas (sg. m.)

This array of demons is, not only on the Schleswig amulet, conjured to protect someone from some harm or illness. All of the items I have selected give some indication as to the nature of the protection expected from the conjuration, so that the demons are called upon:

- On the Blæsinge tablet: *ut non noceatis istam famulum Dei, neque in oculis, neque in membris, neque in medullis, nec in ullo compagine membrorum eius* "that you may not harm this servant of God, neither in the eyes nor in the limbs nor in the marrow nor in any joints of the limbs".
- On the Schleswig text: *ut non noceatis famulo dei neque in die nec in nocte nec in ullis horis* "that you may not harm this [male] servant of God by day or by night, nor at any hours".
- On Romdrup: *ut non noceatis huic famulo dei nicholao in oculis nec in capite neque in ulla compagine membrorum* "that you may not harm this servant of God, Nicholas, in the eyes nor in the head nor in the joints of his limbs".

- On Svendborg: *ut non noceatis famulam dei Margaretam nec in oculis nec in aliis membris* "so that you may not harm this servant of Christ, Margaret, neither in the eyes nor in other limbs [or: other parts of the body]".
- On the Halberstadt tablet: *non habeas potestatem in ista* [...] *dere aut istum amicum dei TADO. Ne nocere possis non in die neque in nocte non in* [...] *su neque non bibenda neque manducando* "so that you have no power over this ..... or this friend of god Tado, so that you cannot harm during the day nor by night nor drinking nor eating nor ...".
- On the both fragmentary and badly executed Viborg amulet we can reconstruct the words: *æb omnis febris* "from all fevers" from the runic sequence **mitius(æ)(o)ni fibri**, although there is not enough left of the amulet to discern any conjuration, only an invocation of God, the Holy Spirit and Mary.

Of all these indications as to the nature of the illnesses meant, the most disappointing is the one on the Schleswig amulet, just asking for protection "by day and by night". However, as the beginning of the conjuration formula is very close to those on the Romdrup and Svendborg amulets, it is possible to infer what the protection was about: Both the latter ones ask for protection of the eyes and the limbs, Romdrup in addition names the head and the joints of the limbs, thus specifying the seat of the illness caused (apparently) by the "demons and elves" called upon by all three texts.

The Halberstadt text is less specific again, but the reference to "day and night" and "eating and drinking" may suggest that the devil called *Alber* here might have something to do with poising or spoiling of food and drink, but this if of course impossible to prove.

The most interesting information, therefore, is the one on the Blæsinge and the Romdrup texts, where "eyes nor in the limbs nor in the marrow nor in any joints of the limbs" and "*in oculis nec in capite neque in ulla compagine membrorum*" are referred to, as well as the new Svendborg amulet, which also seems to mention the eyes and the limbs. A quick diagnosis of an illness that causes pains in the eyes, the head, and the joints of the limbs points very much to a febrile infection of the influenza type, according to GPs consulted. But as mentioned before, the only fevers mentioned, namely on the Viborg amulet, we cannot, due to the fragmentary state of the piece, associate with any particular spirits. All we know is that it was used to avert fevers.

In order to ascertain which spirits are actually causing which illnesses, this leaves us with the most specific of all the known amulets, namely the Blæsinge one, which conjures the Seven Sisters in order to prevent them from doing harm "in the eyes nor in the limbs nor in the marrow nor in any joints of the limbs." This is, of course, very similar to the descriptions given on the amulets from Schleswig, Romdrup and Svendborg, but the conjuration of the Seven Sisters opens up an additional line of interpretation.

Although the Seven Sisters are, to my knowledge, not mentioned on any other amulets found to date, they do appear in several medieval manuscripts, which provide further details. Already Düwel[18] could refer to Stoklund[19] for several invocations calling upon the *septem sorores*, printed by Franz.[20] The most detailed from the *Codex Vaticanus Latinus* 235 (fol. 44–45; 10th/11th century) reads:

> *Coniuro uos, frigores et febres – VII sorores sunt – siue meridianas, siue nocturnas, siue cotidianas, siue secundarias, siue tercianas, siue quartanas, siue siluanas, siue iudeas, siue hebreas, uel qualicunque genere sitis, adiuro uos per patrem [...], ut non habeatis licentiam nocere huic famulo dei nec in die nec in nocte, nec uigilanti nec dormienti, nec in ullis locis.*[21]

> I conjure you, shivers and fevers – who are seven sisters – like the midday ones, the nightly, the daily, the bi-daily, the three-daily, the four-daily, the wood fevers, the Jewish fevers, the Hebrew fevers, or whatever sort you are: I conjure you through the Father [...], so that you may not have leave to harm this servant of God by day or night, neither waking nor sleeping, nor in any place.

The long incantation goes on further below:

> *Epistula contra frigores. In nomine de patris [...] Coniuro uos frigores, VII sorores, una dicitur klkb, alia rfstklkb, tertia fbgblkb, quarta sxbfpgllkb, quinta frkcb, sexta kxlkcb, septima kgncb;*

coniuro uos, de quacunque natione estis, per patrem et filium et
spiritum sanctum [...] *per has omnes inuocationes, coniuro uos,*
frigores et febres, ut non habeatis ullam licentiam, nocere huic
famulo dei N. nec eum fatigare, sed redeatis, unde uenistis, nec
potestatem habeatis nec locum in isto famulo dei amen.[22]

Letter against shivers. In the name of the Father [...] I conjure
you shivers, seven sisters, the first one called klkb, the other rfst-
klkb, the third fbgblkb, the fourth sxbfpgllkb, the fifth frkcb, the
sixth kxlkcb, the seventh kgncb: I conjure you, of whatever origin
you are, through the Father and the Son and the Holy Spirit [...]
through these invocations I conjure you, shivers and fevers, so that
you do not have leave to harm the servant of Christ N. nor torture him, but return to where you came from, so that you have no
power nor a place in this servant of God. Amen.

The second version of the invocation uses a cryptographic method
to encode the names of the Seven Sisters, but the code used is a
very simple one and can easily be deciphered if one replaces every
vowel with its preceding letter:[23] *Ilia, Restilia, Fagalia, Subfogalia*
(recte: *Subfogllia*), *Frica, Iulia, Ignea* (recte: *Ignca*) in the Vatican
text. A Danish formula from the 15th century calls them *Illia,*
Reptilia, Folia, Suffugalia, Affrica, Filica, Loena vel Igne, which
gives a very similar result.[24] However, as the spelling of the names
on the Blæsinge tablet is extremely deviant from any other text,
we cannot really supplant the two missing names there, although
Iulia and *Ignea* are the ones most obviously absent.

However, the demonic Seven Sisters are certainly not only
known from the Blæsinge amulet and the manuscripts mentioned
above, but seem to be far more common in Medieval Europe than
that. Several British manuscripts from the later Middle Ages and
even Early Modern Times mention their names, and also give
some of their uses.

In the British Library manuscript MS Sloane 3853, 143v (16th
century), the "*septem sorores*" are mentioned, but only six names
given, namely: "*lilia, Restilia, Foca, Affrica, Iulia, Iuliana.*" Here,
this is called a charm for "expulsion of elves and fairies", and as
such refers only to the conjuration, but not to its purpose. For this
period, one may add the manuscript MS. Xd 234 (ca. 1600) from

the Folger Shakespeare library, Washington D.C., giving their names as *Lilia, hestillia, fata, sola, afrya, Africa, Iulia,* and *venulla* (variant: *Venila*), which ventures a magic spell to conjure up the Seven Sisters of the Fairies and tie them to you for ever![25]

Another, even later magical 17th century manuscript (British Library Sloane 3825) names them as "*Lillia, Restilia, Foca, Tolla, Affrica, Julia, Venulla.*" As for their function, the similarly magical British Library Manuscript Sloane Ms 1727, 23v (17th century) calls upon them like that:

> I conjure you sps. or elphes which be 7 sisters and have these names. Lilia. Restilia, foca, fola, Afryca, Julia, venulia [...] that from hensforth neither you nor any other for you have power or rule upon this ground; neither within nor without nor uppon this servant of the liveing god.: N: neither by day nor by night [...].[26]

This wording is, of course, very closely related to both the Schleswig and the Halberstadt texts and shows that such beliefs were still known in Early Modern times, but none mentions any illnesses and none of them is as detailed as the Vatican manuscript mentioned above which must, therefore, remain our main guide. The wording in this manuscript shows that the missing words on the Blaesinge amulet must have referred to those *frigores et febres* ("shivers and fevers") mentioned in both versions in this manuscript.

From the detailed description, however, we learn a lot about the seven sisters which does not become clear from the Blæsinge amulet alone: 1. The Seven Sisters are demons for various types of fevers and are individually named, but neither the names nor their numbers bear any direct relationship to the nine types of fevers enumerated in the text. 2. The Seven Sisters are supposedly of different origin (the text says "nation", which refers to geographical direction rather than ethnicity). 3. The aim of the invocation is twofold, firstly to deprive the sisters of their power to harm and secondly to send them back to where they came from.

The earliest instance of the invocation of the Seven Sisters (as seven fevers) is apparently an eleventh-century charm attributed to Saint Sigismund, the so-called Sigismund charm.[27] This refers to King Sigismund of Burgundy, murdered in 523, and early on considered to be useful for invocations against fevers, whether by masses read to call on him or the charm. It is found in a Latin manuscript from Dijon, Bibliotheque municipiale 448, fol. 181r[28] fol, addressing them as follows: "I conjure you, O fevers, you are seven sisters", followed by their names Lilia, Restilia, Fugalia, Suffoca, Affrica, Julia, Macha.[29]

Although the names of the Seven Sisters are far from stable in the transmission, at least in the Early or High Medieval texts they are clearly considered to be seven fever-demons; but as the first of the incantations in the Vatican manuscript names all sorts of fevers, there is no reason to believe that either the incantations or the Blæsinge amulet or any of the others are only specifically aimed at malaria, as Stoklund[30] and Düwel[31] seemed to think, although malaria was known in medieval Northern Europe simply because of the much warmer climate then.[32]

A detailed list of fevers in the context of an invocation is contained in another Vatican manuscript, Cod. Lat. Vat. 510, 168r, dating from the 12th century and probably originating in the French Premonstratensian Abbey of Clairefontaine in Picardy.[33] It certainly was too long to ever have been used on an amulet, but it shows to what extreme detail and completeness a formula for an incantation was able to go to by naming an incredible number of saints, angels and names of God.[34] Despite the fact that it does not name any fever demons, it gives a list of the various types of fevers concentrating to the recurrent types of fevers or malaria:

† *In nomine domini nostri Jhesus Christi coniuro uos febres cotidianas, biduanas, triduanas, quartanas, quintanas, sextanas, septanas, octavas, nonas usque ad nonam graduationem, ut non habeatis potestatem super hunc famulum dei .N.*[35]

† In the name of our Lord Jesus Christ I conjure you daily fevers, bidaily fevers, three-daily fevers, [...] nine-daily fevers, up to the ninth graduation, so that you may not have power over this servant of God N.N.

It seems therefore that the observation made from the description of body parts on the Blaesinge and Romdrup amulets holds true: that it is indeed some general infection, which was only identified by its main symptoms – fever and cold shivers. Such infections belonged, right up to the late 19th century, to the most enigmatic illnesses, especially those with regularly recurrent fever attacks. This is not without good reason, as feverish infections may be caused by viruses (as influenza, three-day fevers/*Roseola infantum*, measles and *rubella*), by bacteria (as in some cases of influenza), or parasites (as with malaria). As none of these sources have any clear or visible reasons, the assumption of demonic origin is obvious. Thus, to look for demonic help or ways of controlling the demonic forces was an obvious way of dealing with them, and this is what our amulets attempt to do.

Notes

1. Simek 2011; 2013; 2017.

2. Cf. *Kormáks saga* Ch. 22.

3. Cf. Stoklund 2003.

4. Imer 2015:14–15.

5. Cf. Muhl 2013.

6. Sørheim 2004:213–214.

7. Cf. McKinnel et al. 2004.

8. Joh. I, 1–14.

9. Imer & Uldum 2015:12.

10. Joh. I, 1.

11. Düwel 2001; Simek 2011.

12. Gastgeber & Harrauer 2001; Düwel 2001.

13. Steenholt Olesen 2010:172.

14. The recently found and as yet unpublished lead amulet from Svendborg is the third such text from Denmark with an identification of demons and *álfar*, after the Romdrup and Schleswig amulets. The equation on the Halberstadt cross of a certain Alber with Satan can be added to these.

15. Steenholt Olesen 2010:172.

16. E.g. Æbelholt-blyamulet Sj 11; Vokslev-blyamulet NJy 57; Køge-blyamulet Sj 14. See http://runer.ku.dk/Search.aspx (as of 1st Feb. 2016).

17. Cf. the close comparison of textual units in Düwel 2001.

18. Düwel 2001:243.

19. Stoklund 1986:207–208.

20. Franz 1909 II:483; cf. also Simek 2011.

21. *Codex Vaticanus Latinus* 235.

22. *Codex Vaticanus Latinus* 235.

23. Cf. Düwel 2003:243.

24. Ohrt 1917–1921 II:1143.

25. I am grateful to Joseph H. Peterson for pointing out the Sloane and Folger manuscripts to me.

26. Briggs 1959:250–251.

27. Wallis 2010:69.

28. Wickersheimer 1966:32–33.

29. Whether the medieval tradition of the demonic Seven Sisters goes back to the pseudo-epigraphic *Testament of Solomo* (4th century), where seven sisters of demons are named, and these in turn originally referred to the seven Pleiades of Greek mythology (but they were called Alkyone, Asterope, Ceaeno, Elektra, Maia, Merope, Taugete, which have absolutely no reflection in the medieval names), or else to the Biblical statement that Jesus had driven out seven demons from the body of Mary of Magdala (Luc. 8,2: *Maria, quae vocatur Magdalene, de qua septem daemonia exierant*), or even have something to do with the legend of the Seven Sleepers (*Septem dormientes*) still needs further investigation for which this is not the place.

30. Stoklund 1986:204–207.

31. Düwel 2001:243.

32. Cf. also Schmid 1904.

33. Schmid 1904:296–297.

34. Cf. Simek 2011.

35. fol. 168v; Schmid 1904:208.

References

Briggs, Katharine Mary. 1959. *An Anatomy of Puck. An Examination of Fairy Beliefs among Shakespeare and his Contemporaries.* London: Routledge & Kegan Paul.

Düwel, Klaus. 2001. Mittelalterliche Amulette aus Holz und Blei mit lateinischen und runischen Inschriften. In V. Vogel (ed.). *Ausgrabungen in Schleswig. Berichte und Studien 15.* (= Das Archäologische Fundmaterial II), Neumünster: Wachholtz, 227–302.

Franz, Adolph. 1909. *Die kirchlichen Benediktionen im Mittelalter.* 2 Vols., Freiburg i.B.: Herder.

Gastgeber, Christian & Harrauer, Hermann. 2001. Ein christliches Bleiamulett aus Schleswig. In V. Vogel (ed.) *Ausgrabungen in Schleswig, Berichte und Studien 15* (= Das archäologische Fundmaterial II), Neumünster: Wachholtz, 207–226.

Imer, Lisbeth M. & Uldum, Otto C. 2015. Mod dæmoner og elverfolk. In *Skalk* 2015, 9–15.

McKinnel, John & Simek, Rudolf & Düwel, Klaus. 2004. *Runes, Magic and Religion. A Sourcebook.* Vienna: Fassbaender.

Muhl, Arnold & Gutjahr, Mirko. 2013. *Magische Inschriften in Blei. Inschriftentäfelchen des hohen Mittelalters aus Sachsen-Anhalt.* Halle/S.: Landesamt für Denkmalpflege Sachsen-Anhalt (= Kleine Hefte zur Archäologie Sachsen-Anhalt 10).

Ohrt, Friedrich. 1917–1921. *Danmarks Trylleformler.* Vol. 1: *Inledning og tekst.* Kopenhagen/Kristiania: Gyldendal. Vol. II: *Efterhøst og Lönformler.* Kopenhagen/Kristiania: Gyldendal.

Schmid, Ulrich. 1904. Malariabenediktionen aus dem XII. Jahrhundert. In *Römische Quartalschrift* 18, 205–210.

Simek, Rudolf. 2011. Elves and Exorcism. Runic and Other Lead Amulets in Medieval Popular Religion. In D. Anlezark (ed.). *Myths, Legends and Heroes. Essays on Old Norse and Old English Literature in Honour of John McKinnell*. Toronto: University of Toronto Press, 25–52.

Simek, Rudolf. 2013. Álfar and Demons, or: What in Germanic Religion Caused the Medieval Christian Belief in Demons? In R. Simek & L. Slupecki (eds.). *Conversion. Looking for Ideological Change in the Early Middle Ages*. Vienna: Fassbaender (= SMS 23), 321–342.

Simek, Rudolf. 2017. "On Elves". In S. Brink & L. Collinson (eds.). *Theorizing Old Norse Myth*. Turnhout: Brepols, 195–223.

Steenholt Olesen, Rikke. 2010. Runic Amulets from Medieval Denmark. In *Futhark. International Journal of Runic Studies* 1 (2010), 161–176.

Stoklund, Marie. 1984. Nordbokorsene fra Grønland. In *National-museets Arbejdsmark* 1984, 101–113.

Stoklund, Marie. 1986. Runefund. In *Aarbøger for Nordisk Oldkyndighed og Historie* 1986, 189–211.

Stoklund, Marie. 2003. Bornholmske runeamuletter. In W. Heizmann & A. van Nahl (eds.). *Runica - Germanica - Mediaevalia* (= Ergänzungsbände zum RGA 37). Berlin: de Gruyter, 854–870.

Sørheim, Helge. 2004. Lead Mortuary Crosses Found in Christian and Heathen Graves in Norway. In *Medieval Scandinavia* 14, 195–227.

Wallis, Faith. 2010. *Medieval Medicine. A Reader*. Toronto: University of Toronto Press.

Wickersheimer, Ernest. 1966. *Les manuscrits latins de médecine du haut Moyen Age dans les bibliothèques de France*. Paris: Centre national de la recherché scientifique.

Response

Olof Sundqvist
Stockholm University

During the last decades several important scholarly works on medieval magic in Scandinavia have been published, such as Catharina Raudvere's *Kunskap och insikt i norrön tradition,*[1] François-Xavier Dillmann's *Les magiciens dans l'Islande ancienne,*[2] and Stephen A. Mitchell's *Witchcraft and Magic in the Nordic Middle Ages.*[3] Different themes related to magic in everyday life are treated there, for instance romance, fortune, weather, malediction, health and disease. In his contribution to the present book, "Tangible Religion: Amulets, Illnesses, and the Demonic Seven Sisters", Rudolf Simek concentrates on this latter aspect, or more precisely, the apotropaic methods of coming to terms with illnesses in medieval Northern Europe, such as magic charms, amulets, and rituals. These strategies may, according to Simek, have their background in the pre-Christian Germanic religion, although they may also derive from the Mediterranean regions. Some of them may even have had a mixed background; such syncretistic expressions are usually called "medieval popular religion".

In previous studies Simek has investigated the role of the mythical beings called Old Norse *álfar* (Latinised *elvos, elvas* etc.) in medieval popular religion.[4] During the Middle Ages these beings were regarded as demons of illness. Amulets and charms were used to ward off their harmful activities and by means of magical-religious methods the causes of the diseases were believed to be removed. In the Old Norse poetic tradition, which may reflect the Viking Age conception of the *álfar*, these spiritual beings, were not primarily considered to be demonic. In the Viking Age context, they were probably regarded as divine beings beside the *æsir*, who could be helpful to humans. In the present study Simek is concerned not only with the *álfar*, but also with other beings related to illness in medieval popular religion, particular the demons called "the seven sisters" (in Latin *septem sorores*). Simek focuses his investigation on six Latin texts (charms) written on amulets, where such beings are mentioned. Four of them are from Denmark, where two were written with runes and two with Latin letters. The other two amulets are from Germany and they were written with Latin letters. All of them are dated to the period 1000-1400.

The purpose of Simek's investigation is firstly, to "look into the types of protection from illnesses named on the amulets" and secondly "to ascertain whether there is any relation between the protection requested and the types of demons conjured". In order to implement these aims Simek compares the amulet texts with some Latin manuscripts, also concerned with illness demons and magic charms. The seven sisters (the illness demons) mentioned in the Blæsinge amulet from Denmark (c. 1200-1400), for instance, and also appearing in the Latin manuscripts, are probably related to different types of fevers. They are described with individual names; however, neither the number of them, nor their names have a direct relationship to the fevers described. According to the medieval manuscripts, the demons originates from different places. The aim of the invocations is to deprive the sisters of their power to harm and to send them back to where they belong. Also, the six amulet texts analysed by Simek probably include similar purposes.

In what follows I will only discuss one aspect of Simek's interesting contribution. In his study, Simek deals with the phenomenon called syncretism, and specifically what happens with old mythical conceptions and beings when they are set in new religious contexts. Some of the demons in Simek's text corpus are called Latin *Elvae*, *Elves*, *Albes*, and *Alber*. In the Schleswig lead amulet (c.1000-1100), for instance, we may read in C3: *c(on)iuro vos demones sive albes ac om(ne)s pestes om(n)iu(m) infirmitatu(m)* "I conjure you, demons and elves, and all the infections of illness, and …".[5] It seems thus as if the *Albes* (ON *álfar*), in their new medieval context have been revaluated; they have changed their character from being spirits with positive aspects for humans to demons causing illness. This demonization of mythical beings is

392 Myth, Materiality, and Lived Religion

not consistent when it comes to the total corpus of the early medieval amulet texts involving protection against diseases. There are
examples where pre-Christian mythical beings have preserved
their power of protecting against demons of illness in their new
medieval context. Þórr, for instance, appears in the text on the
Kvinneby amulet from Öland, usually dated to the early 11th century, but recently re-dated to 1050–1130.[6] This text is carved with
runes in native language. According to Jonna Louise-Jensen,[7] we
may read in one sequence:

þorketih ansmiRþemhamrisamhyR ...

Þōrr gǣti hans mēʀ þǣm hamri (e)s Ām hyʀʀ ...

May Þórr guard him [Būfi] with the hammer with which he strikes
Āmr (a giant = the demon)...

According to Louise-Jensen, Þórr here protects the sick man Būfi
(who is mentioned earlier in this inscription) with his hammer
against the giant Āmr who has caused his skin disease (*erysipelas*).[8]
In my opinion it is quite possible that the carver of this inscription
at least in part is set in a pre-Christian universe of ideas. Āmr
might very well be related to (or identical with) the mythical giant
Ímr, as mentioned in *Váfþrúðnismál* st. 5. The motif that Þórr hits
giants with his hammer is often found in Old Norse mythic traditions.[9] Some of these traditions are also referred to in a couple
of skaldic stanzas containing some kind of liturgical texts (recol-
lections of hymns or prayers) where Þórr is addressed as "you"
who killed "NN".[10] It is thus likely that the carver alluded to this
famous mythic motif as he carved the copper sheet, or perhaps to
a specific myth, when he mentioned that Þórr protected with his
hammer, that is, the hammer that broke Āmr (or Ímr). This does
not have to exclude that the inscription is also about a cure or a
type of folk medicine, where Būfi is the patient, and Āmr is the
giant/demon that caused his skin disease. The fact that Þórr was
invoked for protection against disease is found in other texts referring to pre-Christian contexts. According to Adam of Bremen,[11]
the Svear sacrificed to Þórr if plague and famine threatened (*Si pestis et fames imminet, Thor ydolo lybatur*). The Kvinneby amulet

may thus include an old prayer formula for divine assistance to whoever carried this ritual object. There are, however, images on this amulet indicating that the person who used it was between two universes of beliefs. The fish, for instance, is most likely a symbol of Christ as the Saviour. The whole amulet could thus be seen as an expression of religious syncretism.[12] In my opinion the Kvinneby amulet, which is carved with runes in a native language is thus in some sense closer to a pre-Christian context, than the amulets carved in Latin. Even if on this amulet Þórr is set in a new medieval and Christian context, he has not yet changed to be identified as a demon causing illness, as, for instance, the elves (álfar) mentioned in the Schleswig amulet text. It seems thus as if the first generations of Christians on the island of Öland, at least occasionally, still used the old religious-magical formula when curing illness. Some of them included ancient mythical themes, where the old divinities continued to act as protectors.

Notes

1. Raudvere 2003.

2. Dillmann 2006.

3. Mitchell 2011.

4. Simek 2011; 2013.

5. McKinnell et al. 2004:153.

6. Pereswetoff-Morath 2017:143.

7. Louise-Jensen 2005.

8. cf. e.g. McKinnell et al. 2004:65–67; Düwel 2008:136; and most recently Pereswetoff-Morath 2017:106–143.

9. Lindow 2001:287–291; Simek 2006:219, 316–326.

10. See e.g. Vetrliði Sumarliðason's *lausavísa* in Skj B1:127; A1:135; Þórbjǫrn dísarskáld in Skj B1:135; A1:144; cf. Jackson 2005:492.

11. Adam of Bremen IV, 27.

12. Cf. Hultgård 1988:143.

References

Primary sources

Adam of Bremen. *Magistri Adam Bremensis Gesta Hammaburgensis Ecclesiae Pontificium. Scriptores rerum germanicarum in usum scholarum. Ex Monumentis Germaniae Historicis*. Editio Tertia. Red. Bernhard Schmeidler. 1917. Hanover–Leipzig: Hansche Buchhandlung.

Den Norsk-Islandske Skjaldedigtning. Finnur Jónsson. 1967–1973 (1912–1915). *Den Norsk-Islandske Skjaldedigtning 800–1400*. A1–2, B1–2. Ed. Finnur Jónsson. København: Rosenkilde og Bagger.

Secondary literature

Dillmann, François-Xavier. 2006. *Les magiciens dans l'Islande ancienne*, Acta Academiae regiae Gustavi Adolphi. XCII. Uppsala: Kungl. Gustav Adolfs Akademien för svensk folkkultur.

Düwel, Klaus. 2008 (1968). *Runenkunde*. 4. Auflage. Weimar: J.B. Metzler.

Hultgård, Anders. 1988. Recension av Lindquist 1987. In *Svenska landsmål och svenskt folkliv*, 137–145.

Jackson, Peter. 2005. Thorsmythen. In H. Beck et al. (eds.). *Reallexikon der Germanischen Altertumskunde*. 2. Aufl. Band. 30. Berlin, New York: de Gruyter, 490–498.

Lindow, John. 2001. *Norse Mythology. A Guide to the Gods, Heroes, Rituals, and Beliefs*. Oxford: Oxford University Press.

Louise-Jensen, Jonna. 2005. Södra Kvinneby. In H. Beck et al. (eds.). *Reallexikon der Germanischen Altertumskunde*. 2. Aufl. Band 29. Berlin, New York: de Gruyter, 194–195.

McKinnell, John; Simek, Rudolf & Düwel, Klaus. 2004. *Runes, Magic and Religion. A Sourcebook*. Studia medievalia septentrionalia. 10. Wien: Verlag Fassbaender.

Mitchell, Stephen A. 2011. *Witchcraft and Magic in the Nordic Middle Ages*. The Middle Ages Series. Philadelphia, Oxford: University of Pennsylvania Press.

Pereswetoff-Morath, Sofia. 2017. *Vikingatida runbleck. Läsningar och tolkningar.* Uppsala: Institutionen för nordiska språk, Uppsala Universitet.

Raudvere, Catharina. 2003. *Kunskap och insikt i norrön tradition. Mytologi, ritualer och trolldomsanklagelser.* Vägar till Midgård 3. Lund: Nordic Academic Press.

Simek, Rudolf. 2006 (1993). *Dictionary of Northern Mythology.* Orig. titel: Lexikon der germanischen Mythologie. Cambridge: D.S. Brewer.

Simek, Rudolf. 2011. Elves and Exorcism. Runic and Other Lead Amulets in Medieval Popular Religion. In D. Anlezark (ed.). *Myths, Legends and Heroes. Essays on Old Norse and Old English Literature in Honour of John McKinnell.* Toronto: University of Toronto Press, 25–52.

Simek, Rudolf. 2013. Álfar and Demons, or: What in Germanic Religion Caused the Medieval Christian Belief in Demons? In R. Simek & L. Slupecki (eds.). *Conversion. Looking for Ideological Change in the Early Middle Ages.* Vienna: Verlag Fassbaender, 321–342.

What does Óðinn do to the *Túnriðor?* An Interpretation of *Hávamál* 155

Frederik Wallenstein
Stockholm University

On the following pages I will attempt an interpretation of a well-known, intensively discussed and deeply problematic part of the Eddic poem *Hávamál*, more precisely stanza 155 – a part of the so called *Ljóðatal* section of *Hávamál*.

It is a well-known fact that *Hávamál* is by no means originally to be considered a single coherent work, but rather a compilation assembled, in all probability, before the scribe of the Codex Regius (c. 1270). Usually the poem is divided into several more or less independent parts, often five or six.

The so called *Ljóðatal* section, with which we are concerned here, is a clearly demarcated sequence of 18 stanzas (146–163) that has probably originally been an independent poem – even though it can be connected, in part, to for example *Rúnatal* (the apparent connection with *Loddfáfnismál* though, may well be due to a late interpolation). It consists of a list of 18 *lióð* (magical songs/spells/charms) of which Óðinn claims knowledge and information about the function of each spell (even though the spells themselves are not included). These functions correspond quite well to Snorri's description in *Ynglinga saga* Ch. 6–7 of Óðinn's magical abilities, suggesting either that he knew *Ljóðatal* in some form or that he built his description on similar traditions/sources.

In stanza 155, the tenth of these *lióð* is described in the following words:

Þat kann ec iþ tíunda, ef ec sé túnriðor
Leica lopti á:
ec svá vinnc, at þeir villir fara

How to cite this book chapter:
Wallenstein, F. 2019. What does Óðinn do to the *Túnriðor?* An Interpretation of *Hávamál* 155. In: Wikström af Edholm, K., Jackson Rova, P., Nordberg, A., Sundqvist, O. & Zachrisson, T. (eds.) *Myth, Materiality, and Lived Religion: In Merovingian and Viking Scandinavia*. Pp. 397–421. Stockholm: Stockholm University Press. DOI: https://doi.org/10.16993/bay.n. License: CC-BY.

398 Myth, Materiality, and Lived Religion

> *sinna heim hama,*
> *sinna heim huga.*[1]

Óðinn's tenth *lióð* is obviously a way of dominating other "air travellers" (who "play", "whirl" or simply "fly" in the air) thus asserting his superiority over them. The word *túnriðor* has been translated as "fence-riders" (ON *tún*, "enclosure", "fenced area")[2] and these beings are usually interpreted in the light of a section of "Rättlösabalken" in the Swedish medieval law text *Äldre Västgötalagen* (13th century), relating punishments for insulting women. One of which is saying to a woman that:

> *Jak sa at þu reet a quiggrindu løshareþ ok I trolls ham þa alt var iamrist nat ok daghér*[3]

> I saw that you rode the gate of the animal fold with loose hair and in the shape of a troll when everything was equal between night and day

We will not go further into the fascinating discussion concerning "fence-rider" as a *terminus technicus* for "air traveller" and/or "witch"[4] but only conclude that we can safely assume that we are dealing with female[5] shapeshifters, flying in the air. This has, naturally, led many interpreters to understand this stanza in a more or less shamanistic frame of reference – one that I myself think is reasonable as long as we are aware that we are dealing with "shamanism" in the looser sense. The *túnriðor* are by no means to be considered shamans in the strict sense, but we can safely assume that they are performing a soul-flight. Whether or not this should be called "shamanism" is of little importance. The presence of a soul-flight is further underlined by the use of the concepts of *hugr* and *hamr* which are usually related to what historians of religion call free-soul-conceptions, i.e. aspects of the human soul or psyche that has the ability to temporarily leave the body. *Hugr* is a wide-ranging concept spanning most aspects of man's cognition (such as thought, wish, longing, etc.) but it also clearly signifies the aspect of the human soul believed to leave the body in states of sleep or trance. *Hamr* in similar contexts is the actual shape taken on by the *hugr*. In theory, this demarcation between the concepts is rather clear; in many actual cases, however, they are not so easy to differentiate, a fact we will return to shortly.

Thus far the stanza seems quite comprehensible. But the way in which Óðinn asserts his dominance over the *túnriðor* is not so easy to ascertain. The last three lines of the stanza are problematic, and have been the subject of long and winding discussions, spanning well over a century of research history. The sheer number of suggestions as well as the imaginative power of some of them is quite staggering, but roughly speaking they can be grouped into two basic lines of interpretation (even though these two lines each span a wide range of interpretations as well as differing views of the syntax of the stanza).

1. Óðinn stops their soul-flight and forces them back to their bodies[6]
2. Óðinn leads them astray, making it impossible for them to return to their bodies[7]

The second of these interpretations has been considered possible only by altering the text in one way or another. If we consider the syntax of the later part of the stanza, the problem lies in the syntactic position of the word *heimr*. Had it been in the genitive (sing. *heims*, plur. *heima*), this reading would have been very natural, but since it is here in the accusative, it is not possible to read it this way without some type of emendation.[8] To my knowledge, no one has yet argued for changing the case of only the word *heimr*. Instead, the genitive form is usually produced by making compounds of the words *heim* and *hama/huga* (*heimhama*, *heimhuga*),[9] this has, for good reasons, been considered a lesser emendation. From this operation follows another problem, actually making sense of the two compounds thus produced. *Heimhamr* is unproblematic and quite self-explanatory it refers to the home-shape or the "usual shape" of the shapeshifter, i.e. the body that, left behind, lies inactive as the *túnriðor* are out flying in the air. The *heimhugr*, though, is harder to make sense of. The most usual, and best, attempt is taking *heim-* as meaning "the usual" or "well-known" and thus interpreting *heimhuga* as "the normal mental state" of the *túnriðor*.[10] Although this translation of the otherwise unknown word is quite possible, it feels a little forced and almost *ad hoc*. It is hard not to feel that these interpreters really *want* Óðinn's *lióð* to lead the *túnriðor* astray rather than back to their bodies. As we will soon see, there is good reason for this (better, I think, than most of them realized), but at the same time the problems associated with the emendations made to the text must be considered a major disadvantage of this alternative. Even so, it has become the hegemonic reading of the stanza, followed in all newer editions and translations of *Hávamál*.[11]

On the following pages I will operate from the opinion that, if there is a plausible interpretation to be made without making emendations to the text, it is to be preferred. Before we return to the philological issues though, we need to look to the religio-anthropological context within which to interpret the conceptions discussed.

Seen in the light of comparative anthropological and folkloristic material, the interpretation that Óðinn leads the *túnriðor* astray and prevents them from returning to their bodies actually seems to make a lot more sense. The concept of "soul-loss" is well-known from the anthropology of religion. There are widely distributed conceptions of the dangers associated with the free-soul leaving the body and, for different reasons, not being able to return to it, either because it goes astray and does not manage to find its way back, or because its return is prevented by someone or something. This type of conception has not been discussed in relation to the interpretation of *Hávamál* 155 (or, indeed, to Old Norse soul-conceptions in general). The comparative material that is of interest here is much too extensive for any type of exhaustive or systematic survey, and for our purpose a few illustrative examples from different contexts will suffice.

The Norwegian missionary Isaac Olsen, in his "Lappernes vild-farelser og overtro" (1715) says of the Saami *noaidi* that he always has by his side a young female assistant who sings until he (i.e. his free-soul) returns to his body, and that she also sometimes has to look for him and bring him back so that he may wake up again. If she fails, says Olsen, the *noaidi* dies. He also tells of struggles between different *noaidi* and says that sometimes one *noaidi* may stop the soul of another and prevent it from returning to its body. "Many *Noaidi* die this way", says Olsen.[12]

The relevant comparative examples from Saami religion are many, but here we will limit ourselves to one more: the shamanic ritual described in *Historia Norwegie*. The unknown author here tells us of a group of Christians visiting Saami and witnessing how their hostess suddenly falls to the ground as if dead. The other Saami however tell them that she is in fact not dead but has been abducted by the *gander* of their enemies. Countermeasures are prepared: Their own "wizard" (*magus*), i.e. their *noaidi*, makes the necessary ritual preparations and puts himself into a state of trance to attempt to retrieve the soul of the woman. The results of these efforts are that the woman wakes up, but the *noaidi* dies, and we are told that he, on his soul-journey, had taken the shape of a whale and in this shape had been impaled by his adversary who had taken the shape of sharply pointed stakes.[13] Before this though, he has apparently been successful in returning the soul of the woman to her body. The example thus contains two accounts of soul-loss: the theft of the woman's (free-?) soul and the soul of the *noaidi* that is prevented from returning to its body. Admittedly, it is not led astray but is killed, but the consequences are identical: the soul does not return to the body, and the body therefore dies.

These examples can be related to and, I think, enlightened by a wider comparative anthropological material concerning the concept of "soul-loss". Most of these are taken from more or less shamanistic contexts and cultures, even though the phenomenon itself is by no means limited to shamanistic cultures and religions in the strict sense – this is rather a consequence of the fact that soul conceptions, for natural reasons, have been thoroughly investigated in these areas.

If we begin with some examples from shamanistic areas, it is very clear that the soul-journey of the shaman is considered to be a very dangerous ordeal – primarily for the reason that the shaman may not (for different reasons) be able to return to his body. And when it comes to the shaman's responsibilities as a healer, one of the most common causes of illness is soul-loss, due either to the soul having wandered astray for some reason (for instance during sleep) or to soul-theft of some kind.

Symptoms of soul-loss, apart from death, physical decay, pain and mental problems, range from nervousness, memory loss and mental unbalance to complete madness. Sometimes the symptoms are related to what aspect of the soul has been lost and are usually deepened according to how long the soul has been lost.

402 Myth, Materiality, and Lived Religion

That these conceptions are central in many cultures in the so called "core area" of shamanism was evident already in the travelogues of early explorers as well as the anthropological overviews of Siberian peoples from the late 17th and early 18th centuries.[14] Åke Hultkrantz says of conceptions of soul-loss among Native North Americans (in this case the Shoshoni):

> If the free-soul does not return to the body, and the latter nevertheless returns to life, this may consequently signify that the person's possibilities of apprehending and understanding will be very small. He becomes 'queer', in a number of cases completely 'mad'.
> [...]
> the sickness must be cured sooner or later. i.e. the soul must be restored, if the patient is not to die[15]

These descriptions are very similar to the material presented by Ivar Paulson in his extensive collection and analysis of conceptions of the soul among Siberian peoples. He mentions on the one hand more or less temporary problems such as confusion, neuroses/psychoses, pain and fever, and on the other serious, chronic physical or psychic disease that usually ends with death.[16]

As already mentioned, these types of conceptions are by no means limited to shamanistic cultures in the strict sense, nor are they limited to Scandinavia or even the North-Eurasian area, but seem to be of a very general nature. Carlo Ginzburg, for example, in his famous investigation of the Friulian *Benandanti* in the late fourteenth and early fifteenth centuries, says that:

> These benandanti say that when their spirit leaves the body it has the appearance of a mouse, and also when it returns, and that if the body should be rolled over while it is without its spirit, it would remain dead, and the spirit could never return to it.[17]

Similar conceptions are to be found in Nordic folklore material ranging from the fifteenth up to the early twentieth century. This is especially true of the material in the collections of the folk-memory archives, dealing primarily with material from the late 1800s and the early 1900s. Conceptions of soul-loss are referred to with words like being *vordstolen* (one whose "vård" has been stolen) or *vordlaus* (being without "vård"), or *hamstolen, hamslaus*, etc.

The concept of being *hamstolen* also has a direct counterpart in Icelandic sagas (being *hamstolinn* or *hamslaus*) where it means "having lost one's wits".[18] It is the case, for example in the famous episode in *Egils saga* where the young woman Helga has been made ill by the failed attempts at rune magic by a young farmers son.[19] It is worth noting that this meaning of the word, though not (still?) specifically referring to soul-loss, is completely in line with the thought consequences of soul-loss referred to above, and one may at least wonder whether there is an older conception concealed behind the word as it is used in the sagas.

Nils Lid has discussed a Norwegian trial from 1660 where a woman knowledgeable in the art of witchcraft says that the "word" (voord, vård, vål, etc.) that sits in man's breast is out at night flying around, and that if then a spirit takes it and it is not able to return to the body, that person loses their sanity:

> Der er it word i mennischens bryst, som faar ude om natten, naar dj soffer. Och dersom der da kommer en vnd and offuer den, saa den iche kommer igien till mennischen, saa bliffuer det mennische aff med sin forstand[20]

Conceptions about the risks associated with losing the "vård" have been very widespread, at least in Swedish and Norwegian folklore, and have been especially connected to being suddenly and/or very frightened (*vålskrämd*, *voordskræmd*, etc.) and just like in the case of poor Helga in *Egils saga*, this was considered as leading to "losing one's mind" or "losing one's wits". Another illustrating example can be found in Jón Árnason's (1819–1888) *Íslenzkar þjóðsögur og æfintýri* (1862–1864). Here it is said of the priest Eiríkur (Magnússon) i Vogsósum (1667–1716) that one time when he was out on a *gandreið* his body was found by two boys and that when he returned he thanked them for not having touched the body; had they done so, he says, he would not have been able to return.[21] It should be added, though, that even though there are a few more episodes in this material that could be interpreted in the same vein (some referring to the same Eiríkur), it is hard to find any that are as clear-cut as this one and therefore it is hard to draw any definite conclusions about the occurrence of this conception in Icelandic legend and folklore.

From general folklore one could also mention the very wide-spread conception of the dangers associated with being woken suddenly. Often this is explained by the risk that the soul does not manage to return before the body wakes up, resulting in its inability to re-enter the body. This is common not only in Nordic folklore, but from almost all over the world, and it is not seldom associated with mortal danger. Ivar Paulson for instance, in his book on the soul-conceptions of Siberian peoples writes that several of these peoples "ausdrücklich verbietet, einen Schlafenden vor seinem natürlichen Erwachen zu wecken, da sonst die Seele 'draussen' bleiben kann".[22]

As mentioned previously, the comparative material is very extensive and we could give other examples of this kind for quite some time, but thus far I think we can safely conclude that, while the conceptions of the dangers associated with the soul (or parts of the soul) leaving the body and not being able to return are very widespread and are always associated with grave illnesses and death, magical or religious conceptions of the forcing back of an individual's soul into their body is, as far as I can see, virtually unknown. The conception of soul-loss is more often than not associated with conceptions of especially gifted and powerful people being able to steal and/or (as a countermeasure for this) return the souls of others, but there does not seem to be any examples of shamans, magicians or others forcing the souls of others back into their bodies.[23]

Summarizing the problem, we can conclude that it seems that the wish to read the manuscript without emendations is at odds with the most reasonable interpretation of the stanza. On the one hand we have a line of interpretation that leaves the manuscript untouched and on the other we have one that seems to make a lot more sense but that is forced to make alterations to the manuscript. But let us go back to the first line of interpretation once more. Here we have at least three readings of the stanza that leaves it without emendations (Fredrik Leopold Läffler, Björn Magnus Ólsen and Dag Strömbäck). Of these three, the most interesting and persuasive one is that made by Strömbäck.[24] In fact, on closer examination it seems that the way Strömbäck reads the stanza may actually contain other interpretive possibilities than the one presented either by him or his commentators.

One of the cornerstones in Strömbäck's view of the stanza is his persuasive discussion showing that, even though they are in some cases clearly separable concepts, the words *hugr* and *hamr* should in this case be considered as synonyms, both denoting the "free-soul", and that, accordingly, the "heim hama", and "heim huga" are synonymous expressions meaning the home of the *hamir* and *hugir*, i.e. the home of the (free-)souls (of the *túnriðor*), thus eliminating a source of major problems for many of the preceding interpreters.[25] With this in mind, let us go back to the syntactic issues.

As mentioned, the basic problem is the syntactic position of the word *heim*. Had this word been in the genitive plural (*heima*), says Strömbäck, we would have had an excellent translation: "they go astray, in relation to the home of their souls", but, since it is obviously in the accusative, this interpretation is not possible. He then goes on to give persuasive examples from Eddic as well as skaldic poetry of how the accusative marks the goal of the motion verb. Arguing that the direction of the movement in this case must be *towards* the bodies (the *heim hama, heim huga*) of the *túnriðor*. Since there is no preposition, we cannot say whether they go, *to* their bodies, *into* their bodies or perhaps *towards* their bodies, but from the syntax we can conclude that the direction of the movement is clear beyond doubt. Reading the stanza this way, *villir* has to refer to the mental state of the *túnriðor*. They go, *confused*, towards the home of their souls. Strömbäck uses the Swedish word "förvillade" – "confused" or perhaps "mentally astray".

Thus, concludes Strömbäck, Óðinn's *lióð* makes the *tunriðor* "*villir fara sinna heim hama, sinna heim huga*" – "go, confused, back to the home of their souls"[26] meaning that Óðinn confuses them, takes control over their soul-flight and forces them back to their bodies.

Strömbäck's view of the syntax is very persuasive and I see no grounds for criticising it, but his interpretation (and his translation) does not follow from it logically as the only one possible. As mentioned above, the critical word "to" could just as well be replaced by "towards" (since there is no such exact preposition), which would give a slightly different translation, saying that the *túnriðor* "go, confused, towards the home of their souls".

Well then. What does it actually mean to "confuse", to make someone go mentally astray, at the point of return to the body?

It is actually only said that *at the point of return*, when they go back, they are attempting to re-enter their bodies, Óðinn has thrown the *túnriðor* into a state of confusion, making them go mentally astray.[27] The way I see it this could just as well mean that the *túnriðor* are in a mental state that prevents them from re-entering their bodies, or indeed from actually finding their way back!

If this interpretation has any bearing, we can read the stanza exactly the way that Strömbäck does, but still interpret it according to the other line of interpretation. Óðinn knows a *lióð* with which he asserts his dominance over other beings whose souls are out flying. With it, he has the power to prevent them from returning to their bodies, resulting in the gravest of consequences: he annihilates them.

I would argue that this interpretation is preferable from a philological perspective, as well as a cultural- or a religio-historical, or, indeed, a poetic perspective. It requires no emendations of the manuscript and it does not have to deal with neologisms that are hard to interpret (*heimhugr*). From a comparative religio-anthropological perspective, it is supported by an overwhelming number of parallels (while the competing line of interpretation seems to have none) and from a closer cultural-historical perspective it is coherent with what we know of Old Norse soul-conceptions. It is also, I would argue, more in line with what we know of Óðinn. Destroying his opponents is a more likely action than just stopping their soul-flight and forcing them back. And, at least in my opinion, this much more dramatic action makes more poetic sense in a stanza describing the magic abilities of Óðinn.

Perhaps we even have a few more examples of the concept of soul-loss in Old Norse material. We have already seen a possible remnant of such conceptions in the above-mentioned episode in *Egils saga Skalla-Grímssonar* and there may be others. In closing, we shall look at one such possible instance.

Strömbäck discusses an interesting detail mentioned in *Gǫngu-Hrólfs saga*. In this saga the dwarf *Mǫndull* who is skilled in magic uses something called *seiðvillur* to sabotage the practice of *seiðr* by somehow "confusing" the *seiðmenn*.[28] The use of the word *villr* is of course significant and Strömbäck sees the similarities with Óðinn's tenth *lióð*, but considers the described consequences of the practice as unexpected if (as he would argue) its purpose is forcing back the free-souls of these *seiðmenn* to their bodies. The *seiðmenn* are in fact acting completely insanely. They break their *seiðhjallar*, run around totally disoriented and die by running off cliffs and into marshes. This all seems mysterious to Strömbäck. *If*, though, such an effect can be associated with the return of the souls to their bodies, he says, "then the magic song alluded to in the *Hávamál*-stanza is given an even greater power".[29]

If, however we, like Strömbäck, are to take the details provided in *Gǫngu-Hrólfs saga* of this magical practice seriously, the interpretation must again be altered according to the interpretation presented here. In fact, if we view it in the light of what has been said above on the widespread conceptions of the consequences of soul-loss the description of the *seiðvillur* actually seems to make all the more sense. Indeed, the description of the consequences befalling the *seiðmenn* corresponds completely to this. This is thought-provoking: perhaps this otherwise quite imaginative fornaldarsaga has actually kept the memory of a magical practice functionally equivalent with Óðinn's tenth *lióð*.

Lastly, I would like to add an interesting detail. And quite an odd one. When reading an article by Strömbäck's hand, published 40 years after the dissertation, I found an *en passant* mention of *Hávamál* 155, where he had this to say:

> Odin knows the charms by which they [i.e. the *túnriðor*] can be put out of action. Through him they are led astray and cannot find the place from where they have started their journey, the place where their *hamir* and *hugir* have started their journey[30]

This is, quite obviously, a completely different interpretation from the one he gives in the dissertation, but in the article, he only refers to his own book in the following words:

> I have tried in my time to give stanza 155, which has been discussed by at least two generations of philologists before me, a reasonable interpretation and I shall not now go further into that linguistic matter (Sejd, p. 168–182)[31]

These words are quite surprising, to say the least. Since this is exactly the interpretation that he deems impossible on philological grounds on precisely the pages referred to. What happened to Strömbäck's view of the stanza we will never know. The fact that he would have been persuaded by the arguments of Finnur Jónsson and others seems very unlikely since he was very reluctant to make emendations to the manuscript and argued forcefully against this line of interpretation. Maybe he never changed his mind concerning the syntax. *Maybe he came to see the stanza in the way I do!* But, in that case, he never explained the grounds on which he changed his mind. His silence on this point, much like Óðinn's *lióð*, makes one feel rather confused.

Notes

1. Neckel/Kuhn 1962.

2. Franck 1901:668; Noreen 1922–1924:59–60. For other (decidedly less convincing) explanations of the word, see e.g. Fritzner 1954 (1883–1896), III:731; B.M. Ólsen 1916:71.

3. Äldre Västgötalagen RB V:5, in Wiktorssons edition II:88.

4. But it is worth mentioning the etymological discussion on the word "häxa" (German *hexe*) where OHG *hagazussa* has been interpreted as meaning "fence-woman". See Noreen 1922–1924:60–61. On OHG *hag-* see Noreen 1922–1924:60; Fick et al. 1909:68.

5. Since the *tunriðor* are female, the form *þeir villir* is unexpected. One would rather expect the feminine *þær villar*. This has often led to emendations of the text. Strömbäck, though, wanted to leave the text unchanged and referred to the possibility of there also being male *tunriðor* (Strömbäck 1935:181–182).

6. This is the case with e.g. both Fredrik Leopold Läffler and Björn Magnus Ólsen who debated the stanza in the two Swedish philological journals *Studier i nordisk filologi* and *Arkiv för nordisk filologi* a little over a hundred years ago (see Läffler 1914; 1916; Björn Magnus Ólsen 1916). Also, Dag Strömbäck, who devoted a detailed study to the stanza in his dissertation on *seiðr* in 1935, was of the opinion that

Óðinn forced the free-souls of the *túnriðor* back into their bodies. This, of course, was the *only* thing they agreed on in their in every other way very different interpretations. The case of Strömbäck's view is especially interesting, and more complicated than one might first realize, a fact I will return to shortly.

7. This interpretation was perhaps most forcefully expressed in the work of Finnur Jónsson (Finnur Jónsson 1924; Sveinbjörn Egilsson & Finnur Jónsson 1931), but has been argued in different variants by many scholars both before and since (for the sake of chronology, it should perhaps be pointed out that Finnur Jónsson's views on the stanza are presented already in Sveinbjörn Egilsson & Finnur Jónsson 1913–1916). Early proponents are e.g. Guðbrandur Vígfússon (1883), and, as it seems, even earlier, Fínnur Magnusson (although his is an uncommented translation), see Fínnur Magnusson 1822:142. It was adopted early also by Magnus Olsen (Olsen 1911:32–33; 1917:629) and, in a way, also by Hugo Gering (1904; 1927), although his emendations go further, also changing *-huga* to *-haga*).

8. The philological issues are presented very clearly by Dag Strömbäck (Strömbäck 1935:177ff.).

9. For details see the literature referred to above.

10. This is the interpretation made in the Íslenzk Fornrit edition (see p. 354), as well as Gísli Sigurðsson's edition (1999:57), but it has been argued in variants for a long time. The way I see it, this must be the interpretation made already by Finnur Magnusson in his translation from 1822 (Finnur Magnusson 1822:142). It is also what lies behind the words chosen by Larrington ("their minds left at home") and Orchard ("their proper minds"). It did not impress Hugo Gering (1904; 1927) though, who changed it to *heimhaga* ("heimstätte"), nor Finnur Jónsson who considered the last line to be either "unecht" or a bad variant of the preceding line (1924; 1931).

11. See, for instance, the English translations by Larrington (1996; 2014) and Andy Orchard (2011) and the editions by Evans (1986) and Dronke (2011) as well as the Íslenzk Fornrit edition from 2014 and the edition by Gísli Sigurðsson from 1999. The same goes for the influential edition by Guðni Jónsson (1949).

12. "saa skal hun Joige og Runne saa lenge at hand op vogner igien, og hun skal leede efter hannem med sin konst i hvor hand foer hen, indtil at hun finder hannem, og naar hun da har fundet hannem, saa fører hun hannem til bage igien og saa vaagner hand op igien, de sige self at de finder hannem under tiden i bierge huller langt borte i marcken, Ja og somme tider i Helvede og under Jorden, saa og i vandene, og der som hun er icke forstandig nock, eller icke vel lært, som skal leede effter Noiden, og hun icke med sin konst kand finde hannem, og føre ham til bage igien, saa døer hand viserlig med det samme og aldrig op vogner mer igien"

[...]

"om en annan Noid er vred paa hannemm den samme som ducker under, eller har hafft eller har strid tilsammen, med konsten, og de vill vide hvem som skal være En andens mæstere og over mand i deris konsters strid saa paßer den anden paa i det samme, som hand ducker under, og stopper vejen til for hannem og formeener hannem at kommet til bage igien, og naar det saa er Da døer Noiden ogsaa og aldrig op vaagner meere, Det er mange af Noiderna som saaledis døer i den Zammelli eller ducke færd, i deris troldmesße"

(Olsen, *Lappernes vildfarelser og overtro* 1910 (1715):45–46).

13. *Historia Norwegie* IV, *"De Finnis"*:16–24.

14. E.g. Bogoraz 1975 (1904–1909):332–333 ; Jochelson 1905:41, 61, 101 ; Stadling 1912:19, 24, 93, 96, 98, 99–100, 116, 121 ; Czaplicka 1914:260–261, 282, 287; Nioradze 1925:21ff., 44–45; Shirokogoroff 1935:135–136, 317–318.

15. Hultkrantz 1953:286–287. On the concept of soul-loss in Hultkrantz material, see Hultkrantz 1953:285–291.

16. Paulson 1958:273, 292, 298–303.

17. Ginzburg 2013 (1966):18. This is just one of many instances of this conception in Ginzburg's book. It reoccurs many times in the protocols of the inquisition hearings on which Ginzburg builds his investigation. It also mentions the risks associated with touching, or even looking at the body when the soul has left it. Ginzburg also gives

instances of the conception from a wider area (stretching from Alsace to the eastern parts of the Alps), and further back in time (at least a couple of hundred years).

18. Fritzner: "berøvet sit For-stand", Fritzner 1954 (1883–1896) I:719.

19. *Egils saga Skalla-Grímssonar*, Ch. 72 (ÌF II:229).

20. Lid 1935:12.

21. This episode is also retold by Dag Strömbäck (Strömbäck 1935:190).

22. Paulson 1958:292. Mircea Eliade says of conceptions among Native North Americans: "The soul leaves the body during sleep, and one may kill a person by waking him suddenly. A shaman must never be startled awake" (Eliade 1964:301).

23. At this point I should perhaps clarify that the point of these wide-ranging anthropological and folkloristic comparative examples is *not* to suggest long winding threads of cultural/religious continuity or lines of diffusion or anything like that, it is merely to show that these conceptions are very widespread and general in nature and to suggest that it seems very reasonable to think that this material sheds light on what is going on in this stanza. I am not fishing for the origin of these conceptions or suggesting that they are indicative of certain cultural connections, even though these questions are indeed interesting and worthy of further study.

24. Strömbäck 1935:168–182.

25. Strömbäck 1935:172, see also 173–177.

26. "Förvillade fara till sina hamnars hem, till sina själars hem" (Strömbäck 1935:179–180).

27. On other types of Old Norse conceptions of magic intended to cause similar conditions, see Gunnell 2014.

28. *Gǫngu-Hrólfs saga*, Ch. 28; Strömbäck 1935:181, on his view of *Gǫngu-Hrólfs saga* see also 100–102.

29. Strömbäck 1935:181.

30. Strömbäck 1975:20.

31. Strömbäck 1975:20.

References

Primary sources

Edda. Jónas Kristjánsson og Vésteinn Ólason. 2014. *Eddukvæði I. Goðakvæði. Jónas Kristjánsson og Vésteinn Ólason gáfu út.* Reykjavík: Hið Íslenzka Fornritafélag.

———— Gísli Sigurðsson. 1999. Eddukvæði. Gísli Sigurðsson sá um útgáfuna. In *Mál og menning.*

———— Guðni Jónsson. 1949. *Eddukvæði (Sæmundar-Edda). Fyrrir hluti. Guðni Jónsson bjó til prentunar.* Reykjavík: Íslandingasagnaútgáfan.

———— Neckel, Gustav & Kuhn, Hans. 1962. *Edda. Die Lieder des Codex Regius nebst verwandten Denkmälern. I Text.* Vierte umgearbeitete Auflage von Hans Kuhn. Heidelberg: Carl Winter Universitätsverlag.

———— Gering, Hugo & Hildebrand, Karl. 1904. *Die Lieder der Älteren Edda (Sæmundar Edda).* Herausgegeben von Karl Hildebrand, Zweite völlig umgearbeitete Auflage von Hugo Gering. Paderborn: Ferdinand Schöningh.

———— Magnusen, Finn. 1822–1823. *Den ældre Edda. En samling af de nordiske folks ældste sagn og sange ved Sæmund Sifussön. Oversat og forklaret ved Finn Magnusen.* København: Den Gyldendalske Boghandling.

———— Larrington, Carolyne. 2014. *The Poetic Edda. Translated with introduction and Notes by Carolyne Larrington.* Revised edition. Oxford: Oxford University Press.

———— Larrington, Carolyne. 1996. *The Poetic Edda. Translated with introduction and Notes by Carolyne Larrington.* New York: Oxford University Press.

———— Orchard, Andy. 2011. *The Elder Edda. A Book of Viking Lore. Translated and edited by Andy Orchard.* London: Penguin books.

Äldre Västgötalagen. Wiktorsson, Per-Axel (ed). 2011. *Äldre Västgötalagen och dess bilagor i Cod. Holm. B 59.* Värnamo: Föreningen för Västgötalitteratur.

Gǫngu-Hrólfs saga. Guðni Jónsson & Bjarni Vílhjalmsson (eds.). 1944. *Fornaldarsögur Norðurlanda II.* Reykjavík: Bókútgáfan Forni.

Historia Norwegie. Ekrem, Inger & Mortensen, Lars Boje (ed.). 2003. *Historia Norwegie.* Transl. Peter Fisher. Copenhagen: Museum Tusculanum Press.

Isaac Olsen, *Om Lappernes vildfarelser og overtro (1715).* Qvigstad, J. (ed.). 1910. *Kildeskrifter til den lappiske Mythologi 2.* Trondhjem: Det Kgl. Norske Videnskabers Selskab.

Secondary literature

Björn Magnus Ólsen. 1916. Hávamál v. 155. In *Arkiv för nordisk filologi* 32.

Bogoras, Waldemar. (Bogoraz, Vladimir). 1975 (1904–1909). *The Chukchee. The Jesup North Pacific Expedition.* Vol VII. New York: AMS Press Inc.

Czaplicka, Marie A. 1914. *Aboriginal Siberia. A Study in Social Anthropology.* Oxford: Claredon Press.

Dronke, Ursula. 2011. *The Poetic Edda. Vol. 3, Mythological poems* 2. Oxford: Clarendon.

Eliade, Mircea. 1964. *Shamanism. Archaic Techniques of Ecstasy.* Princeton: Princeton University Press.

Evans, David A.H. 1986. *Hávamál.* London: Viking Society for Northern Research.

Fick, August et al. 1909. *Wörterbuch der indogermanischen Sprachen. Dritter Teil: Wortschatz der Germanischen Spracheinheit.* Unter Mitwirkung von Hjalmar Falk gänzlich umgearb. von Alf Torp.

Finnur Jónsson. 1924. *Havamal.* København: Gads forlag.

Franck. 1901. Geschichte des Wortes Hexe. In J. Hansen (ed.). *Quellen Und Untersuchungen Zur Geschichte Des Hexenwahns Und Der Hexenverfolgung Im Mittelalter.* Bonn: Carl Georgi, Univeritäts-Buchdruckerei und Verlag.

Fritzner, Johan. 1954 (1883–1896). *Ordbog over Det gamle norske Sprog.* Oslo: Møller.

Gering, Hugo. 1927. *Kommentar zu den Liedern der Edda. Erste Häfte, Götterlieder.* Von Hugo Gerling; nach dem Tode des Verfassers herausgegeben von B. Sijmons. Halle: Buchhandl. des Waisenhauses.

Ginzburg, Carlo. 2013 (1966). *The Night Battles, Witchcraft and Agrarian Cults in the Sixteenth and Seventeenth Centuries.* Translated by John & Anne Tedeschi. Baltimore: John Hopkins University Press.

Guðbrandur Vigfússon (ed.). 1883. *Corpus Poeticum Boreale.* 2 vols. Oxford: Clarendon.

Gunnell, Terry. 2014. 'Magical Mooning' and the 'Goatskin Twirl', 'other' Kinds of Female Magical Practices in Early Iceland. In T. Tangherlini (ed.). *Nordic Mythologies, Interpretations, Intersections, and Institutions.* Berkeley & Los Angeles: North Pinehurst Press.

Hultkrantz, Åke. 1953. *Conceptions of the Soul among North American Indians. A Study in Religious Ethnology.* Stockholm: Etnografiska museet.

Jochelson, Waldemar. 1905. *The Koryak*, part I. Leiden: Brill.

Lid, Nils. 1935. Magiske fyrestillingar og bruk. In *Nordisk kultur XIX*. Albert Bonniers förlag.

Läffler, Fredrik Leopold. 1914. Om några underarter av ljóðaháttr. Bidrag till den fornnorsk-fornisländska verslären och till textkritiken av Eddasångerna, tillika en studie över Háttatals strof 101. In *Studier i nordisk filologi 5*. Helsingfors: Svenska litteratursällskapet.

Läffler, Fredrik Leopold. 1916. Till Hávamáls strof 155. In *Arkiv för nordisk filologi 32*.

Nioradze, Georg. 1925. *Der Schamanismus bei den Sibirischen Völkern.* Stuttgart: Strecker und Schröder.

Noreen, Erik. 1924. Om ordet häxa. In *språkvetenskapliga sällskapet i Uppsalas förhandlingar, Uppsala universitets årsskrift* 1924:2. Uppsala: Almqvist & Wiksell.

Olsen, Magnus. 1911. En indskrift med ældre runer fra Huglen i Søndhordland. In *Bergens museums Aarbok* 1911.

Olsen, Magnus. 1917 Norges indskrifter med de ældre runer II. Christiania: A.W. Brøggers bogtrykkeri.

Paulson, Ivar. 1958. *Die primitiven Seelenvorstellungen der nordeurasischen Völker. Eine religionsethnographische und religionsphänomenologische Untersuchung.* Stockholm: Etnografiska museet.

Shirokogoroff, S.M. 1999 (1935). *Psychomental Complex of the Tungus.* Berlin: Reinhold Schletzer Verlag.

Stadling, Jonas. 1912. *Shamanismen i Norra Asien.* Stockholm: P.A. Norstedt & söner.

Strömbäck, Dag. 1989 (1978). Om de nordiska själsföreställningarna. In *Den osynliga närvaron. Studier i folktro och folkdikt.* Hedemora: Gidlunds förlag.

Strömbäck, Dag. 1935. *Sejd. Textstudier i nordisk religionshistoria.* Stockholm: Gebers Förlag.

Strömbäck, Dag. 1975. The Concept of the Soul in Nordic Tradition. In *ARV.*

Sveinbjörn Egilsson, & Finnur Jónsson. 1913–1916. *Lexicon poeticum antiquae linguae septentrionalis – Ordbog over det norsk-islandske skjaldesprog.* København: Det kongelige Nordiske Oldskriftselskab.

Sveinbjörn Egilsson & Finnur Jónsson. 1931. *Lexicon poeticum antiquae linguae septentrionalis – Ordbog over det norsk-islandske skjaldesprog* (2 Udgave). København: Det kongelige Nordiske Oldskriftselskab.

Response

Terry Gunnell
University of Iceland

It should be stated immediately that, while I am a little uncertain about both *hugr* and *hamr* being one and the same thing (in short, both the "soul" and the "shape taken on by the *hugr*", which would appear to me to be different things), I find the overall argument made by Fredrik Wallenstein with regard to st. 155 of *Ljóðatal* convincing, not only philologically but also in terms of Old Nordic religious beliefs and later folklore from the Nordic area. In the short response to the paper which will follow, I will essentially be providing further evidence that can be used to support the idea (and the wider consequences of supernatural figures becoming *villir* 'losing direction'). However, I will also make some suggestions with regard to explaining the apparent change of sex of the *túnriðor* and the possible meaning of that word (with reference to something other than witches as 'fence riders').

It might be said that the most obvious support for the argument made by Wallenstein is found in the detailed account of Þorbjǫrg *lítilvǫlva*'s *seiðr* activities given in *Eiríks saga rauða* where Þorbjǫrg asks a group of women to assist her by singing a *varðlokr/ varðlokkr* (the spelling varies by manuscript: see *Eiríks saga rauða*: 206–9). As Stephen Mitchell has effectively argued,[1] the word in question seems to refer to a "calling song" designed to call the spirit of the *seiðr* practitioner back to her body from a shamanistic journey. The implication is that her activities place her travelling *hugr* in danger of getting lost, and that it needs to be called back safely from the "other side" by the chant in question. While Mitchell sees the first part of the word as referring to women (*vǫrð*), as he notes it might also refer to protective spirits of various kinds (*vǫrðr/ verðir*), as applies in the case of the Norwegian *gardvord*, a word used in later Norwegian folklore for the farm protective spirit (cf. the *nisse* or *tomte* in Swedish and Norwegian[2]).

In a recent article entitled "'Magical Mooning' and the 'Goatskin Twirl': 'Other' Kinds of Female Magical Practices in

Early Iceland",[3] I have noted that the idea of "confusing" nature spirits by means of causing them to lose direction so that they cannot find their way home (invoking a sense of madness) is found on several other occasions in Old Norse literature: in the *Jarlsnið* curse (and so-called *þokuvísur* (lit. 'fog-verses')) which Þorleifr *jarlsskáld* uttered against Jarl Hákon in Þrándheimr, in *Þorleifs þáttr jarlsskálds* (Ch. 4–5); in the curses that accompany Egill Skallagrímsson's erection of a *níðstǫng* ('scorn pole') against King Eiríkr *blóðöx* in *Egils saga* (Ch. 57) in which Egill magically attempts to bring about a situation in which the *landvættir* or 'land spirits' *fari* [...] *villar vega, engi hendi né hitti sitt inni* (lose their way, and do not reach or find their home); and in the similar *Buslubæn* in *Bósa saga ok Herrauðs* (Ch. 5), which also attempts to create a chaotic situation by means of magic: *Villist vættir,/ verði ódæmi,/ hristist hamrar,/ heimr sturlist,/ versni veðrátta;/ verði ódæmi* (May the spirits lose their way, may there be nothing like it,/ the cliffs shake,/ the world go mad,/ the weather worsen;/ may there be nothing like it), which uses the same verb (*að villa*). Once again, the stress is on supernatural spirits getting lost while travelling. Indeed, a similar idea seems to be evident in *Vǫluspá*, st. 50, where, as an image of the ultimate chaos that will come about at *ragnarøk*, the *vǫlva* tells of how *stynia dvergar/ fyr steindurom,/ veggbergs vísir* (the dwarfs will groan/ before stone doors/ the cliff face princes). Here it should be remembered that the *dvergar* are said to secure the cardinal directions in *Gylfaginning*, Ch. 8. As noted in the aforementioned article, several other saga references describe magical rituals which seem to be deliberately designed to invoke a similar kind of chaos in nature, and there is good reason to believe that the same idea lies behind the protective curse in *Hávamál*, st. 155. Indeed, in a world in which sea travel and journeys over mountain passes were commonplace, one can well understand the importance of knowing directions and finding your way home, and the degree to which losing it might be associated with a state of ultimate confusion, chaos and madness.

With regard to the element of an apparent change of sex that seems to occur in *Hávamál*, st. 155, as the feminine *túnríðor* become *þeir*, it is worth considering that a similar thing actually seems to take place in *Njáls saga* (Ch. 157) in the account of the

performance of *Darraðarljóð* in which first we read that **menn**
riðu tólf saman til dyngju nǫkkurrar ok hurfu þar allir (twelve
men rode together to a women's bower, and all of them dis-
appeared) (my bold italics), and then soon afterwards that a group
of *women* were seen chanting verses: *þær kváðu þá vísur nǫkk-*
urar (they [the women] then sang/ chanted some verses). While the
possibility naturally exists that the word *menn* here refers to people in general, it does seem that the idea of some kind of inversion
(often sexual) commonly formed part of female magic practices in
the Old Norse world. I have dealt with this in more detail in the
article referred to above, especially with reference to magic practices that relate in some way to the "other world" of death and the
dísir, in which women commonly take on the stereotypical male
role of ruling, riding horses and bearing weapons.[4]

Bearing the aforementioned *dísir* in mind, and considering the
word *túnríðor* itself, there is also good reason to consider the
account of how two groups of *dísir* are said to ride onto the
vǫllr of a farm during the Winter Nights in *Þiðranda þáttr ok*
Þórhalls (Ch. 2); the accounts of the threats posed by the figure of the ogress Grýla/ Skekla, who is also said to come down
onto farms at various turning points of the year and even literally rides onto a *tún* in a Shetland rhyme:[5] *Skekla komena rina*
tunal swarta hæsta blæta bruna (Skekla [an ogress] rides into
the homefield/ on a black horse with a white patch on its brow);
and the folk legends of the Norwegian "wild ride" known as the
Oskoreia/ juleskrei which was often said to be led by a female
figure known as Guro Rysserover, and was said to threaten farms
at Christmas.[6] There is strong physical evidence (in the shape
of tar crosses painted over stable and barn doors in western
Norway) to prove that this last legend were treated with a high
degree of belief, even in the early 20th century.[7] One might argue
that the word *túnríðor* might well be more applicable to threat-
ening supernatural female figures like these (who all literally ride
horses onto home fields), rather than to witches, even if the latter in the verse in question are said to travel by air. Indeed, the
same was also often said about the *Oskoreia/ juleskrei* which are
often said to be heard in the air and in the wind. In other words,

they, too, were believed to *leika lopti á*, something effectively demonstrated in the final scene of Henrik Ibsen's *Hærmændene på Helgeland* (The Warriors at Helgeland) (1857), where the audience hears "Åsgårdsreien suser gjennem luften" (The Åsgård Ride whistles through the air).[8]

Notes

1. Mitchell 2001:65–70.

2. See references in Gunnell 2014b.

3. Gunnell 2014a.

4. On the *dísir*, see further Gunnell 2005.

5. See further Gunnell 2001; Jakobsen 1897:19.

6. See further Gunnell 2005; Eike 1980; Celander 1943.

7. See further Eike 1980.

8. Ibsen 1962:81.

References
Primary Sources

Bósa saga ok Herrauðs. Guðni Jónsson (ed.). 1954. *Fornaldar sögur Norðurlanda* III. Akureyri: Íslendingasagnaútgáfan, 281–322.

Brennu-Njáls saga. Einar Ólafur Sveinsson (ed.). 1954. *Íslenzk fornrit* XII. Reykjavík: Hið íslenzka fornritafélag.

Edda. Jónas Kristjánsson & Vésteinn Ólason (eds). 2014. *Eddukvæði I–II.* Íslenzk fornrit. Reykjavík: Hið íslenzka fornritafélag.

Egils saga Skalla-Grímssonar. Sigurður Nordal (ed.). 1933. *Egils saga Skalla-Grímssonar.* Íslenzk fornrit II. Reykjavík: Hið íslenzka fornritafélag.

Eiríks saga rauða. Einar Ólafur Sveinsson & Matthías Þorðarson (eds). 1935. *Eiríks saga rauða.* Íslenzk fornrit IV. Reykjavík: Hið íslenska fornritafélag, 193–237.

Ibsen, Henrik. 1862. *Ungdomsskuespill og historiske dramaer 1850–64*. 13th edition. Oslo: Gyldendal, Norsk forlag.

Snorri Sturluson. Anthony Faulkes (ed.). 2005. *Edda. Prologue and Gylfaginning*. Second ed. London: Viking Society for Northern Research.

Þiðranda þáttr ok Þórhalls. Bragi Halldórsson et al. (eds). 1987. *Íslendingar sögur*. Reykjavík: Svart á hvítu, 2253–2255.

Þorleifs þáttr jarlsskálds. Jónas Kristjánsson (ed.). 1956. *Þorleifs þáttr jarlsskálds*. Jónas Kristjánsson (ed.). 1956. *Eyfirðinga sǫgur*. Íslenzk fornrit IX. Reykjavik: Hið íslenzka fornritafélag, 213–29.

Secondary Sources

Celander, Hilding. 1943. Oskoreien och besläktade föreställningar i äldre och nyare nordisk tradition. In *Saga och sed*, 71–175.

Eike, Christine. 1980. Oskoreia og ekstaseriter. In *Norveg* 23, 227–309.

Gunnell, Terry. 2001. Grýla, Grýlur, "Grøleks" and Skeklers. Medieval Disguise Traditions in the North Atlantic? In *Arv. Nordic Yearbook of Folklore*, 33–54.

Gunnell, Terry. 2005. The Season of the *Dísir*. The Winter Nights and the *Dísarblót* in Early Scandinavian Belief. In *Cosmos* 16 (2000), 117–149.

Gunnell, Terry. 2014a. 'Magical Mooning' and the 'Goatskin Twirl'. 'Other' Kinds of Female Magical Practices in Early Iceland. In T. Tangherlini (ed.). *Nordic Mythologies. Interpretations, Intersections, and Institutions*. The Wildcat Canyon Advanced Seminars. Mythology, vol.1. Berkeley and Los Angeles: North Pinehurst Press, 133–153.

Gunnell, Terry. 2014b. Nordic Folk Legends, Folk Traditions and Grave Mounds. The Value of Folkloristics for the Study of Old Nordic Religions. In E. Heide & K. Bek-Pedersen (eds.). *New Focus on Retrospective Methods. Resuming Methodological Discussions. Case Studies from Northern Europe*. Folklore Fellows Communications, 307. Helsinki: Suomalainen Tiedeakatemia/ Academica Scientiarum Fennica, 17–41.

Jakobsen, Jakob. 1897. *Det norrøne sprog på Shetland.* Copenhagen: W. Prior.

Mitchell, Stephen A. 2001. Warlocks, Valkyries and Varlets. A Prolegomenon to the Study of North Sea Witchcraft Terminology. In *Cosmos. The Journal of the Traditional Cosmology Society* 17:1, 59–81.

Author presentations

Kristin Armstrong Oma is associate professor of archaeology at the Museum of Archaeology, University of Stavanger. Her research is focused on human-animal interactions and relationships in prehistory and early history, combining archaeology and the interdisciplinary field Human-Animal Studies. ORCID: https://orcid.org/0000-0001-8249-9332

Maths Bertell is Senior Lecturer at Mid-Sweden University with a PhD in History of Religion. His current work focus on stratification and regionality in Old Norse and Sámi religion, in the Baltic sea region.

Margaret Clunies Ross is an Emeritus Professor of English at the University of Sydney, Australia, and an Adjunct Professor in the School of Humanities at the University of Adelaide. Her research interests are in Old Norse myth and its reception and in Old Icelandic literature, especially poetry.

Christina Fredengren is Associate Professor in Archaeology at Stockholm University. She is currently working on a monograph on sacrifice and the deposition of human and animal remains in wetlands, mainly in Sweden and there focus on human-animal relations and ways of engaging with wetlands. Thereby this work places itself in the wider field of Environmental Humanities. ORCID: https://orcid.org/0000-0001-6431-754X

Frog is Academy of Finland Research Fellow at Folklore Studies, Department of Cultures, University of Helsinki. His current project is entitled *Mythology, Verbal Art and Authority in Social Impact* (2016–2021).

Anne-Sofie Gräslund is professor emeritus of archaeology at Uppsala University. Her research has mainly been on Viking Age issues: Graves and burial customs, religion, conversion and rune stones from various aspects as location, ornamentation, chronology, gender perspective, and as witness of the Christianization.

Terry Gunnell is Professor of Folkloristics at the University of Iceland. Author of *The Origins of Drama in Scandinavia* (1995), he has written a wide range of articles on Old Norse religion, Nordic folk belief and legend, folk drama and performance.

Eldar Heide is Associate Professor of Norwegian at Western Norway University of Applied Sciences. He has a PhD on shamanistic aspects of Old Scandinavian religion, and has also studied maritime topics, Scandinavian dialects, language history, and Old Norse literature.

Anders Hultgård is professor emeritus of history of religions at Uppsala University. He has recently published a book on the Ragnarøk myth and is currently preparing a monograph entitled *Ancient Scandinavian Religion: A Comparative Approach*.

Peter Jackson Rova is Professor of the History of Religions at Stockholm University. Among his recent publications are the two edited volumes *Transforming Warriors: The ritual Organization of Military Force* (with Peter Haldén) (Routledge 2016) and *Philosophy and the End of Sacrifice: Disengaging Ritual in Ancient India, Greece and Beyond* (with Anna-Pya Sjödin) (Equinox 2016). ORCID: https://orcid.org/0000-0002-0742-6640

Merrill Kaplan is Associate Professor of Folklore and Scandinavian Studies. Her current monograph focuses on the Tale of Völsi in the fourteenth-century *Flateyjarbók* manuscript.

Tommy Kuusela (PhD in History of Religions) works at the Institute for Language and Folklore in Uppsala. He has written more than 25 articles on folklore and Old Norse religion.

Currently, he is co-editing a volume on *The Feminine in Old Norse Mythology and Folklore*.

John Lindow is Professor emeritus in the Department of Scandinavian at the University of California, Berkeley. With Jens Peter Schjødt and Anders Andrén, he is co-editor of the forthcoming four-volume work, *Pre-Christian Religions of the North: History and Structures*.

Camilla Löfqvist is an osteologists graduated with an MA from Stockholm University with a substantial experience both from research related osteological projects as well as from contract archaeology.

Ola Magnell is a zooarchaeologist at Arkeologerna, Statens Historiska Museer. He is primarily working in contract archaeology, but also participate in the research projects *Blue Archaeology* and *Fading Heritage* at Lund University. ORCID: https://orcid.org/0000-0002-4861-8067

Stephen A. Mitchell is the Robert S. and Ilse Friend Professor of Scandinavian and Folklore at Harvard University. His current research focuses on Nordic charm magic and the relevance of memory studies for pre-modern Scandinavia. ORCID: https://orcid.org/0000-0002-1468-7558

Agneta Ney is Associate Professor of History at Uppsala University. Her latest monograph focuses on myth and masculinity in the legend of Sigurðr Fáfnisbani http://www.nordicacademicpress.com/bok/bland-ormar-och-drakar/

Andreas Nordberg is Associate Professor of History of Religions at Stockholm University, and archaeologist. His research focuses on religion in ancient Scandinavia. ORCID: https://orcid.org/0000-0001-8583-1505

Sigmund Oehrl is senior lecturer ("Privatdozent") at the Institute of Scandinavian Studies and the Institute of Pre- and Protohistoric Archaeology of the Ludwig-Maximilians-University Munich, and researcher at the Department of Archaeology and Classical Studies at Stockholm University where he leads the project *Ancient images 2.0. A digital edition of the Gotlandic picture stones.*

Judy Quinn is Reader in Old Norse Literature in the Department of Anglo-Saxon, Norse & Celtic at Cambridge University. Recent publications include *A Handbook to Eddic Poetry* (CUP) and *Studies in the Transmission and Reception of Old Norse Literature* (Brepols). ORCID: https://www.asnc.cam.ac.uk/people/Judy.Quinn/

Jens Peter Schjødt is professor in the Study of Religion at Aarhus University. His main field of interest and most of his publications deal with pre-Christian Scandinavian Religion and the methodological challenges connected to studying it.

Rudy Simek is Professor for Medieval German and Scandinavian Literature at Bonn University/Germany. His research interests center round Old Norse mythology, the cultural history of the Viking Age, Saga literature, and Medieval popular religion.

Olof Sundqvist is professor of history of religions at Stockholm University. He has recently published the book *An Arena for Higher Powers: Ceremonial Buildings and Religious Strategies for Rulership in Late Iron Age Scandinavia* and is currently preparing a monograph entitled *The Demise of Ancient Scandinavian Religion*. ORCID: https://orcid.org/0000-0002-4304-9782

Frederik Wallenstein is a historian of religion at Stockholm University. He has published on subjects such as Icelandic sagas, Old Norse conceptions of the soul, berserks, sorcery and ideals of masculinity in Old Norse Culture. His current research is mainly focused on oral tradition and processes of cultural memory in the Icelandic saga-tradition.

Margrethe Watt is senior researcher attached to Bornholms Museum, Rønne. Her current archaeological research focuses on the iconography of the Scandinavian *gold foil figures* as well as on excavations at the central settlement complex of Sorte Muld, Bornholm.

Klas Wikström af Edholm is doctoral student in History of Religions at Åbo Akademi University. His current research focuses on the occurrence of human sacrifices in Old Norse religion. ORCID: https://orcid.org/0000-0002-5563-4065

Torun Zachrisson is Associate professor in Archaeology at Stockholm university and Head of research at the County museum of Uppland. She is currently publishing articles on material aspects of pre-Christian religion and social change in Iron Age Scandinavia. ORCID: https://orcid.org/0000-0001-7755-4982

Index